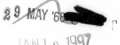

Albert Parry

THE
NEW CLASS
DIVIDED

Science and Technology

Versus Communism

THE MACMILLAN COMPANY, NEW YORK

COLLIER-MACMILLAN LTD., LONDON

First Printing

The Macmillan Company, New York
Collier-Macmillan Canada, Ltd., Toronto, Ontario

Library of Congress catalog card number: 66-15029

Printed in the United States of America

... I close on a note of hope. ...
Now the winds of change appear to be
blowing more strongly than ever, in
the world of Communism as well as our
own. ... Today we still welcome those
winds of change—and we have every
reason to believe that our tide is
running strong.

—PRESIDENT JOHN F. KENNEDY
"The State of the Union,"
January 14, 1963

CONTENTS

PREFACE

This book is about the sociopolitical place of the Soviet Union's new scientists, engineers, and managers. My purpose is to investigate the possibility that the scientific-technical personnel is essentially a group distinct, or potentially distinct, from the Party zealots and that we may expect an emerging political influence and a rising political role for such technocrats in opposition to that country's Party bureaucrats.

I first became intrigued by this possibility some years back, in the process of my more general study of the constantly changing structure of the Soviet Union. For a long time, the changes of particular interest to me were shifts in the roles of the various classes in Soviet society, and also indications of new attitudes of the Soviet man, especially in the upper strata, toward the non-Soviet world. I finally chose the scientific-technical personnel of that land as my main theme because of the obvious growth of science and technology and their singular importance in the Soviet setting.

The chief questions I have asked in my research and in this book are these:

Are the scientific-technical elite of the Soviet Union a harmonious part of the pattern willed and molded by the Communist Party?

Or are they, on the contrary, in actual or potential conflict with the Party?

Even if there are only a few outward signs of rift, the problem still remains whether inwardly these experts are indeed convinced and loyal Communists—whether their individual and group pride in their professional competence and contribution does not gradually overshadow their belief in Communism and their membership in the Party.

The assessment here is one of possible changes not only in the Soviet Union's domestic affairs but also in her foreign policy. One of my aims has been to discover whether the rising influence of these Soviet intellectuals and professionals may truly mean, as some Western observers presume, a more pro-Western and peaceful attitude and policy on the part of whatever ruling group may in due time follow Nikita Khrushchev's immediate successors.

This approach to the new social structure in the Soviet Union and its political ramifications has not, in my opinion, been tried by Western specialists in the field of Soviet studies as boldly and fully as it has deserved. The employment of this approach, then (I venture to hope), is one of the values of this book. The very posing of this significant problem of a possible rift in the New Class, in the country's elite, should clarify at least some aspects of the troubled East-West relations—should help in the world's search for, and chances of, peace.

Ideally this book should have been the result of firsthand research in the Soviet Union. But, since it was unsafe and otherwise impractical for me to do any part of this study on the spot, I had to gather my material outside the Soviet borders.

The impracticability of any investigation within that country was illustrated a few years ago by the experience of Professor Joseph A. Raffaele, director of the Office of International Studies and Research at Drexel Institute of Technology, in Philadelphia. His interest in the Soviet Union was, as he put it to me, in "the context of the relationship between government, trade unions, workers, and the industrial elite."[1] He went to the U.S.S.R. with elaborately prepared questionnaires based on the polls he had previously conducted in Denmark and Italy. But what worked in Denmark and Italy did not work in the Soviet Union. Aside from the difficulty of language communication and the necessity of finding competent interpreters of questions and answers, Dr. Raffaele discovered in the Soviet Union much fear, or at least reluctance to talk, which had not existed in Denmark and Italy. The Soviet citizens queried by Dr. Raffaele gave only stereotyped replies. The net result of Dr. Raffaele's efforts, so fruitful in Denmark and Italy, was nil in the Soviet Union, as he himself sadly confirmed to me.[2]

You have to live with Russians, intellectuals or not, for years, not months; and you have to speak Russian fluently and know quite a lot of Russia's past and present, Russia's customs and morals and her average man's troubles and desires, before your

Soviet acquaintances and neighbors will trust you enough to talk politics with you.

"I think I was more interested in talking politics than they were, and so such conversations were very few and didn't get very far," said Dr. Hubert A. Lechevalier, a young American scientist, on returning from his four months of life in Moscow, where his cultural-exchange assignment was at the Institute of Microbiology of the Academy of Sciences.

The young Soviet scientists with whom he worked those four months in 1958–59 shied away from political talks with this American, and not only because he was a foreigner whose Russian was rudimentary at best, or because he was so new and they needed time to "learn" him while he was learning Russian, but also because they were in a particularly delicate field—the field of genetics, for so long so blighted by the secret-police methods of reactionary Comrade Trofim Lysenko. Among the young Soviet scientists he met and worked with, Dr. Lechevalier "found some who were apparently chary of politically sensitive scientific theories," and even more reluctant to discuss straight, nonscientific politics with any degree of frankness.[3]

But suppose a Western scholar does know Russia and the Russians, along with their language. He thinks he is adroit and discreet enough to ask cautious questions that would bring revealing answers. Still the result is quite disappointing. Take the well-known case of my friend Frederick C. Barghoorn.

This Yale professor, one of our most discerning political scientists specializing in things Soviet, had a record of several years as an observer on the United States embassy staff in wartime Moscow. Later he made six short but worthwhile trips to the Soviet Union, particularly to study the post-Stalin times and moods. On October 31, 1963, as he was about to return to America from the latest of his journeys, he was arrested and held incommunicado in a Lubianka cell on charges of espionage. Only the direct, energetic intervention of President John F. Kennedy (one of his last acts before his assassination in Dallas on November 22) freed Professor Barghoorn.

While pressing for the scholar's release, the President assured the world that Professor Barghoorn was not on an intelligence mission of any kind. And indeed, the scholar's last visit to the Soviet Union was, in his own subsequent words, "to investigate public opinion or the methods by which public opinion and political attitudes are formed" under the Soviet regime.

. . . prior to going to the Soviet Union, I had written a number of letters to university officials and to officials of the Soviet government setting forth quite openly and frankly the activities in which I expected to engage, so that they had every opportunity to know what I wanted to do, and if they had felt that these were matters which were inappropriate, they could have simply not issued a visa.

Even with that Soviet visa, while he was traveling in the country looking for his data, Barghoorn was careful not to carry a camera, nor to go into people's homes, nor to talk with a member of the opposite sex for more than a few minutes. Still, he was arrested and accused. For, as he justly remarked in his first press conference on returning to American soil, discussions in the Soviet Union that "depart somewhat from the official propaganda line are regarded as ideological activity." Thus, he went on, "behavior which we would regard as completely innocent" can and does become in the Soviet Union "a source of police suspicion." Under Soviet law and its interpretation by the Soviet police, "one can be accused of conducting intelligence activity merely by walking down the street."

To try to find out the ways in which Soviet citizens form their opinions and communicate them to their Communist leaders, as Professor Barghoorn attempted to do in October 1963, was useless. Indeed, in my friend's words, "It seems to be difficult for the Soviet Communists to understand that there can be such a thing as objective social research."[4]

II

This is not to say that it is wholly useless to expect any pertinent information from Westerners returning from the Soviet Union. Indeed, such observers have provided a great deal of significant literature directly or indirectly related to my subject. And, both in the United States and in Europe, I have had a number of very illuminating conversations with Western observers who had visited the Soviet Union, especially scientists and engineers who had had contact with their Russian counterparts.

More revealing, however, were my talks with those Soviet scientists, engineers, and managers who have defected to the West, particularly in recent years. All talked freely and not so bitterly as to obscure facts. Candid though they were, some asked not to be identified in this book by name. To their personal stories, and to their views on my subject, I devote a number of pages here and there in this work, availing myself of the points they made during my interviews with them in Europe and America.

Nor does this complete the list of my sources. Prominent among my methods was my careful reading, over a period of years, of Soviet publications as I sought the direct Soviet evidence —often casual and unwitting—of the role and the rift I have aimed to ascertain. Indeed, the more casual or accidental the better. Often, when a published Soviet source starts out by promising to give the truth about Soviet society, its text contains nothing but the Party line. We are not at all, for instance, helped by the recent and rather sudden Soviet recognition of sociology as a respectable science, and not merely as a meek handmaiden of Pentagon imperialism (Moscow still insists that *Western* sociology continues to be such a despicable servitor).[5]

Sociological researches in the Soviet Union have the attraction of a novelty; they are quite workmanlike, but not particularly enlightening. Even when based on written but unsigned questionnaires, they hardly ever reveal anything uninhibited by the official Marxist-Leninist doctrine. In vain would we look in V*oprosy filosofii* (Problems of Philosophy) or any other official academic journal, where the first timid sociological studies have lately been published, for the real interplay of Soviet social forces.[6]

On the other hand, the general Soviet press meant for the man in the street is of real assistance to the scholar. The data I have found on my subject in the nonacademic Soviet periodicals may be judged as highly damaging to the Soviet cause. The fact that so much material unfavorable to the Soviet way of life is found in popular Soviet publications rather puzzles the American public. From my American readers and lecture audiences I often hear these questions:

"Doesn't this prove that there is indeed freedom of the press in the Soviet Union?"

And:

"Why does the Communist Party hierarchy allow and apparently even encourage the printing in its press of so much criticism of the Soviet regime, or what amounts to such criticism?"

The answer to the first question is: No, there is no real freedom of the press in the Soviet Union; the leadership permits and even orders all those exposés of Soviet deficiency, insufficiency and inefficiency, but within limits and for purposes all its own, none of which spells out true freedom of the press.

The exposés form a safety valve for popular irritations over Soviet injustices and inefficiencies. At the same time, they serve as stern warnings to nonconformers, corrupt idlers, clever embezzlers, plain and fancy thieves, blackmarketeers, and all other malefactors, or persons whom the hierarchs consider as malefactors.

But let us note two important points:

1. Leaders on the highest levels of power are not exposed or even criticized as immoral wrongdoers. Even in the rare instances when the top brass are deposed, as were those involved in the June 1957 move against Khrushchev, they are usually blasted as anti-Party elements but not as corrupt criminals. When in mid-October 1964 Khrushchev was overthrown, the Brezhnev-Kosygin-Suslov group of victors accused him of nepotism, harebrained schemes, and undignified conduct, but not of any statutory transgressions punishable in courts of law.

2. The Communist theory is never questioned. The fault of the individual corruption is found embedded in the individual himself, also (sometimes) in the lingering influence of the old tsarist-capitalist times or the invidious effect of modern Western capitalism. But the Soviet regime, building Socialism en route to Communism, is held blameless. The Communist Party is always as pure as fresh driven snow.

Still, there are occasional doubts among the faithful in the Soviet Union that damaging evidence of sin in the Soviet Union, even in the regime's lower echelons, should ever be published. One zealous Communist wrote a letter to a Soviet editor:

> Oh the newspapers . . . these reports about thievery, inefficient transport of cattle, bribery, plagiarism! I cannot calmly work and live, all because of the newspapers. I am hot and bothered when I realize that our newspapers are being read abroad. Why do you publicize all these criminal affairs, even if there are not so many of them? We run into this in our everyday lives; we know this anyway. Why do you carry this trash out of the hut for everybody to see? Better that you send such accounts directly to court, so that the culprits are punished mercilessly . . .

The Moscow journalist assigned by the editor to answer these questions repeats the old Communist explanation that exposés in the press are unfortunately necessary to teach the rascals a lesson and to warn others not to transgress likewise. As for the good name of the Soviet Union which may thereby suffer in foreign lands, why, let "the haters of Socialism" huff and puff, with or without the aid of these Soviet press exposés of the few seamy details of Soviet reality: "We are not afraid. No curtain of lies and slanderous fabrications will conceal from the nations of the world the great social, economic, and cultural progress of Communism now being built, the glorious successes of the creative toil of the Soviet people."[7]

Arkady Raikin, the well-known "loyal" satirist and light-stage performer, echoed that idea, saying: "Our enemies will in any case never say anything good [about the Soviet Union]. What can you expect of enemies? But our friends and other perceptive people, on getting acquainted with Soviet satire, do say that the U.S.S.R. zealously and consistently fights human faults in its firm resolve to overcome the latter."[8]

But of course the Soviet press reveals far more than its editors and satirical writers are ordered to reveal or they themselves mean to reveal. Not mere details of deficiencies, but the entire injustice and the whole retrograde essence of the Soviet regime are unavoidably laid naked. Cobwebbed dogma cannot hide this. Moreover, even if so often crooked, the mirror of the Soviet press does reflect something of a change through which that nation's society is now laboring.

All by itself, it does not suffice; nor is it a true enough source. We cannot always trust the Soviet press when it denounces managers as thieves, engineers as snobs, or scientists as incompetents. But when it is used in close connection with other and more truthful sources, when it is corrected for bias and hysterics, when it is supplemented with our own view of known facts, the Soviet press holds much for the Western researcher and commentator. And that is why I have used it so extensively among my other supplies of data.

Let me note, however, that at some point in 1963 a decision must have been made in the Kremlin's higher councils to reduce and temper such exposés of the regime's shortcomings. Apparently, the writers and editors had by then taken this freedom to criticize a bit too enthusiastically for the leaders' comfort. In mid-1963 not only I, but other Western researchers as well, observed a gradual but unmistakable decrease of the self-critical material in the Moscow journals. Still, even for 1963–66, my notes present a rich enough harvest.

Over the years of my research and writing on this subject, help was given me through grants of varying amounts by several foundations and funds. I am particularly grateful to the Human Ecology Fund of New York; the American Council of Learned Societies; Humanities Fund, Inc.; IBM World Trade Corporation; and the Littauer Grant, this last as aid from the Colgate University Research Council. None of the organizations and their officials who have made my work possible through their interest and assistance is responsible, of course, for any of the views expressed by me here. These are wholly my own.

ALBERT PARRY

Hamilton, New York

CHAPTER I

~~~~~~~~~~~~~~~~~~~~~~~~~~~~

The Problem and the Premise

TWELVE YEARS AGO a highly placed Marxist in Yugoslavia had second thoughts about the historical process in both his country and the Soviet Union. Milovan Djilas saw that in both those new societies the Red elite were taking power and wealth for themselves in the name, and at the expense, of workers and peasants. He wrote about this elite with blunt disapproval branding it the New Class.

By now, thanks to Milovan Djilas and to many other avenues of information and interpretation, the whole world knows about those newly rich and powerful individuals in the Soviet Union. They are the intelligentsia and the privilegentsia. They are at the very top or near the top: bureaucrats and technocrats, Communist Party chiefs and secret-police brass, also marshals and generals and admirals, industrial managers of many levels, desk-bound economists and footloose geologists, all manner of scientists and professors, also surgeons, novelists, journalists, playwrights, composers, and performers.

Talent and education are prime factors in the emergence and progress of these groups. Their numbers rise steadily. Thus, from 284,038 at the end of 1958 the number of science teachers and scientific researchers in the Soviet Union doubled to 565,958 by the close of 1963.[1] In his speech of May 8, 1965, the Party's First Secretary Leonid Brezhnev placed the number of the nation's "scientific workers" at more than 600,000 and the number of men and women "with higher and middle special education" at work in the Soviet economy at more than 11 million.[2] "The intelligentsia are a large and fast-growing social stratum of our society," Aleksei Rumiantsev, a high Party official and propagandist, wrote in early 1965. "They constitute nearly one fifth of all

the Soviet toilers." He went on to deny that this phenomenon
meant the watering-down of the nation's socialism and communism into what he termed as their "second-rate" version—that is,
into a betrayal of Marx's dream and Lenin's design.[3]

Yet, it is these elite and near-elite who have been building
private houses for themselves with increasing frequency and of
ever heightened quality. It is they and their children who crowd
concerts and theatrical productions by the best of the native talent
and by visiting American and other Western artists. They are the
ones who go to all the foreign films, who bootleg modern Western
music, either on the original records brought from abroad or
reproduced by amateur Soviet technicians (often, medical students) on used X-ray films. To them and by them some works, in
Russian translations or in their original language, of Western
writers old and new are at times sold on a kind of black market at
several times their publication prices. It is their children who are
introducing into Russia such foreign imports as skin diving and
water-skiing, costly Western clothes, blond furniture, and even a
few sports cars.

The lowest member of this group may be an engineer just
beginning his career at a mere 150 to 200 rubles per month.
Slightly above him is an older engineer or a plant manager or,
say, an assistant professor (*dotsent*) with a salary of only 300 to
500 rubles a month. Farther up, a full professor draws from 500
to 1,000 rubles, and a scientist between 800 and 1,500 rubles. All
this at a time when the official Soviet rate is $1.11 per ruble, but
its true value is on the average less than 1 dollar.

Do not, however, sigh over the poor Soviet aristocrat. He does
have additional sources of income. The plant manager, called in
Russia "director," has the so-called director's fund at his disposal, the state's bounty given for overfulfilling the month's or
the quarter's quota of production, or for economizing on materials, or, in these days of the Liberman Reform, for making a
profit for the manager's plant. And there are other such occasions
for state bonuses. The manager usually takes the lion's share of
this fund for himself, gives a little less to his closest aides, and
crumbs of varying degrees to those below.

Professors, scientists, and Party chiefs receive all sorts of extra
emoluments, prizes, awards, and perquisites, some in cash, others
in housing, vacations at the seashore, trips abroad, government-
purchased and -maintained cars and state-salaried chauffeurs.
Writers collect royalties. Artists obtain commissions, fees, hono-

raria. And, remember, no income tax in the Soviet Union is higher than 13 per cent of one's income.

Above all, there are sundry kinds of ingenious illegal channels of profit for the elite and the near-elite. Some Western experts estimate that in the Soviet Union "as much as one-third of the country's domestic commerce is carried on by illegal and quasi-legal means."[4] And while some parts of the New Class profit from such "capitalist crimes" more than the others, at least one sector of that Class remains faithfully Communist and antiprofit. This sector resists and fights all the others, all the more vigorously because so many of the New Class have begun to seek that kind of private enterprise and personal profit. The seekers' avidity causes this violent reaction.

There has also lately emerged another dichotomy: the split between some of the young of the New Class and some of its old guard. The emergence of new forms and even of free spirit in Soviet poetry and prose; the appearance of the abstract school in Soviet painting and sculpture; the atonal experimentation in music—all this has come to symbolize the growing split between "the fathers and the sons" (as the young have named this argu-ment, alluding to the historic conflict that raged in tsarist Russia more than one hundred years ago and gave Ivan Turgenev the theme and the title for his famous novel).

By cracking down on the experimenters Nikita Khrushchev emphasized the political nature of the movement. Not once, but several times, he and his henchmen reminded the young Russians that the Hungarian revolt of 1956 stemmed precisely from the originally small and esoteric meetings and readings by Budapest poets. Khrushchev thundered that he would not allow a repetition of it anywhere, and especially in the Soviet Union.

In the Soviet Union, during their restiveness of 1962–63, the young cited Khrushchev's own revelations of Stalinist atrocities; but they refused to blame Stalin alone. They accused Khrushchev and the Party too. "I recall," a faithful Communist woman wrote, clearly horrified, "that one young man said to me that Stalin's cult is a heavy guilt of the old generation accountable to the young, that since these 'fathers' had [in their time] committed so many errors, they now had no right to teach the young . . ."[5] She said she did not like the young man's attitude, even though she herself had for years unjustly suffered at Vorkuta, one of Stalin's worst concentration camps.

Like it or not, sincere or otherwise, this woman who joined the

Party way back in 1918 and would still, after all these long forty-five years of Communist atrocities and stupidities, not admit any disillusionment—this former victim of her own Party's terror, who now so pathetically tried to prove her loyalty to the Party and her gratitude to Khrushchev, did concede one cardinal fact: there was at least one split within the Soviet elite.

I I

And so, to return to Djilas and his thesis: Thankful as we are for his courageous stand, a correction is necessary.

We must say that this is the basic error of Djilas, despite all his merit in depicting the New Class: He wrote of the New Class as something very much of an entity, a united, monolithic phenomenon. He somehow failed to note that already at the time he wrote his book, in 1954, there were within the Soviet elite *several* classes and subclasses, rather different from one another, just as they were a far cry from the rest of the people in the Red empire.

And certainly now, all these years after his work first appeared, we must recognize significant political fissures between group and group within the New Class.

The question I pose in my present work is this: Are the writers and artists now being repressed and scolded by the Party more than a limited group and an episodic movement, or do they represent a catalyst for other and much more important elements within the New Class—elements of socioeconomic and political opposition to the Communist Party, that may not even realize they are such opposition?

Just what more strategic—if less articulate—strata and substrata may there be, now or soon, in opposition to the Party? What groups and subgroups within this New Class, other than bureaucrats and the writer-artists, could there be at loggerheads with those in the political saddle?

Most particularly, are the Soviet Union's new scientists, engineers, and managers so unlike today's professional Communist Party functionaries as to be hostile to the latter? As these scientists and technicians grow in influence, will they ever come to power, either on their own, or in coalition with some other non-Communist or anti-Communist group within their nation? In Russia's foreign policy, will they offer a ray of hope to the world longing for a peace truer and more durable than Communist functionaries have so far given to humanity?

The possible emergence of the Soviet Union's new scientific-technical-managerial personnel as a major sociopolitical force is thus the subject of this inquiry.

I I I

The idea that scientists and engineers are destined to be uppermost in the society of the future is not exactly a new one. One of the very first men of modern times to advance it felt that such an ascendancy could be achieved without necessarily creating a totalitarian society of little or no justice to other groups and classes within the human family of tomorrow. Nearly 150 years ago a French Socialist predicted or at least advocated a rule of engineers and scientists over a future Socialist state. He was Count Claude Henri de Saint-Simon, now remembered not only as a Socialist and a writer but also as a military man and a shrewd businessman.

He fought on the American side in the War of Independence; he returned to France only to be imprisoned by revolutionaries during the French terror, while making his fortune in real-estate speculation. In his Socialist teachings, unlike Karl Marx and other Socialists of the nineteenth century and later, he did not stress any contrast between labor and capital, but envisaged a system where industrial chiefs—an autocracy of industrialists, engineers, and scientists—would control society.

He believed in an aristocracy of merit, not an aristocracy by birth, by privilege, by accident. He usually defined his future elite as a sort of benevolent amalgam of scientists and industrialists, but at times he drew a line between the two and relegated his industrialists to a place below that of scientists.

In such visions Saint-Simon was of course not entirely original. The pioneers from whom he took at least part of his inspiration were Plato with his philosopher-leaders of the *Republic* and Tommaso Campanella and his semimystic, semiscientific *City of the Sun* of 1643, but, above all, Francis Bacon with his *New Atlantis* of 1627, and Marquis Marie Jean de Caritat de Condorcet with his great philosophical work of 1795 on human progress. Both Bacon and Condorcet had written of a future reign of scholars or scientists as a practical possibility. As Condorcet had learned from Bacon, so Saint-Simon adopted ideas from both. But he refined and popularized both, until the image of scientists as future kings appeared to be peculiarly his own.[6]

Saint-Simon was followed, in the first half of the twentieth century, by H. G. Wells, who foresaw a rule of science, a world run by "functional" men, all holding some sort of advanced professional degree.[7]

Wells's prevision of this elite first appeared in 1902 in his *Anticipations*, and in one form and another it persisted to the end of his life in 1946. In his earliest version, the elite was limited by Wells to scientists, engineers, physicians, and other men of scientific training. Later he expanded the governing personnel to include not only managers, but also a sampling of creative professions. Even under the heading "scientists," Wells meant more than such precise professionals as physicists, mathematicians, and chemists. Following the First World War he had increasing confidence also in men of economics, sociology, anthropology, and social psychology. So he began to include social scientists in the elite that were destined to rule society. (Curiously, the Russians have always understood and used the words *nauka* and *uchyonyie* —"science" and "scientists"—in a far more inclusive way than has the West. Science in Russian means all learning; scientists include all savants, social scientists as well as linguists and other men and women of the humanities. With us, however, science means primarily, if not exclusively, the physical and natural sciences. Even the social sciences are held to be too inexact to be included in valid science.)

Yet in his *Open Conspiracy*, published in 1928, Wells doubted that any scientists as such could lead mankind into the golden age of the scientifically arranged world community predicted by him. Men of more general intelligence than scientists, of wider aims in life, should in fact be the guiding spirits, marching in front of the professional men and of the new society as a whole. Still, emphatically disagreeing with most Marxists of his time, Wells refused to picture such guiding spirits as Communist Party leaders. Certainly he placed little if any faith in the monopoly of intelligence and moral virtue ascribed by the Marxists to proletarians.

But the followers of Marx insisted that workers, and no one else, would dominate the future society, until there would be neither workers nor any other classes, until a blissful classless society would emerge—true, pure-red Communism.

However, in 1904–6, while the first Russian revolution was flaring up and dying, two singular books appeared in Geneva, Switzerland. Entitled *The Mental Worker* and *The Bankruptcy of Nineteenth-Century Socialism*, they were written and published in Russian, but their author was a Pole, Jan Waclaw Machajski, who used the pseudonym of A. Wolski. He was a Marxist, yet in his books this remarkable man daringly undertook to tear apart the pretenses of most of his fellow Marxists, who, according to him, only professed to be fighters for the proletariat.

He was bold enough, and possibly among the very first, to say that most Marxists never really cared for the proletariat. He said that they were only using the proletariat to advance themselves as intellectuals, as professionals, as managers, to positions of selfish power.

He wrote that these Marxists wanted to bring down the structure of private capitalism, not to usher in a paradise of equality, of justice for workers and farmers, but to put themselves into the seats of power after they had dislodged those private capitalists.

Instead of private capitalists, these Marxist intellectuals were going to introduce state capitalism, he declared, with themselves as the sinister bosses and sole beneficiaries of the new system. He called these Marxist intellectuals "a rising privileged class, fighting for a place in the sun against the old privileged classes, the landed owners and capitalists." They too, he said, had a kind of capital. This capital was their higher education, "the source of their actual or potential higher incomes."

And they were not going to surrender this capital for the common good as they implied or professed, as they protested or promised they would.

No, in reality they were going to use their capital—this higher education of theirs—to snare all the workers into a revolt against the owning classes, whose seats of power these Marxists coveted. They did not mean Socialism, even as they preached Socialism.

Instead, these intellectuals meant to institute a system of alleged government ownership wherein the means of production would belong, not to the people, and not to the capitalists, but to these educated officeholders (managers, engineers, and scientists), who would receive high salaries and other benefits—in fact, most of the benefits of such a society.

Thus we see Machajski-Wolski as a unique prophet indeed. This Polish intellectual predicted with startling clarity and truth the regime into which the so-called Socialism of the Russian Communists is now being transformed not alone in Russia, but also in Poland, Hungary, Czechoslovakia, and all the other countries seized or influenced by them.

Machajski-Wolski knew what he was talking about. In his youth in tsarist times, for being fearlessly active in the antitsarist,

anticapitalist underground of Russian Poland, he paid with ten
years of Siberian exile. It was in the frozen forests of Siberia that
he first conceived his prophecy of the non-Marxian rule by selfish
intellectuals. Among the revolutionary leaders of the time whom
Machajski impressed, even if briefly, was Lev Trotsky. But
Machajski was soon denounced by true followers of Lenin, and
Trotsky himself presently branded him as an "anarchist."[8]

Machajski lived to see the Communist revolution of November
1917. He hailed it, with grave reservations, and stayed in Moscow
to hold a minor research job with the new Soviet government. He
died in 1927, without having become a Communist or having
changed his views noticeably. Had he lived a few more years, he
would undoubtedly have perished in the Stalinist purges. His
memory was attacked viciously even in the relatively relaxed post-
Stalin days. One year after Stalin's death, "Makhayevism" was
castigated as "counterrevolutionary" and "reactionary" in its
"slander of the revolutionary intelligentsia." The aim of Machajski's teachings was described as "inciting enmity" between the
intelligentsia and the working class. Yet this official statement of
1954 admitted that Machajski's ideas had some sort of following
in Red Russia as late as 1938.[9] And even as late as February
1965 a high Kremlin propagandist writing in *Pravda* on the relations between the Party and the intelligentsia found it necessary to
castigate "Makhayevism" once more, ostensibly as a long-out-
dated phenomenon.[10] But if outdated, why was it necessary to
drag it out? Apparently the Party hierarchy is not too sure that
the Machajski prediction is outdated or otherwise laughable.

And, we may ask in 1966, what higher education is so valuable
now, in the second half of this twentieth century, as modern
scientific and engineering training, with a dash of managerial
skill?

I V

Scientists, engineers and other experts are taking over everywhere—how can the Soviet Union escape the same fate? The
recent transformation of Western technicians into technocrats
seems to bolster those of us who believe in the premise of the
Soviet scientists' and engineers' possible opposition to, and even
rebellion against, Communist ideology and authority.

That in our Western society, or at least in its American sector,
a unique transformation is indeed occurring appears to be a clear
enough fact. It is hard to disagree with Daniel Bell, the noted

American sociologist, when he sees in the United States of the 1960s "a new 'technocratic' elite—scientists, mathematicians, economists, sociologists, with their new techniques of decision making: input-output matrices, system analysis, linear programming—that now becomes essential, if not to the wielding of power, then to the formulations and analyses on which political judgments have to be made." The old elite is passing despite its desperate opposition: "It is these complexities and the rise of the new skill groups which pose the real threat of dispossession to those who once held power by virtue of their wealth or property or gerrymandered political control."[11]

The momentous process is spelled out by Professor Bell in detail:

> The new nature of decision-making, its increasing technicality, forces a displacement of the older elites. Within a business enterprise, the newer techniques of operations research and linear programming almost amount to the "automation" of middle management and its displacement by mathematicians and engineers, working either within the firm or as consultants. In the economy, the businessman finds himself subject to price, wage, and investment criteria laid down by the economists in government. In the polity, the old military elites find themselves challenged in the determination of strategy by scientists, who have the technical knowledge on nuclear capability, missile development, and the like, or by the "military intellectuals" whose conceptions of weapon systems and political warfare seek to guide military allocations.
>
> In the broadest sense, the spread of education, of research, of administration and government creates a new constituency, the technical and professional intelligentsia. While these are not bound by the common ethos that would constitute them a new class, nor even a cohesive social group, they are the products of a new system of recruitment for power (just as property and inheritance represented the old system), and those who are the products of the old system understandably feel a vague and apprehensive disquiet—the disquiet of the dispossessed.[12]

A Soviet parallel is seen by other American observers when they write about the possible result of so much new education, industrialization, and "technization" of Red Russia. Herbert McClosky and John E. Turner state in their admirable volume on the Soviet regime:

> In educating its managers, functionaries, and scientists for industrial and administrative positions, the regime runs a risk that the

thin diet of Marxian ideology may no longer be intellectually satis-
fying and may be questioned or ignored by them. Although some
(a minority) of the intelligentsia in other countries have responded
to the dogmatic appeals of Communism, there is a tendency for
people to grow less doctrinaire as they become more educated.
Moreover, scientists and other scholars who develop habits of objective inquiry and demonstration for their own fields may be
tempted to transfer them to the social and political realms. . . .

As Soviet society grows more complex, greater technical knowledge will be required to operate it—knowledge familiar to practitioners but beyond the understanding of ordinary politicians. . . .
As the technical intelligentsia increasingly become the judges of
their own needs, they move further out of the reach of the political
center and are more difficult to control.[13]

The demand for freedom, the first step toward political power,
may become a slogan of some immediacy. Leonard S. Silk remarks:

If they breed up a class of competent scientists and intellectuals,
in the numbers they will require if they are to overtake us, they
must give their people more freedom. And their people will wonder
—as I think they have begun to wonder already, as I believe the
whole Boris Pasternak affair demonstrated—where do we go from
here? What was the revolution for? How about some peace and
happiness? How about taking your damned foot off my neck?[14]

In fact, whether or not the Party satraps and subsatraps realize
this, freedom of one kind has already been won by their pet
scientists. A recent team of British investigators of the Soviet
scene reported that Soviet scientists are now permitted to spend
some 30 per cent of their time on research projects of their own
choice. As in the West, so in the Soviet Union, the employers of
scientists have learned the lesson "that the practical value of any
piece of pure research is essentially unpredictable, and that the
scientist knows best what lines of research may produce results—
whether of practical value or not." Results cannot be dictated; a
gamble must be taken. Hence the Party has had to allow the
Soviet scientist his favorite pastime, and the Party can only hope
that out of this grant of freedom to the scientist the Party may
incidentally, almost accidentally, gain something for its military
and industrial might. And yet, inevitably, the Party loses something very important, too: "Meanwhile, the scientist's greater
freedom to think about science may lead him to ask why he is not
free to think and talk about other things.[15]

V

Of course, the Communist hierarchs taboo too open a discussion of such ideas in the press of the Soviet Union. But a few echoes of such heretical thoughts can be caught in the Moscow journals, and even more clearly in some works of Soviet fiction.

"Our era is that of technology and science," a Soviet engineer says in a private conversation in one recent novel. "Therefore, those who command technology and science must become the leading, guiding force. Engineers, my dear, engineers! That is you and I—we." His interlocutor, a would-be inventor, agrees enthusiastically: "True, how true! You argue this remarkably, Konstantin Romanovich. We!"

Later in the novel the pair are publicly accused by zealous Party men of wanting to establish "not a dictatorship of the proletariat, but a dictatorship of strong personalities . . . an era of engineers and technicians . . . as if our engineers and technicians are not workers and peasants of yesterday."

But the chief rebel-engineer insists on this sharp line between him and his fellow plotters on the one hand and the Party zealots on the other. He calls to action: "It is not we who should retreat from our positions, but they, they, these types made of reinforced concrete. Their time has ended, they are now living their last, they are dying out. These people with whom we are compelled to clash are all dead. But, as the saying goes, it is not enough to kill, you must yet knock them down to the ground. Well, then, act, knock them down. Nothing should stop you. Victors are not judged."[16]

In another, later, Soviet novel a group of young physicists are far more sympathetically described as daring rebels, or at least as fancying themselves rebels, in the wake of the de-Stalinization. At their half-merry, half-serious parties they read aloud the poems and prose forbidden during "the cult of personality" but now printed once more. Their bold talk has a political tone among others:

> They were excited most of all by the questions connected with the cult's consequences and they were confidently rebuilding this imperfect world. Together with Langmuir, Niels Bohr, Kurchatov, and Kapitsa they commanded the era's most important specialty. They believed that mankind's future depended on them; that they were humanity's prophets, benefactors, liberators.[17]

The Party functionaries are outraged by these young scientists with their own sense of historic mission. The Party declares this

sense wholly unwarranted. A faithful Party writer in *Pravda* denounces yet another such fictional character, a young engineer, as
"totally bankrupt," since he "places himself and his generation in
direct contrast and opposition to the older generation." The
Pravda article complains that the engineer "has in all self-conceit
decided that this era's truth begins with him and with persons as
young as he is; that before their own time everything had been
lies, untruth, falsehood."[18]

The young engineer indeed proclaims that he does not want
"Party secretaries to interfere unceremoniously with man's personal life." The Soviet writer who created this young engineer
makes it clear in his novelette that he is not at all sympathetic
toward the character he drew. In the novelette the engineer only
tries to palm himself off as "a new man of the new time, the time
cleansed of falsehoods and injustice"; but the novelist insists that
his character is not at all virtuous. He portrays the engineer as
somebody very negative, an immoral young man who mistreats
the trusting girl in love with him.

Most importantly, the novelist depicts this cad with an engineer's diploma as someone who goes too far in his criticism of
Stalinism. The novelist protests that the engineer should not "spit
in the face" of the entire generation of his elders, of Stalinists
and of those who had suffered Stalinism meekly or with misguided
enthusiasm. But the engineer (despite his creator's disapproval)
raises his voice against the older Communists quite effectively.
"It is you the older generation who made a mess of everything!"
the engineer exclaims at one point of the narrative. ". . . Consider
that I speak on behalf of many young people of my age." The
man whom he so addresses, his cousin, a former flyer and a
curious blend of Stalinist and Krushchevist, bitterly replies: "I am
afraid that to you the long years of our history are a period of
nothing but lawlessness, lies, and arbitrary violence."[19]

But weren't they? Aren't they still? The young engineer stands
his ground. Whatever his own set of morals may be, he rejects the
entire lawless code of both Stalin and Khrushchev. He—and others
his age—mean to begin their new era.

CHAPTER II

The Case Against

CALM YOURSELVES, citizens. Forget your wishful thinking. All this education, industrialization, and technization can and will only strengthen the Communist regime. Far from undermining and dooming it, science and technology make the Soviet regime the triumphant fact of the present and the wave of the imminent future for all humanity.

So say quite a few experts. Foremost among them until October 1964 was Khrushchev himself. In a speech to Bulgarian peasants, he boasted: "Annually the Soviet Union graduates three times as many engineers as does the United States. And whoever possesses knowledge owns the future!" But he denied any likelihood that these Soviet engineers would own the future without the Communist Party, by abolishing it. With scorn and contempt he revealed to his audience the news of the latest Western hope that education would bury the Soviet regime. "The capitalists, seeing that they won't be able to demolish the Soviet Union, have begun to console themselves with this reasoning: Well and good, with each year Soviet society indeed contains more and more educated persons, and when the entire Soviet society is educated, the people will change their political setup." Khrushchev laughed at this Western argument. He exclaimed:

> We have a saying: To slay a horse by feeding him more hay! Thus do you, imperalistic gentlemen, wish to slay the Soviet Union with knowledge, with education. Well now, your thoughts have brought you to your loss of common sense. You can't indeed be more foolish! But all right, we agree. You just keep on waiting for the fulfillment of your dream, while we will continue to prove to you of what the educated people of Socialistic countries are capable. They have shown you a lot, but that is nothing compared with what they will yet show you! There now you have the Marxist-

Leninist theory in action, there for you is Karl Marx with what you call "the bankruptcy" of his teaching![1]

On October 24, 1964, ten days after Khrushchev's overthrow, the fallen chief's promise that education would never threaten the Soviet regime was solemnly reaffirmed by Fyodor Konstantinov, one of the regime's high-bracket propagandists. Writing in *Literaturnaya gazeta* that day, Konstantinov complained that such "bourgeios sociologists" as Erich Fromm, Raymond Aron, and W. W. Rostow equated the new industrial society of the Soviet Union with that of "the countries of monopolistic capitalism" insofar as both societies were now being increasingly run by managers and engineers. Ah, but there is a vital difference, Konstantinov cried out indignantly: "Under capitalism, the manager and the engineer are servants of the capitalist who owns the means of production. But in Socialist countries the engineer and the manager are servants of the people."[2]

That is, they are servants of the Party and totally obedient to its slightest will and whim. And the Party, as that shrewd young Yugoslav scholar Mihajlo Mihajlov discovered in his memorable Moscow summer of 1964, like "every tyranny, even the most horrible one, lasts because of the support of its honest fanatics." These fanatics are immature in the midst of most mature or fast-maturing industrial societies, Mihajlov notes. *Homo sovieticus* is sad news both to Russia and to the world at large:

> The first characteristic of *homo sovieticus* is that he approves and accepts everything that is decided at the top with complete sincerity. The second characteristic is a naive and unthinking Jesuitism of the type described by Dostoyevsky in the person of Erkel, one of the minor characters of *The Possessed*—honest, sensitive, and pleasant in his personal life, but prepared for the greatest servilities in the name of the "higher Idea."[3]

And not only the lower classes, but also members of the scientific-engineering-managerial intelligentsia can be so naïve and so subservient. How much validity is there, then, to the Western hope that the Soviet technician is the anti-Communist man of the bright future?

I I

Some Westerners who have had dealings with Soviet scientists, engineers, and managers agree with the Party's contention that this particular Western hope is flimsy and foolish.

An American metallurgist, who with two of his compatriots and colleagues visited the Soviet Union in the summer of 1961 and spent much time with highly placed Soviet metallurgists, returned home with no such hope. Speaking for his two colleagues and for himself, Carl E. Hartbower, of Boston, dismissed the Western argument about the dangers the Communist leaders face in giving people more and more education. Obviously, he wrote, Americans placing their anti-Communist bet on this Soviet education have not met and talked with "Soviet scientists who have been brainwashed to the point where they believe that their government" tells them the truth.[4]

These Soviet scientists believed their propagandists that America's "elite and the warmongering military leaders want war." The Communist leadership sincerely wants disarmament (said these Russian professors), but the lords and masters of the Western camp, particularly of the United States, reject all the generous peace-loving proposals of Moscow. On one memorable occasion the American trio "argued that the U.S. is ready for disarmament and wants a continued ban on nuclear testing providing there is agreement between our countries on simultaneous disarmament and inspection, with a neutral third party to assure compliance." Their Soviet host-scientists appeared to agree with this desire almost completely, and one of them said he "couldn't understand why our countries could not come to similar agreement." He blamed the American government for the lack of such agreement. "It was quite clear that our host had been thoroughly indoctrinated with the idea that his country was entirely ready to accept inspection."[5] The Soviet professor just did not know the Party's real stand on inspection.

Talks with these Soviet scientists and engineers of metallurgy left their three American visitors incredulously wondering how these seemingly intelligent Russians could believe such propaganda rot as they were fed by their Communist indoctrinators. But apparently they did believe it. When the three American visitors asked their Soviet host-scientists about Soviet jamming of the Voice of America, the Russian professors answered "that the jamming of Western stations is done only when we [Americans] are telling lies about the Soviet Union." The Communist propaganda is so strong that the scientists of Russia cannot shake it off even when they go on missions to the United States, where they can find out the truth for themselves, but just won't. One of these Russian scientists, while speaking to the American visitors,

"made a point . . . that he didn't believe our [American] newspapers when he was in the United States because they are a
product of capitalistic industry." When this Russian read in
American newspapers anything unfavorable about the U.S.S.R.,
he did not stop to think about it (as we Americans hope we
would) but waved it away as "capitalistic propaganda generated
by our newspaper companies."

Mr. Hartbower's sad but firm conclusion is that the Communist
system, both now and in the foreseeable future, "cannot afford to
breed intellectuals with freedom of thought outside the realm of
science and engineering." Do optimists cite the Pasternak case as
proof to the contrary? But "the suppression of Pasternak's frank
treatment of religion and the revolution illustrated the point" of
precisely this Communist success in controlling the situation.[6]

Yes, of course, Soviet professional men are superior to Soviet
bureaucrats, if only because they have "a sense of professional
ethics and dedication to their work that one is not likely to find
among mere bureaucrats." This we have from Professor Richard
Pipes of Harvard University, one of the few Westerners ever invited to lecture at a Soviet University. From his close association
with Soviet professionals he writes that "scientists, in particular,
give the impression of considerable intellectual independence and
even daring." And yet:

> one searches in vain among them for that undisciplined love of
> theorizing, that receptivity to new ideas, that intellectual sweep that
> was so characteristic of the old Russian intelligentsia. Soviet schol-
> ars and scientists are usually very competent in their specialty; their
> knowledge of the facts and literature is sometimes acutely embar-
> rassing to a Westerner. But this competence is usually of a techni-
> cal nature; it is limited to the utilitarian aspects of the subject, and
> narrowly confined. They seem to have a positive dread of . . .
> originality of interpretation and boldness of conception . . .[7]

Hand in hand with this pessimistic point goes the view often
expressed by Professor Nicholas DeWitt, of Indiana University, that the narrowness of those most excellent Soviet scientists
makes it easier for the Party to ride herd on them. Compartmentalization of Soviet professors and their fields, lack of broad
cross-fertilization among them, allows the bureaucrats to continue
their dominance over the scientists—robs the latter of any chance
to assert political independence, makes them politically timid.[8]

And still another constant observer of the Soviet scene, Dr.
Philip E. Mosely, of Columbia University, notes the increasing

frequency of the hopeful question asked on the Western side: ". . . will not the ideological grip of the Party be gradually undermined by the remarkable spread of middle and higher education to more and more layers of Soviet society?" Will not "the expansion of education . . . not only equip its beneficiaries to serve the system better but . . . 'inevitably' give rise to a spirit of questioning, independent reasoning and critical judgment that will sooner or later destroy the Party's ideological control" and thus in time destroy the Party itself?[9]

But from the advantage of his many years of close acquaintance with, and analysis of, the Soviet system, Professor Mosely replies to these questions in the negative. There are indeed signs of "stirrings of skepticism and dissent" among the educated, but this "spirit of inquiry, dissatisfaction or even dissent" should not be mistaken for revolt, current or incipient. This spirit or urge

> may stem from many causes, including boredom, family memories, the influence of Russia's great literature, or the impact of injustices. But the problem of harnessing scientific progress with ideological conformity is not a new one for the Soviet regime. It has persisted, in varying forms, from the beginning. The Party and its instruments have developed many ways of shepherding the young toward productive and orthodox careers well rewarded by the state, and away from dangerous thoughts.[10]

It is true that these controls can never work as perfectly as the Communist masters wish them to function. But they work with some success, Professor Mosely feels. On the whole, in his view, Soviet youth is "highly conformist," and for this there are sufficient reasons.

> For one thing, the college-level study of politically dangerous subjects, such as history, economics and law, is confined to a relatively few and carefully supervised students. The great majority of students, and often the ablest, are attracted by good stipends and promising careers into technical and scientific fields. For them, the study of world history or foreign literature, even in its carefully selected doses, ends at about 15. What goes by the name of "social studies" after that is simply Party history, Party theory and the current Party program of "do's" and "don't's."[11]

Boredom, yes; rebellion, no. Apathy caused by all this dull propaganda is "probably far more serious than any conscious dissent" among Soviet youth. Expressions of dissent or doubt are noted only among a small minority of Soviet youth, and these are fairly easily spotted, contained and, if need be, repressed by the Soviet authority.

In handling a problem that has plagued it throughout its existence, the Party is alert but not unduly alarmed by its newest manifestations. Unlike some wishful analysts abroad, it is confident that it can train a very large part of its youth to serve the state, especially in engineering and the natural sciences, without letting many of them stray from the approved paths of ideological orthodoxy, reinforced as it is today by national pride and arrogance.[12]

In fact, the conflict does not seem to bother the Communist Party leadership as much as it used to. Professor Mosely explains: "The old conflict between the Party and the non-Party intelligentsia is very far in the past and is almost forgotten by people under the age of 50 or 45." Because of this, the Party feels safe in trusting its own apparatus, at least in part, to precisely those Party members who have come up from this scientific-engineering personnel.

In my two recent visits [Dr. Mosely writes] I have noticed a considerable shift of the position of Party secretary away from Party hacks and into the hands of competent managers, engineers, and scientists. . . . The upper ranks of the Party have been filled up with people who are also competent in their special bureaucratic or technical roles, and in general the Party leadership would prefer to have in positions of Party responsibility people who are both loyal Party members *and* well qualified in their own special knowledge and experience, as this increases the influence they can bring on both Party and non-Party colleagues.[13]

In sum, the Party politicians trust the Party's technicians so well that they are willing to run the risk of technicians as politicians. These technicians are so much blood and flesh of the Party by now that they will not turn into anti-Communist technocrats. In his time Khrushchev insisted that Marxism-Leninism was the final roof, as well as the prime root, of Russia's technological triumph. "Socialism has won this triumph," Khrushchev proclaimed in his interview with two Brazilian journalists on November 21, 1957, right after the success of the first two Sputniks,[14] and he repeated this assertion on many occasions in the seven years between then and his fall.

The leading editorial in *Pravda* of November 1, 1960, echoed the joyful claim for the thousandth time when it stated:

Soviet science is a child of Great October [the old-calendar month of the November 1917 seizure of power in Russia by Lenin], a child of the Socialist regime. The successes of Soviet science are closely tied with the fact that in its progress this science bases itself solidly on Marxism-Leninism, on the tried and genuinely scientific method of learning—on dialectical materialism. Herein is the true guarantee of further fruitful development of Soviet science, the guarantee of the enhancement of the role of Soviet science in the building of Communism.

Thus (to return this part of the argument to where we started it, to Moscow's claim) the Soviet leadership and its *Pravda* agree with us that in the Soviet Union its scientists and engineers are indeed the wave of the future. But they most emphatically disagree with the "too-hopeful" Westerners in defining this wave. They say that scientists and engineers are the Communist wave, and no other.

I I I

But let us not rest "the case against" right there. Let us push on a bit further; let us go on with this case of the technicians' possible loyalty to the Communist Party as it is constituted now, as it—and the entire Soviet regime—are being run by Khrushchev's heirs or may yet be run by their probable successors of the same ilk.

It may be argued that, genuinely impressed with the strong and successful leadership provided to them and to the rest of Russia by the Communist Party, and well paid for their scientific and engineering brilliance, the professional elite are perfectly satisfied with their subordinate role. They are on the winning chariot of history—so why should they try to upset it? Why should they demand a political leadership for themselves and thus risk their own hides as well as Russia's manifest destiny? Yes, one's career is far more important than any squeamishness about subservience to this stern, outmoded, naïve Party dogma and decree. The new intelligentsia face a number of contradictions in the very process of their development—contradictions which breed hypocrisy and careerism aiding the Party, as a keen *émigré* noted:

In many respects education has reached a very high level. Students receive a great quantity of exact knowledge; excellent mathematicians, physicists, chemists, and so on, are being formed in the Soviet school. This is a high mental culture, which doubtless helps also the development of critical thinking—provided, however, that it [such thinking] is not paralyzed by the careerism which is reared in the very same school which gives its students valuable knowledge. . . . I will add: hypocrisy is being reared along with careerism.[15]

It may be further argued that Soviet scientists, engineers, and managers have gone into science, engineering, and technical-industrial management precisely because they are afraid of Soviet politics and want to stay away from that hornet's nest. If so, they are loyal to the Party, even if passively.

Granted that some of them may not be too enthusiastic about the Communist Party. Most of them are indeed devoted to their research and technical production or management. And because they fear Red politics, they obey the Party. Moreover, for the same reason they will continue to do so in the foreseeable future as well.

Some observers disagree with those who argue that Soviet scientists are in fact in politics. It has been said of scientists that their scientific minds are too independent and too searching to be in Soviet politics in any way whatever. At the same time the inquisitiveness and freshness of their approach, while barring them from Soviet politics, are exactly the qualities that make them happy in Soviet science and technology. It is there, in science and technology, that they find freedom—one of the few freedoms existing in Russia today for the Party's subjects.

And Khrushchev did one smart thing among others: he reversed the late Stalin in this matter of treating scientists. Beginning with 1953, Khrushchev relaxed Stalinist restrictions upon, and persecution of, Soviet scientists. Even Stalin had paid handsomely the scientists he did not kill or jail—he had paid them in rubles, in comforts, in well-equipped laboratories. Khrushchev greatly increased such lavish treatment of scientists and engineers. But most importantly, he stopped exiling or killing them. He gave them security from terror.

The expectation now is natural that, in gratitude for such fine treatment, Soviet scientists and engineers would indeed be loyal to the post-Stalinist Party.

I V

The very reluctance of Soviet scientists, engineers, and managers to join the Party, or, if they have joined the Party (or the Komsomol, Young Communist League), their unwillingness to fulfill the Party tasks assigned to them, this whole phenomenon of their boredom and apathy where the Party is concerned may not be a good sign for our side after all. For how else can they make their political weight felt if not through the Party? Can they learn to swim without plunging into the water? Can they take over the monster of the Party and in time either tame or slay it entirely from the outside? The case against the possibility of the technicians becoming true technocrats, against the chance of their coming to power, should include this consideration of their passivity.

And yet another question in the same pessimistic vein: Is it at all natural for scientists and engineers to become politicians and be successful—above all, to be different from the too-common type of corrupt, brutal, power-for-power's-sake politicians?

A decade before the revolution of 1917 Professor Lev I. Petrazhitsky (Petrazycki) of the University of St. Petersburg, the period's great scholar in philosophy of law, remarked to one of his ablest students, who was busy with politics more than with his books: "Politics and science do not mix. To be in politics, one must sacrifice a part of his wisdom, and to be in science during certain historical eras one has to renounce other values."[16]

And if scientists do enter politics in a spirit of rebellion or at least reformation, engineers are not that daring or progressive. Thus the case against the eventual split of scientists and technicians from the Communist bureaucracy must also incorporate the probability of yet another Soviet split—a crevice within a crevice, so to say. This is the possible cleft between the Soviet scientists on the one hand and the Soviet engineers (and, quite likely, managers) on the other.

Not that such a gulf would be a strictly Soviet phenomenon. C. P. Snow suggests the existence of this separation in human society generally. He argues:

> . . . scientists proper . . . partly by training, partly by self-selection
> . . . include a number of speculative and socially imaginative minds.
> While engineers—more uniform in attitude than one would expect
> a professional class to be—tend to be technically bold and ad-
> vanced but at the same time to accept totally any society into which
> they may have happened to be born. The scientists proper are
> nothing like so homogeneous in attitude, and some of them will
> provide a quality which it seems to me we need above everything
> else.[17]

The quality which Lord Snow values in scientists is their ability to change and to help humanity to change. He writes: *"That* is why I want scientists active in all the levels of government." On an earlier occasion, in one of his novels, Lord Snow expressed this idea even more forcefully:

> As an outsider, it had taken me years to understand this rift in technical society. To begin with, I had expected scientists and engineers to share the same response to life. In fact, the difference in the response between the physicists and engineers often seemed sharper than the difference between the engineers and such men as Hector Rose. [Rose in Lord Snow's novel is a British government official.]
>
> The engineers . . . the people who made the hardware, who used existing knowledge to make something go, were, in nine cases out of ten, conservatives in politics, acceptant of any regime in which they found themselves, interested in making their machine work, indifferent to long-term social guesses.
>
> Whereas the physicists, whose whole intellectual life was spent in seeking new truths, found it uncongenial to stop seeking when they had a look at society. They were rebellious, protestant, curious for the future and unable to resist shaping it. The engineers buckled to their jobs and gave no trouble, in America, in Russia, in Germany; it was not from them, but from the scientists, that came heretics, forerunners, martyrs, traitors.[18]

This is an extremely provocative suggestion, indeed. Is there truly such a difference, such a separation, between the two components of the scientific-technical personnel in the Soviet Union today? If there is, then the Party's hand is surely strengthened. For there could be no united front of science and technology against the Party if scientists and engineers among themselves are at loggerheads about it all; if only the scientists are nonconformists, while the engineers give the Communists no trouble.

Of enmity or at least jealousy and coolness between the two Soviet parts of this intelligentsia there is in fact an occasional sign. Scientists in the Soviet Union look down on engineers. Caste is responsible for inner divisions within this milieu perhaps to a greater extent than such stratification is noticeable in the United States. An American visitor observed about the House of Scientists in downtown Moscow in 1961: "Only 'scholars' were allowed to use this club—that is, people with candidate and doctorate degrees (and visiting dignitaries like myself)."[19]

And Soviet engineers envy Soviet scientists. Often they try to prove that they are wiser and more useful than scientists. In a recent Soviet novel a young woman engineer, the daughter of a

scientist, clearly suffers from no father fixation as she voices her
contempt "for these academic institutes with their abstract crazi-
ness and scholasticism." The man she loves, a research engineer,
should quit his vague seeking in those unworldly laboratories. He
should leave his institute for a well-paying engineer's job at the
factory where she works—where no one "mutters a welter of
terminology about the simplest possible thing," where there is no
such "useless paper scribbling, bereft of the joy of a living cause";
she in her girlhood had seen such lack in her father's house quite
clearly.[20]

We know that in the West science and technology are often
confused with each other, but of course they should not be.
Someone has rightly said that the difference between them is
about the same as between ethics and law—one is exploratory,
contemplative, the other is practical, applied. In the Soviet Union
the difference between the two is understood more frequently and
lucidly. Thus, the gap between the Soviet scientists and the Soviet
engineers may prove to be more of a reality than in the West.

But even in the West—in America particularly—the new elite
of the specialists is recognized as far from homogeneous. Daniel
Bell, while pointing out this new elite's growing influence, is not
too certain about its power—exactly because the elite lacks co-
hesiveness. According to him, as already noted, these "technical
and professional intelligentsia . . . are not bound by the common
ethos that would constitute them a new class, nor even a cohesive
social group . . ."[21]

And if in our permissive society American scientists, engineers,
and other technical experts do not constitute one class or even a
group, then under the much more restrictive conditions of the
Soviet sociopolitical order the comparable Soviet intelligentsia has
even less of a chance to get together as a unified force to challenge
the Communist Party.

Or so runs the argument of those who would deny that Russia's
new scientists, engineers, and managers are shaping up as an anti-
Communist force of tomorrow.

V

But other commentators argue that such intelligentsia do constitute a class, and precisely because they are a selfish, near-
sighted class they are no true hope for humanity.

This view, in fact, is not confined to the subject of Russian intelligentsia. A character in one of John O'Hara's novels says that he neither likes nor trusts any scientists. And this is "because they're scientists. Science is their religion and they never have seemed to care much about people."

A woman protests saying that the man is wrong in his condemnation of scientists: "What about the fights against yellow fever, and syphilis and so on?"

The man stubbornly replies:

> I've never thought that the scientists gave much of a damn about the people involved. As people. A scientist is a fanatic, his religion is the search for information. But it certainly wouldn't surprise me if fifty years from now they rule the world. Maybe a cabinet of scientists, an international cabinet, physicists and biochemists. And then God help the world. If it isn't blown up before then, it will be when they start tiffing among themselves. They're just as bad as any ladies' bridge club. Or, if you prefer, a syndicate of gangsters. The North Side mob muscles into the South Side territory, and the shooting begins. The sad truth . . . is that the human race is made up of people who don't get along very well together. And never will.[22]

Certain events of recent years seem to reinforce this argument for both Europe and America.

Where scientists or other scholars or technicians have already become statesmen or aides and advisers to governments, they have all too often proved themselves either inept or vicious or both. In Portugal, Antonio de Oliveira Salazar is a dictator with neither democracy nor justice on his banner, and his iron-heel rule is not mitigated by the fact that before coming to power he was a professor of economics. In America, some thoughtful observers deny that, during World War II and soon thereafter, scientists proved by their action and advice that "they are free of the insincerities and dubious motives of the traditional actors on the political scenes"; they deny that scientists "are interested only in clarification and truth."[23] In the view of such doubters, Western (American in particular) scientists as seers have not been good news to humanity breathlessly waiting for the right political decision. "The notion that, simply by their status as scientists rather than by empirical work on all the major factors affecting such decisions, scientists deserve a special authority is silly and dangerous. We need the methods of science, not merely the authority."[24]

Other, not so recent, historical examples are sometimes cited to demonstrate that the role of scientists and technicians cannot give us any possible hope. I recall that after one of my lectures expressing my hope that such elite may yet prove to be a liberalizing factor in Soviet politics, I heard this objection:

"Historically, the intellectual class has not provided a brake on political demagogues. One need look no further than Nazi Germany for an example. There were thousands of brilliant German scientists and technicians who were not in sympathy with Hitler's drive for world domination. Yet they permitted themselves to become no more than cogs in the Nazi war machine."

And at a certain meeting of American historians I was asked this question:

"Is it not true that while prerevolutionary Russian scientists, such as the great chemist Dmitry Mendeleyev and the celebrated bacteriologist Ilya Mechnikov, came out for the general rights of the general people, today's Soviet scientists demand—and get—rights only for themselves, rights of untrammeled research and sense of human dignity for their own class or group and not for the general run of Russian classes and masses?"

The questioner went on: "Looking into the future, what guarantee is there that should Soviet scientists gain various rights for themselves, and perhaps even political power for their group, they would demand or provide freedoms for other Russians, of the strata below this scientific and engineering elite?"

A Russian émigré writer in New York agrees with the American challenger of my hope. The Russian declares that the old-time Russian intelligentsia were indeed "a carrier of lofty ideas of universal justice."[25] For them, "human dignity was above all, and they demanded that these ethical premises were applied not [alone] for themselves   [that is, not only for the intelligentsia], but for the entire people, particularly for those minorities that could not raise their voice in defense of their rights." Those long-gone Russian intelligentsia were "a phenomenon unique in history" if only because "on the surface they were a social class, but bereft of one of the principal features inherent in a class—namely, the sense of belonging to their own class and the consequent necessity to defend their own class interests." The old intelligentsia defended anybody else's class interests instead. Therein lay their own historic tragedy.

Not so with the new Soviet intelligentsia who have arisen in the last forty-five years. Of entirely different ingredients, the Soviet intelligentsia "are a real social class with a clearly expressed class

self-consciousness, which defends its own rights and privileges."
They will take but not give.

In sum, if any part of the new Soviet intelligentsia—say, the scientists and technicians—finally defy the tyrants and take for themselves the power that should be their own, and not the Party's, they will not share such power democratically with the folks in the basement.

Thus: What hope can there really be that the scientists and other experts, even if they are found in the driver's seat, will be any kinder to the passengers than the present Communist rulers are? Or any friendlier to us, or to the rest of mankind? Hardly any, say even those who do not love the Communist Party and would welcome a change for the better. They just don't see a chance for any good change. In this, however reluctantly, they agree with the prediction made by Khrushchev at the height of his power.

But the main argument remains that the new scientific-technical elite will not make any try for power, either for itself or for the people at large. As Professor Allen Kassof, of Princeton University, has ably summarized "the case against," the post-Stalinist leadership of the Communist Party, far from being swamped or even a little pushed by the rising technocrats, has allowed "only a tactical regrouping on the march from a relatively primitive to a far more advanced theory of twentieth-century totalitarianism."[26]

In other words, he and his fellow-skeptics look at the changes in the Soviet Union and say: Business as usual.

And in this, quite definitely, I disagree with them—with much of their "case against."

CHAPTER III

Peter Kapitsa: Symbol of Resistance

DISAGREEING WITH MUCH of "the case against," I sought confirmation—or refutation—of my proposition in a variety of evidence coming to us from behind the Curtain. Quite early in my researches I found that an excellent bird's-eye view of our problem was afforded by the adult life of one Russian scientist far more than any other. This was the record of Academician Peter Kapitsa,* a physicist of genius ever since his early twenties, now a man in his early seventies, but ever an active and even vigorous leader in Soviet science nonetheless.

In his life's story we can see practically the entire course of historic relations between the Party and the scientific-technical intelligentsia of Russia. We perceive the Party's early neglect of, and hostility to, the scientists (as to any other non-Communist intellectuals) side by side with the scientists' distrust and contempt for the Party. We then pick up a trend of opportunism, of accommodation, on both sides—soon followed by the Party's obtuseness and coercion, with the years growing into sheer terror, from which very few scientists were exempted. We see the scientists' fear and retreat exemplified in Kapitsa, but also Kapitsa's persistent and adroit resistance; his awareness of his increasing influence; and finally his reach for power, however tentative the reach and incipient the power.

All this is typical, and yet atypical too. For there is no gainsaying Kapitsa's unique stature. If you ask any scientist anywhere, East or West, for the name of a Soviet scientist best known to him, chances are overwhelmingly for the answer: "Peter Kapitsa, of course." The name is indeed well known the world over, but not the man himself. Despite all the many years

* In Western sources his name is often transliterated as "Kapitza." This is less accurate than "Kapitsa."

of his appearance in the world's headlines, Academician Pyotr Leonidovich Kapitsa is something of a mystery, and not only to other nations but to his fellow Russians as well.

One of the earliest Russian scientists to come back to the Soviet Union from a prolonged experience abroad, and surely the most important among such repatriates, Kapitsa has never publicly explained certain intriguing details of his return of 1934. And because such details are still not quite clear, they have to be reported in this work by hearsay and almost on speculation.

The extent of Kapitsa's reconciliation with the Communist regime which practically kidnaped him is an enigma. To some observers, equally debatable is the degree to which he may be viewed as a center or a symbol of present-day active opposition of one group within the New Class against another, of scientists against political bosses.

Some say that the great atomic physicist is a loyal Soviet patriot, even if not a member of the Communist Party. At least one of the Russian defectors with whom I have talked expressed his doubt that Peter Kapitsa can be properly regarded as a source of opposition to the Party. This man, a former industrial manager from Leningrad, remarked to me that Dr. Kapitsa "has been vastly overrated as harboring any true sense" of any such opposition; "there is no real independence in him."

But I have found this a minority opinion. Others, in speaking about Kapitsa, recall the strange story of his kidnaping by Stalin, cite instances of his defiance of Stalin and his later differences with Khrushchev, and insist that he is still a rebel—a kind of "Peck's Bad Boy" of the Soviets.

In the last few years Kapitsa has publicly denounced Communist dogmatists for their Stalin-begotten hostility to Einstein's theory of relativity, to electronic computers, to cybernetics as a whole. He has criticized Khrushchevian and post-Khrushchevian interference by Communist politicians in the daily affairs and long-range plans of Soviet science. He has made no secret of liking the officially tabooed work of Soviet abstractionist artists and sculptors. In sum, the available evidence points to the fact that in his long but not too voluntary Soviet period Peter Kapitsa has at times gone against the power that has tried to order him around. If not always in opposition, and certainly not the chief leader of any hidden or open "scientists' movement" against the Kremlin, Peter Kapitsa by his life and work does prove that the New Class is divided.[1]

I I

There are plenty of reasons why both Communists and non-Communists should admire Professor Kapitsa. Director of the Academy's far-famed Institute of Problems of Physics, he is one of Russia's foremost physicists; author of the hydrodynamic theory of bearing lubrication; originator of the hypothesis of spherical lightning; researcher and designer of equipment in heat transfer and superfluidity of helium; and leading experimenter in atomic physics. His scholarly publications are numerous and important, and his work has earned for him a great number of Soviet and international honors and prizes.

Pyotr Leonidovich Kapitsa, born in 1894, comes of West Russian blood—from Belorussia, or White Russia. He is of the same stock as Andrei Gromyko, the Soviet diplomat, but of a much higher social origin than Gromyko, who came from a peasant family.

Peter's father, Leonid, was a lieutenant general in the Tsar's Corps of Engineers; he helped to modernize the old naval base and fortress of Kronstadt, near St. Petersburg (now Leningrad). His mother was a well-known teacher and collector of Russian folklore. Peter was born at Kronstadt. Some of the best schools of tsarist Russia gave him his early education.

The revolution of 1917 found Peter an honor student in the capital's Polytechnic Institute. His first scientific paper was published in the journal of the Russian Society of Physics and Chemistry the very month the Bolsheviks overthrew the liberal Provisional Government and proclaimed their Soviet republic. Kapitsa's official Communist biographer was, in time, to comment: "Life presents most incredible coincidences. Along with the new state a new scientist was born."[2]

Graduating in 1918, the young man worked with Professor Abram F. Ioffe in the Physics-Technical Institute. Ioffe was Russia's earliest atomic physicist. By his side Kapitsa learned as much about the elusive atom as was known at the time. He also worked with Professor Nikolai Semyonov, who many years later (in 1956) won a Nobel Prize. In 1918–20 Semyonov and Kapitsa collaborated in the development of an original method of ascertaining magnetic properties of the atom.

But Russia's civil war and its aftermath were not exactly conducive to the scientists' well-being and peace of mind. Amid the bloodshed and chaos of 1918–21 the Kremlin had little thought for Russian savants. Grandiose plans of government-sponsored research remained on paper. For many scholars and their families there was neither food nor fuel. Some died amid privations. Several reports insist that among such victims were Kapitsa's wife and child, and that Peter himself survived almost in spite of his will. Crushed, brooding, he decided to leave his homeland.

Soviet officials at first wouldn't hear of a foreign journey for Kapitsa. Now that the civil war was over, the Soviet republic needed scientists for its reconstruction, they said. But Maxim Gorky, Russia's most influential writer then living, came to Kapitsa's rescue. In 1921, thanks to Gorky's intercession, as well as Ioffe's recommendation, a visa was granted to Kapitsa.

The official fiction was that the Academy of Sciences was sending him abroad to renew contacts with foreign scholars, also to purchase sorely needed books and laboratory equipment. Shabbily dressed, thin, thoughtful, he sailed for London.

I I I

His reputation had preceded him. British scientists knew of Peter Kapitsa as a brilliant blend of powerful analyst and practical engineer. Lord Ernest Rutherford at once made a place for Peter in his famous Cavendish Laboratory at Cambridge.

Lord Rutherford was the genius who discovered the nucleus of the atom and was the first to change the structure of an atom. In his fission work he valued Kapitsa's aid from the very beginning. Kapitsa was soon recognized as the Old Wizard's right hand. Under Rutherford's guidance, in addition to working on the problem of splitting the atom, Kapitsa busied himself with the investigation of the reaction of matter to the influence of magnetic fields. His spirits soon revived; he was now increasingly confident and even gay.

Yet, a few scientists did not exactly like Kapitsa—for reasons both personal and political. Among these men were his fellow Russian émigrés. They were definitely (and some belligerently) anti-Soviet, but young Kapitsa seemed equivocal at best. To some acquaintances he explained himself as not an émigré but an emissary, that is, a scientist still on a Moscow mission of research and purchase of equipment and books, with a vaguely acknowledged obligation some day to return home to the Soviets.

Professor Stepan Timoshenko, an *émigré* already then making a great name for himself in American academic and engineering circles for his work in theoretical and applied mechanics, met Kapitsa at a scientific congress in Edinburgh in September 1921. Years later he recalled that even in his first few months at Cambridge young Kapitsa "felt no lack of any of his necessities," because "the Bolshevik government furnished him with money fairly generously." It was this money, Timoshenko went on, that indirectly helped Kapitsa gain his initial fame of a sort in England.

He could even afford to buy a motorcycle. On this he began experimenting. He wanted to ascertain the utmost speed that could be attained on it. These experiments ended for him badly. On one occasion, while making a turn at high speed, the motorcycle crashed, and Kapitsa found himself in a ditch. The impact was considerable, but his arms and legs survived intact. His face and chest, however, did suffer. Someone picked Kapitsa up and delivered him to a hospital, where he had to remain for more than a week.

Telling of this adventure the very first evening of his meeting with Timoshenko at Edinburgh, Kapitsa related that in the hospital he "was bored waiting for a full recovery and so, his head still bandaged, went back to the laboratory." The effect was dramatic. One after another his associates came to Kapitsa's cubicle, asked questions in awe, and wished him to get well soon. "Finally Rutherford himself made his appearance, gazed at the bandaged head, and left silently. This made Kapitsa rather well known in the laboratory."

Grudgingly Timoshenko admitted that at the scientific congress in Edinburgh, at the university's dormitory where the visiting scientists were housed, the young and exuberant Kapitsa quickly proved himself to be as popular as apparently he had become at Cambridge.

In the evening, when all gathered in the drawing room, he amused the public by his tricks and experiments. He was extraordinarily bold. When, in the course of an experiment, he needed an assistant, he would unceremoniously pull some celebrated scientist by his sleeve and begin to explain to him just what it was he had to do. Solemn, dignified Englishmen lost their gravity of manner and fully submitted to Kapitsa's decisive actions.[3]

I V

Some of Kapitsa's audacity may have come from his inner conviction that he had something of value to offer to these British and their society. Indeed, he did. As even Timoshenko allowed, "his superiority over young English scientists came from his passage through the excellent engineering school of the St. Petersburg Polytechnic Institute." He therefore could and did design large machinery. "In his scientific work he tended to shift from small physics equipment to big machines, and this change of the experiment's scale gave him a chance to carry out a series of important researches."[4]

In 1923 Peter Kapitsa was awarded his doctorate by Cambridge. The same year brought him the Maxwell Prize, one of the world's highest scientific honors. In 1924 he developed unique equipment for work with superpowerful magnetic fields. More and more the eyes of Britain's scientists were upon him. In 1929 Kapitsa was elected to the Royal Society, the first foreigner (so it was said) to receive this honor in two centuries. By the early 1930s he had been elected also to the British Institute of Physics, to the Cambridge Philosophical Society, and to Trinity College. He was presently a full professor at Cambridge. The Royal Society built a special laboratory to suit his exacting specifications. In 1932 he designed a high-production hydrogen liquefier. In 1934 he began blueprints of his original apparatus for producing large quantities of liquid oxygen (further developed and constructed in 1938). His administrative posts included an assistant directorship in the Cavendish Magnetic Research Laboratory and, from 1930, a directorship in the Cambridge University Laboratory.

In his personal life he was also finding increased stability and happiness: in 1929, in London, Anna Krylova became his loving wife. She was the daughter of Professor Aleksei Krylov. In the early 1930s she bore Peter Kapitsa two children.

Kapitsa's father-in-law was a prominent mathematician, physicist, astronomer, and above all a first-rate ship builder.[5] While at first in his British residence Kapitsa appeared to be on a Soviet mission but later ceased this connection and became a Russian expatriate, Krylov was never an *émigré*. Krylov's years in England, 1921–27, were spent clearly on a mission for the Soviet government: he supervised the building of ships ordered in England by the Soviets and carried out other technical assignments from Moscow. True, he felt independent enough to meet, and eat and drink with those of his prerevolutionary Russian friends and associates who were now *émigrés* in London and Paris; he listened to their anti-Soviet talk, but he was most careful and reserved on any problem involving Russian politics. "Krylov had to return [to the Soviet Union]; therefore he had to be cautious," wrote Professor Timoshenko.[6]

Krylov was destined to play an important role in Kapitsa's eventual fate. But there are two different—in fact, diametrically opposite—reports on the nature of that role.

V

It was in the late 1920s and early '30s that the Soviet government intensified its bold, smart campaign of enticing gifted *émigrés* back into Russia. Stalin wanted certain key men of the arts and sciences to return. His agents—or just nostalgia—had already won several successes. Among the willing returnees were the composer Sergei Prokofiev, and the writers Maxim Gorky, Aleksei Tolstoy, and Ilya Ehrenburg. Some who were sent abroad on missions could have stayed as *émigrés*, but did not. Among such returnees was Professor Krylov, Anna Kapitsa's father.

And now for Kapitsa. As Peter's renown became worldwide, Stalin and his men realized his worth. They now knew that in letting Kapitsa go abroad a grievous error had been made. Two items were just then discovered by Soviet intelligence men in England.

Item One. Anna Kapitsa missed her father. And as her father's letters began to arrive from Russia, she found that she longed also for one more look at her homeland.

Item Two. Nominally, Peter Kapitsa was still a Soviet citizen. He was refusing all offers of the British government to make him His Majesty's subject.

Why was he shunning British citizenship? Was he now pro-Soviet? No. He was merely a patriot of his old fatherland without any love or respect for the government that happened to be ruling it. He felt it was his duty to return to Russia someday for good—to give to his people the benefit of his talent and knowledge.

Some day, but not too soon. This much was plain from Kapitsa's remarks to his friends on the subject of the Soviets. He would return permanently only if and when there was freedom in Russia.

The Kremlin heard of this, but was still hopeful. In 1933, cautiously, cleverly, the Kremlin let out feelers. Would the prodigal son return just for a visit? A scientific congress was to meet next year in Moscow, surely of much interest to Kapitsa. Also it was known that Kapitsa needed a rest. He could, when the congress was over, take his vacation in the Crimea and the Caucasus instead of the French Riviera. He could bring Anna and his car along; drive anywhere in Russia; then go abroad again. His Russian colleagues, from his old teacher Ioffe down to the greenest assistants in atomic physics, were yearning for a talk with him. Stalin himself gave his word to let Kapitsa out once the visit was completed. Now, would Kapitsa come for a while, a brief while?

Kapitsa shook his head. But Anna pressed, Anna implored. And Peter gave in. Reluctantly, but he did. A Russian *émigré*, Boris Nicolaevsky, wrote to me about this moment in the Kapitsas' life: "She greatly longed for her native land. . . . Kapitsa himself was very reluctant to go—I know this from his close friends."[7]

V I

Such was one report, one belief, widely current among the Russian *émigrés* in Western Europe and the United States. But another story, at sharp variance with the preceding, was known less generally, and chiefly to those who were scientists and well acquainted with Kapitsa or at least with his activities.

This second story had it that all through the 1920s Kapitsa went on periodic trips to the Soviet Union and returned to England with no hindrance from the Soviets at all. In July 1926, on a trip to Cambridge, Professor Timoshenko was entertained by Kapitsa "most graciously," as the rather hostile guest conceded.

He was on the Trinity College staff and had his lodgings right opposite the main gate of that College. To honor my arrival Kapitsa arranged in his flat a tea, to which he invited several young physicists. Kapitsa loved to talk. He told many tales about his trips to Russia, whither he was repeatedly invited to lecture about the development of physics in England. But he was not too burdened by such lectures, and he spent most of his time at Kislovodsk [a resort in the Northern Caucasus]. Now he was talking about his latest trip, during which he had managed to visit his old family home, somewhere in the Volyn province. At that he had succeeded in carrying out with him a few items of his family's silver, and here he pointed to the tea set standing before us.

But Professor Timoshenko did not believe Kapitsa. ". . . I thought to myself that he had been given this set out of the 'cigarette-case fund'* as compensation for his lectures."[8]

Toward the end of that summer of 1926, while in Paris, Timoshenko ran into Krylov, Kapitsa's father-in-law, on the street. They had dinner in the company of some fellow-Russians, and Krylov told Timoshenko that he would like to see him soon alone, on a private matter. Several days later, Timoshenko called on Krylov at his hotel. The matter, it turned out, concerned Kapitsa. "Krylov asked me to warn Kapitsa to decline any further invitations from Russia. . . . At my very next meeting with Kapitsa I told him of this warning, but he paid little attention to it."[9]

Timoshenko saw Kapitsa for the last time in the summer of 1934, at a scientific congress held at Cambridge. Despite his dislike of Kapitsa, he was impressed by the physicist's successes in England. Once more Timoshenko explained this triumph by Kapitsa's old Russian schooling: "Physics, in its development, demanded large-scale, factory-size experimentation, and Kapitsa, with the engineering education he brought from the St. Petersburg Polytechnic Institute, had considerable advantage over the theoreticians of the university type." The two talked about Russia again.

> Kapitsa told me that during his years at Cambridge he had been repeatedly invited to Soviet Russia for reports and lectures, and that he found such trips most interesting, since following the reports and lectures it was very pleasant to spend the remainder of a summer somewhere in the Crimea or the Caucasus. I remarked that such journeys were not without their dangers; it was quite possible that one beautiful day the Soviet government might detain him, and he would never return to England. But he only laughed. Such a turn of affairs seemed improbable to him.[10]

Apparently, in returning to Russia in 1934 reluctantly or not, Kapitsa trusted Stalin's word. Why did he?

Some who knew him at the time recall that Maxim Gorky backed Stalin's promise with his own guarantee. Gorky swore to see to it that Kapitsa was not stopped from leaving Russia when ready to go. And Kapitsa believed Gorky, because Gorky had secured for Kapitsa his original exit visa in 1921. And in 1934

---

* This expression, "the cigarette-case fund," was then common among Russians both at home and abroad to denote the valuables confiscated by the Communists, in 1917 and later, from the upper- and middle-class persons in Russia, in many instances before or after their execution by firing squads.

Gorky was even more powerful than he had been thirteen years before. Stalin now openly deferred to Gorky (while secretly plotting Gorky's death, which came in 1936).

Thus it was, in the summer of 1934, that Kapitsa returned to Russia, an Englishman perhaps more than a Russian. His friend Niels Bohr, the Danish atomic physicist, accompanied Peter and Anna.

VII

In Russia, Kapitsa looked around with shrewd eyes. He saw that his old homeland was immeasurably stronger and far more orderly than when he had first left it. He was impressed by certain improvements introduced by the Soviets. He was pleased when he re-examined the scenes of his childhood and youth and again when—after parting with Bohr, who sailed back to Denmark—he and Anna drove in their car southward, to their beloved Crimea and Caucasus.

But though he and Anna were free in their movements, he noticed that not many Russians were. His early disapproval of things Soviet was confirmed. By the end of several weeks he dreamed of his adopted England, his Cambridge, with its freedom and decency. Naturally both he and Anna missed their children. And so the two turned back.

They drove north to Leningrad to supervise the loading of their car and of sundry souvenirs onto a Britain-bound steamer. It was here that the Kapitsas were told:

"Your exit visas have been canceled."

They were stunned. Their worst fears had come true. Peter argued. In vain. He and Anna had to turn back to Moscow.

In Moscow, high officials were poker-faced. Sorry, but Professor Kapitsa was a Soviet citizen and had to stay. His country needed him. Great things were in store for him. He would have everything—even his Cavendish Laboratory. Yes, Stalin ordered that, if possible, the entire laboratory in Cambridge should be purchased for him and brought to Moscow. What would the professor say to this?

The professor said, No. And no, no, no—emphatically, again and again.

The officials shrugged their shoulders. They were polite. In contrast to the usual methods of the Soviet police, no force would be used on the great scientist. Give him time, and he would see

the light. Such were the Kremlin's special orders. Stalin was patient.

The professor tried to outwait the dictator. For a whole year
Peter and Anna Kapitsa lived in their hotel room, hardly stirring
except for a walk, refusing to say yes, demanding their right to
return to England.

Lord Rutherford and other foreign friends of Kapitsa addressed the Kremlin with protest and plea. Stalin hardly bothered
to reply. To Kapitsa, Stalin sent word that he would see him if the
professor wanted to talk things over in a more placable mood.

In time Kapitsa weakened. He discovered that he longed for his
work even more than for England. He would see Stalin. And so
the two met and came to an agreement.

Things began to hum. Stalin's new promise was kept. Not sparing the expense, the Soviet government bought and brought to
Moscow certain items of equipment in the Cavendish Laboratory
—the items which had been used by Kapitsa for producing high
magnetic fields. The British sold these in the interests of science,
since no one else but Kapitsa could use this equipment anyway,
and since the money received for it went to buy England's first
cyclotron.

Much else was done by Stalin for his captive from this point
on. In 1935 Kapitsa was made director of the Institute of Problems of Physics, within the network of the Soviet Academy of
Sciences. A corresponding member of the Academy from his British days (since 1929), he became a full-fledged member of the
Academy in 1939.

The two Kapitsa children were soon brought from England to
rejoin their parents. The Harris tweeds which Kapitsa liked so
well were ordered for him. Even the precise brand of Kapitsa's
favorite English tobacco was imported for his pipe.

An enthusiastic, devoted circle of colleagues and students
formed around him at the Institute in Moscow. His Wednesday
evening at-homes became a celebrated colloquium for years and
years.

Yet, it was not atomic physics that held Kapitsa's primary
attention once he resumed his work. From 1935 on, his major
achievements were in low temperatures and their application in
the liquefying of air. To his credit he added the first discovery and
investigation of hyperfluidity of liquid helium. His small, inexpensive turbine, used to take oxygen out of air, brought him a United
States patent as well as new Kremlin honors.

But clouds were gathering, thickening, threatening. The purges of the middle and latter 1930s struck Russia in a long, agonizing series. Most of the men and women who had ever had any dealings with the West were arrested and shot, or deported to concentration camps and slower death, by the hundreds, by the thousands. All around Peter Kapitsa friends, associates, acquaintances were dragged out of their homes and laboratories to a fate known or unknown. Closer and closer to the physicist the secret police hit.

Among others Lev Landau, a rising Russian star of physics and mathematics, was arrested. A Jew, he was nevertheless accused of pro-Nazi activities. Nearly three decades later, in 1964 (two years after he was awarded a Nobel Prize), Landau recalled: "They charged me with being a German spy. Now, occasionally, this seems amusing to me, but at that time, believe me, I did not feel like laughing. I spent one year in prison, and it was clear to me that I wouldn't last another six months. I was dying, simply dying." It was Peter Kapitsa who finally saved him.

> Kapitsa went to the Kremlin and . . . demanded my freedom. Otherwise, he said, he would leave his Institute. I was freed. It is hardly necessary to say that in those years, for such an act, one had to have great courage, great humanity, and crystal-clear honesty.[11]

VIII

In the early 1940s Kapitsa returned to the atomic field by helping other Soviet scientists in their nuclear researches. He built new instruments for the cosmic-ray observations carried on in the high mountains of the Pamirs and Soviet Armenia by the two Armenian brothers, Abram and Artemy Alikhanov. During the war Kapitsa experimented with uranium and lectured on atomic physics in Moscow's military academies.

And yet the atom didn't seem to be his chief concern. When in April 1944 the Franklin Institute of Philadelphia awarded him the Franklin Medal it was for his nonatomic work. For his discovery of hyperfluidity he received the First Class Stalin Prize twice, in 1941 and 1943. Early in 1945, when the Kremlin gave Kapitsa the title of Hero of Socialist Labor, it was for his researches into the turbine methods of oxygen production.

By 1946 he had the Order of Lenin, the highest award in the Soviet scale of kudos. At this time, in 1945–46, he smilingly denied to foreign correspondents that he was under any duress. Urbane and relaxed, puffing on his briar, he spoke in his colloquial English of all the facilities and honors he was enjoying in the land of the Soviets. In his public speeches he dwelt at length on the glories of the U.S.S.R. Nevertheless, rumors spread that Stalin was not too pleased with Kapitsa.

Stalin was rewarding him constantly, but more in hopes of spurring Kapitsa on to atomic discoveries than in recognition of work already done. Hints were carried to Kapitsa from the Kremlin: Move "closer to actual life"—that is, to the post-Hiroshima reality.

On the news of Hiroshima, Stalin had tripled the salaries of his atomic scientists. As late as December 1945, Kapitsa blandly revealed that his most recent work had been with hydrogen. Unofficially, however, all the world heard by then that Kapitsa was leading the entire effort to produce a Soviet A-bomb. Norbert Wiener, who had known him at Cambridge in the early 1930s, said later that he was not surprised. He recalled that in Russia, Kapitsa "became the pioneer of that large-scale, factorylike type of laboratory which had first been employed by [Heike] Kamerlingh Onnes in the Netherlands for low-temperature research, and which is now the standard means of exploring the nucleus and of designing atomic bombs." In 1945, just as soon as Wiener had first heard of the American atom bomb, he felt sure that with Kapitsa training

> the Russians in the technique of this sort of laboratory it would not be many years before they would have mastered for themselves the principles and techniques of nuclear research, whether or not they might capture our secrets by means of espionage or persuade a group of malcontents to serve their purposes.[12]

At this time, in 1945–46, foreigners—particularly Westerners —seldom saw Peter Kapitsa. In the summer of 1946, to Richard E. Lauterbach, the young American journalist who questioned him about the atom bomb, Kapitsa made a wry face. "To talk of atomic energy in terms of the atomic bomb," he said, "is like talking of electricity in terms of the electric chair."[13]

A man of peace, Kapitsa was hoping for an international agreement to outlaw the atomic bomb. He hoped for mankind's survival. But, increasingly, he criticized the Americans for what he termed as unnecessary stubbornness in safeguarding our atomic secrets.

This is where the new mystery of Kapitsa began. Was he sincere in this criticism? Did he gradually allow himself to be con-

vinced by Stalin's men that we were being perverse in not
destroying our stocks of A-bombs as the Kremlin wished us to do,
and that as a Russian patriot he must do his best for the Soviet
version of the A-bomb? Or was he only *talking* like a loyal Stalinist—to cover up his decision not to lead the Soviet atomic race
against the West?

The mystery deepened when suddenly, late in 1946, Kapitsa's
name vanished from official Soviet news. He was no longer head
of the Institute of Problems of Physics, nor in the lists of Russian
atomic scientists awarded Stalin's prizes and medals. No letter
from him or about him reached foreign parts. Complete official
silence surrounded Kapitsa.

Two long years passed, and then, in 1948, an article of his
appeared in a Soviet journal of experimental and theoretical
physics. In February 1949, another article by Kapitsa was printed
in the official annals of the Soviet Academy of Sciences. But
neither was on atomics—both were on liquids.

Was Kapitsa being *zasekrechen*—that is, surrounded by utmost
secrecy and security—because of topnotch successes in atomics
since late 1946? Or, on the contrary, was he being punished by
Stalin because he either couldn't or wouldn't help the Kremlin's
efforts to produce an A-bomb? All sorts of reports circulated then,
and still abound now, about this period in Kapitsa's colorful life,
but the most authentic facts seem to be these:

In Stalin's final years Kapitsa refused to contribute his genius
to the evolvement or improvement of the Soviet atomic and hydrogen bombs. Stalin, not daring to shoot or even exile the great
scientist, had him confined under house arrest, which may have
lasted several years.

In his *Moscow Summer* Mihajlo Mihajlov, while reporting
on his conversation with the celebrated Soviet writer Vladimir
Tendryakov, noted: "Among other things, Tendryakov told us
that his friend, the Academician Kapitsa, famous as a mathematical genius, was under house arrest for eight years during the Stalin
era."[14] In early 1965 Ilya Ehrenburg revealed how dismayed
Kapitsa's British friends had been on hearing of his arrest. At the
end of Stalin's era, Ehrenburg was in England on a mission for
the Soviet "peace" movement of the time. He was taken on a visit
to Cambridge, where a distinguished physicist and his wife cautiously and unhappily inquired about Kapitsa's troubles. Ehrenburg tried to reassure them; he felt that his hosts "wanted to
believe me but did not dare to." They were slightly reassured

when Ehrenburg agreed to deliver their gift of a few skeins of wool to Anna Kapitsa (who loved to knit).[15]

That Kapitsa was indeed under house arrest for a period near the close of Stalin's era seems now indisputable, if only because mention of the arrest was later, in Khrushchev's time, allowed to seep through in foreign correspondents' dispatches from Moscow uncensored and unrefuted.

Peter Kapitsa returned to freedom and to the world's headlines soon after Stalin's death. In August 1953, when Russia's possession of an H-bomb of her own became known, Kapitsa's earlier role in this achievement was generally recognized. In Washington it was recalled that Kapitsa's particular specialty was on the major matter of the hydrogen bomb—the behavior of materials at very high and very low temperatures. A December 1945 statement by Kapitsa was recalled to the effect that he had transformed hydrogen into a hard, visible metal. The chairman of the United States Joint Committee on Atomic Energy once remarked, with disquiet, on Kapitsa's "special competence in the technical problems relating to hydrogen weapons."

In 1955, two years after Stalin's death, Kapitsa was reinstated as director of the Institute of Problems of Physics. Also in 1955 he made public his hypothesis about the origin of ball lightning, which in some scientific quarters is seriously considered for its potential as a military weapon of tremendous force.

It is quite possible that the Party now favors Kapitsa because the scientist has by this time changed his ideas about bombs that are too destructive: it is known that currently Kapitsa supervises Soviet laboratories for development of atomic and hydrogen bombs and military use of cosmic-ray energy.

IX

And yet his rebellious voice is still raised. To cite an outstanding example:

Men of science and politics the world over sat up and took notice when on March 26, 1962, the Moscow *Ekonomicheskaya gazeta* printed Dr. Kapitsa's lengthy article "Theory, Experiment, Practice."[16] Therein the internationally famous atomic physicist declared that without the science of cybernetics* Soviet outer-

* Cybernetics, the science of those methods of control and communication which are common to living organisms and machines, is used as a term— in Russian perhaps more widely than in Western languages—to cover also linear programming, information retrieval, servomechanisms, and other fields and features related to electronic computing.

space successes would have been impossible. Yet, the scientist recalled, only some eight years earlier certain Soviet dogmatists had the stupid nerve to denounce cybernetics as something capitalistic and thus worthless, unclean, harmful.

With dignified anger Dr. Kapitsa quoted *Filosofichesky slovar'* (Philosophical Dictionary) published in 1954, one year after Stalin's death but still mirroring the official Stalinist negation of computing machines: "Cybernetics is a reactionary pseudo science, emerging in the United States after World War II and widely spreading in other capitalistic countries as well."

Seizing upon the title of the 1954 book, Professor Kapitsa berated its authors as "philosophers" who "committed an error," but who "as philosophers should have foreseen the further development of natural sciences instead of pronouncing their rigid judgments of a past phase" of these sciences.

Never once did he call them Stalinists, nor (of course) did he say that Khrushchev had been one of Stalin's top hatchetmen, responsible directly or indirectly for that era's atrocities. Remarking merely that "this mistake has been corrected," Kapitsa went on to state that already in 1954, if not earlier, Russia's true scientists refused to bow to those Soviet "philosophers," and how lucky this was for the nation! He wrote:

Had our scientists at the time, in 1954, obeyed the philosophers, had they adopted this definition [of cybernetics] as their directive for the further development of this science, we can say that our conquest of outer space, of which all of us are justly proud and for which the entire world respects us, could not have occurred, since it is impossible to guide a spaceship without cybernetic machines.

Nor would the Soviets have emerged with their own atomic bomb when they did, Kapitsa continued, had the Soviet "philosophers" been obeyed in their abuse of another science milestone: Albert Einstein's work on relativity. He pointed out that already in Einstein's time physicists had confirmed his theory by their experiments with atomic particles, but that Soviet dogmatists disregarded this evidence.

To understand these experiments a profound knowledge of the latest physics was needed, but certain philosophers lacked such knowledge. And now physicists confirm the Einstein law, not on separate atoms, but on the scale of the atom bomb. How embarrassed our physicists would have been had they followed those philosophers' conclusions and had they ceased their work on the problem of applying the theory of relativity in nuclear physics!

In his March 1962 article Kapitsa implied that 'way back in those days, in the 1940s and early '50s, he was among the bold ones who shrugged off the anti-Einstein mania and the anti-cybernetic dogma, who went on with their genuinely scientific work. Kapitsa's house arrest (or even direr punishment, if we are to believe certain more sinister reports) may have been caused in part by his refusal to work on the atomic bomb. An additional cause may have been his disagreement with Stalin's "philosophers" on the validity of relativity and cybernetics.

X

Still, what exactly was behind Peter Kapitsa's sudden attack of 1962 on those Soviet dogmatists for their erstwhile sabotage of Einstein's ideas and computer work in Russia? Why his extraordinary review of this particular Stalinist sin, which, like all the other varieties of the late dictator's whims, was supposed to be safely dead by 1962?

Nine years after Stalin's demise, Einstein and computers were at last raised from the limbo of taboo or official neglect by the Communists. Computers in fact were being worshiped all over the Soviet scene. The Party's new program, adopted at the Twenty-Second Congress in Moscow in October 1961, proudly trumpeted that for the next two decades the widest possible use would be made of computing, control, and information machines. Why, then, the outburst by Dr. Kapitsa—the seemingly belated broadside against those Stalinist dogmatists? Was it merely historical, a proud and near-gloating reminiscence of that horrid period's sufferings as a prelude to the latter-day triumphs of true scientists?

Not entirely and not primarily. Professor Kapitsa made it clear that the present and the future of Soviet science and politics were involved no less than their past. Interference in Soviet science by Communist politicians continued, he hinted in his March 1962 manifesto. He sideswiped Trofim Lysenko, the darling of Soviet antigeneticists, without naming him, yet plainly meaning him when he wrote about "the incorrect generalizations made by our philosophers, not alone in the field of physics, but also in biology."

Kapitsa then proceeded to his main target, which was none other than the old sacred cow of Marxism: dialectical materialism. He wrote in his "Theory, Experiment, Practice" cautiously, yet unmistakably:

> Application of dialectics in the realm of natural sciences demands an exceptionally thorough knowledge of experimental facts and their theoretical generalization. Without this, dialectics by itself cannot solve the question. Dialectics is like a Stradivarius violin. To play this most perfect of all violins, one must be a musician and know music. Without this, it would yield false notes just as any ordinary fiddle would.

Somehow he seemed to connect the dogmatists' misuse of dialectics with the fact that young Soviet physicists shunned experimentation. Too little experimentation was being done in the Soviet Union even in the early 1960s, Professor Kapitsa asserted in his significant article. In this lag he saw a danger signal for the future of Soviet science. He explained; he cited facts and figures: as editor of the journal *Eksperimental'naya i teoreticheskaya fizika* he noted that, in the themes of articles submitted to him, theoretical physics outnumbered experimental physics 3 and even 4 to 1. For various reasons, "young people on graduating from higher schools prefer theoretical work to experimental," he pointed out. He warned: "We cannot permit any lag in experimental physics, for this would greatly hinder the normal growth of our physics—would prevent it from occupying leading positions in the world's science along the entire front of most important researches."

While some of the reasons for the young Soviet researchers' reluctance had nothing to do with politics, others did. Professor Kapitsa intimated that fear of Marxist dialectics was among the handicaps to experimentation in the Soviet Union. In sum, he blamed the Soviet "philosophers" who, although less pernicious than they had been in Stalin's time, were still strong enough to oppose true science.

But were there any true philosophers in the Soviet Union in 1962? Was Dr. Kapitsa's outburst not in fact aimed at those Communist Party officials and their Lysenko-like sycophants—rather than any genuine philosophers—who may have still been trying to run Russia's science in a stifling would-be Marxist way?

XI

Early in 1965, in a speech subsequently published in an Academy journal, Kapitsa called for greater freedom for Soviet scientists, when he said that, although they could get money for their research more easily than their American colleagues could, the governmental restrictions made the Soviet research less productive. Let us emulate some of the American practices, he urged. Availability of able researchers, rather than the attraction of this field or that to the government, should be the guiding principle. Give funds to those who can use them fruitfully, not to those in an area of research which may be judged important by the authorities but which may lack truly capable scientists.[17]

At about the same time, in April 1965, in an oblique but again unmistakable way, he demanded freer travel abroad for those Soviet scholars who really needed it, among them himself. He made this demand clear in his article commemorating the two-hundredth anniversary of Mikhail Lomonosov's death, wherein he praised "the international friendship of savants" and pointed out: "These days the necessity of personal contacts between scientists is taken for granted as something self-understood by our as well as foreign savants."[18]

This was doubtless to call the world's attention to the fact that ever since 1934 he, Peter Kapitsa, had not once been allowed to go abroad. And it was to ensure the Soviet government's permission for him to travel to Denmark the very next month, in May 1965, when he was to receive the Neils Bohr International Gold Medal awarded to him by the Danish Engineering Society for his work in the peaceful uses of atomic energy.

On May 23, for the first time in thirty-one years, Kapitsa left Soviet soil—to receive the medal from the hands of King Frederick IX, to tour Danish laboratories, and to deliver a lecture in Copenhagen on high-energy physics.[19]

And then of course he returned home to Moscow. For he still has much work to do in Russia. At the age of seventy-two, Peter Kapitsa is still the faithful sentinel of non-Marxist science in the Soviet Union. Blue-eyed, tweedy, ever puffing on his English pipe, now mercurial and now calm, he is indeed the aging yet very much living conscience of those ever-growing and increasingly stirring Soviet laboratories and lecture halls.

Through the darkest era of Stalinism he preserved at least a spark of the scientist's independence. In the easier post-Stalinist years he has served as a rallying point of resistance to the political bosses and their deadly doctrine. Thanks in a large measure to him, younger men now can carry on with a yet bolder course of scholar's freedom.

CHAPTER IV

~~~~~~~~~~~~~~~~~~~~~~~~~~~~~~

The Soviet Battle over Einstein

IT IS EASY to see why Stalin ordered his minions to attack Albert Einstein: the very word *relativity* must have disturbed him. The rigid Communist deals in absolutes; anything that is said to be relative makes him uneasy, angry, suspicious. A highly political animal, the orthodox Communist takes any talk of relativity in a political sense. If things can be relative, then his own Communist beliefs may be considered by some as only relatively, not wholly, true. And the hated capitalist, moderate, liberal beings and ideas may be viewed by some as only relatively, not absolutely, evil and wrong.

Besides, Einstein's theories were too deep even for many of those Communists who said they were thinkers, the Party philosophers. They did not understand those theories. Of course, multitudes of people in the 1920s and '30s who heard of Einstein's relativity theory and other of his concepts did not understand such complexity either. Among such noncomprehending humanity were many intellectuals. But intellectual or not, the nonunderstanding majority of mankind either did not bother to inquire further when they heard of Einstein's ideas or, having inquired and being still unable to grasp them, they merely shrugged their shoulders and let it go at that—with a certain amount of indifference or vague respect.

Stalin and the Stalinists were very much aware of Einstein's theories. By 1925 Einstein was too much of a world figure for them to disregard him and his work. For one thing, Russian scientists talked of him, and with much deference. At that time, still somewhat independent, Russia's foremost scientists were not afraid to pay homage to Einstein: they invited him to their conferences and laboratories; in 1927 they elected him an honorary member of their Academy of Sciences. Accepting the honor, Einstein nevertheless declined the repeated invitations. Neither then nor at any time later would he visit the Soviet Union. "Einstein realized," a biographer wrote in explanation of this refusal, "that any friendly remark he might make to the country [while on a visit in the U.S.S.R.] would be interpreted by the outside world as a sign that he was a Communist, and any critical remark would be taken by the Communists as a part of a capitalistic crusade against Russia."[1]

Toward the end of the 1920s, as both Einstein's fame and their own power grew, Stalin's Communists were increasingly hostile to the great physicist. Failing to understand him, the Communists could treat him with neither indifference nor respect. They felt an overriding need to decry and attack him and his teachings.

A true intellectual with high-flown ideas is bad enough in the rigid Communist's view. An independent, high-level intellectual who is a Jew, and a foreign Jew at that, outside the Soviet control, is a veritable threat. Not by chance did the original Moscow attack on Einstein coincide with Stalin's mopping-up action directed against the last remaining Trotskyites in the Party and government apparatus, so many of them precocious, critical Jewish intellectuals.

But an "ideological" explanation was in order, one that would give no hint of the real reasons behind the attack. So the official Soviet line on Einstein was that his bourgeois origin prevented this "greatest physicist of our time" to draw proper Marxist conclusions from his own excellent scientific theories. His physics was superior, the Communists said, but his philosophy was confused. True, there were some elements of dialectical materialism in his philosophy, but they were hopelessly interwoven with the predominant idealistic points apparently accepted by him from the teachings of that Austrian physicist and philosopher Ernst Mach,* whom Lenin himself had singled out for a ferocious onslaught. That was why, said Stalin's Communists, Einstein was to be attacked and was being attacked—at about the same time and with many of the same arguments (we should add) that the Nazis were assailing him with. To both the Communists and the Nazis, Einstein was too free a spirit.

As early as 1922 the orthodox Communist "philosopher"

---

* Generally remembered now for "Mach Number" far more than for any of his philosophic theories. ("Mach Number," used in high-speed aviation, is the ratio of the speed of any object—in this case of an airplane—to the speed of sound.)

Aleksandr A. Maksimov wrote sneeringly about "this idealistic
atmosphere" enveloping the theory of relativity. He charged that
in the Germany of the early 1920s "the relativity principle served
exclusively religious and metaphysical tendencies." He repeated
in 1928: "The idealistic atmosphere surrounded the theory of
relativity [in post–World War I years] and still surrounds it."
And again in 1938: "No physical theory has produced such a
stream of idealistic fantasies as Einstein's theory of relativity." Too
bad that "a number of serious scientists" keep company with the
"mystics, clerics, idealists of all shades . . . [who] snatched at the
philosophical consequences of the theory of relativity."[2]

In the Soviet terror era of the 1930s the few Russian intellectuals, Jewish or not, who understood Einstein's theories, were too
frightened to stand up with their explanations and reassurances.
The Soviet scientists, who knew what Einstein's formulae meant in
the exploration and exploitation of atomic energy, protested only
among themselves. It was only gradually, under the leadership of
Kapitsa, that they gained enough courage to use Einstein's contri-
butions—without mentioning him. For by the mid-1930s his
name was a Party-decreed anathema.

And yet, amid all this terror, a young Soviet student dared to
proclaim Einstein's genius publicly. He was prompted not by any
urging of self-sacrifice. He did this, most likely, in his starry-eyed
innocence, typical of a youthful scholar in search of truth.

The consequences for him were tragic, and could have been
fatal. But he survived, and I met him years later, in Western
Germany.

I I

The man who as a young student defied the Soviet authorities
and openly admired Einstein is now in his fifties. He is short,
unhurried, with a light of inner dignity shining through. There is
much thoughtfulness, and a suggestion of past suffering, about
him. He is calmly philosophical in what he says, but there is no
resignation. His is a subdued fire, but a fire.

I met him in the spring of 1963, in Munich, where he is known
under his literary pseudonym of Aleksandr Vardy (his real name
to me is known and it is no special secret, but it is not necessary
to use it here). He is an engineer by his Soviet training and past,
but now he is in communication media. He writes very well, in

Russian, for *émigré* Russian periodicals in Western Europe. His German too is excellent.

He left Russia legally, without officially defecting, in 1957. His wife is Polish, and this gave them a chance to secure passports and visas to go to Poland, and from there westward. But he had been "an inner *émigré*," to use a Russian phrase, a defector in spirit, for many years before leaving the Soviet Union.

He was first arrested in his early twenties, in 1936, when he was a Moscow student interested in philosophy as well as engineering and mathematics. At the time he worked days and studied evenings. In his busy schedule he did not notice how careless he was becoming in his political attitude. (In my opinion, there is indeed such a thing as becoming so harried by your tightly packed work timetables that you lose your sense of caution.) One of his evening professors, knowing young Vardy's interest in Albert Einstein's work, handed him a special assignment: Write a paper on Einstein and relativity, then deliver it at a public seminar of this course.

Vardy should have known how bitterly hated and denounced Einstein was by the Party of the 1930s. He did and he did not. He knew there was this Party disapproval of Einstein. But, perhaps naïvely, he thought that this was because the Party did not really know Einstein. (Which, of course, it did not.) He would remedy matters by telling the Party the truth about Einstein and relativity.

And so he wrote and delivered a paper wherein he praised Einstein and his unique theory. He endeavored to prove at length that Einstein was not anti-Marx; that relativity and Marxism could and did coexist.

There was a storm of indignation in the seminar room. Foaming at the mouth, the Party faithful attacked Vardy. His, they cried, was "a sortie of the class enemy," and it did not make any difference whether Vardy's enmity toward the Soviet regime was "conscious or unconscious, witting or unwitting." It was enmity. Courageously Vardy tried to answer. He stood his ground, but his voice was lost in the vicious hubbub.

His liberty was lost two short weeks later. He was arrested and tried "for agitation against the Soviet regime." His sentence was three years in a concentration camp, and he was sent north, beyond the Arctic Circle, toward Vorkuta, whose very name caused shivers down the spine of any Soviet citizen hearing it.

But he never reached Vorkuta. He was placed in a gang of

convicts surveying and building a railroad to Vorkuta. In swamps, in tundra, amid horrible conditions, with fellow prisoners dying all around him by the hundred, Vardy surveyed and built. Winter and summer he lived in a tent. Luck and his iron constitution were with him. He survived.

He was released in time to be sent into the Soviet armed forces. For the war was on by then. He served throughout the war and again survived. The war over, he was again arrested.

"Why this time?" I asked.

"No reason," he quietly answered. "Except that there was a new wave of postwar terror, you will remember. A lot of us former prisoners were picked up. Oh, yes, there was some sort of formal charge against me, but it was just a routine entry in my record. I hardly remember just how they phrased it. What actually led to my rearrest was that first conviction for my pro-Einstein paper."

The curious point was that by the latter 1940s the Party line on Einstein had changed to very much Vardy's thesis, which had been so costly to him. When I quoted some of Moscow's pro-Einstein statements of the 1940s, Vardy nodded, with a slight, rueful smile. "I was then still in a concentration camp, serving that second term, being punished for precisely such statements."

This term he was in the appalling concentration camp of Vorkuta itself. But, the old hand at survival that he was by then, he knew how to improve his condition by showing his technical skills. As a slave-technician he witnessed the great strike and bloody rebellion occurring at Vorkuta in the summer of 1953, a few months after Stalin's death.

Those who were not executed after the rebellion's suppression received more lenient treatment than they had previously received. And finally, some two years later, Vardy was freed. A technical invention he presented to his slave-drivers in the course of his second captivity somewhat quickened his release. The slave-drivers proved to be that grateful.

This time Vardy decided he had better get out of the Soviet Union before a new campaign of terror would land him in a concentration camp once more. Using the confusion of Soviet officialdom at the time of the Hungarian revolt, he and his wife— with the aid of her highly placed Polish relatives—obtained their Polish visas. A little later, their journey from Poland to the West was comparatively easy.

III

In the Soviet Union by the middle 1940s you could pronounce Albert Einstein's name with due respect and not suffer arrest or any other unpleasant consequences.

One reason for the change was that the great scientist was an active anti-Nazi and thus an ally of the Soviet Union in her dire wartime need; also that he was a resident and a citizen of the United States, surrounded by practically universal deference and even worship by Americans and other Westerners. And this was at the time when the United States and the non-Nazi West in general constituted Russia's hope and support.

Another and far more important reason was the reluctant clarity with which even Stalin and his "philosophers" saw that without Einstein's formulae there could not have been an atomic bomb in anybody's possession; and that if the Communist leadership wanted an A-bomb of its own, Einstein's value had to be recognized.

Thus Kapitsa as Einstein's advocate won the day—even if as late as 1962 he had to remind some of the stubborn anti-Einstein dogmatists that they had better continue their retreat.

Significantly, the change was officially introduced by a scientist and only echoed by a "pilosopher." In 1939 Academician Sergei Vavilov, the world-famous physicist specializing in fluorescence, was allowed by Stalin to come out with a public statement that Einstein's theory of relativity did not contradict the Marx-Engels-Lenin teachings of dialectical materialism: "In Einstein's theory space-time is an inseparable property of matter itself. Such is the basic idea of Einstein's general theory of relativity." It took three years for Stalin's ideologists to confirm Vavilov; in 1942 Mark Mitin, one of the chief Party propagandists, solemnly announced the Party's approval of Einstein's theory—"as a result," he admitted, "of the tremendous work that our philosophers and physicists had carried out . . . of many impassioned discussions."[3] Thus the scientists' pressure and triumph were at last publicly revealed, and, what is more, by Stalin's own high priest.

In a few more years an attempt would be made to legitimatize the Party's retreat by invoking the sacred name of Lenin himself. One Moscow writer of the latter 1940s tried to claim that in his time Lenin surely understood and blessed Einstein, nay, had anticipated him: "Einstein's discovery and its consequent testing in the field of nuclear physics were a brilliant confirmation of dialectical materialism, according to which there is no matter without motion, and no motion without matter. [Thus] the physicists of the twentieth century confirmed the geniuslike prevision of Lenin."[4] A later Soviet comment on Einstein went so far as to say that Lenin had played a prominent role in the world's recognition of the physicist and his theory of relativity.[5] There is of course no evidence of this. Lenin, so prolific on practically every subject in the world, left behind him not one quotation on Einstein. True science barely interested Lenin. (A perceptive anti-Soviet jest in Russia has it that Lenin himself "never was a scientist; else he would have experimented on mice instead of humans.")

IV

But there was more to Einstein throughout the 1940s and the first half of the 1950s than just his theories and formulae so needed by Soviet science. He was also a very active political man, a man of peace speaking and writing on this subject in ways not always to Moscow's entire liking.

In May 1946 Ehrenburg as a "peace" emissary to the United States called on Einstein at his Princeton home. Years later, in his reminiscences of the visit,[6] Ehrenburg was fairly delirious with delight and prostrate with awe. He confessed that at no time did he understand the great man's theories, but he was ecstatic just the same. He was also indignant at the memory of the Nazi and other reactionary onslaughts on Einstein's name and work; he sang Einstein's praises for his "support of Socialism and friendship for the Soviet Union"—all this with not a word about the abuse of Einstein by the Communist press in the Soviet Union and elsewhere in the 1920s and the 1930s, not a hint of the case of Aleksandr Vardy sent to years of concentration camps for a mere student's paper in favor of Einstein.

And soon, precisely because Einstein was a true man of peace, came the proof that Moscow's anti-Einstein days were not entirely over. Eighteen months after Ehrenburg's fawning pilgrimage to Princeton, an official Communist journal in Moscow, *Novoye vremia*, carried a sudden attack on Einstein over the clearly coerced signatures of such academicians as Vavilov (by then president of the Soviet Academy of Sciences), Ioffe, Semyonov, and Aleksandr Frumkin (a celebrity in both physics and chemistry).

This blow of November 1947 had nothing to do with Einstein's scientific ideas, although Stalin craftily designated scientists to sign the article. The attack was against Einstein as a political man; he had, in September of that year, boldly addressed the United Nations with his proposal of limiting national sovereignty for all the world's countries in the interests of all the world's peace. As one of its practical measures, the plan would transfer to the United Nations Assembly much of the power of the United Nations Security Council. This latter body was hamstrung and paralyzed by its members' right of veto, Einstein pointed out, and that was why the cause of peace suffered. Stalin was enraged, for the veto power was his plaything and weapon almost exclusively. Hence the renewal of his anti-Einstein drive.[7]

With dignity and restraint Einstein answered the attack, but there is no evidence that his reply was ever published in the Soviet Union or any Communist periodical anywhere else. For, despite the moderation of his text and tone, Einstein did say some frank words about the caveman nature of the Communists.

It was a pity that in his reply Einstein did not realize, or pretended not to realize, that the four Soviet scientists were captive signers of the attack on him, and that the real author was Stalin. Had he added this point, the effect of his answer would have been even greater than it was.

Einstein wrote:

> . . . we should not make the mistake of blaming capitalism for all existing social and political evils, and of assuming that the very establishment of Socialism would be able to cure all the social and political ills of humanity. The danger of such a belief lies, first, in the fact that it encourages fanatical intolerance on the part of all the "faithfuls" by making a possible social method into a type of church which brands all those who do not belong to it as traitors or as nasty evildoers. Once this stage has been reached, the ability to understand the convictions and actions of the "unfaithfuls" vanishes completely. You know, I am sure, from history how much unnecessary suffering such rigid beliefs have inflicted upon mankind. . . . Socialism as such cannot be considered the solution to all social problems but merely as a framework within which such a solution is possible.[8]

Soviet insistence on "unlimited sovereignty, in the sphere of international politics," Einstein declared, leads to sheer anarchy. The Communist arguments that the United States uses the idea of curtailing sovereignty to camouflage her imperialism, and that "the Assembly of the United Nations is a mere puppet show controlled by the United States and hence the American capitalists," did not convince Einstein. To him they were "a kind of mythology," unworthy of intelligent men.

In his answer he conceded (however mistakenly, or too generously) the Communist assertion that "a Socialist economy possesses advantages which definitely counterbalance its disadvantages whenever the management lives up, at least to some extent, to adequate standards" (as if the Communist Party's management of Soviet economy had ever lived up to any such standards). He admitted certain allegedly inherent inabilities and failures of the free-enterprise system. While regretting the Soviet desire for isolation as "nothing else but the trend toward an almost unlimited isolationism" and thus "no less disastrous to Russia and to all other nations," he mitigated his dismay by saying that this desire was "understandable," almost excusing it by "what Russia has suffered at the hands of foreign countries during the last three decades." Again there was an important omission on Einstein's part: he should have reminded his readers how much the original cause of these sufferings lay in the Lenin-Stalin policies of aggression against the rest of the world.

Still, Einstein's credo of November 1947 rather refutes Ehrenburg's assertion that Einstein, at least in his talk with him in May 1946, showed himself to be a supporter of the Soviet brand of Socialism. Nor can we really believe Ehrenburg's record of Einstein's alleged words about Lenin as "a man with high moral criteria."[9] With all his occasional noble naïveté Einstein could have hardly believed in Lenin as a highly moral man—Lenin who in October 1920, in his widely known preachment to the Communist Youth League, cynically elaborated on Friedrich Engels' declaration of 1877 on morals (that there was no such thing as an immutable code of laws of ethics) by saying that morality was a bourgeois concept, a deception, a fraud, to be discarded by proletarians (that is, by the Communist Party) in their war upon the rest of the world.

It is true that in one interview, in 1945, Einstein said that conditions of life in the Soviet Union, harsh and unfree as they were, did not constitute "a menace to the peace of the world in themselves." To American liberals decrying the absence of freedom in Red Russia he replied that "this reign of a minority which they so deplored was a necessity for a nation deprived of political education and a country that lacked a majority capable of improving its disastrous conditions."[10]

He felt, rather vaguely, for the Soviet Union as he did habitually for any underdog whenever it appeared that Moscow was being snubbed, mistreated, or threatened by Washington and London. He said that the United States, being technologically stronger than the Soviet Union, should feel more secure and therefore act more leniently toward the Moscow autocrats. He was at times almost absent-minded as he remarked in print or, more often, from a public rostrum or to a left-wing visitor, that Moscow had a case—this Moscow of Stalin amid the cold war which Stalin and his Party had deliberately launched and relentlessly pressed!

Such statements by Einstein were used by slick professional left-wingers hovering nearby to utilize any grist that would drift toward their unceasing mill. But despite such naïve and exaggerated lapses, the true political wisdom and honesty of Einstein were too well known to be forgotten or forgiven by the Communists either in Stalin's time or the immediate post-Stalin era. They remembered and detested Einstein's readiness to see the world establish supranational security, even without the Soviet Union, should the Communists refuse to join such a world government. As he agreed with them that they would find it difficult to preserve their regime within such a world state, they were incensed that he felt the world state with its guaranty of peace was vastly preferable to any Soviet regime they could save for themselves by refusing to enter into a worldwide supranational agreement. Thus, when death came to Albert Einstein on April 18, 1955, the many pages devoted to the great scientist in the Western journals were contrasted by the scant three-line Einstein-passed-away announcement hidden on the last page of *Pravda*.

Clearly, dead or alive, Einstein was not a hero to the Communists.

V

But to the civilized, even in the Soviet Union, Einstein was indeed a hero.

Beginning with the late 1930s, at first cryptically, but in the ensuing years with an increasing boldness, particularly after 1953 and Stalin's death Soviet scientists spoke of Einstein with worship at every chance they had. And, finally, in March 1962, when Kapitsa burst forth with his far-famed article in *Ekonomicheskaya gazeta*, the gate was flung wide open.

Now the scientists of the Soviet Union could and did take Albert Einstein away from the politicians' untender mercies completely. No more was the great physicist-pacifist's name attacked in that country, on any pretext, political or not. When in August and September 1962, at Cornell University, at the Tenth International Congress of the History of Science, a multinational Einstein Committee was formed to honor his memory, a Soviet specialist on Einstein's work, Professor B. G. Kuznetsov, headed the body. At the Eleventh International Congress of the History of Science, held in Warsaw in August 1965, Soviet experts on Einstein were active participants in the Einstein Symposium.

In Moscow the Academy of Sciences established an Einstein Committee of its own, its membership composed of Russia's most famous physicists and other scientists. The Committee's head, Academician Igor Tamm, a Nobel Prize winner, said in April 1965, on the tenth anniversary of Einstein's death: "We now witness an extraordinary intensification of interest in Einstein's works. In them science seeks a clue to new and most complex problems."[11]

To satisfy this interest, the Academy's Einstein Committee is now supervising a four-volume edition of Einstein's scientific writings, "the first in the world," noted Tamm, with not a little satisfaction. The first two volumes were on the Moscow presses in 1965; the second two are scheduled for 1966. In addition, annual anthologies dedicated to "Einstein's creative path, to his ideas, and to the most fundamental problems of current physics," will be published in the Soviet Union, the first such volume coming out in 1965.

The defeat of the Communist "philosophers" who sent young Vardy to his concentration-camp slavery for praising Einstein is, in truth, complete.

CHAPTER V

Computers and Politics

THE PARTY'S FEAR of computers and cybernetics was even deeper than its opposition to Einstein's theory. But why such determined antagonism?

The main answer lies in the origin of this new science. The chief reason Stalin and his dogmatists so strenuously opposed cybernetics, including machine programming and other such innovations, seems to be that it was of Western, not Russian, origin. The time of the first major spurt of the theory and practice of computers in the West came right after World War II. The very name "cybernetics," employed in France as long ago as 1834, was applied to the new science 113 years later, in 1947, by that American professor at Massachusetts Institute of Technology—Norbert Wiener.[1] Most of the novel scientific study and its practical applications came from America, and this was at the time—1946–53—when Stalin hated America most. Nor must we forget the circumstance that Wiener was a Jew. As in the case of Einstein, we see here too the hardly camouflaged anti-Semitism of the erstwhile Georgian seminarian who toward the end of his bizarre life waged a phrenetic compaign to root out the "cosmopolite" (that is, mainly, the Jew, but also any foreigner) from any place of honor or recognition he had achieved.

But in addition to this xenophobic* (particularly anti-

---

* Some observers feel that the Soviet fear of the foreign is also the fear of the new, and that it is to be found in post-Stalinist Russia as well. "The Soviet authorities, imprisoned by an inferiority complex and an ideological obsession, frequently refuse to entertain the idea of something new and foreign, simply because it is new and foreign. The Soviet society is weighted down by inertia. Nothing changes easily. Institutions are geared to block change rather than to channel it from creator to public." (Madeleine and Marvin Kalb, "Exchangemanship and All That Djazz," *The Reporter*, New York, July 5, 1962, p. 30.)

American and anti-Semitic) feeling, there may have been in this period also a hidden, sickly fear in Stalin and his henchmen that the newfangled science of cybernetics, of programming, of servo-mechanisms, was just too deadly precise; that, if given leeway, it might somehow prove their vaunted "science" of Communism, its alleged historical inevitability, all wrong. Some of this fear may have been lingering among Khrushchev's own Communist dogmatists, and quite possibly in Khrushchev himself; hence the March 1962 attack by Kapitsa upon the foolish "philosophers" opposing cybernetics.

As in the instance of Einstein and relativity, the official Communist ideologists eschewed the true reasons for their rejection of cybernetics. They simply declared that cybernetics was "a bourgeois pseudoscience."[2] Those who believed in computers were "charlatans."[3]

Late in 1963 a Moscow writer recalled that only ten years earlier cybernetics had been called, at best, "a sterile flower," and that this had happened "through ignorance or because of the limited horizons" of such name-callers. At worst, "the Soviet ship *Cybernetics* had to fight her way through a ferocious storm and mine barriers" set up by the Party dogmatists against the new science, for "anyone's interest in it caused fierce attacks on the part of the dogmatists." The same Soviet writer reminded the reader that as late as 1953 the twentieth volume of the *Great Soviet Encyclopedia* came out with all sorts of silly articles on stupid or obscure topics but not a word on cybernetics.[4]

And yet, to counteract the Stalinist suppression, there was even in Stalin's era—and long before it—a solid Russian tradition of top-flight work in numerical analysis, in part because of the old-time development of applied mathematics in Russia.

Linear programming, the mathematical technique of solving complex problems in economic analysis and planning, found its Soviet Russian pioneer in the brilliant young mathematician Leonid V. Kantorovich in the 1930s. He was only twenty-seven when in 1939 he put down his basic ideas in a pamphlet entitled *Mathematical Methods for the Organization of Planning and Production*. Ten years later he was awarded a Stalin Prize, but little practical use was made of his work. The American rediscovery of linear programming was done quite independently of the Kantorovich achievement.[5] Its wide application in the West, connected with input-output analysis, would have had numerous potential parallels in Soviet economic planning, except

for the ideological cloud and political wrap under which Kantorovich found himself. In this slighting of his achievements, as his
Soviet colleagues later said, "temporary victory belonged not to
those who truly cut new paths in science but to those who more
dexterously manipulated quotations"[6]—quotations taken from Marx
and Lenin, that is, purporting to show that the Kantoroviches
were wrong or worse.

A similar inadequacy of recognition has in the past hampered
Academician Andrei N. Kolmogorov, one of the world's leaders
in researches on the theory of probability, in application of the
theory of functions of a real variable, functional analysis, statistical theory of turbulence, statistical methods of mass production
control, and automation.

But Norbert Wiener discovered a great affinity between his own
mind and Kolmogorov's. The American professor declared that
they had followed each other's thought, sometimes unknown to
each other, but on occasion fully aware of each other's work.
Thus Wiener's World War II prediction theory as applied to antiaircraft fire was antedated by Kolmogorov's work of the 1930s, but
Wiener learned of this quite some time after he had authored his
own theory. To quote Professor Warren B. Walsh, of Syracuse
University, on this point:

> Professor Wiener has also been heard to say that Kolmogorov's
> work, like Wiener's own, is readily applicable to hardware [military
> weapons]. He believes that Kolmogorov was first made aware of
> such possible applications through learning of Wiener's experiences,
> and says that some of Kolmogorov's theories have been applied to
> computers but that the application was not made by Kolmogorov.[7]

I I

Despite the disapproval by Stalin and his "philosophers," and
because the race with the West demanded it, systematic scientific
work in mathematical cybernetics was begun in the Soviet Union
in 1950.

That year the Academy's Institute of Precision Mechanics and
Computer Technology was founded in Moscow. Its head and
moving spirit was Professor Mikhail A. Lavrentyev, famous for
his research in the theory of functions of a complex variable,
mechanics of continuous media, and hydromechanics. Stalin was
to live some three years more. During those three years hardly
any digital computing machines were made available to research-

ers in Russia. "I began my career as an engineer in 1953," a Russian woman reminisced in 1962. "At that time we used to frighten children with the word 'cybernetics,' but at my Institute I did not hear it [discussed] although my specialty was radio-electronics. . . . We ridiculed cyberntics for an impermissibly long time. Now we have to catch up. And we are catching up fast."[8]

In March 1953 Stalin died, and that year the first respectable computer—BESM-I—was completed at Lavrentyev's Institute. The same year the STRELA computer joined it. Several copies of this machine were soon produced. Later a number of other, even better computers appeared, and not only in Moscow, but in the provinces, too.

From 1957 on, wide-ranging research in mathematical economics was done, chiefly under the leadership of Academician Vasily Nemchinov, who brought together a select group of gifted graduates of higher economic schools and with their help opened the nation's first Laboratory of Economic-Mathematical Methods.[9] Increasingly and with great fanfare in the press, conferences on cybernetics, linear programming, computers, and automation were held in Moscow. In May 1959 the American Exchange Delegation on Computers went to the Soviet Union, and was received with much cordiality. Norbert Wiener was welcomed and highly publicized even in July 1960, despite the considerable souring of Soviet-American relations in the wake of the U-2 incident. In the words of Maurice Hindus, who was in Moscow that summer (and who knew Wiener as the son of Harvard's Professor Leo Wiener, under whom Hindus had studied), "Norbert Wiener was dined and wined everywhere, even in the privacy of the homes of Russian scientists. Whenever he appeared in the lobby of the hotel, Russians who recognized him from newspaper pictures came up to him and shook his hand."[10]

At the University of Moscow a Chair of Numerical Analysis was established in 1955, and by 1959 about 40 per cent of the mathematical students at the University were specializing in that subject. To draw young men and women into this field, the government stipend to students of numerical analysis was raised to a point 50 per cent higher than for other mathematical students. Moreover, the general rule that a single "C" cost a student his stipend was waived for numerical analysis majors. But a complaint was soon heard that the inducements had brought some weak students into this field, and a weeding-out process was ordered.

The post-Stalin missionary zeal for the new science was so

great, and it carried Khrushchev's government along so swiftly, that presently all Soviet college students of mathematics, whatever their specialization, were required to take courses in numerical analysis and programming. All had to show some practical experience with computers. The success of the Sputniks and the Luniks from 1957 on, so clearly depending on computers, brought new waves of adherents among both scientists and students. In 1961, Professor Saul Kravetz, of Rensselaer Polytechnic Institute, observed: "More and better mathematicians are connected with computers in the Soviet Union's computing centers than anywhere else in the world."[11]

In Moscow, to supplement the Institute for Precision Mechanics and Computer Technology, and the Numerical Analysis Chair at the University, there is the computing center of the Academy of Sciences, and another computing center at the University, also the Steklov Institute (the Academy's Mathematical Institute). In the summer of 1962 the Academy announced its plans to establish an Institute of Mathematical Problems of Cybernetics and "to develop an experimental base for an Institute of Theory of Information," these and other institutes "to be a solid foundation for further researches in the field of cybernetics."[12]

Away from the capital, the University of Leningrad has a computer center, and so do Soviet Georgian professors in Tbilisi. In the Ukraine, Kiev's scientists are immensely proud of their pioneering work with computers. In November 1963 an engineer wrote: "Ten years ago, who would not have thought such a combination of words as 'mathematical linguistics' incredible! But today the University of Kiev has such a chair."[13] In addition to the university's computers, there is in Kiev also the Institute of Cybernetics of the Ukrainian Academy of Sciences. And the Academies of Armenia and Lithuania have computing centers in Yerevan and Kaunas respectively. So does the University of Rostov in the Don country.

At Sverdlovsk, in the Urals, two computing centers are thriving, one of them a branch of Moscow's Steklov Institute. There is the Automatic Computer Factory in Penza in East European Russia; and last but not least comes the newly burgeoning forest of large-scale computers at Science City in Novosibirsk, Western Siberia, under Academician Sergei L. Sobolev heading the celebrated Institute of Mathematics, with Academician Kantorovich himself second in command but first in fame. "I believe," Dr. Sobolev declared to a Moscow reporter in July 1962, "that the time is not far off when a network of computing centers will cover our entire country from the Pacific to the Carpathian foothills."[14]

In November 1964 a group of visiting American experts on computers found "a lot of talk about cybernetics—as if the whole Soviet Union was run by a vast computer." They agreed that "the Soviet theoretical work on control systems is excellent, but their process data are not so well developed . . . the Soviets seem to do relatively better with analog computers than with digital [which] tend to be for general purposes and are therefore harder to plan for."[15]

This suggests that not all the growth and planning in Soviet cybernetics has proceeded smoothly. In May 1965 the state economy within the Soviet Union's largest geographic unit, the Russian Soviet Federated Socialist Republic, commanded seventy computer centers, but they were not used to their full capacity, because the machines were "employed mainly to solve engineering problems and least of all to mechanize economic-planning calculations in management."[16] In places, computers were not only too many, but also too small. "The large number of small computing centers demands increased expenditures to erect their building, to maintain their service personnel, etc. All this raises computing costs and lowers the effectiveness of computer technology."[17] The complaining Soviet official recommended fewer but bigger centers of cybernetics.

As if to prove his point, it was reported in September 1963 that "a miracle machine," an electronic computer ordered by the Moldavian Academy of Sciences, had been lying in the Academy's courtyard and conference hall at Kishinev for one whole year, unpacked. The lament from Kishinev, signed by a group of cybernetics experts, read:

> Our electronic experts have found themselves in a deplorable situation. Each morning they must scratch their brains: what to do today? And so, our young engineers betake themselves to the conference hall and begin once more—for the umptieth time!—to inspect the crates containing the computer's parts. After all, they must not sit idle! And so it goes, for months at a stretch. The young specialists ask: "When will our knowledge be used at last? We are after all ashamed to take our salaries."[18]

The whole snag was caused by some higher bureaucrat's refusal to vacate a centrally located building that had been allotted to the Academy for its computer. Some archive was housed there, and its protector would not budge. Was this part and parcel of the continued anticybernetics by the "dogmatists"? Or just ordinary Soviet inefficiency? The answer may be either or both.

If it was indeed sabotage, Sobolev and his group would dauntlessly and ingeniously fight it. If it was mere inertia and slumber, they would shrilly wake the sleepers. In sum, the computer era will forge on.

I I I

Now in his middle fifties, Sergei Sobolev is a passionate mathematician-analyst and a dynamo of energy, a man of originality and daring, with a youthful, springy step. A graduate of the University of Leningrad, and a former professor in Moscow, he is presently one of Russia's outstanding scientists; he works in Siberia, but he has a telling influence all over the nation. He is more than director of the Institute of Mathematics at the Academy of Sciences in Novosibirsk—he heads the entire development of numerical analysis in the U.S.S.R. He is known to mathematical analysts abroad as well as at home for his work in partial differential equations.

A member of the Communist Party since the age of thirty-two, Sobolev is impatient of those in and out of the Party whom he suspects of anti-intellectualism. On one occasion he publicly upbraided the Soviet press for publishing "just one line, without any details," of the news that a group of Soviet scientists had given a series of important lectures to greatly interested audiences in a certain East European country. And yet, he went on, the same press at the very same time ran a long story about a football match that occurred simultaneously. He waxed sarcastic as he enumerated the painstaking detail with which the match was reported while science was cold-shouldered.[19]

Above all, Professor Sobolev deplores this modern Soviet philistinism when it hurts his beloved mathematics, particularly mathematics serving the computer field in Russia. He was, for instance, frankly critical of the "proletarization" of Soviet education decreed in late 1958 by Khrushchev. This, you will recall, required of many Soviet high-school graduates two years of manual labor before admission to college. In the process, Sobolev and his colleagues protested, many youthful mathematicians were prevented from proper development into geniuses.

Sobolev proclaims that mathematics is the queen of all sciences; that more and more it acts "as a singular cement" binding all sciences into one harmonious entity. Cybernetics to him is the unifying agency par excellence. He speaks of the "mathematization" of all sciences through his batteries of electronic computers. He says that he and his associates at the Science City in Novosibirsk "consider as their foremost task the uncovering and the propagandizing of new and yet newer opportunities for the utilization of speedy electronic computers in science and life."[20] He and his colleagues run through the list of sciences from anthropology to zoology as breathlessly waiting for computer aid. In April 1965 his Ukrainian counterpart, Academician Viktor Glushkov, having exhausted one such list of fields to an interviewer, was asked, "And in what other fields of human activity can cybernetics be of help to us?" He answered, "Better put your question this way: Is there any field at all in which cybernetics cannot be of great service to us?"[21]

I V

Such boundless enthusiasm cannot fail to annoy at least a few scientists, as well as whatever unrepentant Stalinists or other anti-eggheads may lurk among Communist Party functionaries.

Certain scientists, in the Soviet Union no less than in the Western world, do indeed resent and even fear the intrusion of machines into their studies. They cherish a quieter life and a more leisurely pace of research than Kapitsa and Sobolev urge. Even among mathematicians there are some groups that wish contemplation without computers. They are irritated by the missionary ardor of their machine-mad colleagues. They try to resist the Kapitsa-Sobolev drive to enlist and engulf them in the whirr and clang.

Of course, there is nothing Stalinist or anti-intellectualist about such resentful or reluctant professors.* But chances are that the anti-intellectualists among Communist functionaries have been quick to observe the smoldering academic opposition to computers; that behind the stage of Soviet politics they have begun to use the academicians' arguments against too much cybernetics; and that this was one of the chief reasons why Professor Kapitsa

---

* This is the proper place to remark that Western scientists also disagree among themselves on the extent to which machines should be used in research. But in our society the argument has nothing to do with political ideology, and the government is not involved in it.

raised his powerful voice against "the philosophers." His attack, as I have already indicated, was primarily against the nonacademic dogmatists still living in another age, and still trying to catch Khrushchev's ear. Yet the Kapitsa outburst also may have been a notice to those of his academic colleagues who, though not Stalinist, were attempting—not without an occasional half hearted nod from Khrushchev—to halt the computer tide.

Lysenko still enjoyed Khrushchev's favor, and some Soviet biologists still rallied around Lysenko. Professor Kapitsa's reference to those biologists who did not believe in computers was preceded by a similar sally by Professor Vasily V. Parin, a prominent space-medicine expert, in *Literaturnaya gazeta* a month before Kapitsa's manifesto. Dr. Parin had written of certain biologists' "lack of confidence in experimental methods, which were implacably invading their field of research and were based on the achievements of modern physics, chemistry, and cybernetics."[22] Parin too meant Lysenko and his coterie.

Dr. Parin cited sniping by one such Soviet biologist at the use of computers in biological research. The sniping took the form of a review of some work on cybernetics in biology published by the Academy of Sciences. The reviewer, according to Dr. Parin, insisted that "old research methods are so good that science can get along without any new ones." Dr. Parin asked: "Did such a review appear accidentally, and, at that, as late as 1961?" His own answer was No. This anticomputer sortie, he said, was no isolated occurrence; and he hinted at a campaign. "Fortunately," he observed, "such biologists are few in number." We may add, however, that the small group's influence must have been rather large, otherwise Professors Kapitsa and Parin would not have bothered to object with such verve.

The few anticomputer biologists are sometimes joined by men and women of certain other disciples. Economists, for instance, were conspicuous by their absence from a mammoth Conference on Philosophic Problems of Cybernetics held in Moscow in early June 1962. The name of the Conference, let us note, was quite interesting. This may have been an attempt by some post-Stalinist philosophers to prove to Professor Kapitsa that they were a different breed from the "philosophers" whom he attacked in March for their resistance to cybernetics. *Pravda* reported that philosophers were indeed present among the more than one thousand participants of the Conference. But economists were not

there, and chiding them for failure to appear, Professor Aksel'
Berg, in his capacity as head of the Academy's Learned Council
of Cybernetics, said in an interview in *Pravda*:

> It is a pity that certain branches of science and technology do not
> as yet recognize the tremendous opportunities being opened up by
> cybernetics to increase the effectiveness of human labor. Our Con-
> ference was devoted to the philosophic problems of cybernetics,
> and these are to a considerable extent economic problems also. Yet
> economists did not come to our Conference. And it is precisely in
> economics that wide opportunities are being unfolded for the appli-
> cation of the successes of cybernetics.[23]

Others, however, did fall into line. Khrushchev, whatever his
vacillations and doubts on the subject may have been, was far
more for cybernetics than against it. Computers were indeed
sweeping the world. And so *Pravda* reported that at the Conference, in addition to mathematicians, engineers specializing in
electronics, physicists, and philosophers, the following professionals were present: psychologists, biologists, medical experts,
and representatives of various Soviet industries.

In Siberia (the wonderful center of Sobolev's influence and
orders), if not in Moscow, economists showed great interest in
cybernetics. In June 1962 Academician Ilya N. Vekua, head of
the up-and-coming Novosibirsk University, and himself a celebrated mathematician, boasted that on his campus mathematics
and physics were being diligently studied not only by mathematicians and physicists, "as is good and proper for them," but also
by economists. Their main interest was in linear programming;
their chief tools were computers. "I don't have to argue," Professor Vekua remarked, "how important this is in our day and
age."[24]

In the group described by Vekua, geologists, biologists, and
linguists are also included. Siberian fans of cybernetics further
insist that electronic machines should be utilized in anthropology,
ethnography, archaeology, and numismatics as well. One day, at a
session of the Learned Council of the Social Sciences at the
Novosibirsk University, a young scholar was defending his thesis
for the degree of candidate of sciences (slightly above the American degree of master, slightly below our doctorate*). A varied
group of professors and students came to the session, among them
economists, historians, archaeologists, linguists, and a number of

---

* For a fuller explanation see footnote 19 in Chapter II.

outstanding mathematicians headed by Dr. Sobolev himself. This prompted a Soviet journalist to write: "What do the historians and the mathematicians have in common?"

The answer was in the title of the dissertation under discussion —"Certain Problems of Applying Electronic Mathematical Machines in the Science of History." The author of the thesis, Valentin A. Ustinov, wrote it as the result of his participation in a Soviet team of researchers who deciphered certain Mayan inscriptions with the aid of computers. Electronics in this case, it was said, shortened decades of labor to just a few days. At the Novosibirsk meeting, Professor A. P. Okladinikov proudly declared: "We are witnessing an epoch-making fact. We stand at the very beginning of a splendid experiment. How pleasant it is that our country is the one that has done it."[25]

V

But as cybernetics continues to rise triumphantly in the Soviet land, its overtones of political unorthodoxy persist. And it is the youngish Academician Sobolev perhaps even more than his senior friend and patron Kapitsa who appears to be the political leader of the new science.

Sobolev operates from the periphery, it is true. Yet he does have the world-famed Kantorovich at his side and such powerful allies in Moscow as Kapitsa and Berg, who occasionally come to Novosibirsk for lectures and seminars, and also to maintain contact with Sobolev and his group. And Sobolev visits Moscow frequently, too, of course. He keeps up a prolific stream of articles and interviews not only in learned publications but in Moscow's general press as well.

With seeming loyalty Sobolev quotes the Party's program and other Red announcements and rules while he blows his own horn for computers and adds his own bold interpretations of, and variations from, the Party's credo. He would, for instance, remove certain baneful influences of collectivism itself from young mathematicians and other budding scientists of Russia. In an article entitled "Let's Teach Them to Think," Sobolev declared:

> When we say that modern science is in essence collectivist, this does not mean that, in the process of collective creativeness, individuality is "erased" or "dissolved," that today's laboratories need little people to be used as cogs in a machine, whose chief virtue is their blind obedience. . . . Modern science needs talented people who have an aptitude for independent research.[26]

He called upon his fellow Soviet educators not just to go after
an ever higher number of persons to be trained but even more to
improve their quality. And the quality, he said, would come if his
colleagues would "train genuine thinkers and creative researchers"
—in short, if the professors would "teach them to think."

This is strong and novel language in Soviet science and politics,
a language that Communist politicians themselves would not use
so readily and do not relish when it is uttered by others. Yet,
apparently, they have to accept such talk from the privileged
scientists in their midst.

To Stalin, such talk would have sounded like rank heresy, as
cause enough for a punishment sterner than mere house arrest. It
could not have been music to Khrushchev's ears either; but he
had to pretend that he liked it, that he accepted it willingly.
Brezhnev and the other post-Khrushchevian leaders dislike it a
little less, but having been brought up largely in the Stalin-Khru-
shchev Party school they do dislike it. As did Khrushchev in his
time, so they in theirs accept it nevertheless. For it may well be
that Brezhnev's Party needs the Sobolevs and the Kapitsas far
more than they need the Party for their survival and success in
these mid-1960s.

CHAPTER VI

~~~~~~~~~~~~~~~~~~~~~~~~~~~~~~~~~~~~~

Retreat and Attack: Genes and Grain

NOWHERE DID THE PARTY'S RETREAT before science come with such sharp clarity as in the case of Trofim Lysenko and the harm he had for so long done in the field of Soviet genetics.

The retreat of the Party dogmatists supporting Lysenko began soon after the end of the nightmarish era of Stalin. It was a reluctant retreat, full of zigzags and replete with sudden rallies and sallies against Mendelism, but it was a retreat nonetheless. Eleven and a half years after Stalin's death, came Khrushchev's downfall; and the last desperate holding operation of the Lysenko dogmatists seemed to collapse.

A joyous victory celebration by the Soviet Mendelians marked the very first week of the post-Khrushchevian era dawning that mid-October of 1964. The puzzled uncertainty descending upon most of the country's population when Nikita was sent down the trap door did not include the Mendelian geneticists. They knew that they had just clinched a triumph. For Lysenko had counted Khrushchev as practically his last supporter of any weight in the Party.

Denunciation of Lysenko by scholars enlivened the Soviet print from mid-October 1964 on. Neither Lysenko himself nor any one of his cohorts was given a chance to reply. Through the rest of 1964 and well into 1965 they were dismissed in droves even as they ran, in vain, for cover.

In late January 1965 anti-Lysenko scientists began to reorganize his pet Institute of Genetics; the biological laboratories once closed by him as heretical were reopened; new and even more modern ones were established or planned. The Western-minded geneticists of Novosibirsk led in the gigantic task of junking the millions of schoolbooks based on Lysenko's fallacies, of rushing into print stacks of truly scholarly manuals, and of re-training the nation's 100,000 teachers of biology.

Lysenko was removed from his high post as head of the Insti-tute of Genetics, and his aide-de-camp Mikhail Olshansky lost his helm at the Lenin Academy of Agricultural Sciences.[1]

Genetika, a new monthly journal, was announced by the Acad-emy of Sciences in late May to be dedicated to the Mendelian theory of heredity, so long fought by Lysenko. The very first issue was to carry a eulogy of Nikolai Vavilov, the great geneticist whose death in a Siberian concentration camp in 1940 had been caused by Lysenko.[2]

I I

Trofim Lysenko's shunning of computers in biological research was, of course, not the only and certainly not the main reason for the emboldened post-Stalin-era scientists to criticize him and those Party dogmatists who still aided and comforted him. For years Lysenko feared any solid scientific method, particularly a method using mathematical calculations, which might have proved his botany and biology wrong. Already in 1949 Professor Conway Zirkle, of the University of Pennsylvania, noted (perhaps a bit too sweepingly) the "overwhelming evidence that the sim-plest mathematics is quite beyond Lysenko's reach."[3]

But here we deal with a question of far more than method. It was a problem of substance. And the substance of Lysenkoism, and of the modern Soviet scientists' protest against it, especially against its succor by the Communist Party, rested in Lysenko's and the Party's stubborn reactionary refusal to give up their ig-norant notion that acquired characteristics could be inherited.

For some twenty years before Stalin's death, with an ever-increasing ferocity, the Party and its darling Lysenko carried on their fight against modern Western genetics, destroying all traces of it in the Soviet Union. There are several reasons why the Party attacked—and essentially still dislikes—Mendelian teachings on genes. The principal explanation is that Soviet leaders want to transform nature. In this, they feel, they are thwarted or delayed by the laws of hereditary phenomena discovered in the 1850s and '60s by the Austrian monk and botanist Gregor Mendel and, since the dawn of the present century, rediscovered and accepted by modern science. In the apt phrasing of Julian Huxley,

Communism has practical achievement as part of its ideology. It is part of the job of man, at least of Communist man, to change nature for his own ends. . . . Mendelian heredity, with its self-copying genes and its random indirected mutations, seems to offer too much resistance to man's desire to change nature, and to elude the control he would like to impose. . . . [Soviet leaders war upon Mendelism] because it can be taken to imply human helplessness in the face of genetic predestination. . . . if a man is what his genes make him, what is the use of human aspiration or effort?[4]

Most disturbingly for the Communists, what use is their peculiar, emphatic insistence on changing human nature, human genes?

Early and late the Communist leadership has promised to elevate the masses through bettered conditions of their life and work —elevate them to what amounted to better genes. The leaders set out to prove that brain and virtue could become a kind of monopoly of the masses under their (the leaders') inspired guidance; that the lofty Communist ideal, along with such brain and virtue, could be bred into lowly humans; that once acquired, all this genetic bounty could be passed on to the children and grandchildren of those humans—until "a few generations of life under improved Communist conditions would level up the genetic quality of the population of the U.S.S.R."[5]

Jean Baptiste Lamarck, the French naturalist of the eighteenth and early nineteenth century, taught that acquired characteristics can be inherited—so why not wisdom and Communism as such acquisitions? Communist leaders liked Lamarckism because it promised genetic control by man, which Mendelism denied.

And Lamarckism held out an offer of speed and simplicity, which were lacking in Mendelism. Here we should observe that, despite all its customary verbiage, Marxism is at bottom too simple a view of social problems to accept Mendelian genetics. Mendelism is just too involved and complex to fit into the essentially crude, black-and-white, blood-and-thunder ideology of Marx and Lenin. The teachings of Mendel and his latter-day followers and continuators insist "on elaborate and abstruse procedures which are beyond the comprehension" of the obtuse Marxist defined by Julian Huxley as either "the uninstructed farmer," a broad hint at Lysenko, or "the uninstructed politician"[6]—such as Stalin was at the time he unleashed the uncouth Lysenko to campaign against Western genetics.

In keeping with Stalin's general mood, anti-Westernism was another factor in the declaration of war against this science. To be sure, Lamarck also was a Westerner, but now ridiculed and rejected by Westerners. But Mendel was a Westerner very much revered by modern Westerners. Therefore he should be denounced. Besides, even Lamarck did not have to be emphasized. Instead, Ivan Michurin, a Russian pro-Lamarckist, could be stressed, and was so stressed, as the prophet who proclaimed holy truth in botany and biology. And Michurin was not only a Russian. He was also a Marxist, or so he said.

Weirdly, Stalin and Lysenko lumped the Western Mendelians with Hitler's racists who lauded their "pure Aryan" blood as something superior to any other blood, certainly 'way above the Slav and other Eastern human stock, and surely a value with which the master German race was born. Curiously, Soviet anti-Mendelians failed to notice that they and the Nazi theoreticians were guilty of the same sin: both extolled genetically one group of humans at the expense of all the others, the Soviets one class (proletarians), the Nazis one race (Germans).

Nor should we forget that, young as Marxism is (comparatively speaking), this movement is already hog-tied by traditions which the Communists do their worst to follow blindly. Thus, Mendelism was to be opposed because it taught human inequality in genes—"human beings are not merely different from each other, but often differ in respect of a greater or lesser genetic endowment of desirable characters like health or intelligence."[7] Already in Lenin's days, but surely in the Stalin and post-Stalin eras, Russian Communists could and can be reasonably charged with abandoning the traditional Marxist egalitarianism, with a gross betrayal of Socialist-Communist premises and promises. They have by now created a new class society of the haves and the have-nots, of the privileged and the oppressed. Still, ideology demands that they keep on parroting their theoretical egalitarianism, in which actually they no longer believe. As someone has remarked, it is no longer ideology, it is only phraseology. But they must dislike Mendelism because their feeble pretense is still that of egalitarianism.

They felt they had to fight it for tradition's sake also because the founders of Marxism believed in Lamarck, not in Mendel. And here is how this historical tale unfolds:

It happened that Charles Darwin, as part of the erroneous consensus of his fellow scientists of mid-nineteenth century, accepted Lamarckism. He was not a Marxist, of course. But Karl Marx endorsed Darwinism and, with it, Lamarckism. So did Friedrich Engels. So did, later, Vladimir Lenin.

It is true that in time Engels corrected Darwin's "mistake" of endorsing also Malthusian views of population pressures. Therefore Soviet leaders denounce Malthus. But neither Marx nor Engels ever "purged" Darwin of his Lamarckism. Thus Lamarckism remained a sacred cow of Communism.

In fact, Lenin strengthened Lamarckism in Russia by unduly praising Michurin, that homespun Russian naturalist and Lamarck's devotee, that office clerk turned into experimenting nurseryman, who toward the end of his long life (1855–1935) violently raged against Mendelism. This he did practically in his senility, "when his Bolshevik record and Lenin's approbation had raised him beyond the criticism of mortals."[8]

The result of this sorcerous blend of Lamarckism and Marxism, of Michurinism and Stalinism, and of the combined drive by Stalin and Lysenko against Western-style genetics in the Soviet Union, was disastrous. To quote a summary from an earlier book of mine:

> Scores of reputable Russian scientists lost their jobs, and many their liberty and their very lives, when they dared to oppose Lysenko, even if mildly. The ugly record began in 1932 when two cytologists, G. A. Levitsky and N. P. Avdulov, were sent to concentration camps. It drew its first blood in 1935 when I. J. Agol and L. P. Ferry were executed by the Soviet secret police, the first two Russian geneticists to be put to death. Two years later Avdulov was shot, and so was S. G. Levit, former head of the celebrated Moscow Institute for Medical Genetic Research. In 1940 the great Professor Nicholas Vavilov himself, for decades the guiding light of Russian biology and the pride of the world's genetics, was arrested by the Stalin-Lysenko police. Two years later, a prisoner in Siberia, Vavilov was dead. Nor is this numbing list complete: whole staffs of anti-Lysenko scientists died similarly, in prison and labor camps, of quick bullets or slow mistreatment.[9]

The appalling onslaught reached its peak in 1948–49 when the pogrom of the Soviet biological institutes and laboratories assumed its mass proportions, and when Stalin and Lysenko no longer bothered to camouflage their savage tribal dance with any semblance of propriety, and even less of justice. The surviving Mendelians among the Soviet scientists managed to save themselves only by an abject public recantation of their views.

Mendelism as a deadly sin had by then been extended by the Soviet executioners to the three-part crime of Mendelism-Morganism-Weismannism. This was a Communist attack on Thomas Hunt Morgan (1866–1945), the American biologist celebrated for his formulation of the theory of the gene as a carrier of inheritable characteristics; and on August Weismann (1834–1914), the German biologist who proved that characteristics acquired by man from his environment were not transmitted to his progeny. In 1948–49, the Soviet scientists humiliated by Lysenko heartbrokenly abjured Morgan and Weismann in the same crushed breath with Mendel's name.

A horrifying detail was that, in the torrent of abuse directed at the Mendelians, one of the Soviet accusations was that these scientists were guilty of idealism, a cuss word among the Russian Marxists. The recanting Russian scientists humbly swore that they were not idealists, and that they too hated idealism.

The world of Western science gasped at the spectacle—not seen since the days of Galileo—first with disbelief, then with helpless protest.

I I I

The story of that astonishing massacre of a science is told here as a prelude to the question, Precisely what happened in this particular field after Stalin's death? We have already made note, in the preceding three chapters, of the post-Stalinist stirrings among the anti-Lysenko biologists and their sympathizers in other sciences, such as Professors Kapitsa and Parin. But how much good did this renewed protest do up to the day of Khrushchev's dismissal?

The answer is that Lysenko's decline was slow in starting. For several years after Stalin's death Lysenko continued with his exalted posts and sundry honors. It was true that arrests and recantations of the few stray Mendelians ceased, but Lysenko kept his headship of the All-Union Institute of Genetics, in Novorossiysk, in South Russia, and of the Institute of Genetics of the Academy of Sciences, in Moscow, which he first assumed in 1940. Even more significantly, he was still president of the Lenin Academy of Agricultural Sciences, a foremost national organization, the post given to him by Stalin in 1938.

Gradually, in 1953–54, a few Soviet scientists began to criticize Lysenko openly. In 1954 evidence was published that some of Lysenko's "proof" of his theories had been falsified. Still, Lysenko retained his high command. It was only in April 1956, three years and one month after Stalin's passing, that Lysenko was finally deprived of his headship at the Lenin Academy. It is significant that he stepped down from the presidency at the very beginning of the official campaign of de-Stalinization launched by Khrushchev with his "secret" anti-Stalin speech at the Twentieth Party Congress in Moscow in February 1956.

Some in the know mentioned also a very personal reason for demotion. Khrushchev had just before this juncture become enamored of hybrid corn, and this had dismayed Lysenko as a near-Mendelian heresy. He had voiced his Lamarckian opposition to Khrushchev's beloved corn, and so he had to go.

However, even this spat did not mean a complete break. The Lenin Academy of Agricultural Sciences stayed in the hands of Lysenko's followers, unrepentant Stalinists like himself. Behind the scenes, Lysenko was still a great man to Nikita. This became especially clear in the period of reaction which followed the quelling of the Hungarian revolt. In February 1957 Khrushchev praised Stalin's pet: "I think few scientists understood soil as well as does Comrade Lysenko." On October 4, 1957, *Pravda* published Khrushchev's public speech wherein he chided those resurgent Mendelians who "greatly vied with one another in accusing Comrade Lysenko of all kinds of sins at the time of his presidency of the Academy of Agricultural Sciences."[10] In mid-1958 several Soviet delegates about to appear at the International Congress in Montreal were replaced with others, who read papers written in a Michurin-Lysenko style.

Repeatedly, Lysenko's advice was sought by Russia's post-Stalinist leadership, and he was included even in plenary sessions of the Party's Central Committee devoted to discussions of Soviet agriculture. Each time the Party's official communiqués made a point of stressing the nominal fact that Lysenko was "a non-partisan," that is, not a member of the Communist Party. This was, of course, an uproarious joke in and outside the Party; it fooled nobody about Lysenko's real status.

But the Mendelians were rising. Two learned publications in the Soviet capital were now in their hands: *Botanichesky zhurnal* (Botanical Journal) and *Byulleten' Moskovskogo obshchestva ispytatelei prirody* (Bulletin of the Moscow Society of Nature Researchers). More and more openly these journals carried attacks on Lysenko for the damage he had done, and was still doing (in however diminished measure), to Soviet science and agriculture.

By the end of 1958, encouraged by Khrushchev's renewed support, Lysenko and the party's dogmatists tried to counterattack. Their target was Academician Vladimir Sukachev, a venerable and much respected botanist, editor of *Botanichesky zhurnal*. On December 12, 1958, *Pravda* published a vitriolic indictment of him and his editorship. The result was that soon after this Dr. Sukachev was removed from his post, and a more accommodating academician, Vasily Kuprevich,[11] was appointed in his stead.

Yet—a sign of better times!—Sukachev was neither arrested nor forced to recant. Nor were any new kudos of any significance bestowed upon Lysenko. The greatest honor given him was the headship, in 1960, of the Soviet delegation to the All-Hungarian Conference on Maize Cultivation Problems, in Budapest.[12] The Academy of Agricultural Sciences, even after he had left its presidency in 1956, remained a citadel of his followers, but *Pravda* (March 29, 1960) had to report the acrid criticism, voiced at the Academy's general assembly, of the feeble work of the Academy's most important institutes. Lysenkoism was not covering itself with glory. In particular, the institutes of animal husbandry, of plant crops, and of mechanization were singled out for strictures.

The realization that in the master's absence the movement was doing poorly may have decided Khrushchev to return Lysenko to the presidency of the Academy of Agricultural Sciences in 1961.

He resumed the presidency on August 8, and one reason now was that, like Khrushchev, he favored practical farm work over laboratory experiments. Let Soviet farmers decide whose theory was right! But 1961 was the year of the Soviet Union's outstanding successes in manned space flights. First, in April, Yuri Gagarin soared; then, in August, Gherman Titov orbited. Surely the new space age called for laboratories—and for bold and imaginative biology in laboratories. Both plants and men could not be left to the primitive, outdated mercies of Lysenkoism. Not in vain did 1962 start with two major attacks on Lysenko and his lickspittles, first by Academician Parin in February, next by Academician Kapitsa in March.

As already noted in these pages, Dr. Parin is a foremost Soviet expert in space medicine ("cosmic medicine" in the Russian phrase). With much sorrow and ire he wrote of certain biologists' "lack of confidence in experimental methods."[13] It came as no surprise, then, that on April 5, 1962, so short a time after the

Parin-Kapitsa onslaught, Lysenko once more resigned from the presidency of the Lenin Academy of Agricultural Sciences.

The official reason was Lysenko's health. And nearly a month earlier, on March 9, 1962, from Khrushchev's closing speech at the plenary session of the Party's Central Committee the Soviet people must have been surprised to learn that Lysenko had really never wanted to be that Academy's president. He had not, you see, wished to head it even the first time in 1938 when Stalin called him to the post. "Lysenko journeyed then from Odessa to Kiev," Khrushchev fondly reminisced, "and begged me to do everything to spare him this promotion. He said, 'I can't work in the Academy, I need soil, I must experiment [with soil], I can't live without it.' And I did all I could, but my power was not enough, and he had to take that post."[14]

Now, in 1962, as he left the presidency again, Lysenko once more made sure—not without Khrushchev's aid, of course—that the Academy would remain his fortress even in his absence: Mikhail Olshansky, a selectionist and agronomist of extreme Lysenkoist views, became his successor.

Yet, the anti-Lysenkoists would not be downed. Young scientists, unafraid, were increasingly active among them. Centered in Leningrad and Novosibirsk, and to a lesser degree in Moscow, they researched daringly and wrote and published copiously. Even in Moscow, the *Bulletin of the Moscow Society of Nature Researchers* survived in their possession. In 1962–63 they raised a new issue: the role of DNA or deoxyribonucleic acid in determining heredity. They, as well as Western scientists, saw a great triumph in the work done since the early 1950s in solving the mysteries of the DNA molecules. They viewed the role of these molecules in the chromosomes of cells as furnishing the basic pattern—the genetic code—for duplication of each species and its members from generation to generation.

But all this went against the very core of Lysenko's Lamarckism-Michurinism. Again, desperately, he counterattacked, and Olshansky with him. Khrushchev once more lent his support; in January 1963 there was some more praise for Lysenko in the Soviet press as it widely featured his pseudoscientific report on the "theoretical principles of controlled changes of heredity in plants."[15]

Yet, at this very time, the Party was still retreating. It allowed the State Atom Publishing House to publish two books by Academician Nikolai Dubinin, a biologist of Novosibirsk, wherein with rare nerve he praised Western genetics and "completely ignored the Michurin movement in biology," or so in August 1963 lamented Olshansky. There were other such recent books, too, he complained. And he cried out that the Moscow *Bulletin* still printed those "nonobjective articles containing falsehoods about the Soviet biological science."[16]

I V

Five months earlier, in March 1963, Olshansky came out in another Party publication with an attack on those Soviet scientists who made bold to support the Western view of DNA. Once more here was Lamarckism on a rampage as Lysenko's Comrade Friday denounced not only Russia's resurgent Mendelian biology but also the "baseless promise of some chemists, physicists, and mathematicians" of the Soviet Union to solve the problem of heredity along Western lines, not in Lysenko's pattern. Those Soviet biologists of the anti-Lysenko camp, and their allies in other, nonbiological disciplines in the Soviet Union, had the gall to deny the possibility of regulating heredity through acquired characteristics and, "most harmful of all," had the effrontery of influencing "young specialists who do not yet have any experience of their own" in such weighty matters.[17] Again and again Olshansky sang paeans to what he described as the fruitfulness of the Lysenko school in applying his kind of biology to Soviet agriculture—this on the eve of one of the most disastrous seasons in the U.S.S.R.'s farming of recent decades!

As bad luck would have it for Lysenko and Olshansky, the latter's article coincided with the appearance, in another Soviet magazine, of a most remarkable anti-Lysenko document to appear in the Russian press since Stalin's death. This was a thoughtful, comprehensive essay by two Soviet authors, Zh. Medvedev and V. Kirpichnikov, on the "prospects of Soviet genetics."[18]

Fearlessly the two writers explained and applauded Mendel's historic experiments and teachings (even supplying a diagram as their illustration); expounded the connection between genetics and cybernetics, between genetics and modern biochemistry, between genetics and medicine, particularly space medicine, and between genetics and farming; and in their conclusions issued this clarion call:

> Any and all attempts to ignore the practical and theoretical importance of modern genetics, attempts to limit the development of

Soviet biology by the narrow confines of only one—any one—school, must be rejected decisively. To the service of the Soviet people there must be summoned all the efforts of Soviet scientists and all the methods and achievements of the biological science tested by time and worldwide experience.

The question unspoken for so long was at last asked:

How did it happen that in our country the development of modern genetics was held up for such a long time? Why did we for such a lengthy period of time surrender to the capitalistic states such a large and fruitful sector of the scientific front with the excuse that the classical genetics is a bourgeois science? Surely we do not speak of "bourgeois physics," "bourgeois chemistry," "bourgeois physiology." On the contrary, in these and other areas we closely follow all the achievements abroad and strive to use everything new and interesting. . . . Only in biology certain persons still stubbornly try to draw a sharp line between the Soviet science and the world's science; they ignore everything that is done by representatives of other scientific schools.

Why so? The answer was very simple, the authors declared. The answer was in Stalinism still alive in Lysenkoism. Without naming either Lysenko or Olshansky, the two authors pointed their accusing fingers at "the attempt of certain scientists to isolate the Soviet science from world science—this harmful vestige of the cult of personality [the Russian euphemism for Stalinism], refusal to face reality, this fear to acknowledge honestly mistakes committed in the past and to repair them."

Earlier in the article, the baneful year 1948—the year of Lysenko's triumph—was mentioned by the two authors. Thus, both at the beginning and at the end of the article the blame was bluntly placed at Lysenko's door.

In his March 1963 article Olshansky said nothing about this attack by the two Mendelians. No one, apparently, had informed him that their article was to appear the same month; no one had brought him or his boss Lysenko any advance galleys of the onslaught. A few months later, however, in his August article reprinted by *Pravda* from *Sel'skaya zhizn'* (Rural Life), Lysenko's bootlicker loudly wailed in pain. In that angry piece Olshansky cried out that the two anti-Lysenkoists were guilty of "slander," that they had no right to denounce the 1948 triumph of his chief, that in Soviet biology there could be but one school—the Marxist-Leninist school, with no recognition of any value for any Western genetics.

In giving its *Pravda* columns to Olshansky, that is, to Lysenko, whom he represented, the Party made one more try to halt its retreat. But the Party did not—and does not—dare to repeat Stalin's terror, Stalin's destruction of the offending scientists.

In fact, already in January 1963, as the Party's Central Committee (jointly with the U.S.S.R.'s Council of Ministers) issued its resolution that more biologists were to be henceforth trained for the nation's needs, it recognized at least by implication that Lysenkoism had been costly. For years the memory of the Lysenko-Stalin terror had stopped brilliant young men and women from entering this field. Now, as the Party's plans for recruiting such students for 1963–65 were made public, the text of the resolution praised—as one way of enticement—many achievements of the Soviet bilogical science made *despite* Lysenko and *contrary* to his views and orders.

Thus the retreat was unmistakable. Little salve to Lysenko in the clumsy effort of the Party scribblers of the resolution to ascribe these anti-Lysenko accomplishments to Lysenko![19]

V

What still irks the triumphant host of Lysenko's foes at home is that amid all the chorus of denunciation of Stalinism and the rehabilitation (often, alas, posthumous) of its victims, never once is Lysenko himself officially charged with the sufferings and death of so many scientists in the bloody period of 1932–53. On no single occasion since 1953 did Khrushchev allow Lysenko to be personally charged with Nikolai Vavilov's tragic end, with the murder of so many scientists no less than of a whole science. Nor is the official post-Khrushchev policy on Lysenko any different in this particular respect. Thus the victory of true scholars in this field, although a definite fact and growing in its importance all the time, continues to be short of all the final justice it needs.

The reasons for Khrushchev's continued protection of Lysenko were several. First and foremost was his personal complicity in Lysenko's past crimes which might have risen to the surface were Lysenko's misdeeds officially brought into the open. Secondly, Khrushchev's Communist hierarchy was still as committed to Lamarckism as Stalin's leadership had been, and for the same reasons, although of course Khrushchev's Party was not as articulate or vengeful about it. Times were, after all, different.

Last but not least, there was Khrushchev's ever lively and

rather naïve admiration for Lysenko as a practical agronomist if not a theoretical biologist. Indeed, there is no denying Lysenko a certain flair as a clever botanist with a green thumb. But he—and Stalin's propagandists and secret police—exaggerated this reputation vastly, until even in the West something of this exaggeration was believed. It was repeated even by some of Lysenko's bitterest enemies among Western scientists in the 1940s at the height of the gory massacre caused by him. Thus Julian Huxley, amid all his denunciation of Lysenko as a murderous fraud in biology, remarked that "he enjoys the confidence of the peasants and agricultural workers in general; and . . . this has certainly contributed to the success of the methods he advocates."[20] But who said that there was such confidence and success for Lysenko in the Soviet Union? Stalin's and Khrushchev's publicity organs and police agents?

Far more judiciously, already in the same 1940s, other Western scientists proved that vernalization, for which Lysenko was praised by Stalin, was not original with Lysenko, that it was "old hat" in America and elsewhere in the West and obsolete by modern yardsticks.[21] And in our own times, in 1963–66, the question is asked both in the Soviet Union and in the West: If Lysenko's methods with grain were so good, why was there this near-catastrophic shortage of bread in his country, and why was it necessary for the Kremlin not only to "borrow" wheat from Rumania but also to buy vast quantities of it in Canada and the United States?

It is of note that by the end of Khrushchev's reign the Soviet press was saying hardly anything about any experiments or proposals emanating from Lysenko concerning grain and how to grow more of it and of better quality. Instead, Lysenko was publicized mainly in connection with his work aimed at improving the breed and the milk yield of Soviet cows.

In 1963–64 he did this work in his capacity as director of the Institute of Genetics of the Soviet Academy of Sciences, on its experimental farm Gorki Leninskiye near Moscow. Solemnly he conducted tours for those Moscow biologists who were still his followers, showing off his cows to them and supervising the resulting write-ups in *Pravda*. Profusely, warmly, he was praised by Khrushchev in his marathon speeches on the agricultural situation.

But even this Lysenkoist pretension was bitterly denounced and torn to pieces after Khrushchev fell. In late November 1964 a

member of Lysenko's own staff attacked him viciously in an official Soviet agricultural periodical. Using vast amounts of statistics
he proved that Lysenko's bulls and cows did not at all improve
either the breed or the productivity as the old pseudo master
claimed. Immediately the new onslaught was picked up by the
general press, and thus went the last shred of Lysenko's erstwhile
fame, sired by Stalin's Party and for so long defended by Khrushchev and his aides.[22]

V I

One of the main points Khrushchev usually made was that
Lysenko did his experimenting in the countryside, where such
work belonged, while most other Soviet agriculturalists refused to
come out of their city offices. "Take your institutes from asphalt
pavements to the farms!" was Khrushchev's repeated, angry cry.
The typical retort by Soviet agriculturalists was, "And what sort
of conditions are there, in those grassroots? In the sticks, and no
communication with the world at large—what kind of science
could it be?"[23]

In December 1963, Khrushchev, while praising Lysenko for his
bucolic preferences, upbraided his vassal Olshansky for the latter's predilection for Moscow comforts. And in a surprisingly
unorthodox statement for the Communist leader who condemned
almost everything Western, particularly everything American,
Khrushchev pointed to the United States and its agricultural research center, which he saw on his American trip in 1959 as a
wonderful example to emulate:

> Where is this center? In Washington? No. It is situated a score or
> two of kilometers from Washington, at Beltsville. Not in Washing-
> ton, but out there, in the countryside, the Secretary of Agriculture
> of the United States and his associates demonstrated scientific
> achievements, various experiments on plants and animals. And this
> is quite understandable. Whoever really wants to guide science
> should not separate himself from soil.[24]

Thus did Khrushchev find his target: agricultural scientists who
kept away from soil, who (unlike Lysenko, of course!) did not
understand soil, and who mistreated that lovely Soviet soil, with
the calamitous result of the perennial Soviet grain crisis. He
would not blame himself and his hierarchy, nor the Communist
idea and practice from which he and his Party and government
proceeded. He would chide these hapless scientists. If he must

retreat, in whatever zigzags, from Lamarckism, he would advance, in a headlong and ferocious Party line, against these sinister soil savants.

Khrushchev was essentially anti-intellectual. He disliked the necessity of praising and rewarding so many of his scientists and engineers. But he depended on them for catching up with the West, in his plans some day to vanquish the West. The peasant-potentate must cater to his intellectual subjects.

So much the greater was his vicious joy when he saw a chance to pull down at least one category of his scientists—the agricultural group. It was late in 1961 and early 1962 that he began his anti-*travopol'ye* campaign, with Russia's foremost savants of agriculture as his whipping boys. Soon the onslaught was in full swing.[25]

The Russian word *travopol'ye* means the grass-arable system. For years a revered concept and a firm practice in the Soviet Union, in 1961–62 with dramatic suddenness it became a curse, a sin, an anti-Soviet crime. Sarcastic bitterness marked Khrushchev's speeches against the method. Administrative sternness imbued his measures abolishing it.

The method, used by Russian peasants for centuries but refined and sanctified as "Socialist" by a few Russian professors in the 1920s and '30s, counted on perennial grasses to increase soil fertility. It almost neglected mineral fertilizers. It allowed a certain large percentage of Russian soil the luxury of "recuperating" from grain production by being "under grass." This made Russian agriculture extensive, in contrast to the intensive farming ways elsewhere, particularly in the West. On the cue of the pretense that the method was Socialist, the country's leading center of agricultural science—the Timiryazev Academy in Moscow—for decades sang hosanna to *travopol'ye*. In 1948 the Communist Party bosses decreed a compulsory use of the method in all of Soviet farming.

Following Stalin's death, first tentative criticism of the grass-arable system was heard from Khrushchev in 1954–55. The method was not fit for steppe and arid regions, he said. But everywhere else in the vast country it continued to reign unquestioned. And then, in 1961–62, came the big denunciation and the complete change. For 1962 alone, a diversion of some 55 million acres from grasses to grain and forage crops was ordered.

You can still find unexpunged in the *Great Soviet Encyclopedia* (1949), Volume 1, the earlier official praise for the grass-arable method as based on "the theory of a single soil-genetic process and soil fertility representing the crowning achievement of modern pedology" and proving itself "the scientific basis of production on state and collective farms, and the most progressive farming system in the world."[26]

Beginning with 1962, Soviet newspapers and journals were filled with desperate letters of recantation by Soviet scientists of agriculture. The Timiryazev Academy itself went on record with a letter by its Learned Council apologizing for its many years of support for grass. Humbly the professors agreed with Khrushchev as they scored the now-banned method for its "entire lack of scientific and practical basis."[27]

By fixing his wrath on the grass-arable system as one single convenient scapegoat, Khrushchev in essence proclaimed a change from the traditional extensive Russian system of farming to the intensive Western system, to the use of what he called "Big Chemistry"—mineral fertilizers galore.

Curiously enough, the greatest advocate of the grass-arable system in Russia (and now the chief culprit in the Party's eyes) was a scientist of Western origin. He was Vasily Robertovich Vilyams,[28] born in Moscow in 1863, the son of Robert Williams, an engineer who had come either from England or from America to work in tsarist Russia's newly burgeoning industries (according to one report, to help Major George Washington Whistler, the famous painter's father, build Russia's first important railroad—the one between Moscow and St. Petersburg, now Leningrad).

Vasily Vilyams was educated in scientific agronomy, traveled and researched abroad as well as in Russia, rose in reputation and rank until he gained the chair of pedology at the Timiryazev Academy, and finally, in 1928, joined the Communist Party. His celebrated version of the old *travopol'ye* had four main points: crop rotation wherein perennial leguminous and cereal grasses played a big role; employment of a special tillage system; fertilization of the plant, not the soil; establishment of forest windbreaks.

The basis of his ideas was not new. Russian peasants had long known the good effect, on soil fertility, of the root system of perennial grasses. Certain old-time Russian agronomists, particularly Vasily V. Dokuchayev in the late nineteenth century, proved the value of the grass-arable method and of windbreaks on their experimental farms. But by announcing, as Vilyams did, that all this was "Socialist," and by promising to raise the ebbing soil fertility in Russia by some 1,000 per cent, Vilyams won Stalin's favor sweepingly. When a few scientists tried to argue against certain points of the Vilyams theory, they paid for their daring with their jobs and some with their liberty or even their lives.

It was amid Russia's purges, in 1939, that Vilyams died peacefully and happily, at the ripe age of seventy-six, a greatly respected—and much feared—man. For another period of twenty-two years his name was uttered and printed with awe; his method continued in use throughout Russia.

But it should not have been used so universally, so uncritically. It may have been good—it may still be good—for certain small areas of Russia's terrain. Yet, on the whole, it failed because, as N. Novak-Deker correctly points out, "the vast area of land under cultivation in the Soviet Union, which incorporates all types of pedoclimatic zones but the tropical, was the arena of a grandiose experiment aimed at reducing a complex industry to a single method of production."[29]

VII

Nevertheless, just as the Vilyams system should not have been the only method in Soviet agriculture, neither should it be now blamed so spitefully as the main fault plaguing that country's farming.

Vilyams' "sinister" science is not the sole trouble with the U.S.S.R.'s grain production and other food yield. Few non-Russians realize that nature herself is against an ever full granary for Russia. She is Stepmother Nature to that country.

The Soviet Union occupies quite a share of the Old World— roughly one half of Europe and one third of Asia. It is about two and a half times the size of the United States. Yet, only some 10 per cent of Soviet territory is truly arable. And only one tenth of that arable area can bring good harvests without extra investments of manpower, machinery, and fertilizers.

Large expanses of Soviet terrain, mainly in the north and east, are either too cold or too arid, or too poor in the quality of their soil, for farming. Permafrost occupies 47 per cent of the Soviet Union's territory. Most of the land under cultivation in European Russia runs north of the 44th parallel—the parallel of the southern tip of our state of Maine!

Man-made troubles add to the Soviet farmer's grief. Ruthless deforestation in European Russia has led to much soil erosion. Overenthusiastic plowing of virgin steppes in southwestern Siberia and northern Kazakhstan since 1954 has intensified dust-bowl conditions.

And the greatest man-made handicap, for which of course no Russian scientist is responsible, is the fact that the Soviet farmer is a reluctant and angry serf.

All farming is nationalized and socialized in Russia. Even the small plot of land, about a half acre in size, permitted to each peasant family for private crops and dairying, belongs to the state, not to those families. The farmers' collective duties to the state take precedence, by law, over whatever private effort they may expend on such postage-stamp-sized lots.

This peculiar system, now several decades old, is the greatest man-made hindrance aggravating the natural shortcomings of Russia's poor terrain and harsh climate. Here is really the main reason why there is not enough food for Russia's increasing population and for the Party's ever more ambitious doings and plans at home and abroad.

The peasant is angry because the Communists disregard totally his opposition to any kind of socialization of farming. His anger is passive, however. His resistance has not even a hint of a revolution abrewing. But he shows his feelings by being sullen, inefficient, unproductive in his collective duties—and by being the opposite of all these unlovely traits when he can labor on his tiny "private" plot. In 1959 more than 80 per cent of all eggs produced in the Soviet Union, and almost one half of all meat and milk, came from those nonsocialized plots.[30] In 1962, 70 per cent of the country's potatoes and 42 per cent of the vegetables were grown on private plots.[31] In 1963 private plots produced 42 per cent of the nation's meat, 45 per cent of its milk, and 75 per cent of its eggs.[32] If only grain could be grown in sufficiency on such small plots! But of course it cannot.

Clearly, the Soviet peasant wants a farm of his own. He is resentful, he lacks ambition. He did not respond with enthusiasm to any of Khrushchev's plans for intensive farming, or corn planting, or more Virgin Land plowing—so long as Soviet farming remained collectivized into those neofeudalistic, serfdom-blighted, state-run units called kolkhoz and sovkhoz.

He wants a farm all his own. But this was not granted him by Khrushchev. Nor is it being granted by the Party chiefs of Khrushchev's ilk succeeding Khrushchev. For, if granted, this would start a whole chain reaction of private enterprise in the nation, and of a non-Soviet political structure in consequence.

And so the Red regime lives on, boisterous and belligerent, advancing in science and technology of the most modern kinds, yet with its giant heel sore and not healing.

A tragic jest, indeed, for the Party to blame the heel's illness on the only Soviet scientists that can be frightened in these post-Stalinist and post-Khrushchevist days—the agricultural eggheads!

CHAPTER VII

A Deep Bow to Economists

TWO PROBLEMS HAVE BEDEVILED the Party throughout the nearly half century of its rule over the empire it seized and continued to expand. About one of them, agriculture, the Party has tried to do a number of things, but—as shown in the preceding pages—the measures have so far proved feeble palliatives, not cutting to the heart of the matter. The scientists in this area, always more castigated than consulted and heeded, have so far won no victory. But it is different with the other of the two major problems, the consumer's pressure.

Here the post-Stalinist battle between the Party and the scholars was centered on the very essentials of the problem, and after a rather brief period of hesitation, the Party in effect admitted its retreat. Officially, of course, it denies the dogma's rout. It tries to fit its dogma into the pragmatic change. But Mao Tse-tung and the West, for once agreeing, insist that Khrushchev's heirs in their backdown before the consumer-favoring economists are indeed betraying Marxism.

The theme of this argument is the Liberman Reform, freeing Soviet economy from the sacrosanct Plan and gradually wedding it to the idea and practice of profit, all for the benefit of the customer. During its brief hesitation, the Party allowed some of its top chieftains to assail the Reform. Thus, in 1962–63, when it was first proposed and discussed, the Libermanization of Soviet economy was fiercely denounced at home no less than in China, by Communist dogmatists, as truly a retreat from the holy beard of Karl Marx. And it was Professor Yevsei Liberman, along with the growing host of his supporters in the high seats of Soviet power, who hotly denied that any such retreat or betrayal was occurring or would ever result from the Reform. Gradually, in 1964–66, the Reform won out, its domestic foes subsided, and

Liberman now argues back about the Marxism or non-Marxism of his Reform less and less. He does not have to. The victory is becoming too clear to bother about justifications.

So definite was the economists' triumph by 1965 that the Party merely waited to be told by Liberman and others what to do next. The delay of the next moves was caused, not by any opposition from the hierarchs, but by some minor academic arguments among the economists themselves. In early January 1965, at a symposium at Columbia University, Professor Alex Nove, the knowledgeable specialist on Soviet economy, was asked from the audience: "But don't the Party chiefs try at all to stop these economists?"

"On the contrary," Professor Nove replied, "the Party chiefs only ask the economists to hurry up and make up their minds."

I I

In one sense at least the Libermanites in their curious pro-Marxian protestations may be right: their attack on the Plan may not be anti-Marxian if only because the Plan was never mentioned either by Marx or Engels.

As for Lenin, he came to the Plan quite late in his thinking—at the end of World War I and in the middle of his own civil war. His inspiration, singularly enough, came from the accounts he had read of wartime capitalistic-militaristic planning in the Kaiser's Germany. He was impressed also by a little book in praise of planning written by a White Guard professor in General Denikin's anti-Red camp.[1] Thus did the Plan emerge as a most definite article of Communist faith and practice. Not historically Marxist, it became almost hysterically a Party matter, particularly under Stalin, who introduced his toil-and-thunder series of Five Year Plans.

The Plan was cumbersome and wasteful, especially of human lives and values, and the miracle was that it did produce results in heavy industries, war technology, and of course outer-space accomplishments, but surely not in consumer goods. As the empire grew and its economy expanded, the scope of planning became too much for the mere humans running the Plan, and at times more than consumer wares suffered.

The Plan loomed up a self-perpetuating Moloch, an unwieldy monster demanding sacrifices instead of being there to serve.[2] So all-embracing was its mode of supervision that the construction of a new steel mill was spelled out down to the location of each nail, in ninety-one volumes totaling 70,000 pages. The Plan's committees and councils multiplied so prolifically that one factory received seventy different ukases from fifteen governmental bodies, every one of which had the authority to issue such instructions. Another plant was showered with 111 instructions from nine planning committees, and the bulk of these contradicted one another. A regional Council of People's Economy submitted its plan and in due time received it back approved, but in the next six months there came 137 supplements and orders changing the plan out of recognition.

Between six and ten million persons are estimated to be busy in Soviet planning. One Russian critic of excessive planning estimated that, at the present pace of multiplication, by 1980 every other Soviet citizen was sure to be a planner.

The consumer suffered in particular because the Plan favored heavy industries, even if clumsily. It was in light industries that the Plan frequently lost whatever grain of sense it originally held. Even after Stalin was gone and first Malenkov and then Khrushchev decreed some increased attention to the shopper, the Plan made it necessary for managers to produce not what the consumer really needed and wanted but what the Plan's quota demanded or a given assembly line allowed. A factory produced its chandeliers bigger and heavier, until they pulled ceilings down, but such sizes prevailed only because the weightier chandeliers consumed more metal and the quota could thus be fulfilled that much more quickly. Another plant painted all its output of lamp shades an ugly orange color since more than one hue would have called for more complicated manufacturing processes. Shoddy clothing, inoperable appliances, merchandise with parts missing, all this went to the market in the Planners' supreme confidence that the goods-starved citizens would snap it up in any condition and at any price.

And they did—until the latter 1950s and early 1960s, when the Soviet customer had more money and spunk and began to show his newly found choosiness. Unsold merchandise was piling up in the state stores and warehouses. Three billion dollars' worth of unsaleable goods, about 3 per cent of the nation's disposable annual income, was estimated to have accumulated by 1965. The well-known Podolsk factory near Moscow, having expanded from the Singer sewing machine plant nationalized during the Revolution, reported in late 1964 that more than 150,000 sewing

machines clogged its warehouses with no prospect of market.
"The plant's management begged the Moscow Council of People's
Economy to reduce the plan. Came the answer: 'Keep on making
sewing machines. Carry out the plan.' And so, for the last few
months, the plant has been working, not for the consumer, but . . .
for the plan."[3]

I I I

Yevsei Liberman was born in 1897 and remembers the prerevolutionary times.[4] He attended an old-time *gymnaziya* (secondary school); he was twenty when the revolution broke out; he
took his law degree at Kiev University in an atmosphere of non-
Soviet liberalism; he went on to study engineering at Kharkov
with an open, critical mind.

For about fifteen years he worked in various Central Ukrainian
factories. One especially enlightening part of this time—six years
of it—was spent by him as chief planner of a large farm-machin-
ery plant. During World War II he was shifted to a Moscow job,
but after the war he returned to Kharkov, to teach at the Engi-
neering-Economic Institute, to act as a part-time consultant to the
local industries, and to continue his own education. In 1956 he
won his doctorate in economics; in 1959 he was named a full
professor.

At the Institute the professor was training factory managers.
This was a rare occupation, for, in the Soviet Union, most managers are not trained specifically as managers. To him came eager
men not only from all over the Ukraine but from the entire wide
sweep of the Soviet Union. Liberman knew their problems as
hardly any other Soviet economist-engineer could. At the same
time, in the freer air of the late 1950s, Liberman sharpened his
English, read American and other Western literature in his field,
and met with visiting American economists and engineers.

In 1956 Liberman wrote an article for the Moscow *Kommunist*
in which he argued, almost timidly, that a local Soviet plant could
improve both its efficiency and quality if it emphasized its profitability. The great mathematical economist Academician Vasily
Nemchinov spotted the modest proposal and invited Liberman to
Moscow. Nemchinov, steadily losing his sight and otherwise ailing, used the last few years of his long life (he died in November
1964 at seventy) in persuading the Communist hierarchs to
become pragmatic. It was Nemchinov more than anyone else who

in 1962 prevailed upon Khrushchev to give Liberman his first important green light.

The argument at first stressed the goodness of profitability rather than the evils of planning. Shouldn't even the new Soviet man be rewarded economically if he worked more efficiently and fruitfully? Was there not an early and rather consistent Soviet precedent of deviation from the Marxian principle that all men be paid equally?

Indeed, Stalin, while permitting neither blame nor blemish to be ascribed to Marxism and himself, had already committed the un-Marxian sin of combating *uravnilovka*, or the egalitarianism of the early phase of the Soviet revolution. Unequal pay was introduced by Stalin, and it remained the very non-Communist hallmark of Soviet life for three decades up to his death.

Since Stalin's demise the personal "material interest" of the Soviet citizen has been even more fostered and encouraged. This is the way to march toward Communism: through bonuses and prizes for individual performance. So said *Pravda* proudly in October 1961 as it reviewed the whole series of governmental measures, meant to reward eager beavers in industry and agriculture, decreed by the Party since Stalin's departure.

Yet it was nearly another year before the Party, prodded by its rather un-Marxian economists (who did no more than respond to the facts of life), made a truly significant step away from its dogma by re-examining the very base of that dogma: the question of profit in economy.

Beginning with September 9, 1962, a lively debate was launched in the Soviet press on whether each plant, factory, mine, or any other state enterprise should operate on that old capitalistic principle of profit. In his article "Plan, Profit, Bonus," prominently published in *Pravda* of that day,[5] Professor Yevsei Liberman proclaimed in effect that profit was not necessarily capitalistic, that it could also be socialistic, and therefore clean and altogether lovely. Reduced to its essentials, Dr. Liberman's proposal consisted of these points:

Net profit made by a Soviet enterprise, not its gross output or gross profit, should be the only yardstick for the manager's success or failure. This net profit, figured out in terms of the fixed and working capital, should be the goal of an incentive system for each and every plant in the Soviet Union.

A great deal of decentralization would be necessary for this new system to operate effectively. Wages, productivity, costs—all of these, now dictated from above, would become the concern of the plant's manager only. True, further capital may not come from the center either, but then the manager would put a part of the plant's profit into an incentive fund, from which the manager would on the one hand take money for further investments at the plant and on the other would pay bonuses to both his labor and management.

The central authority of the state would still control the prices of the goods produced, and would keep its watchful eye on the proper use of the incentive fund. As for the rest, the manager would have his complete freedom to elaborate his own plan of production and sales, to enter into contracts with other enterprises, to improve machinery and methods, to reduce costs—and thus make profit.

I V

If Nikita Khrushchev was not directly instrumental in the initial appearance of Professor Liberman's article, by at least acquiescing in the printing of it in the chief Party organ, he certainly took it up after its publication as a point of departure for a nationwide debate. There was a startling amount of freedom in the discussion. Wrote a shrewd American observer: "Unlike other recent economic disagreements, this one is marked by freedom and openness. Absent is the use of doctrinal citation and flag-waving. In contrast to the average Soviet economic discussion, almost no appeal is made to Marx, Lenin or even Khrushchev for ideological justification."[6]

Some Soviet intellectuals, when talking to foreign visitors in Moscow, went so far in their evaluation of the debate as to say that Professor Liberman "proposed jettisoning all the classic Marxist-Leninist economic principles in favor of the capitalistic profit notion." When an Italian guest remarked that only a short time earlier Liberman would have ended up in prison, his Russian acquaintances assured him that "it was the Party itself—and the very top people in it—which was first to perceive that ideology can no longer be permitted to determine whether an object should be made out of plastic or steel"—that it was the Communist Party which had initiated Liberman's onslaught on the old Marxist dogma.[7]

If so, it is interesting to note that the Communist Party apparently feared to come out directly as the originator of those new "pro-capitalistic-profits" ideas and the starter of the momentous debate. It needed the shield, the prestige, of such learned professors as Dr. Liberman even to suggest a retreat from the sacred books of Karl Marx.

The press discussion which followed Liberman's first article went on for months, and it had a spirit of urgency.[8] Critics sprang to their feet and typewriters to declare that Liberman was wrong, that profit should not and cannot be a sole or even main measure of viability in socialistic economy, that it had not been and it ought not to be. Professor Liberman, in a radio broadcast, likened such critics to those administrators of tsarist times "who had opposed the introduction of the motorcar in their districts until horses got used to it.[9]

But, for Soviet mores, this and other criticism of Liberman's plan was indeed surprisingly mild and modest. No critic called for his head; no one accused him of being a Trotskyist, a renegade, or a Wall Street lackey. Some criticized him for details rather than for his proposal's essence. Even those who did not at all like the proposal seemed to concede that Soviet planning was not working properly; that surely it was silly to reward the managers merely for meeting and overfulfilling their assigned quotas of production even when the output clogged Soviet warehouses unwanted by the consumers because of either its poor quality or its high price or both.

A few critics were actually Liberman's supporters; they criticized only to show that Liberman in his argument did not go far enough. Thus, notably, Academician Nemchinov added two logical points:

First, he said, the state—to be truly realistic—should charge each enterprise some interest for the investment capital furnished by the state.

Second, the state's central authority should give up its monopoly of supplying the enterprises with the materials and components they need; the plants themselves should have the right to buy and sell such necessities from one another.

O shades of the free market of the West!

V

Months later, in early 1963, it seemed that the controversy had been allowed to fade and die, with no discernibly novel, non-Marxist measures taken by the Communist Party as a result of the discussion. Faint was the heart of the Party's top elite, if in truth it hankered after this Libermanite liberation of the manager. Shy seemed the professorial group that wanted this far-reaching change.

Yet, the first word of the new sermon had been uttered. Slowly, cautiously, while not approving the Liberman idea officially, the Communist Party began to introduce certain parts of it in Soviet practice. By mid-1964 two state clothing firms, one in Moscow and the other at Gorky (formerly Nizhni Novgorod, on the Upper Volga shores), were ready to experiment.

Starting July 1, 1964, each of the two Soviet firms moved from its erstwhile meek role within that vast, clumsy, central plan to a decentralized blueprint of its own. That old central plan had been prepared by the higher authorities too far ahead. The new independence of the Soviet consumer was rapidly, contemptuously leaving it behind. As a Soviet newspaperman tried to explain it:

> Formerly it was deemed necessary to foresee *ahead of time and in detail* literally everything in the plan: where, how much, and what goods will be produced. But life marches on. The consumer-goods industry swiftly advances. People's material needs and possibilities have grown immeasurably. Reality has shown that under such conditions the planning of consumer goods output—the well-ahead-of-time kind, the meticulous type, up to the last button, so to speak—does not always answer life's demands.[10]

Consider the plight of the wearing-apparel industry in the Soviet Union: In the spring and early summer of 1964 it was still producing models approved by the central authority in the spring of 1963 and, even in 1962. These were approved by "the center" on the basis of orders sent in by Soviet stores throughout the nation, and the stores were then reflecting the 1962–63 fashions or popular demands.

> But in these two years, naturally enough, fashions have shifted; new textiles have appeared; tastes have changed. What to do? To correct the plans of the apparel factories quickly? The fact is, however, that you can't do this *quickly*. And so the result is that the apparel-makers (and not they alone!) work more "for the plan" than "for the customer."

Liberman was right. Thus, on the first day of July 1964 the two clothing concerns, "as an experiment so far," abandoned the old plan, cutting through the red tape and dealing with stores and their customers directly, with no intervening guardianship from the central authority slowing down the orders and causing the ridiculous outdating of suits and dresses. The two firms now need not report to any superior offices in Moscow or elsewhere about anything except the final result; need not account for anything save one thing: its profit.

For this profit is the proof positive that does "compel an enterprise to work with a maximum economic effect." Thus, it will not be "the chase after that proverbial 'gross' that will shape the work of the enterprise; the tastes, the expectations, the demands of the customers" will constitute the driving force. "True," concluded the enthusiastic Moscow journalist, "this is only an experiment. But an experiment, as is well known, is essayed with the aim of trying and testing something new, prior to the time when doors into life will be flung wide open for it."[11]

The firms, an American economist commented, "completely freed from any economic plan set by higher authority, . . . will make their own production plans on the basis of orders and contracts with their customers—that is, in much the same way as an American clothing producer plans his own output." Prices too will thereby be affected. For the apparel-firm managers "will also have much greater freedom than before to set the prices at which their clothing will be offered to representatives of Soviet wholesale and retail trade."[12]

By 1965 the experiment of the two clothing firms was pronounced a resounding success. Suits and other apparel coming from their factories were of better style and quality, just what the store in their direct dealing with the firms had requested. The goods sold quickly, at lower prices, and brought higher profits to the firms and sizable bonuses to the staffs—tailors, sales force, managers, and bookkeepers. And so, in January 1965 an order was issued from Moscow expanding the Reform to nearly 400 factories in the clothing and footwear industries throughout the nation.[13]

But difficulties too have been encountered by the first two successful firms in Moscow and Gorky. One is that the planners still refuse to stand aside, even when told specifically to give these factories their complete leeway in making deals, each with twenty-two stores. The planning committees and councils "simply cannot get rid of their habit." The other difficulty is that the firms' suppliers still obey the Plan. The machinery, the dyes, and other supplies needed by the two "liberated" firms just don't arrive when the firms need them. "The chain of the enterprises operating by direct contact has proved to be incomplete. For the chemical and machine-building factories are not within this chain." Because of this and the consequent lack of machines or raw materials, "the textile factories often cannot fulfill their customers' orders."[14]

The answer is, of course, to liberate from the Plan not alone those clothing and shoe and other consumer-goods factories but, increasingly, heavy industries, too. The first such experiment was announced by Moscow in May 1965: a Ukrainian brown-coal mine had by then been functioning on a profitability basis for some five months.[15]

Indeed, what succeeds in the apparel market should succeed in other fields as well. As its plenary session of September 27–29, 1965, the party's Central Committee decided to change the management of the nation's entire economy to the Liberman methods —this without mentioning Liberman's name in its final resolutions, yet spelling out all of the measures proposed by him and already tried out in those specially selected cases. Now Councils of People's Economy, noted for their interference with efficiency and profit, were to be abolished throughout the land, and their "cleansed" functions centralized in Moscow ministries, some of which to be brand-new; planning and central control were to be preserved but in diminished doses; and, above all, managers in all the industries without exception were to be given enhanced independence and fresh power. On October 1, the Supreme Soviet (parliament) of the Soviet Union was summoned to convene in order to approve the momentous change. This it did promptly, being no more than a rubber stamp to the Party.[16]

VI

Thus, in late 1965, the Liberman Reform won out, sweepingly. It now remains to be seen whether further implementations of the reform, coming yet closer to Western practices, follow and, if so, how soon.

Some Western observers say that, yes, such further changes are inevitable.

The Communist Party may even come to accept Academician Nemchinov's amendment to Liberman's plan about adopting that Western usage of charging interest on investment capital. By early 1964 this was already done in Hungary: a 5 per cent annual interest charge was introduced by the state on all the capital (including the cost of machinery and supplies) received by the state plants from the government. The purpose, the Hungarian chiefs insist, is "not to raise money for the state, but to force businesses to handle capital more efficiently by making them pay for its use." Still, the funds thus gained by the government must have come in handy: the interest charge on the capital so far represents an estimated $400 million yearly boon to the state's treasury.[17]

Victory of the science of economics over the pseudo science of Marxism? Oh no, protested another Soviet top-notch scientist, a specialist on automation, Academician Vadim Trapeznikov, writing in *Pravda* on August 17, 1964:

> We hear the opinion that interest on capital is a phenomenon of the capitalistic society. This is not convincing. In actuality, the form here is indeed similar, but the essence is not. In the capitalistic society capital is a source of income, and interest on capital is the capitalist's profit. But with us receiving interest on capital is not the state's income (after all, the pocket is one and the same, the state's pocket), but a form of economic pressure, quickening the capital's turnover.[18]

But Hungarian capitalists of the Communist Party, the regime's chieftains already introducing capital interest charges, let the cat out of the bag when they admitted, even if obliquely, that Marxism is certainly being revised or even dropped. Said Comrade Sandor Kopacsy, deputy general manager of Hungary's Investment Bank, which collects the interest for the state: "In the past, capital did not figure in plant costs, due to theoretical principles which no longer hold true."[19]

Thus we see the beginnings of the Soviet retreat from the stifling, nonworkable theory, or, shall we say, the Soviet advance to greater freedoms, which the new technological day demands of the Red camp so insistently, so clearly.

VII

The argument is by no means settled, and Liberman's innovation is not yet a sure winner. Indeed, many high-placed dogmatists keep on fighting to preserve the Plan. Some of them had even shifted, dramatically, from their former fear and hatred of cybernetics to a hope that, of all things, computers will save the Plan. They argue that the Plan has grown unwieldy and illogical only because of the greater magnitude of the task at hand. Just change abacuses for computers, and the Plan will become workable and smooth.

The sharpest argument is about profit and interest: Can these indeed be Marxian? When Liberman and his followers complain in the press that the Western commentators are unduly triumphant about the un-Marxian features of the Reform, particularly about the element of profit, the complaint is addressed to the domestic critics no less than to the West. For some die-hard faithful the Reform is unholy because it is to Profit that the Plan is sacrificed.

The pro-Profit eloquence runs thus (quite similar to Academician Trapeznikov's defense of interest):

> The heart of the matter is in who owns the means of production. On this depends just who gets the profit. In a Socialist state it accrues to the state, to the toilers themselves, while in a capitalistic state the profit goes to the entrepreneurs, to the monopolies.[20]

And:

> When and by whom has it been said that profit is natural to capitalism but alien to Socialism? . . . under capitalism, in consequence of exploitation of man by man, profit accrues to the owners of the means of production, while under Socialism it goes to all of society and is spent on expansion of production, enhancement of the people's welfare, and the nation's defense.[21]

The main fault of this argument, seen by the West but hardly perceived by those Communists who sincerely believe in the purity of Soviet profit, is this:

The result of the Soviet experiment of nearly half a century has so far been gross inequality and injustice instead of the promised equality and justice. It is true that practically all the means of production and most other property belong also to the state, but the state and its profit do not belong to the people. These belong to the New Class of the privileged and to their children, who inherit and widen their fathers' new socioeconomic and political power.

Professor Liberman may indeed be convinced that he is steadying, not rocking, the false premise on which the Soviet state rests. Then again he may be fully cognizant of the epochal role he and his fellow economists are playing in tearing the premise apart.

CHAPTER VIII

~~~~~~

Hail the Healer

THEN AGAIN, there comes a time when out of the blue the Party concedes its defeat even more clearly and bows before science with no hems and haws. Wonder of wonders, the Party pronounces that science is sovereign, that politics—Communist politics—has no business dictating to science. Thus it admits implicitly if not outright this triumphant erosion of Communist dogma by scientific pragmatism. It eats humble pie in a way that would have been unthinkable in Stalinist days—aye, even in Lenin's era.

Such sudden confession was first made in 1962 concerning just one learned field, that of medicine. Yet, one phrase of the admission spelled out the general nature of defeat; it proclaimed a principle which should be valid for, and can yet be applied to, all the other sciences now known or yet unborn.

A Leningrad man named A. T. Kochugin, a medical experimenter without a medical degree, for several years prior to 1962 had tried to treat cancer of the bladder by using chemical compounds consisting of semicarbazide chloride and cadmium iodide. He rallied to his support a group of doctors who said they would be willing to experiment with his method if only their medical superiors gave them the go-ahead signal.

Charlatanism and quackery, said Dr. Nikolai N. Blokhin, president of the Soviet Academy of Medical Sciences. He did his best to prevent those Leningrad doctors from experimenting with the Kochugin method. But other powerful influences prevailed, and on March 22, 1961, the Soviet Ministry of Health issued an order allowing the employment of the method in a Leningrad hospital. Still Dr. Blokhin, together with a doctor who was a high official in the Ministry of Health, in one manner and another prevented the hospital from even starting the experimentation. At last, in January 1962, the work was begun. On April 24 the Ministry of Health sent a committee to check on the results. Exactly one month later, on May 24, it issued an order stopping any further experimentation with Kochugin's chemicals.

Kochugin and his friends flared up. They vowed they would not give in. They went around Leningrad with their lament; they presented their side of the story so convincingly that soon nine well-known writers and journalists wrote an indignant letter to the Central Committee of the Communist Party.

In the protest, the group demanded the top hierarchs' intervention in the matter. The patients on whom the chemical compounds had been used were hopeless cases anyway, the argument ran. Treatment given in the few months when this was permitted did bring the patients relief. Even if not always beneficial, the method was harmless, so why not continue its use? The higher medical authorities who issued their prohibition of the Kochugin method were "inhuman," "callous," "conservative," "bureaucratic," and "antistate." The Party's top-stratum bosses should immediately cancel the prohibition, and Dr. Blokhin and his colleagues should be charged with obstinate dereliction of duty.

The leadership was not long with its answer. On August 1, 1962, nearly all of page 2 of *Pravda* was devoted to the intriguing case. The angry letter of the nine writers and journalists was published—side by side with a still lengthier rebuttal by Blokhin and fifteen of his colleagues, members of the Academy of Medical Sciences and other famous medical professors. Not the least among the latter was Academician Vasily Parin, the Soviet Union's great space-medicine expert.

The rebuttal branded the Kochugin method a fraud and a delusion, totally devoid of any scientific value. Kochugin should have used the method on laboratory animals before trying it on humans. If any of the Leningrad patients did feel well, it was a temporary relief only, "a psychotherapeutic effect quite often observed in medical practice." Some who thought they improved thanks to Kochugin were not cancer patients at all, as the diagnosis of their trouble had been wrong in the first place. Kochugin practiced medicine illegally; he was "a demagogue," interfering with the true medical scientists, whose progress in treating cancer has been unspectacular and slow, yes, but fruitful nonetheless.

I I

The most remarkable feature of *Pravda's* page 2 for August 1, 1962, was the short introduction to the complaint and the rebuttal. The introduction was the Party's own answer to the argument—the Central Committee simply refused to take sides in the argument.

In effect, however, it sided with the academicians against the protesters. For, after all, the refusal meant that the order prohibiting the amateur cancer healers from further experimentation was left standing. Thus, for the nonce, came Kochugin's fiasco.

The striking part was the language of the pronunciamento by the Party's Central Committee as it declined to rescind the academicians' order:

> The Central Committee of the Communist Party of the Soviet Union does not consider it possible to assume the role of arbiter in approving methods of medical treatment. Only medical scientists can ascertain the correctness of using these or other methods of treating illnesses. *Attempts to dictate in science by injunction cannot bring any benefit,** and, as is known, such attempts in the recent past led to the undeserved accusation and discrediting of certain leading scientists and physicians of our country (the "doctors' case").

In short, the Central Committee said, let us avoid repetition of Stalin's error of terror. The doctors' case, to which the Committee so meaningfully referred, involved fifteen prominent Soviet physicians, most of them Jewish, who in January 1953—a short time before the old dictator's death—were arrested on charges of killing and plotting to kill high Party officials of Stalin's entourage by the use of incorrect medical treatment. In April, a month after Stalin's demise, the doctors were freed.

The phrase, "Attempts to dictate in science by injunction cannot bring any benefit," was quite an admission to be made by the Party guilty of far more than the infamous "doctors' plot." This was the Party that initiated, blessed, and was then still condoning, even if halfheartedly, the gory sin of Lysenkoism. This was the Party that still tried to make some sound laws of economics subordinate to the "unscience" of Party politics; the Party that blamed agricultural scientists in particular for all of the Party's blatant transgressions in the vital problem of Russian farming.[1]

A Russian *émigré* wondered in a New York newspaper:

* Italics are mine.

Just a moment, citizens, but what may the result be? In your
hurry you blurted out quite something! If the scientists of medicine,
and not members of the Central Committee of the dearly beloved
Communist Party, are the proper persons to judge about treatment
of diseases, then perhaps architects themselves are to judge about
architecture, and composers and conductors can judge music, and
some historians with a petit bourgeois deviation can judge history.
Where will it all end?[2]

III

We may well probe for reasons for this unprecedented action
on the Central Committee's part. Look closely: Not only did the
top leaders fail to make a secret of the trouble in the Soviet medical
paradise they publicized the argument in their most authoritative
Party paper—and they openly proclaimed, possibly for the first
time in Soviet history, that henceforth the Party would not and
should not "dictate in science by injunction." Why did they?

One reason may have been that Party doctrine was not involved in the Leningrad quarrel. So the Party could afford to turn
the other way, to appear liberal and magnanimous, objective and
noninterfering.

This in itself was rather a substantial change since Stalin's long
reign. In Stalin's time the Party "shoved its nose" (as the Russian
saying goes) into everybody's business, doctrine or not. If there
was no doctrinal reason, the Party invented one. Didn't Stalin
become an outstanding expert in linguistics, laying down the law
on what in his opinion constituted Communist and anti-Communist morphology and phonetics?

Another reason, however, may have been the exalted stations
—in the medical science—of such academicians as Blokhin and
Parin. The ruling of the Central Committee of August 1962, and
especially the wide publicity given to it by the Party, may have
been the Party's notice to amateurs and lower-echelon politicians
to respect the luminaries of true science, to stop attacking or even
criticizing them in any way whatever.

This may have been notice of a change far exceeding the scope
of the medical field alone. Those in opposition to any and all
science (except, as noted in an earlier chapter, to agronomy)
were warned to desist. No longer would the Party protect, much
less encourage, any ignoramus tilting at science in the name of
truth or antibureaucratism or Communism or what have you.

The Party's well-known "interferiority complex" was at last to be abandoned, in some cases at least, if science indeed and insistently demanded such a retreat.

IV

Note well, however, that the bow to the healers was made by the Party at the highest level possible; that the medical profession as a whole did not appear to be particularly honored. "Take the physicians who treat you," Khrushchev reminded a farm conference in a Virgin Land district in November 1961. "They get less pay than tractor drivers."[3] This was his tranquilizing rejoinder to the Soviet peasants then clamoring for better wages.

Western observers confirmed time and again that, of all the sciences, conditions were worst for the vast majority of Soviet medical practitioners. In 1957 an American mission of health specialists returning from the Soviet Union reported shrewdly: "The average Soviet physician does not have the same status as a Soviet engineer, although he spends more time in training and gives more of himself to his fellow men." Not so shrewdly the mission added: "He receives a lower salary and consequently has a lower standard of living, presumably because it takes the State longer to train him as a physician and, having invested more, the State can claim more of his time and effort for less compensation."[4] This is a rather clumsy rationalization, and one wonders whether the visiting Americans had a brainstorm of their own, inventing such a tenuous presumption rather than hearing it from some solemn but stupid Intourist guide. The real truth is, of course, far more basic and simple: Machines are of more value to the Communist hierarchy than men. Engineers are therefore (just naturally for the Soviet Union) paid better for taking care of machines than physicians for healing humans.

As late as April 1964, an American news agency reported from Moscow: "A graduate doctor can expect to start with a salary of 75 rubles a month, a little over $80. He may be assigned to a remote area where living is disagreeable and promotion slow."[5] Little wonder that the bulk of lower-rank physicians in the Soviet Union are women. Men, if they can at all help it, try their utmost to push their way to the higher strata of the medical profession—or do not enter that field at all.

But it was in the same month of April 1964 that in a short story published in *Izvestiya* the population was warned to be nice to doctors, to respect their education and mission, and not to set ferocious dogs upon them.[6] In June 1964 the same newspaper

chided a Party bureau in the countryside near Moscow for siding
with the enemies of a newly appointed physician who tried to
bring order into a neglected and mismanaged sanatorium for
tubercular children.[7] Also in June it was announced that beginning January 1, 1965, any and all car or truck drivers were
obliged to place themselves at the disposal of any medical worker
demanding emergency transportation.[8]

Finally, in mid-July, with great fanfare, Khrushchev announced
nationwide salary increases to doctors: from 72 rubles 50 kopeks
to 90 rubles a month; from 75 to 100; and so on, to the top rank,
from 151 rubles a month to 170—this to a physician with more than
twenty-five years of practice in the countryside and over thirty
years in the city.[9]

But still, how niggardly this homage to the medical helots, how
inadequate the occasional hymn in praise of an obscure but talented doctor that in these post-Khrushchevian times appears in
the Soviet press.[10] The truth is that, not only the Soviet state, but
Soviet society too fails to value the physician as highly as does
Western society, particularly that of the United States.

In the Soviet Union the engineer is ahead of the physician in
the popular esteem, also in the young citizens' plans and ambitions for careers. But in the United States it is the other way
around. In fact, American respects go to engineers after those to
the lawyer, who is only slightly behind the doctor. A 1960 table
of a marriage broker's fees in New York demanded from a girl's
family $500 for her marriage to a doctor, $400 to an attorney,
and only $300 to an engineer (but a dentist lagged in this proces-
sion with just a $250 fee). A prestige poll conducted by the Na-
tional Science Foundation across the United States in 1963 and
'64 ranked Supreme Court justices first; then—in this order—
came physicians, nuclear physicists, scientists, state governors
and government-employed scientists, followed by a tie among
Cabinet members, congressmen, and college professors. In this
roll call of popular American esteem, engineers were not even
mentioned, while physicians came near the top, ahead even of
scientists.[11]

How unlike the Soviet picture, indeed.

V

Does the Soviet physician protest? Is he to some degree a rebel
against the regime? The usual charge is that he has gone along
with Communist oppression too easily. In June 1965, Dr. Sergei

Mardashev, vice-president of the Soviet Academy of Medical Sciences, publicly called shame on his profession's record in Stalinist days. Take the case of the great heritage of Ivan Pavlov's ideas and discoveries: from the "rich teachings of this genius of Russian physiology" Soviet medical researchers and practitioners "selected just one division—dealing with man's higher nervous activity, and at that in the arbitrary interpretation given to it by certain savants who assumed the role of infallible commentators of I. P. Pavlov's teachings, [setting themselves up] as his direct and sole heirs." Dr. Mardashev did not say what every doctor and biologist in the Soviet Union had known for years: it was the Party of that dark period who had narrowed the use of Pavlov's theories to whatever could be crammed into the Party's credo. Nonetheless, in 1965, Dr. Mardashev felt free to decry a few of the Party's prohibitions if not perversions of Pavlov's heritage:

> . . . all other [of Pavlov's] physiological directions (various other aspects of research in the nervous system, evolutionary physiology, physiology of cells, physiology of endocrine organs, and so on) were declared under ban unless they were connected with the study of higher nervous activity in its exclusively dogmatic interpretation.

Great damage was caused by those medical bootlickers in Stalin's Russia who in their so-called physiological research "revolved in the closed circle of dogmatism" and "sent to the winds rather than enriched the heritage left behind by I. P. Pavlov." And some of this harm to the Soviet science of physiology still lingers behind; aye, "there are even some repetitions" of this damage to be noted in these mid-1960s.[12]

Where the Party ordered—and, in certain ways, still orders— this de-Pavlovization of the late great Pavlov is of course in the fields permitting the application of his teachings to the human psyche.

Of all the Soviet medical specialists laboring in the Soviet Union ever since the regime's beginnings, psychiatrists and psychologists have had the hardest time. And in no report coming to us from Russia is this made clearer than in a work of fiction smuggled out of that country to the West a few years ago: a book telling the world about the post-Stalinist decision of the Moscow hierarchs to send intellectual rebels to insane asylums instead of concentration camps or execution chambers.

The author Valery Tarsis, confined to a Moscow asylum for writing anti-Communist books to be published in the West,

tells in *Ward No.* 7 (meant to be the Soviet sequel to Anton
Chekhov's immortal "Ward No. 6," written in 1892) of his and
his fellow inmates'' experiences. Most of the doctors in this docu-
mentary novelette are not true physicians; they are jailers, cow-
ardly though not necessarily cruel. But two of the physicians are
clearheaded and honest about the crime they are compelled to
commit in the name of the Soviet state and society. They are
helpless to mend matters except in minor ways by occasional
kindness to their charges. One of the two, Doctor Andrei Nezhevsky, the chief psychiatrist of the Ministry of Health, was

> tall, well-formed, his crew-cut gleaming dully with silver, his eyes
> wise and penetrating, merry, witty, agile despite his seventy-four
> years, a scientist of worldwide repute, a frequent attendant of vari-
> ous congresses, conferences, symposia, and seminars abroad.

At the Moscow asylum where Tarsis was imprisoned, this doctor was shown "the most interesting patients of whom the [other]
doctors stood in fear, whom they were afraid to treat with usual
means." Dr. Nezhevsky knew what to do in each such case, "but,
still better, knew that real treatment was of course impossible in
the Soviet setting." For this wise physician

> was a follower of Gandhi, thoroughly studied Indian philosophy
> and certainly understood that the Soviet reality had mangled all
> human souls with its decades of terror, crimes, wars, fear, violence,
> and lack of confidence in one's tomorrow; that, generally speaking,
> there exist no humans with entirely healthy psyches, and there
> could be no such completely healthy people in these inhuman con-
> ditions; and that the only true medicine for psychic disturbances
> was a decent way of life. . . . Therefore he thought it was ridiculous
> to say that some Soviet individuals suffered from a mania of per-
> secution—these individuals who for forty years have been perse-
> cuted, whose fathers were executed by firing squads or tortured to
> death in concentration camps.

Mental health could be restored in the Soviet Union if only the
authorities would stop the "persecution of humans for their lack
of enthusiasm for the Soviet regime," when and if the Soviet-
liquidated democracy was restored, and "freedom given to
people, freedom of movement first of all, since so many—so very
many—are threatened with real insanity and pushed to suicide if
they continue to stay in the Soviet paradise."[13]
This realization by Dr. Nezhevsky of the true illness of Soviet
multitudes, and of the only genuine cure for the mass sickness,

makes it abundantly plain why the Party early and late censored
Ivan Pavlov's great teachings—why it never wanted Russia's doctors and researchers to have anything to do with the real substance of psychology and psychiatry.

VI

And yet, the advent of the space age made for a change in this
field also. By the middle 1950s the post-Stalinist oligarchs began
to show their increasing respect for some great luminaries of the
healers' Olympus, for the academicians of Dr. Parin's caliber. For
these men were developing an entirely new science so needed for
the cosmonauts then already in training—the science of space
medicine. And this space medicine included, most importantly,
space psychology. Thus was psychology rehabilitated, after a
fashion.

Psychologists and psychiatrists are now permitted their untrammeled research if it has to do with the Soviet man not here on
earth but out there, in the orbiting capsule. For "the cosmonaut's
psychological preparation" serves the Soviet version "of the most
complex task ever faced by man"—the task of mastering outer
space.[14]

Let us hope that, emboldened by his novel freedom, the Soviet
outer-space doctor some day may seek the same independence for
his earth-bound, run-of-the-mill colleague as well.

CHAPTER IX

Anonymity for Rocket-Men

THE INVOLVEMENT OF Academician Vasily Parin in the Leningrad medical case was particularly noteworthy. He and his space medicine may not have been directly concerned in this question of treating cancer of the bladder by Kochugin's eccentric nostrum. Still, his prestige was sought by both sides in the argument. In their naïve appeal to the Central Committee to intervene, the nine writers and journalists proposed Parin as first among the three experts whom they wanted as arbiters in the conflict. The other two would have been Academicians Vladimir Chernigovsky, also a space-medicine specialist, and Aksel' Berg, the cybernetics celebrity.

No arbitration with or without the suggested trio was arranged, but Parin's name appeared in *Pravda* among the sixteen condemners of the Kochugin method. The protesters had banked on support which just wasn't there—which, in fact, went over to their enemy, to Dr. Blokhin's side.

In Parin's person, Soviet space medicine endorsed Dr. Blokhin's antinostrum stand. This alone would have been enough for the Party bosses to bow to Dr. Blokhin's wish and to say, as they did in August 1962, that politics could not, should not, and would not interfere with science.

For Dr. Parin is a shining light of the great and growing realm of rocketry with which the Party has no wish to quarrel. Before rocketry and its space medicine, even more than before medicine in general, the Party bosses genuflect with the deepest respect imaginable.

Yet, it is more than respect. Even as it claims credit for rocketry and its achievements, the Party leadership stands in genuine awe and fear of the wizards of space technology. Yes, fear. Which leads us to a significant phenomenon in recent relations between science and politics in the Soviet Union: enforced anonymity for certain persons and groups within the rocket field of that country.

The builders and the guiders of the *Vostok* spaceships and other great Soviet rockets are being constantly decorated by the Moscow government. Their names, however, are never made public.

The very first brief recognition of this motive power behind the Soviet man-in-space flights and the other, nonmanned rocket triumphs came on April 14, 1961, two days after Yuri Gagarin's orbiting. It occurred at the official reception in the Great Kremlin Palace in honor of Gagarin, which incidentally was also to honor (as the governmental description of the reception later read) "the outstanding feat of the scientists, engineers, technicians, and workers who made possible the successful completion of the world's first flight of man into space." But the men and women thus honored were not identified. No photograph of this sector of Russia's elite was published then or has appeared since.

Two months later, on June 17, details of their decoration were announced officially. On June 18 a photograph of the April 14 reception in the Kremlin was run on the front pages of *Pravda*, *Komsomol'skaya pravda*, and *Krasnaya zvezda* (the daily newspaper of the Soviet Ministry of Defense). But all it showed was Khrushchev, Anastas Mikoyan, and other political leaders smiling at Major Gagarin in front of two microphones, one for Nikita, the other for Yuri. In the background there were a few more men and, rather vaguely, two women, but none of these was identified in the caption. Most likely they were political aides and not the rocket masters who were being honored. Apparently, the photograph was taken from where the rocket-men were seated, listening to yet another of Khrushchev's orations.

The list of honors to Russia's rocket personnel, as made known in June 1961, opened with "the second gold medal 'Sickle and Hammer' to seven outstanding scientists and engineers" who had previously earned the title of Hero of Socialist Labor. Neither the dates nor any other circumstances of those earlier honors were recalled in connection with the new citation. It would, however, be safe to surmise that these experts became Heroes and won their first gold medals for some prior astronautic accomplishments, probably for their role in the launchings of the first few Sputniks and Luniks.

Next in the June roll came mention of award of the Hero of

Socialist Labor title to ninety-five "leading engineers, administrators, scientists, and workers" of rocketry. This was followed by a catch-all reference to unspecified "orders and medals" for 6,924 other rocket scientists, engineers, technicians, and workers. Collective honors were also distributed among "a number of research institutes, design offices, and plants" in the rocket-and-missile industry. A more detailed breakdown spelled out the Order of Lenin to 478 persons, the Order of Toiler's Red Banner to 1,218, the Order of Red Star to 256, the Order "Sign of Honor" to 1,789, and simpler medals to 3,183.

Mid-June of 1961 was the time when Khrushchev called in Moscow a nationwide conference of his scientists of all fields and categories. The honors to the rocket personnel were patently connected with the conference and the headlines it caused. Here was a perfect opportunity to publicize one of the most remarkable successful branches of today's Soviet science and technology—but without divulging the identities of the honored.

Subsequent years and rocket feats in the Soviet Union brought more of such wholesale awards to anonymous scientists, engineers, technicians, and lower crews of the space field, but never again were rocket-men singled out with as much trumpeting as was done in 1961. For one thing they were bunched together with specialists of other fields; for another, the Party gave them much less publicity than formerly. The award announcement of April 29, 1963, was typical; it was brief and not displayed in the Soviet press[1] too prominently, and it revealed that, not only rocket-men (those specializing in military weapons solely), but also experts working on atomic submarines and rocket-carrying surface warships were given new honorary titles and medals. Of these, thirty-six leading scientists, engineers, designers and other personnel were made Heroes of Socialist Labor, while more than six thousand others were awarded sundry orders and medals. And again, as before, anonymity was the word. No name was divulged; no photo was published.

I I

The Party pays these wondrous experts not in medals alone. Their salaries are high, too; their living conditions are privileged. And if there is any whisper of restless envy on the part of any nonprivileged Russians, the Party is quick to chide the whisperers and to explain again and again how well deserved the rocket-men are of such emoluments. Speaking to the peasants of his native village of Kalinovka in the Kursk Region of July 28, 1962, Khrushchev himself pointed out:

> One must incessantly raise the productivity of one's labor, and this is what is being done by educated people who have mastered technology. Some may say: "And what are we to do, we who have not mastered technology?" I will answer: Study, so as to raise your labor productivity. If you don't want to study, don't at least envy the man who was improving his skill while you were wasting your time playing cards. A skilled worker is within his rights when he receives proper pay for the labor which he is contributing to the common cause. The scientists and engineers who have created rockets are being paid well by the state. If not for such pay, the development of our science and technology would have been stymied.[2]

But money and medals should be enough. There should be no publicity, no fame, as part of the compensation. That these experts' identities shall remain secret is, then, a most definite policy of the Soviet government.

This unique policy was first proclaimed publicly by Khrushchev on July 9, 1958, nine months after the first Sputnik had blazed across the skies, in his speech to the staff of an electrochemical factory at Bitterfeld, East Germany. In effect pleading with the skilled Germans of his audience not to defect to the West, the Soviet boss painted in red-and-rosy colors the lives of their Russian counterparts—of Soviet engineers and scientists, particularly those engaged in the most crucial branches of science and industry: in rocketry and atomics.

He was holding out to the East Germans the very same high pay rates and lush comforts. Yet his talkative tongue slipped, and he admitted that those Soviet Russian "scientists and engineers working in atomic and rocket technology," although well paid and otherwise signally pampered, did "have to suffer somewhat in one respect: to the outside world they are, for the time being, anonymous."

Why so? Khrushchev had a facile explanation:

> We highly value these people, we prize them and protect their safety from hostile agents who might be sent to destroy these outstanding people, our valuable cadres. For the sake of the safety of the country and of the lives of those scientists, engineers, technicians, and other specialists, we may not as yet make public their names and their photographs.[3]

This intriguing passage in Khrushchev's speech can be interpreted in several ways. To wit:

Some Soviet experts on rockets, missiles, and atomics may well resent this anonymity. Amid their splendid triumphs they may have begun to grumble. The Soviet chief, at least on that occasion in July 1958, felt obliged to take note of some such complaints of his advanced-technology men against the anonymity imposed on them. He tried to soften the effect of this restriction by saying that it was really the only discomfort or offense they had to bear. They should not feel slighted, he said—look at the ample salaries, fine country villas, and other plush perquisites he gave to his savants and technicians in return for those atomic and hydrogen warheads on the ICBMs and IRBMs, and for the Sputniks, Luniks, and other spacecraft.

Yet he must have felt that he had to explain this anonymity—by blaming it on evil forces which were, "for the time being," beyond his control. The sole reason, he declared, why he did not publicize the identities of his rocket, missile, and atomic miracleworkers was to protect them and, with them, Russia's scientific and military secrets from the spies and kidnapers of the Pentagon, Central Intelligence Agency, British Intelligence, and other such hellish agencies.

In that speech of July 1958 Khrushchev did promise that in good time the names and photos of Red rocket and missile makers and atomic experts would be published. "We shall," he said, "erect an obelisk to the people who have created the rocket and the artificial earth satellites. We shall inscribe their glorious names in gold to make them known to posterity for centuries. In due time the photographs and names of those glorious people will be widely known by the people."[4] But he did not set even an approximate date for such publicity.

Evidently the proper time is not yet here. As cosmonaut after cosmonaut rose into orbit through the 1960s and, in 1963, the first woman joined the illustrious roster, their names were dutifully published and they themselves lionized, but not the names of the scientists and engineers who labored—and are still toiling—behind the scenes to make these achievements possible.

III

In all fairness to the bizarre Communist mentality, we must concede the possibility that the Moscow hierarchs may be quite sincere in their fear of the outside world. They may really be afraid, and not merely pretending such fear, that American and British intelligence services would try to kill or kidnap the Soviet rocket scientists and engineers if the names and faces of those gifted folk were known.

Just because we in the West won't have as our way of life the sort of paranoidally closed society that the Soviets maintain, does not mean that the Communists only claim to like such a system but actually do not want it. We cannot deny the topmost Communist leaders their sinister pleasure of taking their fear of us so seriously. We must recognize also the probability that the Communist leaders cannot tolerate even the thought that our way of life might some day replace theirs. Our open society is as repulsive to them as their closed society is to us—repulsive and fearsome.

Their fear of us is being exaggerated by the leaders and their diplomats and propagandists, constantly and deliberately, for purposes of over-all Soviet strategy and tactics. But, basically, the fear is there. Essentially, it is not make-believe. They have come to believe so many of their lies about us.

Yet, greater than their fear of us and, in this case, of our intelligence services, is the Red leaders' fear (whether or not they admit this to themselves and to one another) of their own population, particularly of their better-educated men and women—in this instance, their own rocket experts. And here is where we may find the chief reason for the Moscow policy of secrecy in this special area of their science and technology more than in any other field: the Party fears that once revealed and publicized these true geniuses of the new rocket age may yet want political plums. These the Party does not wish to yield.

However, before exploring this reason more fully, let us acknowledge that another and perfectly laudable reason for secrecy is in the following consideration: The principal scientists and engineers of Soviet rocketry, thus put under wraps of anonymity, have a greater opportunity to concentrate on their work. They are not distracted by puerile banquet appearances and wasteful television paneling, by popular article or book writing, and by pointless conference attendance, as some of our rocket-age wizards are obliged (or unfortunately glad) to undergo.

For this sort of public-relations babble for the masses, the Kremlin has long since detailed a few less important scientists and engineers. They are competent enough to speak and write in this field, yet they are not truly of the very top bracket in their specialties. Thus they can easily be sacrificed for purposes of propaganda—and to serve as a sort of smoke screen for the real geniuses of their trade, who are therefore left undisturbed to do their work.

Of such handy decoys, best known on this side of the ocean is Professor Leonid I. Sedov, a fairly frequent visitor to conferences held in Western Europe and the United States. An able astrophysicist and a man of charm, he was the first Soviet scientist to be elected—in September 1959, at a congress in London—president of the International Astronautical Federation, a twenty-six-nation organization. On April 12, 1961, when Gagarin orbited the earth, Sedov happened to be in Boston attending the celebration of the one-hundredth anniversary of the Massachusetts Institute of Technology. That he was not kept back in Russia for Gagarin's feat but was free to go to America for a mere festive assembly, is in itself a measure of his relative unimportance in Soviet rocketry.

Yet, everywhere Sedov goes he is billed by Moscow propagandists, unwittingly echoed by our own communications media, as "the Soviet Space Spokesman." It was in this capacity that early on the morning of April 12 he was interviewed on Dave Garroway's television program, with my interpreting help. Friendly and affable as ever, Sedov said practically nothing. Part of it was, of course, caution so typical of any scientist representing a government, especially a Soviet scientist speaking for the Soviet government. But another part was sheer ignorance. At one point Sedov grinned and said to me: "I know no more about Gagarin's flight than you do." To be sure, he knew rather more; but in some respects this claim was not mere modesty or playing the security game.

That same day, in Italy, another official spokesman of Russian rocketry also betrayed a lack of knowledge of the latest details of his field. This was Professor Anatoly A. Blagonravov, a learned specialist in aviation arms and missiles, who holds the military rank of lieutenant general in Soviet artillery. Used by the Kremlin for international conferences almost as much as Sedov, Professor-General Blagonravov was in Florence on April 12 as head of the Soviet delegation to the International Symposium on Space Research. Asked by eager journalists about Gagarin's Vostok, Blagonravov made the blunder of asserting that Russian rocket capsules did not have any portholes such as Gagarin mentioned in his explanation of just how he was able to see the earth from outer space. Blagonravov's error indicated how remote from the most recent Soviet rockets this spokesman was kept by the Kremlin between his travels. Soon, in some embarrassment for Blagonravov, it was brought out in Moscow that while earlier Red rocket capsules did not have any portholes, later ones did.

A third spokesman does not travel as much, but he writes a great deal. He is Professor Georgiy I. Pokrovsky, a major general in the Soviet engineering troops, and a foremost expert on ballistic missiles. He may indeed have much to do with actual laboratory work and launching pads these days—more than Sedov and Blagonravov do—and that is why perhaps he travels abroad less than the other two. He is too valuable to travel.

Inevitably there is also a woman—Dr. Alla G. Masevich, a youngish (still in her forties) and rather personable astronomer, with not much of scientific achievement to her name, but with a good command of English and a pleasant manner. She is repeatedly sent to foreign conferences and is often assigned to guide visiting celebrities through Soviet institutes and observatories. Compatriots with sharp tongues call her "our astropolitician" behind her shapely back. But the Party is highly satisfied with her performance.

These four persons and a few lesser lights in the same field are not sealed in anonymity, because they are not the real high-level creators and launchers of Russian rockets. They are built up in the public eye at home and abroad because the Party had to provide some plausible personal representation for the real but anonymous heroes to receive the public's plaudits and to satisfy its curiosity.

I V

Khrushchev himself claimed to be many kinds of expert, but rocketry was too complex for him, with his rudimentary schooling, to appropriate it as one more of his fields. He was aware that he would appear entirely too ridiculous were he suddenly to step forth as an oracle on astrophysics. Occasionally some sycophants tried to give him academic honors—as did four cosmonauts (Yuri Gagarin, Gherman Titov, Andriyan Nikolayev, and Pavel Popovich) in November 1962, when in a co-authored panegyric they hailed Khrushchev as "the man who developed in himself the work endurance of a miner, *the thinking ability of an academi-cian,** and the stamina of a veteran warrior."[5] However, unlike Stalin, the earthier Khrushchev knew better than to accept any intellectual laurels even when they were proffered to him on a golden plate of flattery.

The most Khrushchev could do was to claim administrative, rather than scientific or engineering, credit for the tremendous advances made by Russia in this epochal realm. And this admin-istrative credit he did take. On June 17, 1961, as he distributed honors to those anonymous heroes of the laboratory and the launching site, he appropriated for himself one more Order of Lenin and one more (third) gold "Sickle and Hammer" medal. The citation, signed by his heir Leonid Brezhnev, applauded Nikita for his "leadership in the creation and development of the rocket industry, science, and technology and the successful com-pletion of the world's first space flight"—politico-managerial kudos, clearly, and rather deserved, at that. In this sense, as the stubborn, hard-driving, inspiring boss he may indeed have earned the compliment of "the first discoverer of the space era" with which two Soviet journalists honored him in July 1961.[6]

But Khrushchev did long for a closer relation to astronautics than this, for something that would prove to be more genuinely scientific. The best he could hope here was for *a* Khrushchev, rather than *the* Khrushchev, to become a real rocketman. So, a decade ago, he sent his son Sergei to learn rocketry. The result was not spectacular. Sergei was passionately devoted to collecting butterflies instead. With his father's fall in October 1964 his chance to succeed in anything as important as rocketry dimin-ished considerably.

Men like Sedov, Blagonravov, and Pokrovsky could be used by Khrushchev, and can now be used by his successors, as Russia's spokesmen of space science quite safely, without too much glamour attaching to them, because of two circumstances:

First, the Kremlin's propagandists see to it that this trio and others like them are publicized but not glorified.

Second, there is apparently no danger that any such spokesman would get dizzy ideas of becoming a politician—of moving into a decision-making position—if only because these men are getting along in years. They are past the age of beginning any active

* Italics are mine.

adventures on the Soviet political stage. Blagonravov was born in 1894, Pokrovsky in 1901, and Sedov in 1907. To start a political career in today's Russia one has to be much younger than this.

Indications are that the real wizards of Russian rocketry, missilery, and atomics—those kept so carefully hidden—are mostly in their thirties and forties, and only a very few in their fifties. The Party cannot and will not allow such younger men to be publicized. Once identified and praised, they could "go places," politically—and they would have plenty of time in which to do it. It is much safer for the Party to give the smart young ones those medals and titles without divulging their names and faces.

And it is far more expedient to concentrate all the fanfare on Gagarin, Titov, Nikolayev, and other cosmonauts—and, latterly, one woman cosmonaut, Valentina Tereshkova-Nikolayeva. These young airmen are very probably ambitious, but their appetites can easily be kept in check. Did their counterpart in America, Astronaut John Glenn, want to run for the Senate? Had he thus set a political example to the Soviet cosmonauts? No such fear in the minds of the Kremlin. The Party can make all the cosmonauts of the Soviet Union members of its parliament in an instant, and there will be no political changes thereby. For the Supreme Soviet in Moscow is but a rubber stamp, with no real power.

And these cosmonauts are by and large not scientists, nor engineers, whose knowledge and skills might be difficult for the Kremlin to control politically. The Gagarins and the Titovs, the Nikolayevs, and the other orbiters are mere passengers on ships of Communist destiny, and each of them will remain a tractable, exploitable fare to the end of the trip.

Let smarter men build those spaceships. Let the Gagarins ride the wonderful craft to the stars. Let the charming, pliable professors advertise the Soviet Union's rockets to audiences native and foreign. But Khrushchev did take care that he and, after he was gone, other Party leaders would alone continue to control all these marvels of science and technology.

At least, such is the Party's intention; such is its shrewd effort.

V

Not just a few geniuses at the very top of this field of rocketry, but whole legions of men and women are, in the Russian word, *zasekrecheny*, or "secretized," that is, security-restricted. A tremendous industry working for both the military and the civilian sides of the rocket effort is involved. Indeed, "plants where rocket-carriers of spaceships are being made are closed plants. And they will remain closed until the day when the threat of war is fully liquidated, when the Soviet proposals of universal and complete disarmament are accepted."[7] How many "secretized" scientists, engineers, technicians, and workers does this mean?

John Scott, an American journalist, tried to arrive at an approximation of the vast number. Visiting Moscow in the summer of 1961, he noted that more than 7,000 medals had just been distributed to Soviet rocket personnel, and that, in addition, collective honors were awarded to a number of research institutes, rocket-design offices, rocket-making plants, and launching sites. From a Soviet friend, John Scott heard that, all together, counting the staffs of the decorated organizations, "about 10,000 individuals got personal decorations."

To this, Scott remarked: "I'm guessing that if 10,000 got high decorations, twenty times that number did not. This would mean that nearly a quarter of a million people have been working on your space program. And these people, many of them, have to be highly qualified."

But it would seem that more than 250,000 Russians were then, in 1961, in the space program. This estimate came from Scott's Soviet friend as he said: "I think your numerical guess is on the low side, though I don't know." He agreed that they were highly qualified—"our best people," he boasted. "For many years now the rocket research projects have gotten the very best of personnel and resources, and all sorts of extras—bonuses, new houses, trips abroad . . . everything."[8]

These observations were exchanged between the American and the Russian 'way back in mid-1961. In the years since then the number of the Soviet rocket personnel has certainly increased, at least twofold, if I may offer an educated guess. But the utter and total secrecy has not changed.

Who makes up this multitude? What are their thoughts, plans, ambitions? "We don't know, we can only guess," declared a Soviet writer in a special article on this subject of rocket-men's anonymity, published in *Izvestiya* on April 12, 1962, the first anniversary of Gagarin's flight.

> They live among us. Most probably they are very much like ourselves. They also love their children; they read the same books we do; they sing the same songs. They sit next to us at the movies; we bump into them on the street and in the trolley buses.

These people have done everything for immortality. Only we do not know their names yet, and their faces are unknown to us. But we love them just the same—these nameless yet great contemporaries of ours, these men who have invented, calculated, built these most wonderful space ships, who have sent them into the cosmos. . . . But what sort of humans are they?[9]

The journalist quoted Gagarin to the effect that the age of this anonymous personnel ranged from twenty-five to fifty-five; that, in short, they grew up under the Soviet regime. But this remains one of the very few statistics or facts ever given out in the Soviet Union about these enigmatic people. The wholesale mystery is sternly decreed and strictly enforced. If a Soviet man or woman is even a small cog in the vast Soviet network of rocketry and missilery, he or she is forbidden to voice the merest hint of this, much less to reveal anything about the job itself.

The very fact of this mandatory anonymity is only rarely mentioned in the Soviet press. The few times it has been taken up, the Soviet reader has been assured that the scientists, engineers, and other rocket-making personnel do not at all mind their submerged status, that they accept it as a necessary, temporary measure of precaution.

A Moscow reporter met a young scientist of his acquaintance in the festive crowd of August 9, 1961, celebrating in Red Square the grandiose welcome for Cosmonaut Titov. By the scientist's side stood a short man, in a gray suit, on the coat of which the little golden star of the Hero of Labor shone. "We became acquainted. . . . And in a few minutes I learned that I was conversing with one of those responsible for the day's triumph. I cannot yet mention the name of this *dotsent*, this physicist, this man who has been distinguished by the Fatherland's highest award for his participation in the creation of the spaceship Vostok."

The reporter confessed that he was consumed with curiosity—oh how he wished he could ask the physicist just what his work was, precisely what part he had played in Titov's achievement. But he restrained himself. "He wouldn't answer anyway. So far it's a state secret. A secret perforce, because the world is not peaceful; because some persons beyond the ocean, and in Europe also, daydream of war. . . . That is why for the time being the Physicist will not say a single word about his work. That is why for the time being we cannot mention his name."

Still, the reporter asked the physicist about his anonymity: "Tell me frankly, don't you resent it?"

"Frankly, no," was the answer. "I am doing my work. I serve the cause of peaceful science. The Party and the government have valued my modest accomplishments highly. The time will come when our names will also be made public."

The reporter concluded: "I will wait. And I will see this happen. Absolutely!"[10]

Nonetheless, constant propaganda is deemed necessary to remind the scientist that he should be a good Party man, and that as a loyal Communist he should remain modest about his scientific achievements. A message of this type is considered that much more effective if the Party succeeds in putting it into the mouth of the scientist himself. In late April 1963, at the All-Union Conference of the Best People of the Movement for Communist Labor, V. P. Sigorsky, a mathematician with a doctorate in the technical sciences from the Novosibirsk Science City, orated: "In this movement a scientist of a new type is emerging, in whom his deep scientific quality is intertwined with a high Party-mindedness, and whose modesty increases the greater the obtained result; who incessantly strives to carry out the Party's directives on the development of science."[11]

Occasionally Soviet propagandists point out (quite possibly on explicit instructions from above) that these "miracle-workers" deserve far more of a public incense than they are given. "Here are the men before whom it is worthwhile to bend our knees; here are the persons who should be presented wreaths of glory so rightfully earned by them." But such open recognition is out of the question, the Party line hastens to assure the curious world at large. "As are all of us, they are simple Soviet toilers, for whom the meaning of their life is in service to the Fatherland." These remarkable scientists and engineers know the reason for their enforced anonymity: "Here is precisely where the greatness of these geniuses lies, of these geniuses who are at the same time so modest while creating their ingenious machines—not for a moment do they think that they should be singled out and glorified." Despite the magnificence of their inventions, "they march in the same ranks with all the builders of Communism, they conduct themselves with no show and without throwing their weight around, while giving birth to such truly astounding wonders."[12]

Only very infrequently does a detail or two escape the propagandists that gives us a glimpse of these concealed elite. We spot in the Soviet press brief descriptions of the physical appearance of the mysterious Chief Designer: he is rather slow in his movements, although well-built and quite muscular; his face is of the "pleasant Russian" cast; his slightly squinting brown eyes are shrewd and wise.[13] These eyes are also described as faintly tired but penetrating: "Such eyes see everything." At all the cosmonaut launchings he wears the same light-colored hat[14]—perhaps, we may ask, regarded by its wearer as a good-luck piece?

From yet another source we learn that the Chief Designer is

> a great mind, a fine organizer. He can find talented people, enthusiasts, for this work. He will never refuse to help a man, but he recognizes practical men only. At conferences he is never the first to offer solutions. He listens, he forces others to think. Men respect him boundlessly, and he has been given the highest awards possible. His hobbies? Serious music and work in his garden.[15]

The Chief Theoretician is described as a man whose sun-tanned face is energetic yet a wee-bit tired, and whose shock of hair is touched with gray. He can be found always not in solitude but in a beehive of fellow scientists "with whom he solves the most complex problems of cosmonautics." On the wall of his study prominently hangs a fantastic landscape of an imaginary planet.

> Beyond the window a street is bustling, but the scientist, absorbed by a multitude of earthly concerns, sits with his back to the window. Is the landscape hanging on the wall not his window? Is it not from there that light streams upon his work-laden desk— the light of the feasible real future? . . .[16]

Their very names—Chief Designer (*Glavny Konstruktor*) and Chief Theoretician (*Glavny Teoretik* or, in another version, *Teoretik Kosmonavtiki*)—are used somewhat in the style of dramatic science fiction. The cosmonauts who have been trained by them, and who are still under their ceaseless guidance and supervision, go lyric and ecstatic at the very least mention of these scientists who have made modern space miracles possible. Gagarin and his fellow cosmonauts in an article in *Pravda* said: "Had Thomas Edison, that great American, been alive today, he would have respectfully doffed his hat before them."[17]

On the very rare occasions when articles about or by the two mysterious leaders—the Designer and the Theoretician—appear in the Soviet press the authorities are careful not to let them say anything significantly new in astronautics, or anything revealing either about themselves or the Soviet space plans.[18]

VI

By late 1963, as if in defiance of the Party's edict, it was common for people in Moscow to try to guess those forbidden names of rocketry. There is no freedom of speech in the Soviet Union, but in this post-Stalin era of thaw there is a freedom of conversation, at least among trusted friends. How long in such a comparatively relaxed period can the Party succeed with this prohibition, this secrecy? Five or six years, no more. People begin to wonder, to exchange guesses; in time it becomes a game, first a parlor game, next a public contest.

And so in November 1963, despite the Party taboo, Muscovites began to whisper to one another that Valentin P. Glushko and Sergei P. Korolyov must be these heavily veiled Chief Designer and Chief Theoretician of Soviet rocketry. Only no one seemed to be sure which of the two was the Designer and which the Theoretician.

Westerners in Moscow, freer with their tongues and typewriters than their Russian acquaintances from whom they heard the surmise, at once communicated the guess to their contacts in America and Western Europe. The story of the news appeared in the Western press,[19] but the Soviet journals continued their solemn silence on the subject.

Standard Soviet reference books supply Glushko's and Korolyov's official biographies, but without any of their latter-day rocketry connections. We learn that both men are nearing sixty, Glushko born in 1908, Korolyov in 1906. The former is a combustion engineer, the latter a specialist in mechanics. Glushko joined the Communist Party in 1956, Korolyov in 1953. Both have been identified with Soviet rocketry since their young days, Glushko experimenting with liquid oxygen and nitric acid as fuel in the first Soviet rockets of the early 1930s, Korolyov busying himself with building a liquid-fuel rocket engine for a plane in 1940. Both were admitted as full members to the Academy of Sciences in 1958, in the triumphant wake of the first few Sputniks.[20]

Gossips in Moscow noted that both Glushko and Korolyov were present at the last two congresses of the Communist Party, and that among the dozen or so academicians at those congresses the pair were the only engineers—the other academicians represented such orthodox nontechnical fields as politics and economics. And wasn't this, the agile guessers asked, proof enough that Glushko and Korolyov were precisely the mystery men for so long camouflaged as Chief Designer and Chief Theoretician of rocketry?

If indeed they are, the Party is not telling. Nor is it allowing any such guessing to appear in the Soviet press. For the moment, the policy announced in 1958 is still in effect. It is anonymity for rocket-men, not just these two, but a quarter million or half million of them, and most of them younger than Glushko and Korolyov.

The Party is still not sure that it could control the fame that may come to these miracle men of science and engineering if their identities are revealed at last.

As this chapter was being proofread, news arrived from Moscow that Sergei P. Korolyov died somewhere in the Soviet Union, of heart failure during cancer surgery, on January 14, 1966. The official announcement spoke of him as "a distinguished scientist and designer in rocketry and space research."[21]

VII

A limited departure from the rule of no publicity for rocket scientists came at the very end of Khrushchev's reign. In mid-October 1964, the day he had already fallen but did not yet know it, Khrushchev talked by radiotelephone with the latest trio of Russians then orbiting this planet. He was warmly congratulating them. He was telling them to keep in good shape for the reception he would give them in the Red Square on their landing. Alas, when the rocket capsule landed, his heirs and betrayers—Brezhnev and Kosygin—were in his place in the Square to greet the orbiters.

The departure in the rule of anonymity for space scientists was in the fact that, of the three men in the latest orbiting crew, two were scientists. This was the first time that scientists were sent into outer space along with a pilot; it was a tremendous advance and a real credit to the Soviet space effort, and in announcing the achievement the Soviet leaders had to reveal the names of the scientists.

The two were Konstantin Feoktistov, thirty-eight, an engineer-scientist with considerable experience in space-craft designing, and Dr. Boris Yegorov, twenty-seven, a research physician specializing in space medicine. One of them—Feoktistov—was not even a

Party member and did not seem to be eager to join the Party now that the Party acclaimed him.

Yet—and this is a point to be watched from now on—far less publicity has so far been given to this pair than to all the other Soviet cosmonauts. It is as if the Party leadership were saying: Yes, we must send real scientists into outer space, and thus necessarily show them to all mankind. But the world's applause for them must be tempered by us—so that it does not give these and other Soviet scientists any dangerous ideas.

CHAPTER X

~~~~~~~~~~~~~~~~~~~~~~~~~

The Rise of the Military Engineer

AND WHAT OF THE military in the laboratories and on the launching pads of the Soviet Union? Do they feel their enhanced importance to a point of wishing to supersede the Party in the nation's politics as well as in military strategy?

No, they do not, say the Party politicians in military uniforms detailed by the Party to write and edit the press of the armed forces. This problem of the possibly heightened role of the warrior in charge of the computer and of the rocket, "so sharply debated in the American press," hardly exists in the Soviet Union; and if it does, "it is solved under our conditions painlessly and [thus] is no problem." To be sure, "the role of scientists, engineers, and other specialists in our country grows from year to year. This process occurs also in the Armed Forces, but it is not accompanied by the antagonism characteristic of the United States."

Computers are no threatening juggernauts to the Soviet military establishment. For, thanks to the faultless essence of the Soviet sociopolitical system, "cybernetics becomes a most valuable aid to strategy, but does not presume to take its place, just as a computer helps man to think but will not replace its creator's brain."[1]

But a defector whom I met in London in the spring of 1963 evaluated this complex phenomenon quite differently. This was Dr. Gregory A. Tokaty, head of the Department of Aeronautics and Space Technology at Northampton College of Advanced Technology, in the British capital, and a frequent contributor to British and American technical publications. There was little in his British appearance and Briticized speech to suggest the Soviet military engineer, Colonel G. A. Tokaev, who chose freedom in Berlin in 1948.

Among the Soviet defectors I have interviewed at length, he was the only one who had fled in Stalin's era. All the others were of post-Stalinist defection. I had sought him out because, despite the long span of years since he last saw the Soviet Union, he had kept up with Soviet events, albeit from afar, and he had remained in touch particularly with the facet of his native country of the greatest interest to me—the sociotechnological development.

In Moscow, on the eve of his defection, he was chief of the Aerodynamics Laboratory of the Military Air Academy. Both in that position and in his post–World War II service in occupied Germany, he was concerned with Soviet rocketry and atomics. On one occasion he was summoned from Berlin to report on German rockets personally to Stalin and his Politburo. In my book *Russia's Rockets and Missiles,* written before I met Tokaty-Tokaev, I quoted his 1954 statement: ". . . there is reason to believe that intensive work is now being carried on in the U.S.S.R. on guided missiles capable of carrying small atomic bombs. It is possible that in a year or so these weapons may affect the whole course of Soviet strategy."[2] I stated about Tokaev: "He brought to the West enough evidence of Stalin's acute interest in rockets and satellites to warn us that artificial satellites were very much on the Soviet program." I commented: "Tokaev's warning was not noticed . . ."[3]

In London, in March 1963, we talked about the latest situation —the state of science in politics, and of politics in science, in the latter-day Soviet Union. From his constant study of the current Soviet scene Tokaty gathered that there was indeed a close and firm connection between science and technology on the one hand and politics on the other. He said to me:

"In the Soviet Union now there is no such thing as just a scientist, or just an engineer, or just a plain citizen. Everyone is a political animal, whether or not he knows and admits this. He is a scientist-politician, an engineer-politician, or a citizen-politician. All of them have gotten their political education as an inevitable part of their scientific, engineering, or what-not training. Some may *seem* to shy away from politics, but actually they don't. Because, you see, they can't shy away from it even if they would want to. They got political dogma along with mathematical formulas and other parts of their school learning."

But the dogma itself is changing, Tokaty pointed out. At least its practical consequences are not what the earlier Marxist manuals proclaimed them to be. And some of this change, he said, is due to the advice and pressure of precisely those technicians who, according to him, do not consciously or deliberately question the dogma.

The defector went on:

"What has happened is this: Pure Marxism used to emphasize man, who, according to its doctrine, could change and sway and dictate anything and everything. But man has created so much perfect machinery that now the machine is omnipotent and man retreats before the machine. In antiaircraft defense, for instance, manned planes—interceptors—recede and fade out before those new push-button rockets. It's true, of course, that rockets, like planes, are operated by men. But there is a difference: rockets are far less personal, far more automated, than intercepting planes.

"The role of ground forces—infantry, artillery, tanks—is also now subordinated to nuclear energy, to rockets. Men will merely back up or clean up *after* the new weapons systems will do the main job. Thus Marxism, with its emphasis on man's role, re-treats—changes—under the impact of the science and technology created by man himself!"

Here the professor came to his main point:

"Aggressiveness can no longer be national, or, in fact, interna-tional policy. The Soviet Union—and actually, any other modern nation, too—can no longer plan to attack. It cannot press a genu-inely aggressive policy when other nations have, or may soon have, atomic bombs and nuclear-warhead rockets of their own. It is sci-ence and technology that have produced this mutual deterrent, the heaviest blow Marxism has experienced since its inception.

"That is how Russia's own scientists and technicians—particu-larly the military scientists and technicians—are able to claim credit, if they wish to, for this basic change in Soviet foreign policy."

I I

With the space age, a new kind of aristocracy has indeed emerged in the Soviet armed forces. "You will live in a big city, and they won't constantly blow reveille at you, and you will fre-quent the theaters, but the main thing—you will become an engi-neer!" These wistful words of envy were spoken by his fellow officers to a Soviet lieutenant who was being detached from his unit to learn rocket engineering. They bade him farewell at the exit gates of a military settlement somewhere in Russia's deep provinces, and he and his young wife joyfully began their "road into the future"—as a military correspondent phrased it while describing this particular journey.[4]

But this Red "road into the future" is not only the lieutenant's path to a more expert knowledge of his rocket specialty. It is also his route into a brand-new sector of Russia's elite.

The elite of today's Soviet armed forces are not alone marshals, generals, and admirals. Increasingly, prestige and all manner of privileges and preferences accrue also to those of the colonels, majors, captains, and even lieutenants who have had modern engineering training and are the much-needed technicians of the Red troops. Naturally enough, this means rocket and missile specialists first of all.

The importance of rocketry and missilery in tomorrow's possible war has led to the separation of the U.S.S.R.'s rocket troops from other services into a command all its own and to its elevation above the other branches. This was done in 1959 and officially revealed in early May 1960, close on the heels of the triumphant Moscow claim that the U-2 of Francis Gary Powers was shot down by Red rocket-men.[5] Officially the new rocket command has from the very beginning been on an equal footing with the Soviet army, navy, and air force. In reality, in the Orwellian phrase, it is now "more equal" than the others.

The privileged status of the military rocket command is evident not only from the frequent praise bestowed upon it by the Presidium members, by Marshal Rodion Malinovsky, and by other leaders. The preferential treatment strikes our eye also via the details of the cuts in Soviet armed manpower: demobilization of the personnel in the latter 1950s and early '60s was repeatedly effected at the expense of nontechnicians—of "conventional" officers and men.

As new rocket units are added to the standing Soviet force, young experts are graduated from special military schools for the novel branch; old specialists are not demobilized but stay and get promoted. Together these young men and their knowledgeable elders play an ever weightier role in the Soviet war machine, if only because they now physically constitute a greater ratio within the smaller (though deadlier) military establishment.

We have some interesting figures, which shed light on the increased ratio, from the Kremlin's own sources. The lead editorial in *Krasnaya zvezda* for November 24, 1960, revealed that already by January 1959 the proportion of engineers and technicians in the commanding personnel in the Soviet armed forces was three times higher than at the close of the Second World War. By November 1960 "the wide introduction of the most complex rocket technology increased this ratio yet higher." Some six months later, Marshal Sergei Biryuzov, chief of Russia's antiaircraft defenses (by then heavily missile-equipped), proudly declared that in the troops under his command the number of engineer and technician officers exceeded that of officers who came from nonengineering schools and academies.[6]

In early 1965, for the 3,300,000 men under arms, constituting 6.4 per cent of all Soviet males in the 15-to-64 age bracket,[7] it was officially announced that the number of military engineers and technicians among these officers and soldiers was three and one-half times the immediate end-of-the-war figure; and that in the rocket, antiaircraft, and naval units, out of every 100 officers, 65 to 70 were engineers and technicians.[8] And, Marshal Malinovsky declared at about the same time, "nearly 90 per cent of our officers, generals, and admirals are Communists or members of Komsomol."[9]

I I I

However, all signs point to the fact that their engineering competence is of much greater importance than their Party or Komsomal card.

But in the Party's view, an officer and a soldier or sailor of the Soviet Union must be a good Communist, card-carrying or not, precisely because of the tremendous demands of this rocket and nuclear age. So said the front-page editorial of *Krasnaya zvezda* on June 15, 1965:

> The appearance of new, rocket-nuclear means of armed struggle has caused a veritable revolution in the military art—in the organization, forms, and methods of operational-tactical training of troops. . . . The role of scientific guidance of troops, of scientific prevision in military work, has risen to an unprecedented height. It is quite clear that to know one's way in all this thoroughly, to understand profoundly the inevitability and trends of the development of military work, to guarantee a high scientific level of guiding the troops, is possible only on the basis of deep knowledge of Marxism-Leninism, of its methodology, by the military cadres.[10]

In the fall of 1957, heartened politically by the success of his first Sputnik, Khrushchev dismissed Marshal Georgiy Zhukov from the nation's top military command, giving as one of the reasons the indubitable fact that Zhukov had been systematically depressing and even negating the role of political commissars in the Soviet armed forces. Political orientation had taken a sharp drop under Zhukov. Now Zhukov was dropped. From late 1957 on, well into this year, 1966, the Party has been busily staging a militant comeback into the military establishment.

And so, the standing order, ever and again drummed and hammered up and down the ranks, is: Preach and be preached to, study the holy books and saintly brochures of Communism and make others study, too.

Still, the bigger the brass the freer it feels to stay away from church. Marshal Malinovsky once complained: "It so happens that real, demanding control over political self-education reaches, at best, up to the regimental command, but higher on its fire decreases and in final analysis comes to nothing."[11] In other words, a few colonels do read Marx occasionally, but generals and admirals don't; a few do preach as ordered, but most decline the duty.

A professional propagandist with the rank of general in the Political Office of the armed forces lamented that in the Leningrad Military District "certain officers and generals did not visit a single meeting" of their political study groups "all year long." Evening schools of Marxism-Leninism, officially designated as "universities," are shunned; "for instance, from among the officers and admirals of the staff and the headquarters of the Red Banner Baltic Fleet not a single man studied in the evening university in the last two years." Where officers do go to such "universities" and other Party schools, "attendance is very low." And those who come do not show either any preparation or any interest. "Commanders, political workers, and Party organizations fail to effect a strict control over the listeners' preparation."[12]

Where generals are assigned, as part of their political task, to chair seminars on Marxism-Leninism, they are supposed to undergo preliminary training by attending certain "lectures of Marxist-Leninist preparation," but in the Kiev Military District such generals refused to come to these lectures, and the official complaint against them in this connection was that "they conduct themselves snobbishly." The political boss of the Kiev Military District assigned a special leader "to make sure that high quality is achieved in the political education of officers and generals," but the man simply slumped on his job—he was "not demanding enough of these people."[13]

Down the line, for colonels and majors, for captains and lieutenants there is less chance of escape—there is more supervision and coercion from political agents clad in military uniforms and holding ranks similar to those of their victims, all in an effort to make propagandists out of the latter.

Still, the victims try to dodge, and occasionally they succeed. Typically, a captain of the tank forces was told to attend a political seminar in order to learn how to be a political mentor of his subordinates. He came looking bored. While all the other officers took notes, he sat idly, his hands folded. "Doesn't this concern you?" he was asked. "All this is clear to me anyway," he replied haughtily. "I can get along without a seminar." Later an inspector, checking on the political class led by the captain, judged it a complete failure. The authorities cracked down on the unruly captain, and in time he "reformed," even writing articles for the unit's newspaper on the wonderful help given by the Party to the unit's military preparedness. But then other officers in the same unit began to show the very same political ills—they handled their soldiers "with no regard for the Party organization . . . not having learned to see in the Party organizations their true support."[14]

To a political talk at an air force unit by a visiting speaker only one third of the summoned officers came; some of the other two-thirds were seen in a room adjacent to the auditorium, playing billiards.[15] In another group of Marxist-Leninist orientation, only one of the seventeen participants—a major—was conscientious enough to read the assignments and take notes.[16] A third seminar revealed that a captain, commanding a battalion, as a recent graduate of a military academy knew "the role of man and technology in modern warfare," but was woefully ignorant of Marxist classics; "in the entire past school year he had read only two articles by V. I. Lenin" and no books whatever.[17] In yet another garrison, a captain, a major, and a lieutenant colonel showed their ignorance, respectively, of the fate of private property under Socialism, of the Party's role in the building of Communism, and of the relations between the East European countries and the Soviet Union.[18]

In a certain naval garrison, a captain who ran a political study group came ill prepared to preside over its session. "Trying to hide this," an informer's report read, "he killed a whole hour in a needless discussion of organizational problems. Then, for fifteen minutes, he droned quotations from a textbook of political economy." His topic was "The Worldwide Historic Significance of the Great Socialist Revolution, of the Final Victory of Socialism, and of Building Communism." But, the informer lamented, this "serious and important theme remained untouched." The speaker had just returned from a leave, had not been attending special training seminars for such officer-propagandists as himself, and that was why this meeting was a fiasco. To his audience "the propagandist finally had to confess that he had not studied this topic, and so stopped the study session altogether," sending his listeners back to their barracks.[19]

In the same garrison a class in the Party school housed in the sailors' club drew less than one half of its enrollees, and even some of these were outrageously late. All sorts of formalities were blamed. One group's driver lacked a seal on his pass. Another group failed to come because somebody had lost the note with the telephone message from the political office about the day and hour of the class.[20]

In this garrison's "Evening University of Marxism-Leninism," out of the 98 students registered for the course, only 54 came to the first lecture. They found it difficult to concentrate on the speaker's words, because the garrison's ensemble of song and dance was rehearsing in the very next room. Nobody bothered to transfer the rehearsal to another, more distant hall. The result was that only one third of the audience stuck it out to the end of the lecture. Among the officers who quit, the indignant informer named four most prominent Party secretaries of the garrison. "Formalism in ideological work," fumed the informer, "careless attitude toward enhancement of political knowledge of Communists . . ."[21]

A major acting as his unit's Party secretary candidly described Party and Komsomol meetings under his jurisdiction as monotonous and "quite like sour apples—they set your teeth on edge."[22] Numerous complaints come from regiments, companies, squadrons, and ships that during such orientation meetings hardly anybody listens as the official speaker intones from a book, a newspaper, or his own manuscript—all equally hateful to himself and to his audience. Men in the audience read something more lively, chat, or even nap. Why have professional agitators at all, some officers ask, "when all our soldiers are now literate, and there are so many newspapers around in the barracks"—surely the soldiers can read these papers without coming to meetings?[23]

A favorite method is to disregard the shrillest or otherwise

silliest among the materials prescribed for officers as their polit-
ical-teaching handbooks. In the Baltic Military District the propaganda office prepared a special series of brochures, manuals, and
display materials on "the aggressive nature" of the American and
West German armed forces. While some officer-teachers use this
data, in certain other locations of the district—particularly in
such elite and specialized sectors as air force units—"all these
texts gather dust in bookcases." When reprimanded for this negligence, officers declare: "But these materials are not mandatory,
after all." The chief of the political office of the district grows
sarcastic: "Strange as it may be, in some such places the exposure
of the aggressive character of the imperialistic armies is considered a secondary matter."[24]

One young officer was heard deploring his transfer to the job of
a Komsomol agitator for two years—"lost years," he wailed.[25]
Frank sabotage is rife: a captain, placed in charge of his unit's
Party Bureau, did not call a single meeting of the members for
four whole months and openly boasted: "I get along without any
meetin' fuss.'"[26] A military engineer, who for a time doubled as
a member of his unit's Party Committee, said to two of his misbehaving subordinates: "As your superior and by my Party duty I
should call you to order, but as a human being I forgive you."[27]

Party politicians are shocked when officers in command do
nothing to nip in the bud whatever hostile ideology may readily be
noticeable among the lower ranks. In one unit a smart private was
discovered, with a high-school education, who "reads a great
deal, expresses his ideas literately, and writes poetry." On the
surface he appeared to be "a model soldier and an activist." But
actually he was a heretic. "Much of what he read he compre-
hended incorrectly. According to him, man must question everything. He recognized no authority. Advice of his superiors was
considered by him as superfluous and unnecessary." There were
thus apparent some awful "gaps in his ideological upbringing."
Were his superiors in a blissful ignorance of this soldier's non-
conformity? Not at all. "The soldier's immediate superiors knew
of his incorrect and mistaken argument, but attached no importance to it, and so failed to refute it—to subject it to stern public
judgment."[28]

But what can you expect of officers who in their own clubs
encourage concerts with repertories full of "imitations of rotten
Western art," and whose libraries "at times artificially fan the
interest in decadent bourgeois authors"?[29]

I V

The reasons they give for sidestepping the Party and its message are many and good. A highly placed propagandist, a lieutenant general in charge of political supervision of the Soviet troops in East Germany, indignantly cited the alibi of those professional military men who neglected indoctrination—they say that "in the intricate and tense situation [of these days] there is no time for Party work." "How profoundly mistaken!" exclaimed the political chief.[30]

But a colonel argued: "Let's have some straight talk. In the rocket troops, should there ever be a battle, a propagandist [*polit-rabotnik*, literally "political worker"] can't count on a large audience; he won't have to urge men to get up and go over the top against the enemy. What's more, at the tensest moment of battle, when the operators spot and trace their targets and the starters get ready to launch their rockets, speeches would surely be out of place: they may distract the men and cause damage."[31] A lieutenant colonel added: "What help, for instance, can be given by a propagandist to a young flyer in the mastery of methods of hitting ground objects when the propagandist is not a flyer and does not know how this is done? What can he tell him about conduct in an air battle when he himself has never been in one and has never lived through the tension of its minutes?"[32]

When a professional military person is ordered to become a propagandist among his colleagues and subordinates, on either a part-time or a full-time basis, he pleads his lack of preparation for agitation and the superabundance of his proper technical duties. It is a common expression in the Soviet air force that "a good flyer is not always a good propagandist."[33] A captain said: "To talk is not my business. To convince, to explain, this is the political workers' official task. My job is to command."[34] A naval officer "would speak of technology with pride and love," but fell silent whenever a superior shifted to the question of his political duties. At best he would remark: "I am an engineer. My business is technology."[35]

Not only do they refuse to be the Party's messenger boys, they also dislike training the ranks technically or having anything to do with soldiers. Their job, they insist, is only to look after equipment. Let the sergeants and the privates get their technical know-how somewhere else, but not from them. And let the non-engineering officers command the troops.

But in some recently formed or reorganized units there are no other commanders but engineer and technician officers. Increasingly a rocket engineer is his unit's top officer. As such he must supervise his personnel both technically and politically. He is not allowed to leave the boring or messy Party assignment to others, since there are no others. He must improve his own Red orthodoxy and continue indoctrinating everyone under him.

Some military engineers argue that the reason they dislike stepping outside their technical function is the complexity of modern war technology—the fact that it is growing so vast and so difficult to master that it leaves no time for anything else. "The specialist's load is very heavy," wrote an engineer officer. If an engineer does not devote at least some of his limited spare time to learning new things in his field, "his work loses meaning." Suppose, the officer continued, the engineer "shifts part of his time to training his men in nontechnical matters, what then will be left for the engineer's own improvement?" This particular officer rather agreed that the Soviet military engineer should indeed give some of his valuable hours to the technical instruction of his subordinates. But in the same breath the officer proposed that the military engineer "be relieved of secondary matters"—that is, of the necessity to spend his time and effort in Communist indoctrination of the lower personnel.[36]

A few military engineers suggest, however, that, although political propaganda may indeed be a good and necessary task, it often miscarries through overdosing. One engineer wrote:

> Personally I head a group of political study. I am a member of the Party Bureau. I am carrying a number of other such assignments. All this is necessary, but one must admit that such a plenitude of various assignments hardly leaves me any opportunity for technology. Apparently, when it comes to an officer-technician, the problem of load distribution should have a better solution. In short, the question of drawing engineers into educational-social work should be decided with thought and care. It is not enough to assert that every officer should be such a mentor.[37]

Meetings, conferences, discussions—there is much too much of all that. A colonel complained: "Let us not conceal this sin: we still have far too many conferences, summonses, and so forth, which tear the commander away from his work and keep him from concentrating his attention on the study of technology."[38] Still another engineer-officer demanded: "It is necessary to cut down the number of conferences sharply. In some places these are called with cause and without cause, robbing commanders and engineers of their precious time."[39]

Disregard of, or at least complaint about, nontechnical duties is not confined to the rocket and missile branch. Older services too figure in the Soviet military-press denunciation of "snobbish" officers by Party politicians. We may surmise that the new praise heaped by the Soviet leadership on the role of science and technology in modern warfare has given technicians in nonrocket troops additional cause for the superior feeling they had harbored long before the Sputnik and Cosmonaut era blazed forth.

Indeed, respect for military engineers in Russia goes all the way back to the times of Ivan the Terrible in the sixteenth century and Peter the Great in the eighteenth, when the Western science and art of building fortifications and undermining the foe's fortifications was imported and fostered. During the Crimean War of 1854–56 the Russians made a pet hero of their German engineer, Colonel (later General and Count) Eduard Totleben, who built the brilliant defense works of Sevastopol. He has remained a legend to this day.

The centuries-old superiority complex of Russian naval officers was in a large measure based on the greater technical complexity of their duties and knowledge as compared with those of their colleagues in the army. The latter, even if grudgingly or at least reluctantly, recognized naval officers as their betters for this reason and no other. A Soviet naval officer, defecting to the West in the latter 1950s, has recently told me that some of that superiority and recognition of superiority began to disappear with the advent of rocketry in the land forces. "The land forces are now themselves full of technology," he remarked, "and thus they need not feel in any sense inferior to the machine-laden navy. Yet, part of that tradition survives. The army boys still regard the navy officers as more of technicians than they themselves are."

V

Gradually but surely the Party's hierarchs realize that military specialists, forced to become Party secretaries and propagandists, on the whole do not have much stomach for such alien work; that the engineers and other officers quickly learn how to get away with a lukewarm minimum of what is expected of them in this line.

What should be done? Never easily routed from its positions, the Party looks for new solutions. Some are found that are not so new. One method is to turn things around—give Party hacks a modicum of training in military technology and make their propaganda a mixture of political preaching and weaponry teaching. Above all, the Party sermons might be accepted by the warriors with more respect if the listeners knew that the preachers mastered this difficult technology, too. In the process, the propagandists would become more self-confident.

A propaganda chief of the Moscow Military District wrote: "Technical know-how adds boldness to a Party propagandist's activities. It helps him to find his way profoundly both in his positive experience and in his shortcomings. It transforms him into a passionate fighter for better results."[40] Political boys could not hope to learn everything about these complicated rockets, but they could master one or another vital area of the new arms. "Only this," one superior urged, "will make your [political] guidance work expert and authoritative."[41] In every branch of service, but particularly in rocket units, a political officer "should be ready any minute to act as an engineer, technician, weapon operator, ship pilot, or other specialist."[42] In June 1965 the political chief of the Baku Military District boasted that more than 70 per cent of his propagandists were engineers and technicians.[43]

But some failure has been admitted here, too. A high political officer of the Carpathian Military District confessed: "Our training of political functionaries is weak. Some of them do not know how to carry on military-technological propaganda in connection with learning new weapons and means of defense."[44]

In sum, if you want modern prestige for your propagandists, their deft political sermons are not enough. They have to display technological knowledge too, and it has to be a rather solid kind of expertise. A small amount and a slight quality will not do. For propagandists to display their semi-ignorance of matters technical is worse than to admit frankly their full ignorance.

But other troubles too exist for the Party. Some of the military politicos who learn something of the modern war technology and realize its complexity tend to become infected with the viewpoint of the professional technicians and practically cease being propagandists. One propagandist, attached to an air force unit, sympathized with the flyers' refusal to listen to political talks. He said: "See how much we fly! How can we think of lectures here at all?"[45] Some superiors, taking advantage of the fact that political officers now have some technical knowledge, keep them exceptionally busy as professional military, deliberately taking them away from their propaganda duties; "they use them even at work that has no direct relation to their proper service designation."[46]

And the old, old enmity of the professional commander for the professional commissar emerges again and again: a superior succeeds in transferring a political agent from his unit to a distant post;[47] a lieutenant colonel throws a Party secretary out of his office when the functionary dares to visit him without a summons or an appointment, and the same officer yells at a Komsomol Committee meeting of his soldiers: "Enough babbling! Break it up!"[48]

VI

How serious can this dissatisfaction of the military engineer with the Party become?

In 1963 some Western observers thought they saw a most significant phenomenon in the treason case of Oleg Penkovsky. Penkovsky, until his arrest by the Soviet authorities in Moscow in October 1962, had been deputy chief of the foreign department of the Soviet State Committee for Scientific Research and Coordination.[49] Before that, in 1956, he had served as assistant military attaché in Turkey. His rank was that of colonel in the reserves, and his decorations included eleven wartime medals, among them the Order of the Red Banner. He was an official of science rather than a scientist himself. Above all, he was an intelligence man of that modern type which specializes in things scientific and technical.

In his five-day Moscow trial in May 1963 (his only codefendant a Britisher), the forty-three-year-old Soviet expert was charged with betraying his country by working for British and American intelligence for as long as seventeen months, in 1961–62. It was alleged that he had turned over to his Western employers some five thousand frames of film of secret Soviet documents on Red rockets, on the numbers and location of Soviet armed units in East Germany, on the current state of Sino-Soviet relations, and other such crucial matters. (Later, the Soviet government tried to reassure its subjects that Penkovsky had lacked truly worthwhile contacts in the Soviet rocketry setup; that he had managed to smuggle out of the Soviet Union a few details of some obsolete rocket weapons only.)

During and for a time after the trial there were unofficial sporadic hints in Moscow that Penkovsky had committed his treason, not really for money or women or other Western luxuries as the Party insisted, but for some political, ideological reasons, which, however, were never brought out fully or clearly enough even by any Western commentator. At the trial's conclusion Penkovsky was sentenced to death by firing squad. On May 16, 1963, it was officially announced that he had been executed.

Late in May, another official announcement stated that Chief Marshal Sergei S. Varentsov, a foremost Soviet expert in artillery and rocketry, was demoted "in rank and post" for his past patronage of Penkovsky. Two other military persons, one a major general, the other a colonel on the same Committee for Scientific Research and Coordination, were given "severe disciplinary punishment" for having shared with Penkovsky certain secret data, which he carried to his British and American employers.

The political-ideological reasons prompting Penkovsky's treason to the Party were finally spelled out amply, two and one half years after his execution, in his *Papers* published in New York in November 1965. The internal evidence of the book, and even more so the frantic assault on the book's veracity raging in the Soviet press that November and December, convince me that the volume is not a forgery. From his *Papers* it is clear that Penkovsky was an anti-Soviet nonconformist, that his betrayal of the Party was a deliberate political act. He was alone in his conspiracy, aided by his few Soviet bosses (such as Marshal Varentsov) and associates (fellow military on the Committee) through their negligence, not complicity.[50]

But all this is a far cry from any real evidence that the new scientific-engineering military group in the Soviet Union has ever produced any concerted plot against the Party or, indeed, is truly capable of asserting itself through any pro-Western subversion.

The process of their rise to power may prove to be more gradual, less violent. With their growing prestige, their higher salaries, with many and various perquisites, these military engineers and scientists feel their own value and demonstrate a certain amount of independence from both the nonengineering commanders and the political officers of their units. It is this special part of the armed forces that I would single out as particularly influential and up-and-coming among "the newly educated and powerful groups of managers and army officers" who, in Professor John N. Hazard's words, "will exert pressure upon the members of the Presidium and the Communist Party's Central Committee to expand the circle of those who share power to include more of their number."[51]

Professor Hazard, however, thinks that these elements of Soviet society still accept the doctrines of Marx. He declares that "it is not possible at present to imagine that these groups would press for the opening of routes to power for the holders of non-Marxian ideas or for those who do not belong to the Communist Party." But this chapter's evidence of the military engineer's attitude toward Marxist indoctrination, and the still earlier proof (given at the very opening of this chapter) of the change wrought in the Marxist dogma itself by the military scientist, combine to show that, contrary to Professor Hazard's prognosis, the officer may yet play a rather non-Marxist role.

Time is not what Marx or Lenin thought it to be: the inevitable swallower of any and all class systems. Nor what Stalin and Khrushchev—or Malinovsky and his like—threatened in the name of inevitable time: perdition of the West and its way of life, and triumph of Communism, Russia's brand of it. With time, Malinovsky and his contemporaries, all quite old already, will die or retire, and to the seats of these conventional warriors will come those most unconventional ones—the present-day captains, majors, and colonels with scientific degrees. They, the uniformed men of the prestigious laboratories and the powerful launching pads, are the generals and the marshals of the very near tomorrow. A new class system will arrive, quite different from the Party-dominated structure of today, and with a military caste much unlike what has existed under the Party's aegis so far.

CHAPTER XI

~~~~~~~~~~~~~~~~~~~~~~~~~~~~~~~

The Civilian Technician: Coercion and Courtship

How FARES THE PARTY's organizational control over the civilian part of the nation's scientific-technical establishment? Not so well, the Party itself admits.

As the nonmilitary scientists and engineers, similarly to their military colleagues, grow stronger in their new social status and political stature they begin to shed the fetters of the Communist Party's actual, day-to-day control that for so many decades have so heavily pressed upon them. The Party naturally reacts. Taking due note of the increasing boldness of this professional elite, the Party hierarchs frown and threaten.

At an important Party meeting, a secretary of the Party Committee for the city of Moscow voiced his painful surprise that the Red capital's 700 scientific establishments, with their more than 350,000 scientists, engineers, and technicians, were not governed by the Party tightly enough. His lament ran: "All the necessary conditions are being afforded for the creative activity [of this unique army of brainpower], but the Party organizations have not as yet succeeded in raising the work of the scientific-research institutes, engineering-design bureaus and technical-project offices to the level of demands made by the Twenty-Second Congress of the Communist Party of the Soviet Union."

To decipher this heavy-footed and rather enigmatic charge: The scientists and engineers of Moscow seem to be going about their tasks as they please, amid all the comforts and conveniences extended to them by the Soviet government and the Communist Party. They do not heed—or do not heed well enough—whatever orders or injunctions may rain down upon them from those Party units that are assigned to watch over them.

At that Moscow meeting, the secretary and other Party activists went on to spell out the timidity of the Party units in this particular field:

> ... often the City Committees and the District Committees of the Party give only superficial guidance to the Party organizations within the scientific-research and technical-project establishments as well as engineering-design bureaus. They do not penetrate the life of these scientific collectives deeply enough. . . . Party Committees and Party Bureaus of many scientific-research establishments betray their timidity in the posing and discussion of questions of scientific work, in the analysis of the content of scientific researches; they do not take advantage, in full measure, of the right to control the activity of the administration [of these scientific and engineering establishments], the right given to them by the By-Laws of the Communist Party of the Soviet Union.[1]

But the Party, at least on occasion, appears to be of a divided mind about its own lack of resolve to run the professors and the engineers. Some Party members seem merely to envy the scientists and the technicians their newly found freedom from excessive Party controls. Some even wish the same liberty for themselves —if they happen to be not only Party members but also skilled nontechnical professionals of some kind or other.

Thus from the nation's highest rostrum, at the Party's Twenty-Second Congress, Nikolai Gribachev, a well-known writer, wistfully commented that "engineers-designers and physicists do not even have special Party organizations [for their professions], yet are succeeding rather well—they are already in outer space." This was part of Gribachev's hint that perhaps Soviet writers too did not really need a special Party unit to supervise them.

The minutes of the Congress session, as officially published by the Party, noted at this point: "Merry liveliness in the hall. Applause."[2] The Party hacks were applauding, of course, the Soviet scientists' successes in mastering outer space, not their increasing freedom from the Party's commands. Yet the scientists could well have derived yet newer boldness from the mere fact of this applause, disregarding the real cause of the plaudits, and taking the applauders for the fools that they surely were when they clapped at this particular juncture of Gribachev's speech.

I I

In all the years of its absolute reign the Party has never deviated from the practice of allowing the existence of only those organizations which were created and controlled by itself. For the scientists and technicians as groups there may be no special Party organizations, but individually they better be Party members—in general Party units.

The Party does its utmost to rope these specialists in, not only as members, but also as propagandists, secretaries, and other servitors. Some specialists succumb or even join willingly. But a surprising number of them resist the Party quite successfully. We see here a pattern very much like that of the military technicians' reluctance.

True, most of these civilians are Party members. In this part of recruiting, the Party does succeed. The element of resistance comes in when, as Party members, the specialists refuse to be Party activists. In the process some display or pretend amazing naïveté. A young Komsomol girl of Kazan wrote to her District Committee:

> Respected comrades! I don't even know whom to approach, whom to tell about a catastrophe that has happened in my life. I have just learned that you intend to put me in charge of a Komsomol political study group. I am so shaken by this unexpected news that I simply can't imagine how I, a mathematics teacher, can be a propagandist. We were not at all taught this at the Institute. . . .[3]

This, then, is one of the soundest and most effective excuses they use: *I have not been trained to be a Party propagandist or any other kind of activist. I have been trained as a technician—a real specialist, too valuable to the state to be used in any other way. Therefore leave me alone.*

A young hydrologist, attached to a Soviet fishing expedition prowling the Indian Ocean, refused the request of the ship's political officer to write for the ship's newspaper and to deliver a propaganda talk to the crew. "This is not part of my duties," he said.[4] In the Ural machine-building industry, machine designers —particularly young ones—were accused by Party officials of being "not at all concerned with their Marxist-Leninist erudition." These men "as a rule do not participate" in Party or Komsomol work, "they shy away from the collective," and their alibi is: "I am an engineer, my business is technology."[5] In the city of Elektrostal in the Moscow Region, a senior engineer declined a propaganda assignment, saying to the Party functionary who tried to press him into it that he was trained for engineering only: "Orienting others is not my business." This was indignantly quoted at a meeting of the city's Party activists as a truly horrible case. But it was not a unique case. At the same meeting a similar "none-of-my-concern" statement was cited as emanating from another technician in the same area.[6]

Propaganda tasks and other routine Party and Komsomol assignments are covered in the Party's vocabulary by the high-sounding euphemism of "social work" (*obshchestvennaya rabota*). But the fine sound of it does not at all inspire or shame young specialists into running the Party's errands at the expense of their professional interests. The hacks who hear the specialists' refusal make believe they are puzzled.

A young woman, a Komsomol organizer at the celebrated Volgograd (formerly Stalingrad) Tractor Plant, is quoted[7] as saying "in alarm" about the young engineers who have recently been graduated by the Volgograd Mechanical Institute to work at the Plant: "I am surprised, but it is precisely the young engineers who are the hardest of all to be drawn into social work. And from where do they get so much indifference and lack of interest?"

The Komsomol secretary of the Institute, who quotes the comrade lady, answers her question bluntly: "From where? From the Institute . . ." At the Institute, he explains, these young men and women study hard not only their engineering profession but also the sly knack of evading their Komsomol assignments or Party work.

Be hard-boiled, don't accept any excuses, loyal Party men urge one another. "When a student says that he does not want to be on duty in the Committee, that he does not wish to be a Communist organizer, that generally he will not occupy himself with social work because this hinders his study, remember that an egotist is facing you! Studies for him are but a handy shield."[8]

Far more plausible is the explanation by good students why some of their classmates *do* want to become Komsomol organizers. "Others did not want this—they were busy with their study. But he did not want to study, and that is why he was straining to become an activist," said a girl about a fellow-student, a light-brain comrade, a hypocrite who "was looking for an easy life." Grateful to him for sparing them the distasteful job and letting them study in peace and quiet, they allowed the organizer to copy his institute assignments from them![9]

And thus one more argument is offered by students and graduates as they plead to be excused from Komsomol and Party errands. "Let others busy themselves with politics—each person should know his own business. I know my drafting table, my mathematics, or my medicine, or my designing work. Let me be engrossed in it completely. Only chatterboxes try to do several things at once . . ."[10] One of the shrewdest, weightiest points stressed by the specialists in their passive resistance to the Party runs: *It is much more practical—far more modern and efficient —for every Soviet citizen to do what he can do best. Division of labor!*

You Party men do your work and we specialists will do ours. We will do much better work if you don't bother us with your political sermons or, worse yet, make us echo your orations and editorials. At the far-famed Science City of Novosibirsk, at one of the institutes, a public debate was held on the subject of "Communist Labor in Science." Some official orators apparently urged the audience to proclaim "a Communist Competition"—a kind of Red race between eager beavers of laboratories. A forty-year-old scientist, holder of decorations for his work on the atomic icebreaker, demurred:

> As you know, our work is creative. It demands the entire man. No one can intensify a scientist's labor more than he himself. In other words, if a scientist is devoted to his work he toils Communistically. Of course we can accept obligations and even carry them out, but I think this will rather be our concession to form.[11]

III

Some answer the pressure by not belonging to the Komsomol or the Party at all. An ingenious dodge is to say that one is a member in spirit. A character in a Stalinist novel, an engineer, has something like this in mind when he explains why he has not joined: "It always seemed to me that entering the Party is only a formality and that it is enough to feel your Party essence within you . . ." But this adroit excuse is immediately followed by the engineer's confession of his real motive—the motive most commonly given by those not wishing to join: "In my institute and during the first years of my engineering work I figured that, should I join the Party, its work and various other such loads would take me away from study, from my deep preoccupation with technology. And in fact I witnessed just such a case involving one of my comrades."[12]

You want a sacrifice for Party or Komsomol work? As his

reply, in these post-Stalinist days, a member may give up his Party or Komsomol card with a sneer: "I don't long to be a hero."[13]

In Kharkov, a young engineer refused to become a member of a quasi-police detachment (*druzhinnik*); boldly—almost boastfully—he said to his Komsomol superiors and associates: "I am afraid. I don't need any posthumous medals. I am a coward." The other Komsomols argued with him long but fruitlessly. Finally they said: "But you are a Komsomol. Don't you value your Komsomol card?" Coolly he replied: "Expel me if you find it necessary." And he was expelled.[14]

Such individuals do not hesitate to break their family ties, their marriages, if they feel that the Party's excessive demands are made through their loved ones. A loyal Communist told of bumping into an old classmate whom he had not seen since their institute days. In the course of their conversation it developed that the old classmate had divorced his wife because as a Komsomol organizer she "had remained a big child" and too "idealistic" a burden to the man and his get-rich-quick ways.[15]

Friendships, too, go overboard if a specialist, or a student preparing to be a specialist, is cursed with a Party or Komsomol job because of a sly chum. At a Komsomol meeting of the Cheliabinsk Pedagogic Institute a dean heard this conversation behind his back:

"I am going to nominate Seryozhka Kubitsky."

"What for?"

"I will play him as dirty as he played me: he nominated me last year."[16]

I V

Desperately, pressed by the demands of this increasingly complex technological age, the Party reaches out for engineers and other specialists, pampers them, cajoles them, draws them into its ranks, and more and more depends on them. Gone are the times —the 1920s and the '30s, the '40s, and even the early '50s— when the Party could consult them yet insult them; when it could and did arrest and murder them as easily as it used and flattered them. Now, as the Communist hierarchs run their tightfisted ship of state, they invite the specialists to share the wheel.

The Party thinks that the invitation is still on the Party's own terms, that the Party has nothing much to fear from any differing

ideology or separate, selfish ambitions on the part of the specialists. Indeed, says the Party hierarchy, we trust these intelligentsia,
these specialists, so thoroughly that we will accept them as our
fellow leaders in the Party, at least in that leadership's lower and
middle echelons.

And so, witness now the intensification of a most remarkable
process: the replacement of Party hacks with the technical intelligentsia, particularly with engineers; the drafting of veritably
thousands of engineers into the network of full-time Party functionaries.

It has been estimated that, in absolute figures, engineers are the
largest part of the present-day Soviet intelligentsia. At the beginning of this decade, the Soviet Union's adults between twenty-five
and sixty years of age totaled nearly 90 million, and of this number more than 1,100,000 were engineers (the two next biggest
categories of professionals were the more than 420,000 physicians and the 400,000 scientific personnel). In the late 1950s and
early 1960s the total of Soviet engineers increased by 10 to 11
per cent annually (compare this with the 6 to 7 per cent yearly
increase for scientific personnel and the 4 to 5 per cent for physicians).[17]

In the Party, too, engineers constitute one of the highest ratios.
They are six or seven times as numerous on the Party rolls as men
and women of any other occupation. Only Soviet military officers
are as numerous in the Party's membership as engineers.[18]

Engineers are so plentiful in the Party, not only because there
are so many of them in the population at large, but also because
the Party's hierarchs make a particular effort to attract them into
its ranks. Two reasons account for this effort: First and foremost,
engineers in this technological age are prestigious everywhere, but
especially in the Soviet Union, and the Party needs this prestige;
secondly, engineers are commonly known as a practical, business-
like breed of people, and the Party needs their technical know-
how, their pragmatism. Now, more and more, the Party wants
them as Party functionaries of various categories, particularly as
Party secretaries.

From Karaganda in Kazakhstan comes the cry that the Communist organizer of a large industrial-building project must know
more than the mere art of human relations—"he needs also a
certain minimum of engineering knowledge." It won't do to appoint a half-educated comrade, who may have got "stuck" in his
second year of technical study, to the most important Communist-

functionary post on the project. But he was appointed, and he just did not know enough technology to "think statesmanlike thoughts, to look far ahead, and not allow himself to be swamped by daily routine."[19] Reason enough to replace the half-baked comrade with a full-fledged engineer!

This is true of agriculture as it is of industry. "Indeed," echoes a Party secretary from the Stavropol Territory in the Northern Caucasus, "the development of farm economy now proceeds not so much in its extensification as in depth—along the path of intensification. This places entirely new demands on the cadres, on the leaders of all grades. The time has come when an organizing talent alone will not suffice. Production calls for knowledge, and knowledge again!" This is what a Party leader should now remember: "To rule, one must be competent, must know all the conditions of production, its technique and technology. In short, one must have a certain scientific education."[20]

But what happens if a local Party Committee does not know the technology of a given industry or branch of farming? Ah, then "Party Committees must abandon any and all attempts to hand down 'leading orders,' directives, and recommendations on how to run economy." For this work there are experts: "agronomists, zoological technicians,* engineers."[21]

Thus are the Soviet Union's young engineers and other experts replacing the dull Party hacks—the men and women who all their adult lives have known only how to read or write directives and obey or shout orders but have lacked any technical knowledge of the industry or the agriculture they were supposed to boss.

V

Solomon Schwartz, a Menshevik *émigré* in New York and for many years a keen student of Soviet affairs, observes that in the Soviet Union "the Communist Party is becoming basically a party of technical intelligentsia." We may add, "for better or worse," and try to answer the questions: Better for whom? Worse for whom?

Mr. Schwartz states that, increasingly, engineers and other technical personnel in the U.S.S.R. become Communists, and Communists become engineers. Soviet statistics on this trend are

---

* *Zootekhniki* or "zoological technicians" are low-ranking Soviet farm experts with a modicum of special education fitting them to advise farm managers on the care of cattle.

fragmentary, yet emphatic. Mr. Schwartz relays to us, from Soviet sources, a table showing the numerical increase of Communists among the Soviet Union's "specialists with higher or specialized secondary-school education," an official category denoting mainly professionals with engineering and technical training.[22]

From the Party's own statistics of its over-all membership, the percentage of such specialists in the Communist Party appears to be constantly growing. When we look back to 1956 we discover that on January 1 of that year, out of the total Party membership of 7,173,521, specialists with higher or specialized middle education numbered 2,001,176, or 27.9 per cent of the total. Six and one-half years later, on July 1, 1961, in the Party of 9,626,740 members, these specialists increased to 3,076,228, or 31.9 per cent.

Early in 1961 a Party publication revealed that "in 1960, the number of engineers, technicians, agronomists, physicians, teachers, economists, and other specialists accepted into the Party as candidate members was larger by 31,500 than the corresponding figure of the preceding year, and their ratio among employees accepted into the Party was 68.5 per cent." (The Russian term *sluzhashchiye*, "employees," is used to distinguish white-collar personnel from proletarians and peasants.)

It was inevitable that with the number and percentage of engineers, technicians, scientific personnel, and other specialists in the Party steadily growing, there would occur a rise of their categories to the Party's surface as Party Congress and Supreme Soviet deputies, delegates, orators (even if the speeches were written for them or at least approved by Party pros), and holders of specific Party honors and even actual Party functions and jobs.

The hierarchs' effort to make engineers into Party secretaries and other functionaries is not exactly recent. The earliest change from hacks to technicians in Party posts was caused by the purges of the 1930s. So many Party professionals were wiped out in that fratricide that new men—preferably with some education—had to be found to replace the victims. Thus young engineers were made into functionaries; that was how the Brezhnevs and the Kosygins got their start. But such recruits, after a few years in Party service, ceased to think of themselves as technicians. They were Party men and nothing else. So the Party was safe.[23]

Yet it was not too safe two decades later, when, following Stalin's death, the tapping of engineers for Party posts became particularly intensive. Boris Antonovsky, one of the defectors who answered my questions, recalled out of his own experience as a Soviet industrial manager of the middle 1950s that there was trouble for the Party when it tried to bring a whole new crop of technicians into its functionary strata. Antonovsky said: "Some such engineers, chemists, intelligent foremen and the like became too independent for the Party's comfort, even as they ostensibly did the Party's bidding, which actually they did not. Yet the Party's high leadership did not think of removing them right away. It was three or four years before those sassy young men were removed."

From 1956 to 1958 new engineers were appointed Party secretaries. This time, according to Antonovsky, the Party bosses in charge of the selection were more careful; the engineers' early Party membership records and latest Party zeal were scrutinized thoroughly. "And perhaps this time the Party was not disappointed," said Antonovsky. "Now in the 1960s such engineers in Party posts show less independence than the group showed in 1954–57."

Significantly, he added: "Still, they are a great deal more independent that a comparable stratum was in Stalin's time."

V I

On January 1, 1959, throughout the Soviet Union, Party Committee secretaries with higher education constituted 34.8 per cent of all such secretaries, and the ratio rose to 58.6 by January 1962.[24] But the most recent and decisive spurt in this process of replacing hacks with knowledgeable technicians occurred in late 1962 and early 1963.

In November 1962, at the plenary session of the Central Committee of the Communist Party in Moscow, a decision was made to divide Party organizations throughout the nation into two distinct categories, industrial and agricultural. The move was accompanied by the well-publicized directive to intensify the 1954 idea that new Party secretaries and other functionaries should have engineering or technical training. In his penetrating comment, Solomon Schwartz summarized this reform as "replacement everywhere in the field of conservative-minded Party bureaucrats, of professionals of Party administrative and ideological work, by Communists who have grown up directly in production and as production managers."[25]

In early 1963 a typical example for industry was widely

trumpeted, namely: In Soviet Georgia, the Party committees of four industrial regions reported that before the reorganization hardly 10 per cent of their member-functionaries were engineers and technologists, and that secretaries of district Party committees lacked special technical training yet tried to run these industries. But after the reorganization, in all four districts more than one half of the Party Committee membership had higher and middle technical education. The manager of an important cable-making plant, an engineer by profession, became one of the region's main Party secretaries.[26]

A similar success in replacing Party bureaucrats with Party men possessing technical training was claimed for Soviet agriculture. The rapidity with which this metamorphosis was undertaken from the very start of the reform was illustrated by a member of the Presidium of the Party's Central Committee, Leonid N. Yefremov. On March 11, 1963, speaking at the special conference of Party secretaries of the Russian Socialist Federated Soviet Republic (the Soviet Union's largest component) summoned to Moscow, he announced that in the forty-two territories and regions of the Republic there were 84 first and second Party secretaries, and that of these men and women fully 77 had higher education, and of these 67 were trained agronomists and zoological technicians.[27] In July 1963 a regional example of this transformation was cited for the Don River area: "Specialists who know their business run economy. Thus, for instance, all the twenty chiefs of Party production offices are agronomists and zoological technicians, and out of the twenty Party Committee secretaries sixteen have higher education."[28]

The November 1962 decision to divide Party organizations into the industrial and agricultural categories was in itself a cause of yet greater inefficiency and even chaos for the Party. It did not last beyond Khrushchev's reign; soon after his October 1964 downfall the Party's two-way division was abolished, and the old unitary system was restored. But this restoration did not in any way slow down the Party's effort to make engineers into Party secretaries, to replace mere hacks with sheer technical geniuses.[29]

VII

The Party thinks it is discovering the psychological, disciplinary value, in addition to the purely technological worth, of the engineer as Party or Komsomol secretary, of the man who continues to work as an engineer while carrying out the duties of his secretaryship.

The Party welcomes this value. Its propagandists frankly point out that when a Komsomol or Party functionary happens to be an engineer, and an able one at that, "his ideological influence upon the young is doubtless greatly strengthened by his professional authority in their eyes." Such was the case of Kenes Zhandy-bayev, a Komsomol secretary on one of the largest collective farms in the Alma-Ata Region in Kazakhstan. He was the farm's chief engineer and a diligent instructor of mechanics in the area. "The dependence of the authority of Kenes the Communist func-tionary on the authority of Kenes the engineer is entirely clear."[30]

Yet there are doubts among the Party's pros. Does the new system actually work? And even if it does, is the price being paid by the Party and the Komsomol to these engineers-turned-politicians not too high? Is there not too much emphasis on secre-taries with technical training and engineering diplomas? Are they indeed good Communists or even efficient functionaries—really the important ingredient for the Party apparatus to have in order to survive? Worriedly the hierarchs or at least their faithful henchmen are asking such questions. They are answered by life's disquieting surprises.

Some engineers and other specialists seem to be cynical about the "ideological influence" they are supposed to exert as Com-munist functionaries. From the Donetsk Region in the Ukraine comes a lament about the low quality of lecturers in the outlying districts; yet, the argument runs, it would be so easy to replace such "insufficiently trained" speakers with the college graduates now manning the Regional Committee of the Donetsk Komsomol, whose entire staff consists of "persons with higher education—pedagogues, engineers, jurists." It is they, "the Komsomol lead-ers, who should be propagandists at the meetings of the young." But these new Komsomol secretaries dodge such speaking dates, and "following their lead, the other Komsomol Regional Commit-tee personnel also look for a chance to shirk the necessity of lecturing."[31]

And then there was this unpleasant illustration reported from Yerevan, capital of Soviet Armenia: For two years, a young en-gineer named Vladimir Khachaturov served as secretary of the Komsomol organization of the republic's main radio station. Eyebrows were raised at the time of his original appointment, for it was known that as a student he had been reprimanded for some sort of anti-Party behavior, and the punishment had been duly entered in his personal dossier. Then, for two years, he did hardly anything on his job as the radio station's Komsomol secretary —except losing his Committee seal. For two years, the ensuing complaint about him read, Khachaturov also forgot "even such an elementary duty as collecting membership dues in time." Because of him, "life in the organization stood still."

The District Committee in Yerevan, under whose jurisdiction young Khachaturov's Komsomol unit was supposed to operate, tried to teach the young engineer-secretary his duties, tried to help him—then discovered that the Committee staff's chief task was just in locating him. Nobody seemed to have seen him lately; he had to be summoned to the Committee's office so that its functionaries could upbraid him. On his own initiative he appeared in the Committee's office only once, and "at that, did his best to avoid a frank talk." Even when ordered to come to the Committee Bureau's sessions, he only promised to attend but did not come. Finally, in November 1962, his own radio station's Komsomol membership voted no confidence in Khachaturov.

Imagine then the surprise of Khachaturov's District Committee superiors when four months later, in early 1963, the young engineer was once more introduced to them—as the holder of a yet higher Komsomol post. And who had promoted him? Why, the top authority in Soviet Armenia's Komsomol, its Central Committee. Didn't the Central Committee know (the plaint went up from the District Committee) of the engineer's horrible record as a Komsomol member and functionary?

None of your business, rejoined the Central Committee. Its first secretary summoned the chief complainer in the District Committee to hear the riot act. The complainer was cussed out as "a dirty, low man" and was at last dimissed with a reprimand "for behavior unworthy of a Komsomol functionary." Another District Committee secretary was warned that it was his duty "to look after the education" of such mischief-makers as the complainer on his staff. However, to even up matters, Engineer Khachaturov was also reprimanded for "concealing his past."

But other Komsomol zealots spoke out against Khachaturov. One of them publicly asked the important question: "What, after all, motivated the Bureau of the Central Committee of Armenia's Komsomol to confirm Khachaturov" in his promotion? The zealot answered his own question brutally: "The only motive was that Khachaturov has the diploma of a communications engineer."

The protester went on to say that another promotion by the same Central Committee was also based on the new appointee's engineering profession. This second engineer was no better a Komsomol functionary than Engineer Khachaturov. "He has never done any Komsomol work, and he has but a vague notion of his new duties. . . ."

Case after case of such new appointments was cited in the indignant outcry—appointments of young engineers and technicians inexperienced in Komsomol work and indifferent to it, sometimes even cynically so. The complaint summed up:

> The method of choosing Komsomol functionaries in our republic on the sole premise that "so long as there is a diploma, all is well" has long since proved its bankruptcy. We have the right to expect that the Komsomol's Central Committee abandon its activity methods, to which it has grown accustomed but which are no good whatsoever and that it correct its errors in the process of reorganization. But so far nothing has changed.[32]

VIII

But engineers, as they are pulled and pushed into Party posts, also have their problems. One is of livelihood. For an engineer to be appointed to a Party secretaryship often means losing half of his salary. We find an indication of this in a Soviet novel: "Experienced, knowledgeable engineers were, most frequently, fathers of large families, and they earned twice as much as Party Bureau secretaries; the lowering of their earnings was for them a catastrophe."[33] This difficulty is now being solved for the engineers by the Party, which increasingly decrees that they be paid their high salaries as engineers even when they become Party functionaries.

Then there is the problem of too many Party jobs heaped upon a capable engineer. At the famous Likhachev automobile plant in Moscow a senior engineer, Mikhail Ryss, found himself saddled with at least eight major Party offices as his permanent duties, plus an astonishing variety of "one-shot," emergency tasks. His two chief associates, both also senior engineers, were likewise given eight to ten Party jobs apiece. They, too, were called upon to perform sundry additional Party errands. "These giants are torn to pieces. They are mobilized on the least excuse. Hardly do they return from one conference when they are summoned to one more. There are days when they sit at three sessions nearly simultaneously. And while they are sitting there, their main work stands still."[34] What self-respecting engineer in his right mind would want to become a Party functionary, opening himself to such a rat race?

And then, of course, there is the engineer's fear that he would become rusty as a technologist were he to take on even one Party job, not to mention the multitude showered on engineers at the Moscow auto plant. That the fear is ever present can be illustrated by the following case:

At the huge automobile factory in Gorky, the executive committee of the local Komsomol organization totaled fifteen members, and eight of these were engineers. The engineers' assumption of this Party work was a recent phenomenon. "Yes, new leaders now stand at the steering wheel of the Komsomol organization in industries. They are knowledgeable people, deep-probing, striving to dig down to the very 'roots' of production. Increasingly do young experts, engineers, come to run Komsomol organizations."[35] A young engineer was appointed to the secretaryship—the highest post—of the Gorky plant's Komsomol. But car technology was his passion. He was known as the originator of certain improvements in the gear shift of the Soviet automobile Chaika (Seagull). His work on the gear shift had been published in the Moscow magazine *Avtomobil'naya promyshlennost'* (Automobile Industry). And now came the momentous problem: "Some secretaries are tortured by the question 'But won't my technical qualifications be lost in Komsomol work?'"

The Soviet propagandist writing about the case gave her reassuring answer: "In the last year Aleksei Novikov has grown perceptibly both as a [Komsomol] leader and a specialist."[36]

I X

But in reality the answer cannot be as simple as the one given in the Gorky case. First of all, the conflict between Party function and professional career may go beyond the lower levels of leadership. The developing transformation has so far involved the Party leadership up to that of regions and territories; a similar transformation above this level seems destined to come. When it does, it will mean "a change in the sociological face of the higher links of the Communist Party too—of the Central Committees of the Party in the republics and of the Central Committee of the Soviet

Union's Communist Party." This phenomenon "inevitably leads to the enhancement of the *social weight* of specialists and particularly of engineers and technicians in the nation and, correspondingly, to the increase of their influx into the Party."[37] To this observation by Solomon Schwartz, we should add our judgment that hand in hand with an increase of social weight a heightening of political importance also occurs.

Thus the two main problems we should pose here are: Will the change-over bring engineers and technicians (as well as scientists) into the highest organs of the Party, until such new personnel indeed becomes a majority of the committees at the very top of the nation? If so, how soon? And: Will the new Party functionaries of this engineering and technical origin, in committee jobs high and low, indeed lose their identities as true technicians? That is, will they become more Party men and less technicians? Or, to put it yet another way, will the Party change them in its own image rather more rapidly and thoroughly than they would have any chance to change the Party in their own "sociological face" with far-reaching political implications?

These problems are something for the Party to worry about. The Party's nontechnical personnel do worry.

Thus, in May 1963, a Party secretary, boss of the Industrial Party Committee at Zaporozhiye in the Ukraine,[38] reported with considerable alarm "the mistaken view, of late beginning to spread in some places, that questions of ideology" should be removed from the Party's hands and turned over to those new intellectual functionaries and "volunteer" propagandists of Communism. The secretary protested and warned:

> Any and all attempts of the Party organizations to stand aside from the guiding of ideology do nothing but damage to the cause of the Communist development of the Soviet people. It is necessary not to slacken but to strengthen the Party and state guidance of ideological activity in all its sectors. It is not at all permissible to allow any initiative in our society to develop by itself. We must guide whatever spontaneous social activity exists in the realm of ideology.

Certainly, the Party hack agrees, the effort of the Party Committees throughout the nation to bring into their network, as secretaries and propagandists, fresh elements from among the scientific-technical personnel and other intellectuals is laudable. For "this enhances the scientific level and the force of influence of our work in the field of ideas." This new, active participation "of the best scientific roster and of the wide circles of the intelligentsia in the Party's propaganda makes it truly profound and effective."

But, the Party pro insists, this does not by any stretch of hostile imagination mean that the Party should abdicate. Indeed, in the guidance of the new intellectual secretaries and propagandists by the old professional Party hacks the zealot sees "the guarantee of new successes in the political education of the masses, and of the raising of the idea-level and of the effectiveness of [the Party's] ideological work."

Let us Party professionals (*Pravda* closed the year 1965 with its urgent sermon) teach such engineers and the like our own "ways and methods of political approach to problems." Let us Party stalwarts prevent such engineers and other diplomaed experts from using their "executive-managerial methods" so different from good old Party patterns.[39]

In sum, it is all right, the Party holds, nay, it is necessary, to recruit those confounded engineers and technicians as Party functionaries, but in the process the Party's control over them must be tighter than ever, lest the Party be eroded by them, lest the Party be molded by the technicians into their own image and tool.

The very presence of these particular problems, the very fact of the Party's concern about them, cannot but suggest that a new danger is indeed arising for the Party.

CHAPTER XII

~~~~~~~~~~~~~~~~~~~~~~~~~~~~~~~~~~~~~

The Managerial Evolution

A STORY OCCASIONALLY HEARD in Eastern Europe relates that a Western visitor is shown around a Soviet plant. The manager tells the guest about the plant's wonderful achievements. The visitor compliments the manager, who modestly concedes: "All our plants are managed by smart and industrious Communists." But after a moment of hesitation the manager adds candidly: "However, if a manager is smart and industrious he is not a Communist. If smart and a Communist, he is not industrious. And if industrious and a Communist, he is not smart."

There is a grain of truth in this anecdote, but not the whole truth. A smart and industrious manager will not necessarily do his best to avoid Communist membership. Holding or not holding a Party card is not the important dilemma that it used to be. Where the story rings true is in its implication that a shrewd and hardworking manager cannot be a *convinced, sincere* Communist, and the Party better not bank on him as such.

Of course, Soviet fiction, particularly of Stalinst times, is full of alleged heroes—managers who are thoroughly devoted Communists. But in reality, as the engineers and the scientists, so the managers are prouder of their professional competence than of their Party cards. Many are patriots of their country rather than of the Party. They rejoice in the scientific, technological, and industrial progress of their homeland, but very seldom do they, down deep in their hearts, praise the Party for it. They attribute the nation's successes to the genius of the people. Even more often they ascribe it to the talents and hard toil of such elite as themselves.

They have come to their positions and their feeling about their own rule not suddenly, not through some dramatic upset in recent

Soviet history, but slowly, gradually, almost imperceptibly. But the phenomenon is there, and they are aware of it.

Today's manager is indeed a much more assured and demanding man than was the harried factory administrator and the hectic Red executive of the descriptions given by Professors David Granik and Joseph S. Berliner in the 1950s.[1] In relation to this new boldness and independence the Liberman Reform may have been both a cause and an effect. Its grant of managerial freedoms may have contributed to the group's new stature. But in part the Reform was the result of the manager's restlessness and rise.

The Party knows this, too, and the Party does not like it. In one way and another the Party tries to check or change the managerial evolution before it becomes too dangerous for the regime. It calls upon its hacks to wake up from their stupor, to be vigilant against the managers' growing cheek. In the words of the complaint coming from the first secretary of the Leningrad Party City Committee, "we have frequently met with situations where Communists of various Party organizations did not thwart executives who strove to be assigned smaller quotas of production and thus live without trouble . . ." The first secretary lamented that in Leningrad (as in other places all over the Soviet Union, to be sure) "Party men at times do not discipline officials who disregard deserved criticism, Party men will not nip in the bud attempts to blacken and blame men of principle who refuse to make peace with men's failings"[2]—the euphemism "men of principle" meaning here those who inform on managers and other wrongdoers.

Even close to Moscow, right under the eye and ear of the highest authorities, the Party command has discovered with dismay that many Party committees "tackle problems of industry and construction only after some failure occurs" in the planned work of the industrial and building projects involved. "This," the Party admonishes its subordinate committess, "is, of course, incorrect and inadmissible."[3] Managers and all other executives should be checked and ordered around constantly and consistently, and not only in emergencies.

In the provinces, too, the Party hacks' slothful omission or wrong commission is frequent. At the Penza air-compressor plant, affairs were at sixes and sevens for years. The plant's Party Committee habitually waited until problems piled up threateningly. When equipment broke down and its repair was imperative, the Party Committee woke up sufficiently to "try their solution all at once, wholesale." It called Party meetings, it hurled thunder and lightning at the plant's managers and engineers, it set time limits within which the equipment was to be repaired. "But the time limits would pass, and the matter would not move off its dead center. And again resolutions were adopted, and speeches full of exposés were delivered. But the Party Committee . . . never once punished" the engineers and managers guilty of neglect. Finally just one man, the plant's chief mechanic, was removed. But the main thing, "the much needed enhancement of the role and the militancy of the Party Committee," was still not done. The plant's engineers and managers just didn't pay any attention to the Committee.[4]

In another case, at a ball-bearing plant in Kuibyshev, the offending manager was "an honest man," or so the two Party secretaries assured an investigator. "Even if he used unlawful steps, this was not to make profit for himself."[5] Thus did the Party functionaries find excuses for erring or even thieving managers. At Gorky the manager of a sausage factory for years tolerated petty thefts of the plant's products by staff members and their visiting friends. The Party Bureau warned him repeatedly, and finally ordered that he be fired. Was he? And arrested and tried? Not at all. It was not proved, you see, that he had participated in the stealing. His only guilt was his "personal principle" that small-size thefts of state property by his crew were wholly permissible. And so he remained comfortable "in his leading armchair—he sits and leads, and allows to multiply, in accordance with his personal convictions, those who love to take state property" for their own needs or sale. The Party was helpless; the manager won.[6]

I I

The frequent complaint of the Party is that only too often managers disregard Party organizations completely. The secretary of the Party Committee at a large chemical plant in Leningrad is peeved because the area's Council of People's Economy* persistently neglects Party organizations of the factories and plants under its jurisdiction. When the Council's executives—managers and engineers—visit a plant "they do not call on its Party Com-

---

* All Councils of People's Economy were abolished in early October 1965, paradoxically to give managers of individual plants more freedom of action. (See above, Chapter VII.)

mittee; they are not interested in the latter's opinion on this problem or that." It seems that some such visitors (Oh, horror!) "do
not even know just where the Committee has its headquarters."
At this particular chemical plant the secretary does not recall a
case

> where the Party Committee's secretary was invited to come to the
> main office of the Council of People's Economy, so as to express
> his view of this or that acute question. There has never been a
> single telephone ring [from the Council's main office]. The Coun-
> cil's executives do indeed meet often with the plant's manager, chief
> engineer, and chief technologist, but as for us, no, stubbornly they
> do not want to meet us. Is this right? How is it possible to direct the
> plant's activity thoughtfully without the advice of the Party organi-
> zation? It is no secret that the Party Committee and our manage-
> ment hold divergent opinions. The Council of People's Economy,
> as it makes its decisions, should take this divergence into considera-
> tion. But in actuality we see the opposite: they do not listen to the
> voice of the Party organizations, they pay no attention to it.[7]

A lower-level Party official at a large paper factory in the city
of Balakhna in the Gorky Region complains:

> I am upset by the relations that have evolved between the busi-
> ness leaders and the Party organizations at our plant. Say, a work-
> shop at the plant gets its new chief. By whom is he appointed and
> confirmed in his duties? His "go-ahead" signal comes from the
> plant's personnel director, from the plant's manager, and, if we are
> lucky, also from the plant's Party secretary. But the Party Commit-
> tee of the workshop in question is left out. . . . This Committee's
> opinion is considered unneeded and goes unheeded. Too bad.[8]

The aggrieved Party official cites this case: The repair workshop of the paper plant had to welcome to its design department a
brand-new chief appointed "contrary to the opinion [expressed
on the appointment] by the Party group" of the workshop. In
protest, three of the five dissenting Communists quit their jobs,
transferring to another plant. "But nobody was upset over this.
We hear: 'The Party group was wrong.' Perhaps. But won't they
explain to the Communists just what their mistake is? Why didn't
they even bother to convince the Communists that they had been
wrong?"

As scientists and engineers, be they military or civilian, so
managers also duck assignments to Marx-Lenin groups either as
propagandists or as spare-time students. They simply declare they
have no spare time. When a North Russian industrial manager

was summoned by his city's Party Committee to speak of the measures he would take to improve his workers' understanding of Communism, he took an are-you-kidding stance: "Why do you ask *me*? For this we have the Party Committee, the trade union, and the Komsomol organization. This is their business . . . I have enough of my own worries about production . . ."⁹

Indeed, so cocky do some managers feel that they do not hesitate to disrupt or even nullify the local Party Committee's efforts at propaganda if they feel these efforts are in production's way. The manager of a Diesel-machinery plant in Khabarovsk, Eastern Siberia, needed space for the offices and drafting rooms of his engineer-designers. With no qualms he took over for this purpose the plant's Red Corner—the Party propaganda hall where the workers and employees listened to speeches and read Communist literature. A Party Committee man complained; the Committee called a hearing and summoned the manager. The Committee man offered to find other space for the designers, but the manager remained adamant, saying to the Committee: "Well, if you here listen to him, let him be the manager, let him issue commands!" And so the Red Corner was not restored, and the Committee man—after a few more losing fights with the manager about sundry other matters—resigned his Committee post at the plant.¹⁰

Often managers look pained when they are asked to account to Party or Komsomol meetings. At a Kazakhstan state farm the chief manager came to a Komsomol session and listened to complaints against him. "A heavy-set man, there he sat, fanning himself with his hat, and the chair under him creaked piteously. He gave a little laugh now and then, and kept silent. We asked him to say his say. At that, he rose and made his way to the door, demonstratively, with the air of an insulted man." No wonder that Komsomol members on this huge farm "do not give battle to the disorder" caused by the manager who "fails to listen to the young ones and does not take into consideration their just demands . . ."¹¹

At an ore-concentrating mill in the Kemerovo Region a thirty-year-old shop manager, an engineer who had finished his studies and got his diploma only some six years earlier, refused to come to a Komsomol meeting, saying: "I am past that age bracket!" An indignant reporter wrote that, despite his youth, the manager seemed to him "a very old man with cold eyes, his heart long since cooled off," who had himself dug "an impassable abyss between the collective and himself."¹²

A manager does not come to his plant's Party meeting even

when especially invited; he "does not find it necessary to come."[13]
But sometimes a local Party organization shows signs of opposition and strength to such an extent the plant's manager feels he
must mix in its affairs. In such cases he makes it a point to come
to its meetings even if uninvited—to fight and dominate it. Thus
the head of a factory at Kazan, accused by Party functionaries of
dishonesty and inefficiency, tried to run the plant's Party organization as part of his managerial prerogative. At one Party meeting
the functionaries attempted to snub and punish him by omitting
him from the membership of the presidium. The manager strode
to the head table and arrogantly took a seat right next to the
chairman. Protesting voices came from the audience, but the
manager ordered the chairman: "Put an end to this bazaar!"[14]

At times a manager won't even let a Party meeting be summoned at his establishment. This happened at a district headquarters of a state agency in charge of cattle-fodder supply in the
Tyumen Region, in Western Siberia. When Communists on his
staff planned to call a meeting to discuss what they considered to
be his mismanagement, he blew up: "You want to criticize? A
meeting? I forbid it! I am the boss and not subject to account to
anyone here . . ." The local Party functionaries tried to complain
to a higher Party authority—to the District secretary—but he
refused to hear them out. They wrote him a letter, but there was
no answer.[15]

When a Party secretary is properly cowed or otherwise impressed by a manager, he may even suppress a Party Bureau
resolution aimed at the manager. This happened at a machine
shop in Kazan, where such a resolution included an order to the
secretary to relay it to the higher Party Committees. The secretary
simply hid this antimanager resolution.[16]

Sometimes a Party secretary balks at the manager's attempts to
control him. This happened at a state building-and-repair agency
in Odessa, and so the manager called a clandestine meeting of the
agency's Communists to plot the undoing of the secretary and of a
few of his friends, even though summoning Communists to a
meeting without the knowledge of their Party Bureau is a deadly
sin in the Party's book.[17]

III

On occasion Party functionaries come out against managers
not in the name of the Party (or Komsomol) but on behalf of

other organizations ostensibly independent of the Party but actually set up and run by the Party, such as trade unions, cooperatives, and cultural groups. In a typical case of this kind Yevgeny Menzelintsev, manager of a large state farm in Western Siberia, was charged with arbitrariness and arrogance: first he failed to provide his tractor drivers and mechanics with enough work, then he fired thirteen of them "for absenteeism." One of the thirteen had in the past won various medals and other prizes as a hero of Virgin Land campaigns. Two of his awards had come from the Regional Party Committee.

"Why are you breaking the law?" the manager was asked by Party men.

"More than one thousand persons work under me," he answered. "I threw out a mere thirteen. What percentage does this constitute? One and three tenths only."

When the case of the discharged holder of awards was cited to him, the manager disdainfully replied: "But what is just one man for the state farm? This is not even one per cent, but a miserable fraction of one per cent. Don't I have the right to throw him out to maintain order?"

The Party men who came to this manager to argue with him were representatives of the trade union. But Menzelintsev paid little heed also to this variety of Party organ. When the state farm's trade union decided to give a certain worker the much-needed living quarters in a newly built house, the manager announced: "It does not matter what they have decided." He gave the space to a more favored employee.

The manager was supposed to make his frequent appearance at the local union's meetings, but in two years he came to just one meeting. The regional presidium of the union twice discussed the manager's arrogance and each time passed a resolution deploring his behavior, but no measures against him were recommended to the Party and the state. The decisions in the matter "ended in very mild appeals to him to behave better." Complaints lodged with the manager's personnel-office inspector were of no avail, because the inspector turned out to be the manager's own wife. But his real power rested in the protection, or "hand," as the Russians call it, somewhere in the higher echelons. And those who complained against him and his wife ended their tale dolefully: "In such a matter, of course you have to have a hand."[18]

Defying the trade union, a manager will decree overtime hours and "often will not even pay for them." He will capriciously move

the day of workers' rest from Sunday to some other day of the
week, and order their payment for Sunday toil at regular rates,
not the higher rates officially set for labor on holidays.[19]

At an Omsk plant the manager announced to the workers on a
Saturday that "tomorrow is not Sunday but Friday, and we will
work as usual," thus robbing his crew of the weekly respite just
because his plan was in arrears. In the Kirov Region, in the Urals,
a submanager declared that Sundays were "shown erroneously in
the second half of each month." There were to be no Sundays! In
Leningrad a manager warned: "I will fire those who refuse to
work on holidays."[20]

The manager of a Donets Basin coal mine made the first shift
come to work on all Sundays, crediting the output now to Saturday, now to Monday, "depending on the [degree of] fulfillment
of the weekly plan."[21]

Neither the Party authorities nor those other faithful servitors
of the Party—trade-union officials—do much to stop such managers. Yet, following Stalin's death, in the mid-'50s, the presidium
of the Supreme Soviet reminded the trade unions of their rights
vis-à-vis managers, if only to cut down the number of individual
labor-abuse complaints by then cluttering Soviet courts. Each
factory, plant, and mine was from then on to have its own commission on labor disputes, composed of an equal number of representatives of labor and of management. Should a worker be
dissatisfied with the commission's verdict, he could appeal to the
executive committee of the local trade union. Cases were to go to
people's courts under extreme circumstances, only when the local
commissions and committees failed to settle them. But in the '60s
it was still found that "trade-union organizations do not always
avail themselves of the rights extended to them."[22] In many instances and in many ways managers still did as they pleased.

Often a wily manager attempts to be literally a law unto himself. He clothes his orders into as legal a form as possible, even
though there is no Soviet legality behind these orders whatever.
When a Moscow investigator called on the manager-satrap of a
Ukrainian lime mill, the man proudly displayed a bound volume
of the orders and directives he had issued. "I am not an anarchist," he declared. "Everything is formalized, for everything there is
an order." But one of his orders included his own decree setting
aside not only a trade union's decision in a labor dispute but even
a district court's verdict against him.[23]

I V

Quite revealing is the main reason given by local Party organizations or individual functionaries for their retreat before managers, for their reluctance or refusal to take measures against the executives' misdeeds, or for the outright cover-up the local Party organs provide for those misbehaving industrial gentry. The reason is, usually, the managers' competence and efficiency.

In the case of one arbitrary manager at Novokuznetsk, in southcentral Siberia, the plant's Party secretary said in answer to subordinates' complaints: "We know that Fedortsov is rude and doesn't like criticism. But he is, after all, a good specialist. And as leader he has plenty of will power." A correspondent commented indignantly: "The Party Committee's secretary holds that these qualities outweigh everything else."[24]

Frequently the local Party functionary adds to his defense of the manager the argument of the latter's indispensability. Good men are scarce, so what if they are arrogant or embezzle a little or even much. It isn't so easy to find a replacement. The sacrosanct plan must be fulfilled. "Yes, our manager is rude, but look at his energy. Does he fulfill the plan? Yes, he does. No great harm if he is a little rude." Just see to it that a Party secretary trying to deal with him can shout back. But Peter Gazarov, manager of a tobacco factory in Samarkand, is so tough and the plant's Party secretary so mild (once she slumped over in a heart attack when the manager roared at her) that "the Party Bureau actually removed itself from any control over production." Indeed, "how can it implement its right of such control when the Party Bureau secretary fears to enter the manager's office?" And thus Gazarov "does not permit criticism and is convinced of his immunity."[25]

A Komsomol official came to a North Caucasian manager with a request to set aside a room in the plant for young workers' boxing. The manager yelled at him "Turn left. What do you see? The door? That's right . . ." The official obediently marched out.[26] Utter meekness is the hallmark of some Party functionaries in their reaction to managers. The manager of the Omsk ventilation-equipment works behaved "like a feudal princeling." He cursed his subordinates for the slightest mistake; he pocketed one quarter of the bonus fund as prizes for his own work, and he shouted at those who objected: "I am the boss here. What do you understand—I myself am an engineer!" And so objections sub-

sided in fear. A newspaper correspondent noted: "As you analyze
the minutes of workers' meetings and of the Party Bureau's sessions, you will nowhere find any criticism of the manager." Also
in Omsk the manager of a tire factory was "a very knowledgeable,
educated, wise, but haughty man." Engrossed in the factory's
production problems, he increasingly neglected to be good to his
workers, to take care of their needs. And what did the plant's
Party Committee do about it? Nothing. "Sparing his sensitivity,
they kept silent. After all, he was so well known in the city."[27]
In Kursk, thefts committed by two submanagers at a shoe
factory were discussed at a closed session of the local Party Bureau, which voted a reprimand, but decided not to bring the case
to the attention of an open meeting of all the Communists of the
factory. "It would somehow be awkward to publicize it at the
meeting," one Bureau member said. "After all, men of a higher
category, leaders, are involved. Their authority may suffer . . ."
The other members of the Party Bureau agreed.[28]

In Arkhangelsk on the White Sea a subordinate exposed his
manager publicly for some faked figures in reports. The manager
responded by branding the subordinate, also in public, as "a
demagogue." Several days later the subordinate was summoned
into the august presence of a Party District Committee secretary,
who praised the author of the antimanager sally for his courage,
for his "Bolshevik standing up for principle," for his "intolerance
of what hampers our progress." But the secretary wound up his
panegyric by suggesting that the critic "not make any more noise
about it," so as "not to undermine his [the manager's] authority."[29]

Not infrequently the manager and the Party combine forces to
prosecute the manager's critic through the courts. Thus in Odessa,
at a roofing-materials plant, a Communist worker in charge of a
special Party Control Commission was investigating the manager's efficiency and honesty. He uncovered considerable theft of
roof iron, but, for his pains, was himself charged by the manager
with stealing the iron. Action was taken on the charge; the Communist zealot was suspended from the job, and while the charge
was being investigated the luckless man spent his days idle, waiting at the plant's gates, and the manager rubbed his hands in joy:
"Got caught, little pigeon! Now you will know how to criticize
and inform on us!"[30]

The least that may happen to a manager's gadfly is demotion.
In Ryazan, at a fiber mill, a young Komsomol member reported

to his superiors that two submanagers were "cheating the state" in all sorts of "dirty machinations." Neither the manager nor the mill's Komsomol supported him. "Moreover, they gave him short shrift: he was dismissed from the Komsomol Committee and demoted from his foreman's job to that of janitor."[31]

Some managers are not at all shy in reminding the would-be fighters about the dangers of fighting them. In the Donets Basin, the manager of a coal mine boasted to the local Party functionaries: "You can't take me with bare hands. I have a 'hand' myself." In this case, the protecting "hand" was a kinsman who happened to be the managing director in charge of a number of mines, including this one.[32]

The futility of fighting such managers is all too evident. At the Michurin locomotive-repair shops in the Tambov Region, "people stopped going to the Party Committee to complain" against the manager's irregularities. "Just try! The manager will get even with you."[33] In a sports-goods store at Lipetsk, in southcentral European Russia, two managers stole some money, but when an inspector found a shortage they forced several innocent salesgirls to make up the missing sum. The poor girls had to hock or sell their coats and borrow rubles from kind neighbors. When they finally went to complain to a Party secretary, that worthy said he was too busy to listen to them. While dashing past them to an appointment he counseled them "to write and complain as little as possible." And another official agreed: "Yes, you had better keep quiet. Don't buck the tide . . ."[34]

To prove to the complainers how risky indeed it is to complain, there is a steady and perfectly astonishing procession of reports in the Soviet press detailing, in case after case, dismissal of those who dare to complain or inform against arbitrary or thieving managers.

In Tula, near Moscow, Boris Baranov, a plant's Party secretary tried to upbraid his manager and his immediate aides for drinking and other "un-Party" behavior. His wife Maria Baranova, also a Party faithful, encouraged him to be implacable in his criticism. The manager struck back. He and his cronies accused Baranov of being "a slanderer and an idler, politically immature." The Party's District Committee relieved Baranov of his post as secretary, and the manager fired him from his job. Maria wrote a letter of complaint to the Moscow *Sovetskaya Rossiya*. The letter was printed, and the readers were invited to comment.[35] While some readers wrote in to applaud Boris and Maria, others said the

couple were not realistic. From the Voronezh Region, N. Samoi-
lenko philosophized:

> Maria Baranova is naïve. She should have known that the one-boss
> system or the so-called "power on the spot" is the base of our social
> relations. How can you under such conditions talk about principle?
> Only that person lives well who can cuddle up [doglike] to the legs
> [of the boss]. Baranov would have been working in peace and
> quiet even now, if it had not been for his wife with her insistence
> on principle.

D. Cheliayev, from Irkutsk in Siberia, echoed the sentiment:

> The plant manager's opinions and deeds, no matter what they may
> be, are always supported by Party and trade-union organizations.
> That is why there are so few Don Quixotes who dare to stand up
> for truth in an argument with the manager.

They sum up: "Don't fight the one in power."[36] And the
managers are indeed the ones in power.

Sometimes a critic of the manager is harassed so much and so
skillfully that finally he resigns himself. Typically this happened in
Murom, the Vladimir Region, where the manager of the railroad
transport section of the Upper Volga Council of People's Economy protected an engineer on his staff against charges of wheeling-
dealing. The charges were pressed through Party channels by a
lower-echelon Communist on the staff. The manager began his
campaign against the Communist: he "picked on him at every
turn, threatened him, was rude to him." And the faithful Communist could not stand it; he wearily resigned. When a higher
authority tried to tell the City Party Committee secretary that the
manager should be fired, the reply was that "the Committee con-
siders him irreplaceable."[37]

In case after case the managers' critics are reprimanded by the
Party. Sometimes, however, the manager too receives a reprimand. Although such a rebuke is entered in the man's Party file, it
is generally viewed as a mere formality by all concerned, is never
taken seriously, and is promptly forgotten. A loyal newspaper
correspondent indignantly defined the Party reprimand to a manager as "a kind of safeguard certificate for a man with nerve, for a
criminal."[38] Having received such a censure, the managerial
wrongdoer usually feels he has thereby paid his debt to Soviet
society and can from now on continue with his stealing and
wheeling-dealing ever so more boldly.

The manager of a large flour mill in Siberia illegally established a private farm, with flocks of ducks, geese, and chickens, with a cow or two supplying his personal table with fresh milk, and with a hired woman to look after all this. He bought three cars—two for his sons, one for himself. Looking ahead to either retirement or another job in warmer climes, he shipped lumber (filched from the state yards) thousands of miles away, to a delightful spot in the Ukraine, where trusted contractors built a house for him. And when he was caught by the state authorities, he "found high-placed defenders" of his conduct, and for his punishment "he got by with a reprimand" from the Party. Bitterly commenting on the manager's luck, one Siberian citizen advised another: "No one needs your honesty, modesty, and principles. Look how they live, learn to live from those who work as little as they wish but get more than they need."[39]

V

An important factor in the ascendancy of the manager over the Party organization is of course his control of the nation's economic assets. If he is a clever manipulator, and often he is, he can in ways blunt or subtle share his particular factory's goods, services, or money with the Party functionary assigned to supervise him. The Party no longer being a fanatical or idealistic category of Russians, its functionaries turn out to be human enough to want a share of the manager's loot. Thus, many a Party hack ceases to be the gadfly that the hierarchy in Moscow wishes him to be. He becomes a junior accomplice of the manager.

At Yoshkar-Ola, in the Mari Autonomous Republic (former Cheremiss area) on the Upper Volga, two managers of a business-machine factory lined their own pockets lawlessly, but "the plant's Party Committee did not expose in time these business executives who took the path of cheating the state." And this happened because most likely the secretary of the Party Committee himself had accepted several "illegal bonuses."[40] At Ki-selevsk, in southcentral Siberia, in a period of two years some fifty scarce automobiles were bought by managers from the state wholly against the law. The men "later resold them at black-market prices," making juicy un-Communist profits for themselves. When informers brought the matter to the attention of local Party organizations, one committee passed the buck to another, until the City Party Committee "quashed it." One of the disappointed informers exclaimed: "You will ask, Why?" And he gave his own answer: Because officials of the Party Committee were "unashamedly" in on the deal, at least two of its secretaries getting their rake-off in cars.[41]

A local Party secretary can sometimes be taken over by an enterprising manager at the cost of a rather small handout. A Moscow brewery was exposed as a nest of inefficiency and thievery while officially boasting of overfulfillment of its production plan and, just before its exposure, arranging a television demonstration of nonexistent automation of its bottling. When the mess was exposed, the cry went up: Where was the plant's Party Secretary all the time? The answer came at once: In partnership with the thieving manager. The manager had been clever enough to appoint the Party secretary to the job of the plant's chief engineer-designer—although the secretary had neither a diploma nor any prior experience qualifying him for the job. But the trick was well turned: the secretary barred any and all complaints against the manager from ever reaching the Party meetings at the plant. Soon the grateful manager saw to it that the secretary received a cash bonus for his allegedly excellent "engineering" work.[42]

Two terms have appeared in the Soviet Russian language to define the wrongdoing of officials, particularly of managers: *ochkovtiratel'stvo* and *pripiski*. These mean, respectively, "pulling wool over the eyes" (literally: "rubbing the eyeglasses") and "bloating the record" (literally: "adding fake figures"). To explain: A plant may actually be behind in its official plan and quota of production. Yet its manager, with the connivance of nearly everyone on his staff, uses clever sleight-of-hand bookkeeping and misrepresents the shortages of his production as laudable surpluses. For this alleged overproduction he receives money bonuses from the cheated but gullible Soviet state. Full of caution no less than trickery, the manager shares the bonuses with everyone of consequence. In this, the local Party officials are also involved. It is very seldom that they are blissfully ignorant of the managerial peculations. They are in the know and in some indirect sharing of the bonuses. They accept from the managers bribes in money, goods, and services.

Even if some do not accept such a rake-off, they cover up for the managers because it is too late in the season to expose the irregularities. The chicanery could have been thwarted at its very start, yet the Party functionaries were too negligent when the game was as yet young and could have been stopped. Now that the cheating has rolled up to a sizable total, the exposure of the managerial thievery would bring Moscow's wrath not alone upon the managers but upon the local Party functionaries as well, on the logical premise: "Where were you all this time?" And so the Party secretaries, in the plant itself, and in the city, district, and regional headquarters, sit tight and keep quiet, sometimes counting their own share.

Thus for a number of uneasy years the Party secretaries in the city of Irbit in the Urals hoped for the best and expected the worst. They knew that the manager—and practically the whole staff—of the local truck-trailer plant lied and stole as they sent to customers hundreds of trailers without brake equipment or spare wheels, which were nevertheless triumphantly included in the "overproduction" reported to Moscow. When an occasional Communist worker wrote his complaints about this to a local newspaper, and the newspaper dared to publish it, the Regional Party Committee men chided the editors: "Was it indeed worthwhile to write about the Irbit case once again?"[43]

VI

The evolution of the relationship between the manager and the press is intriguing. In Stalinist practice the appearance of an attack on a manager in a Soviet periodical either presaged, or was concurrent with, a court action—more often a secret police move —against the victim. Not so now in these post-Stalinist times. At best, many managers simply disregard the exposés of their misbehavior; at worst, they take action against the journalists and editors.

In a typical case reported from Divnogorsk, in the Krasnoyarsk Territory (Central Siberia), the manager of a plant making reinforced-concrete equipment declared to the local Party Bureau secretary: "If you dare to write to a newspaper we will fire you from your job." The plant's newspaper nevertheless printed a few articles protesting against faked figures in production reports, and naming those responsible. One of the named, a submanager, sought out the author of the article in which he was accused, and beat him up. The editorial office started a criminal court case against the submanager, but the local Party Committee secretary summoned the beaten writer and forced him to make peace with his assailant.[44]

It is no wonder, then, that in some cases Soviet workers are fearful even to sign their own names under the complaints they send against their "grandee" managers to editors of Moscow newspapers. Such an example was cited for a state timber-rafting enterprise near Gorky on the Volga; the complaint's "authors were apparently afraid to launch an open battle against injustice, and so they hid themselves under names that were not theirs."[45]

A campaign against rural managers in the Lazarev District of the Krasnodar Territory in the North Caucasus was decided upon by the higher authority of the Party. The Party chieftains in Krasnodar, the capital of the Territory, ordered the middle-rank Party chieftains in the affected district to call a plenary session of the District Committee and there give the kolkhoz managers proper hell. The charges against the managers read that they had allowed state cattle to go down in number and productivity while individual farmers were permitted to acquire or breed an undue quantity of privately owned stock as well as to devote generally much more time and effort to their own plots and orchards at the expense of the neglected kolkhoz (that is, state) interests.

The middle-rank Party functionaries were not at all happy at the prospect of summoning such a session and hauling the managers over Marxist coals. And even less were they pleased when a reporter from the Territorial Party newspaper *Sovetskaya Kuban'* came to cover the proceedings. Chances are they knew that the session would inevitably involve their own dirty linen as well as the managers' underwear. On the legalistic excuse that the reporter was not one regularly assigned to the District, its Party chieftains barred him from the session: "You don't belong to our bush." When pressed by the reporter, the secretary of the Territorial Party Committee took the side of the District Party functionaries: "We gave no assignments to your editorial office, and there is nothing for you to do here."[46]

Some managers dare to disregard the exposés printed even in such powerful central newspapers as *Izvestiya* and *Literaturnaya gazeta*.

In 1960 workers of the Karl Marx State Farm at Mineralnyie Vody complained against the arbitrariness and rudeness of the farm's manager, who showered his crew with fines and reprimands, fired his men for no excuse or reason, and yelled at the critics on his staff: "I'll throw you out!" and "I'll skin you alive!" His friend, the City Party Committee secretary, persistently and skillfully shielded him against all such complaints—until finally someone wrote an article about it in *Literaturnaya gazeta*. This did it. The manager was dismissed. But imagine the surprise of the Moscow editors when in 1961 a fresh complaint against the arrogant and selfish manager reached *Literaturnaya gazeta* from the crew of an alcohol-making plant in the Krasnodar Territory, where the man, once dismissed, was now enjoying his promotion to the job of chief engineer.

Here again he was abusive to his workers. Also, he used the plant's workers, at the plant's expense, in the remodeling of his private apartment. Out of spite for one of the workers he ordered the sewage pipe of his apartment to be connected, not with the town's general cloaca, but with that worker's cellar. He used the plant's gasoline for his personal car and put his personal chauffeur on the plant's payroll. Last but not least he prohibited a political discussion to which the workers were summoned by a Party functionary on their own time. *Literaturnaya gazeta* was aghast. Who put this humpty-dumpty together again after that influential paper had once caused its fall from the wall? "Let us hope," it lamely concluded in its bill of particulars, "that the Krasnodar Territory Party Committee will bring clarity into this question."[47]

Even more shocked was the Moscow *Izvestiya* when nearly six months passed since it had first published a blistering exposé of managerial misconduct at the heavy-machinery plant in the nearby city of Elektrostal, but nothing was heard about any corrective or punitive action. So the editors telephoned the first secretary of the Elektrostal City Party Committee, and heard this calm reply: "We did not respond to your article because we considered it erroneous." *Izvestiya* exploded: "Where does this aristocratic scorn for the press come from? . . . Ignoring [the press] is a form of fighting against criticism, and, at that, not a nice form."[48]

Sometimes a manager, with the aid of subservient local Party chieftains, suppresses the paper itself—when it is small enough thus to be punished. In a railroad settlement in the Novosibirsk Region, an assistant stationmaster was satirized in a wall newspaper for his inefficiency in organizing snow and ice removal in his bailiwick. He forthwith demanded immediate removal of the offending newspaper from the walls. This order was carried out at once. The public exhibit of the newspaper had lasted a mere three hours. The authors of the satire brought their complaint before the secretary of the local Party Bureau, who promptly called a

Party meeting—and publicly blasted the protesting authors. Need-less to say, the critical newspaper did not reappear on any wall. It found its final resting place in the Party secretary's safe.[49]

Similarly, at Prokopyevsk in the Kuznetsk Basin, Siberia, the secretary of the Party Bureau at a coal mine confiscated the entire issue of an already printed local newspaper for daring to publish the news that a member of the mine's managerial staff had created a drunken scandal on a street. Another issue of the same news-paper was held up by another Party secretary for printing a fable about an arrogant manager. "Why did you print it?" he roared at a woman member of the editorial staff. "At whom is this fable hinting?"[50]

VII

The Party cracks down on those of its secretaries and other functionaries who cover up a manager's sins. Yet it is quite pos-sible that the Party has purposely, through its press in particular, overdrawn the picture of the managers' sins.

One purpose is to beat the rising managers down with the same stick the managers have used (in gossip and grumbling) against the Party functionaries: charging them with being inefficient, cor-rupt, superfluous, nonproducing drones and thus halting the man-agers' possible sociopolitical emergence.

Secondly, and more importantly, we see here the Party's effort to curry favor with the long-neglected and much-abused prole-tariat—by shifting the blame for the neglect and abuse from the Party to the managers.

In blackening the managers perhaps more than they deserve to be, the Party has encouraged the workers to oppose these execu-tives. Already in February 1956, at the Twentieth Party Con-gress, Khrushchev noted with sorrow that many union officials in the nation appeared to avoid disputes with industrial executives. On May 8, 1956, in a front-page editorial *Pravda* urged unions to have "a good wrangle" with their factory managers. There was thus, for a time, an attempt by the Party to use labor unions as "a new safety valve for labor tensions."[51] Characteristically, it was right after the anti-government riots of workers and students in the summer of 1962 at Novocherkassk on the Don and elsewhere that the Party, in a *Pravda* editorial, put its stern finger on "cal-lous" managers as the cause of the workers' troubles. Said the editorial:

The Party demands a careful, tactful attitude toward every man and knowledge of the needs and requirements of the workers. The Party organizations cannot tolerate that some leaders of the economy [i.e. managers] who endeavor to fulfill the plan at any price forget about the alleviation of working conditions in the workshop, care nothing . . . about labor safety and plant sanitation conditions. . . . It is necessary to be tactful toward people no matter what they may approach you with . . . and to bring to their senses callous officials who behind all their papers do not see man. . . .[52]

Thus history seems to repeat itself. In 1917, the Communists (then Bolsheviks), led by Lenin, excited and inflamed Russian workers against their capitalist bosses—against that era's upper- and middle-class factory owners, managers, and engineers. In many cases the owners and their executives and technicians were barred from even entering their premises. Some, already in their offices, were carted out ignominiously in wheelbarrows, amid hooting and curses. Later came arrests and executions of those who did not succeed in hiding or emigrating in time.

By 1966 the old classes of such owners, managers, and engineers are of course gone. The Party is now the owner. Soviet-reared managers and engineers have long since replaced their counterparts of the tsarist and Kerensky eras. But to keep its own threatened position of ownership, the Party must excite Russian workers again, this time against the new managers. Once more the Communist drones pretend to be not only a very much needed, productive element in the state but also the workers' sole protection.

But the campaign differs from that old 1917–18 outburst in one significant respect. It is not a revolution—the Party wants nothing violent. It is an evolution, or, shall I say, a counter-evolution to oppose the managerial evolution toward status and power just noted in these pages. It is a nervous but peaceful struggle against the managers who do their encroaching, which too is short of any sudden, daring coups.

CHAPTER XIII

~~~~~~~~~~~~~~~~~~~~~~~~~~~~~~~~

Underground Capitalism

ONE OF THE PARTY'S most petulant and at times ferocious charges against the technical-managerial elite is that they are too fond of comforts, and that in this fondness they either encourage illegal entrepreneurs to cater to their appetites or they themselves become illicit dealers in commodities and luxuries. In short, the Party blames much of this elite for much of the country's underground capitalism.

Theft and other crimes as part of Russia's new underground capitalism are often exposed in the Soviet press, and the accusing finger is on the managers, submanagers, engineers, and other employees of the state. An official government report revealed in the summer of 1964 that "about 20 per cent of all crimes [in the Soviet Union] involved theft of government property, 30 per cent of such thefts being committed by employees of the government organizations and agencies affected."[1] A typical investigation of the state trading network in Soviet Moldavia brought up the startling fact that managers and salesmen were stealing in every fifth one of 748 inspected stores.[2]

Where does this "worminess" in the seemingly "rosy apple" of the Soviet system come from? "If there is worminess this means there is a worm. But how did the worm first appear and why did we, those who live and work side by side with it, miss seeing it?"[3] To this question by a *Pravda* journalist, two *Trud* newspapermen replied that certain Soviet citizens, "by going into private enterprise, have decided to resurrect in our land the order which the revolution destroyed almost a half century ago."[4] The implication was that the Soviet people were so confident of the complete destruction of the old order of private enterprise that the latter-day wrongdoers caught the populace by surprise; that they attempted to restore private production and private trade by stealth, as it were, and certainly against the will of the overwhelming majority of the Soviet people.

But is it indeed so? In reality, private enterprise—no matter how forbidden and persecuted—never in the Soviet era died completely. And, actually, the Soviet consumer always wanted at least a modicum of private enterprise.

In 1921 Lenin had to yield to popular pressure, and he had to rescue the country from the starvation and economic chaos into which his earlier policies had plunged Russia: he gave the Russians his New Economic Policy with a limited freedom of farming, manufacture, and trade. In 1929 Stalin abolished the NEP, but private enterprise continued underground, even if precariously. In 1953 Georgiy Malenkov promised more consumer goods and, by default more than by outright permission, suffered some private enterprise to come to the surface. Late that summer I wrote in a newspaper article:

Since 1929, when the original NEP died its violent and much-lamented death, and to this day the Soviet customer has been deprived of goods in both quantity and quality; has stood in lines for hours to get the little and the shoddy that he was sold at the exorbitant prices of the state stores; has been cheated through short-weighting and short-measuring . . . has been served badly and arrogantly; and yet has never seemingly dared to complain—at least, not audibly.

So why this governmental concern for his needs now? The answer is in the Kremlin's own press, which is unwittingly frank as it declares, in so many words and quite frequently:

"The customer has money now. The customer demands."

Though there have been uprisings in Pilsen and East Berlin, none has occurred in Moscow or Kiev. The Kremlin, however, doubtless feels that there may be trouble (not necessarily in the form of outright uprisings) in its own Russian cities, and soon, unless the consumer is given better and cheaper goods, accompanied by salesmen's smiles, not snarls.

The Kremlin's fear is not of trouble from the mass of the low-paid Russian workers and peasants. They have no real purchasing power and thus are not the customers to be courted. But the new middle and upper classes, from the Stakhanovites up, do have rubles, for which they want even more comforts than they now enjoy.

Numerically small, a mere well-fed handful in the Soviet sea of misery, they are nevertheless strategically placed, both socially and geographically.

They run things for the Kremlin in the larger cities. As a technical intelligentsia and managerial group, they have risen to their
money and appetites in the last eight to fifteen years. The looting of
the satellite states since the war has speeded up the process of their
enrichment, first started at the expense of the Russian peasants and
workers (the classes from which incidentally they themselves or
their parents came). They have grown bolder, more restless. They
have to be provided with more goods, with newer and better comforts, if the Kremlin is to continue counting on them as its main
pillar.

By now it is an axiom that revolutions seldom come on empty
stomachs. More often they come on full or half-full stomachs. The
anti-Romanov revolt of March 1917 began in the prosperous
Petrograd whose women resented a temporary closing of a dozen or
so bakeries.

The question is: Can the Soviet state prevail upon its managers,
distributors, and salesmen to improve the present system of production and sales without using the real essence of Lenin's old NEP—
private enterprise?[5]

By this time, nearly thirteen years after I wrote the foregoing
paragraphs and asked my question, the answer is clear. More than
ever before in the Soviet Union private enterprise has become
inevitable, even if still denounced and banned, repressed and punished. Not only have the upper and middle classes of the country
grown yet more insistent and choosy as consumers, but increasingly larger groups of the lower strata—workers and even peasants—have come clamoring to the nation's stores and markets
with their meager rubles in search of goods and food.

The lower classes are not being paid appreciably better in these
1960s than they were in the early 1950s. But the fact of their
higher awareness of lovelier standards of living than their own;
also the land's generally freer air and thus the greater tendency to
protest against the continuing shortages and occasional price
hikes—all this has sharpened the Party's problem. And, implacably, it has emboldened the nation's illegal and semilegal
chastniki, the private entrepreneurs.

So much so that on May 5, 1961, the Party found it imperative
to strike back by reintroducing the death penalty for theft of state
property—a measure aimed at the resurgent, rampant private
enterprise, and soon widened to include bribery, forgery, and
blackmarketing of currency and other valuables as punishable by
shooting.[6]

In the summer of 1962 the consumer, aggrieved against the

state and the Party, went into a kind of action that had hardly seemed possible in 1953: he rose in riots in Novocherkassk and other Soviet cities, protesting the increase of prices for meat and butter just announced by the government. The riots were bloodily suppressed. Still, both the consumer and the illegal entrepreneur continued—the former by grumbling, and by patronizing the underground capitalist; the latter by persisting with his enterprise.

Thus did the populace of all classes answer the question of 1953 throughout the eleven years of Khrushchev's reign. And this is still the people's reply to the Party in the post-Khrushchevian times as well.

I I

The large-scale, elaborate organization of this "economic crime" against the Party is wondrous to behold. Its broad expanse and high frequency come to light in the arrests of its practitioners. (The thought, of course, always occurs: How great must the underwater part of the iceberg be! How many more cases of illegal enterprise go undetected and unpunished!) To cite a series of notable examples of Soviet life and trade in the 1960s:

More than 900 lathes from several Central Russian machine-making plants were sold "on the left" (the Russian expression for "illegally") by a ring of several managers and engineers. Their partners and clients represented blackmarketing interests spread over Central Asia, the Caucasus, and other provinces. One branch alone did business in thirty-five cities. Two women engineers, employed in a central government office in charge of Soviet machine-building, covered up the ring by issuing fake documents which authorized the sale of the lathes. When arrested they said they were insulted "to be placed on the same level with thieves." They admitted they had taken bribes, but protested: "We took them not from any dirty fly-by-night broker but from completely decent intellectuals . . ." The two women drew ten years of prison each, and those who bribed them were jailed for twelve and fifteen years. The leader, a machine-plant manager, was shot.[7]

In Frunze, capital of Kirghizia, a ring consisting of fifty-four members was uncovered. It was led by the head of the State Planning Committee of the Kirghiz Republic, a deputy minister of trade, two textile factory managers, and a number of other plant and store executives. The charge against them was embezzlement of a total of 3,100,000 rubles through illegal production and sale, for their own profit, of textiles in several Soviet republics. At one of their factories they even organized a special department, solely for their black-market business, equipping it with machinery bought in Moscow, Poltava, and Alma-Ata, in some cases facilitating such deals with bribery, in others brandishing their official or semiofficial documents at naïve state chiefs in charge of the equipment which they had the right to maintain but not sell.

The ring manufactured curtains, carpets, and other consumer goods, using silk, wool, artificial viscose, and other materials in short supply. Thanks to the wide range of talent among the members, their functions were distributed properly, along the lines of a solid private enterprise: some supervised manufacture, others were in charge of transportation and sales, still others saw to the concealment and protection of operations. Regular meetings of the members, and the dividing of "the black treasury," took place in the office of one of the managers.

But finally somebody slipped, and the ring was undone. In a public trial four chief defendants were sentenced to be shot; a number of their lesser associates were sent to prison for varied terms. The "unclean" profits of the ring members, confiscated at their arrest, included more than 23 kilograms of gold, 30 kilograms of silver, and a million or so of rubles in cash and property, this last including passenger cars, villas, and "objects of luxury." One of the managers had a weakness for rugs: 20 of them were found in his house.[8]

The presence of a bookkeeper among conspirators is imperative—to juggle records so as to "lower all ends into water" (a Russian folk saying for "successfully conceal"). In fact, sometimes a bookkeeper, rather than a manager, is the head of the plot. In Baku a bookkeeper was chief of eleven conspirators, most of them shoe-factory and shoe-store managers; they were responsible for the theft of 56,000 rubles' worth of footwear. The modus operandi was clever yet simple: the bookkeeper issued fictitious documents claiming that shoes failed to arrive from state factories as ordered, or that other shoes were returned to the factories; the stock of shoes thus accumulated was sold through the stores where the group had accomplices, and the receipts divided. The bookkeeper was shot, and the other ten were given long jail terms.[9]

A highly placed staff member of the State Planning Committee (Gosplan) in Moscow was found to be a bribe-taking accomplice of a many-branched underground combine dealing on a large scale in automobile tires (sold at three times their state-decreed price),

roof tiles and roof metals (at hundreds of rubles' profit per ton),
and other merchandise in short supply and therefore eagerly
blackmarketed.

Yuri Saksagansky, one of the ring's leaders, was officially employed by a kolkhoz as an expediter, and this gave him the needed
cover to live in Moscow and to buy, sell, and barter with quick-
fingered state factory and store managers all over the Soviet empire. He and his men moved large shipments of lumber, glass,
rubber, and other commodities to and from Moldavia, Karelia,
Georgia, Moscow, Voronezh, and other areas.

Among the fast-dealing partners were the two Dunduas, father
and son, the father a retired engineer, the son a physician specializing in cancer research and treatment. The father had moved
from his native Georgia to Moscow to initiate his surgeon-son
into the intricacies of illegal commerce. The elder Dundua said to
the younger one: "You know half of Moscow. Find me people
who could help me ship lumber to Georgia. There is good money
in it nowadays."[10] This was how, most likely, such high-level contacts as the Gosplan men were reached and drawn into the ring—
if you are a cancer expert you may easily have intimate acquaintances among the mighty patients at the Soviet top.

Speaking of medicine, at least two cases have been brought to
court involving the use of mental patients in state hospitals as
workers in underground capitalistic enterprises. The excuse for
such employment was its therapeutic value. In both instances
knitted goods and other wearing apparel or textile goods were
illegally produced and sold for private enrichment.

In the first case, at Lvov in the Western Ukraine, the chief
physician of the psychiatric hospital agreed to the proposal made
by a group of entrepreneurs, to establish at the hospital "a cure-
through-labor shop" on the condition that the apparel produced
would be kept for the needs of the hospital itself and of other
health establishments of the city. But once entrenched, the entrepreneurs disregarded this rule. They shipped and sold the output all
over the Soviet Union. The ring's profit reached 250,000 rubles by
the time the authorities caught up with the scheme. Its leader was
shot, and the others sent to prison for long terms.[11]

The second and yet bigger case occurred in Moscow and resulted in three million rubles' profit for twenty-three participants.
A total of fifty-two plants, cooperatives, and collectives found
themselves eventually connected with the ring's business somehow
or other. The ring bought 460 tons of wool in Lithuania, North

Caucasus, Central Asia, and other parts of the Soviet empire. They purchased 58 knitting machines and other equipment in Leningrad, Poltava, and Moscow itself. All these deals were strictly against the Soviet law, but the ring managed them well. To supplement the work of mental patients at the hospital where most of the sweaters and jackets were produced, the partners established additional shops in rented basements elsewhere in Moscow. They made a deal with officials of two state factories to which they sent the patient's output for dyeing and other improvement. They bribed hospital chiefs and other health officials, police officers, and labor inspectors. Managers of stalls and stores at railroad stations and on the cities' markets in poor sections shared in the profits as they sold the production. The material was often shoddy, as the ring tried to economize on the wool content. After the arrests it was noticed that the ringleader, when brought from his cell for questioning, wore a different woolen shirt every time, and each shirt was new and of foreign make. He was finally asked why he was not using shirts of his own manufacture. He replied: "I am not a fool to wear rags . . ." More than 100 kilograms of gold were confiscated from the ring members, of which quantity 52 kilograms were taken from the leader. Besides, there were diamonds, platinum, and cash. The sentence was death by shooting for the leader and severe jail sentences for the others.[12]

One imaginative citizen not only organized an illegal factory in the basement of his house but prospered and dared enough to turn a state plant in the same industry into a virtual branch of his underground enterprise.

His name was Nikolai Kotliar, and his business record went back to pre–World War II days when he was a modest state-employed retail-stall manager at a Moscow market. Already then, despite his small salary, he had put aside sufficient funds to buy and furnish excellent living quarters near the capital and to invest in various illegal trade deals. He sat out the war in the safety of Central Asia, then returned to Moscow to steal and sell scarce chemicals, also to deal in foreign money. In 1957 he was caught and sentenced to ten years in a concentration camp; but, with the aid of influential friends, he was paroled in December 1959.

It was then that, in partnership with another man, he organized his own basement factory for making lipstick. He had three modern machines; he installed all the necessary utilities: water, gas, electricity; "he lined the walls with blond ceramic tiles." His working staff included his wife; his daughter, a student at the Moscow Engineering-Economics Institute; and a nephew, who was a dental technician at a nearby state farm but apparently was seldom, if ever, on his proper job.

The machines were copies of the installations used at a certain state factory in Riga. It was from the same factory that Kotliar began to receive lipstick cases. In 1960 alone a total of 59,000 such cases were obligingly delivered to him by a special courier in a car or by rail. More and more of the Riga factory's executives went on Kotliar's payroll (over and above their regular state salaries). They and Kotliar viewed the Riga plant "as their own patrimony." The group included the plant's manager, chief engineer, two bookkeepers in charge of the plastics department, and others. They shipped to Kotliar their Riga plant's chemical formulas, equipment, and lipstick cases. Some of the latter were, however, manufactured not at the plant but in a kind of cottage industry, established by the conspirators in the private homes of Riga workers in need of extra earnings.

Profits of Kotliar and Company were considerable, and their living was high—at seashore resorts, in expensive restaurants, with travel in their own latest automobiles, with purchase and piling up of diamonds and other valuables—until the police got on the group's trail and arrested them. Kotliar and one of his codefendants were shot, and the others sent to prison for long terms.[13]

Nor does one have to return from exile to become an illegal entrepreneur. The perfectly astonishing case of one V. Seredkin, better known as "the King of the Taiga," was reported from northern Siberia, where this colorful man made illegal deals for four years before he was caught and sentenced to twelve years in prison. A true inheritor of the best traditions of the old-time pioneers who had once opened and settled Siberia, this man took lumbering and transportation contracts to bring timber and other goods down the difficult rivers and across the wild forests. He hired gangs of men as free in spirit as himself; he cajoled and browbeat Party officials to help his unique private enterprise most illegally. But he gave the people and industries of Siberia what they needed.[14]

III

Soviet court cases involving black-market dealing in gold, platinum, silver, diamonds, and foreign currency are at times particularly spectacular. When such underground trade is uncovered and the "firms" are arrested and tried, it becomes a matter of wonder that so many men could flourish in this business for so long, each group with branches or agents in so many cities, without detection. But when they are nabbed and their valuables are seized by the state, the richness of the government's loot is both a yardstick of the vastness of the culprits' operations and an explanation of why they had been invulnerable to detection for such a lengthy time.

The explanation, freely whispered all over the Soviet Union, is that the black-market dealers in gold and money exchange are purposely left alone by the secret police for weeks and months: to let them accumulate those stocks until they are large enough to be of some use to the state treasury. American dollars and British pounds sterling, Swiss francs and Swedish kronor—in short, all "hard" *valyuta* (currency)—are needed for the state's trade, diplomacy, and secret service abroad. The under-the-counter jewelers and the back-alley exchange brokers are a breed most necessary to the Party's grand design.

If any surprise is in order at all it may be our puzzlement over the childishness of these Russian entrepreneurs: Don't they know that the secret police keep their eye on them all the while, that the police simply allow these underground gold-and-dollars men to fatten the inventory before grabbing the valuables and killing or exiling their owners and traders?

But, most likely, each operator hopes that *he* will escape detection and arrest, that *he* will be able to enjoy his trade and his growing property of valuables to the natural end of his life, many years hence. And some perhaps do evade the net of the secret police and do survive in full illegal possession of their property and prosperity. A few may even escape ruin thanks to, not despite, the secret police, by making, in good season, supersecret deals with a few individual policemen, who then extend their ironclad protection in exchange for payment. Such contracting parties may very well succeed against all the odds, even as they live with one another in a kind of uneasy amity.

I V

The presence of engineers, technicians, and other such professional intellectuals was notable among the defendants shot or jailed for long terms in the Rokotov case, one of the earliest to be widely publicized by the Soviet government when it began its anti–"black-bourse" campaign in earnest, in 1961.[15]

True, the ringleader himself, Yan Rokotov (nicknamed Yan Kosoi, or John the Cross-Eyed), only pretended to be an intellectual. In his lapel he wore the coveted pin to which a Soviet college graduate is entitled (*universitetsky znachyok,* or university badge), but which he had not earned, since he quit school in his middle teens. He now said he had the degree of candidate of the juridical sciences; but at times he said he was an astronomer. He looked the part of a professional intellectual, for his "face was well cared for."

But his closest associates, who dealt with him in gold, platinum and foreign currency totaling millions of rubles, did have genuine degrees and diplomas. Vladislav Faibishenko was a graduate of the Electric Energy Technicum who refused to take a job in the provinces to which the government tried to send him in 1957, but remained in Moscow, to spend the four years until his final arrest in "chasing after foreigners," buying and selling gold and currency, making huge profits—between brief and mild jail sentences.

Yustin Lagun was a construction engineer and a bona fide "young scientist," as he liked to introduce himself to his black-bourse clients and, later, to the judges at his trial. Indeed, he had completed all his graduate work and was, at the time of his arrest, "five minutes short of being a candidate of the technical sciences." His publication record included fifteen scientific-journal articles. His young wife, Eleonora Lagun, was a ballerina at the Bolshoi Theater. His middle-aged mistress, Yelena Polianskaya, was assistant director of the Central Scientific Research Institute of Building Designs. It was she who helped to place Lagun on the Institute's prestigious staff, where he was given the opportunity to write his dissertation. Polianskaya also helped Lagun by serving now and then as a middlewoman in currency transactions. The court proceedings did not quite bring out whether Lagun's mistress aided her lover in bribing the personnel officials of Bolshoi Theater into giving Lagun's wife that wonderful job as ballerina. Lagun loved his beautiful wife, but he was pleasant to his useful mistress when in his frequent phone calls to Yelena Polianskaya at the Institute he would tell her that he wouldn't show up at the office or laboratory: "Pussycat, I have a little headache after last night. I'll stay home today."

Sergei Popov was a pianist, and his wife Nadezhda Edlis an

official of the Central House of People's Creativity. Yan Rokotov's own girl friend, Tatiana Umnova, was for a time a student
at the Moscow Institute of Fine Chemical Technology. When she
was expelled "for immoral conduct," Yan suggested that she
conceal this calamity from her folks at home. To substitute for
the student's monthly stipend which she had lost through expul-
sion he began to pay her a subsidy out of his own voluminous
pocket.

The ring was active from 1957 to 1960, when it was rounded
up. The trial took place in Moscow in June 1961, and at first
resulted in no death sentences. Yan Rokotov, Vladislav Faibishenko, and Nadezhda Edlis, the three leaders, were given fifteen
years' "deprivation of freedom" each (in a concentration camp
rather than in a jail, most likely). Yustin Lagun was among those
sentenced to eight years. The group's confiscated property included 12 kilograms of gold coins alone, a large quantity of foreign currency, and much other valuable property.

The higher authorities found the sentences too lenient; the
Moscow judges were clearly unaccustomed to meting out death by
shooting, a punishment which had been reintroduced just one
month before. On review, the Supreme Court changed the sentences of Rokotov and Faibishenko to death. Soon thereafter the
two were shot.

Another engineer was among the five leaders of a gold-and-
foreign-currency concern operating illegally in Minsk, the capital
of Belorussia, its network extending to more than a dozen Soviet
cities, among them Riga, Kaunas, Vilnyus, Kishinev, Lvov,
Leningrad, and Kiev. All five were sentenced to death, and thirteen others—ranging in age from twenty-five to sixty-five—were
sent to prison for terms of five to fifteen years.[16] In a Vilnyus case,
the turnover of diamonds, gold, and foreign currency was estimated at 1,300,000 rubles. In the American money handled by
this combine, one operation involved a one-thousand-dollar bill
that somehow found its way into the ring's coffers. In the final
reckoning four of the firm's members were shot, and four others
jailed for four to ten years.[17]

Similar cases, ending in death sentences and stiff jail terms,
have in recent years been reported from Chernovtsy in the Western Ukraine, Kishinev in Moldavia, Tbilisi in Georgia, Baku in
Azerbaijan, and Alma-Ata in Kazakhstan. At Rostov on the Don,
one Ivan Avanesov displayed the humor of the doomed when he
described himself to the judges as "the king of the black market, a

millionaire."[18] The hiding places for his gold and foreign currency were under an asphalt pavement near his house, a flour bin in his barn, and some chicken dung in the coop. At Alma-Ata, secret-police agents had to use a mine detector to find two kilograms of gold stashed away by another dealer.[19] The cache of a ringleader at Mineralnyie Vody yielded, among other valuables, a quantity of Japanese yen.[20] The treasury of the group seized in Chernovtsy included, not alone gold ingots, diamonds, and foreign money, but even a check payable at the Bank of England.[21]

That some of these surreptitious dealings involve a direct connection with foreign banks and foreign sources of purchases of gold and other valuables, has been brought out in several cases. In the trickle of Soviet citizens going abroad these days, mostly on governmental missions, a few daring men now and then decide to make small fortunes in illegal gold and currency transactions. From Soviet Georgia, a technician named Parmen Stazhadze was sent to serve as an expert on a railroad-building project in Iraq. But "he was envious of American businessmen, and instead of occupying himself with his mission, Comrade Stazhadze made a deal with an Arab merchant," buying gold from him—apparently to smuggle it into Russia for a profitable resale. But he did not have enough money of his own to pay for the gold, so he made up the purchase price by turning over to the Arab the drugs meant for the treatment of Soviet specialists in Iraq, to which valuable medicine stores he apparently had access.[22]

V

Despite all such draconian legislation as the May 5, 1961, death law and all the other earlier and later harsh decrees, the black-marketeer of the 1960s knows how to protect himself or herself against detection and punishment—for some time, at least. He is a polished and accomplished man or woman—clever, suave, quick, slippery. He is

> not the petty bag-dragger of the 1920s. He does not use his fists to gain for himself the third upper shelf of an overcrowded railroad car. He does not implore a railroader aide for Christ's sake to let him take a sack of potatoes along. He does not shake in his boots at a mere glimpse of a distant policeman's cap. Today's black-marketeer has learned to use up to 200 per cent all the wide rights that Soviet society affords a toiler. And he tries his utmost to camouflage himself as a toiler. Even if the camouflage fails him, the black-

marketeer knows how to appeal to the souls of men standing on guard over our laws; how to play upon them in order to escape the penalty.[23]

To their arresters and grillers, and later in the dock to their judges, these "economic criminals" may plead guilty and admit that there was really no excuse for their transgression of Socialist laws. But very few of them are actually convinced that they have done wrong. Justifications which they and their clients often use among themselves are many and self-righteous.

"What sort of private entrepreneur am I?" a Belorussian contractor exclaimed to the prosecutor's staffmen questioning him. "I am a toiler. The moneys I made are a toiler's kopeks." And he flung on the questioners' desk his labor book in which his friends, industrial managers in the area, had properly and officially testified that there was nothing illegal in his work of building and remodeling furnaces. The labor book did not, of course, say that, in addition to his own honest labor, the contractor used help which he hired and put on the payroll, and that on his contracts the managers paid out state sums twice as high as the law allowed —two serious transgressions of Soviet Socialism.[24]

Managers and their Party guardian angels—Party secretaries who aid and abet them—justify their participation in underground capitalism by asking: "And do you think that other managers don't risk such deals? One must build, but there are no building materials. And so one must take a risk! If he is not caught, he is lucky."[25]

A sinning submanager of a kolkhoz was caught and reprimanded; he was asked by a Communist zealot: "How do you now meet the eyes of the people whose leader you are? After what has happened?" The submanager jeered: "Oh go on, and who is without sin? Nobody's conscience is clear." The zealot was in despair: "He is not tormented by his conscience, his repentance. . . . Here it is, the thief's philosophy—it seems to him that everybody steals."[26] "We are not the only ones, and others take more than we do," ran the staff's excuse at a sugar refinery in the Ukraine where stealing and illegal selling of sugar was uncovered.[27]

If a man ventures into underground capitalism he takes chances, and this also should be considered as a mitigating circumstance. The manager of a state cattle-purchasing station in the North Caucasus was exposed in his illegal private machinations. Yet, at his trial, his lawyer's plea won him acquittal: "Yes, Albegov indeed faked those prices [and thus made profits for himself], but he [at times] suffered losses, too. Therefore how can you talk of a crime here!"[28]

In another nearby area of the North Caucasus, buying of spare machine parts on the black market was explained by the postulate that "such is life." An official said: "Legally it is a crime, but in practice this is our daily life." In other words, human nature is stronger than dogma, and a law or a set of laws is invalid if it goes against life, counter to human nature. As the result, black markets in certain districts of the North Caucasus "have become almost legalized and open!"[29]

An appeal is heard at many a factory as zealous Communists are about to expose their fellow employees in stealing of state goods for private resale: "Be human!"[30] The constant refrain everywhere is: "The state will not become the poorer for it."[31] It is the Soviet populace who is poor, not the state. "I need money, you need money, everybody needs money."[32]

Socialism or not, this Soviet society is still a money society. As in the world of private capitalism, so in the Soviet Union money covers a multitude of malfeasance—or what only seems to be malfeasance but down deep in its substance isn't. In Moscow Aleksandr Sinis, a young engineer, in his spare time acted as a long-distance chauffeur to a ring of underground capitalists, transporting from city to city diamonds, gold, jewelry and other valuables. When he was arrested, his office superiors and associates were questioned. They testified that "at his job Sinis was an industrious engineer who carried out all his assignments, and who willingly did his Komsomol tasks, too." Yes, they knew that after work hours Sinis drove those cars for somebody—an uncle of his, they thought. But his immediate office superior, a woman engineer, was surprised at the charges against Sinis and his spare-time work. She said: "Yes, but after all Sinis worked, and was paid for it. Nothing immoral in that." To those questioning him about Sinis, a man technician and fellow employee argued back that "any work is moral if it is well paid."[33]

Those who inform on the lawbreakers are often ostracized. A teen-age girl reported her own mother for dishonesty at her state job of food-and-drink selling. The mother was fired from the job, was tried, and was given a suspended sentence. Another woman in the same selling line exclaimed: "Such daughters should be strangled by their mothers' own hands!" When the girl tried to find a job, every manager refused her curtly. A senior bookkeeper was horrified at the very thought of giving employment to the applicant: "But she will send all of us to prison!"[34]

Thus are the tables turned upon the zealous Communists who spy and inform on the stealers and manipulators. The popular view of the zealots does not credit them with public-mindedness, honesty, and general pure Communist conviction. To the contrary, the populace holds them guilty of the very greed of which they accuse the underground capitalists. In people's eyes any informers (disliked everywhere, but particularly in Soviet society) are selfish, pushing busybodies ever on the make. The common phrase addressed to them is: "*Chto, tebe bol'she drugikh nado?* (What, do you need more than others do?)" This is truly part and parcel of the modern Russian language, a question heard in the Soviet Union every day on every side.

Noninterference with transgressors of Soviet morality is a rule with many citizens. When a Komsomol employee was asked by the authorities how it was that she had never noticed and reported the wrongdoing of an associate at work who ran a private woolen-goods manufacturing shop on the side (with wool stolen on his state job), she replied: "Of course I knew that he lived beyond his [legal] means, and had a car of his own. But after all that was his own affair . . ."[35]

The ingenious range of some justifications is marvelous to see. A man accused of using his state-farm job to establish a private business on the side flared up: "What of it? We live not in America—we have full rights . . ."[36] This is to say: You Soviet propagandists buzz our ears with the story about how people in America are deprived of all sorts of rights, and how we have all the human rights there are, so we take you at your word.

Parasites? Illegal capitalists? Why, Friedrich Engels himself once wrote that "individual parasites will survive even under Communism."[37]

But the most sensible, practical, sober argument remains the indispensability of the private trader in this Soviet society. The populace argues something like this: We Soviet citizens should be grateful to him amid all the deficiencies, insufficiencies, and inefficiencies of the state system of production and distribution forced upon us. To cite an example: Tamara Porfiryeva, a woman doctor servicing the pilots and other personnel at the Sheremetyev Airport in Moscow, was finally caught in her longtime successful black-marketing of women's woolen jackets and other scarce merchandise. A fellow woman doctor at the airport declared to the investigator from the prosecutor's staff: "Personally I am very pleased by my purchase; I consider that Porfiryeva did me a favor." A petition, signed by a number of Doctor Porfiryeva's associates at the airport, pleaded for her that she "and her transgression do not threaten society with any great danger, since her transgression has not led to any harmful consequences."[38]

Underground manufacturers and sellers of phonograph records "do not, contrary to the commonly held opinion, make their *bizness* [only] of their rock-'n'-roll production. . . . They take advantage of the fact that many popular—and good—melodies are absent from the store counters. If a melody is liked by the public the businessman needs two or three days to issue a recording. But in the [state] stores it [a state-made record of the hit] appears only six months later!"[39] (Note that the illegal rock-'n'-roll record production is branded by the offical Soviet writer as *bizness*—the derisive Russian transliteration of the English word "business.")

The Soviet consumer needs raincoats made of synthetics, for "they are light, inexpensive, and do not let moisture through." But for a long time the Soviet state industry was sending very few such raincoats to the market. Here came private craftsmen who said: "None in the stores? Fine. We will have them on our market stalls." The private craftsmen got busy, "and displayed such inventiveness that our state personnel of planning and selling such goods could do well to learn it" from the private entrepreneurs.[40]

A private entrepreneur sees the consumer's need that can be satisfied easily, and he acts quickly, whereas the state usually flounders and blunders. At one time dust was gathering on the heavy plaid shawls piled up on the Soviet store shelves. Yet mufflers of exactly the same material were in short supply, actually nonexistent. Young Valentina Gaidamak, a graduate student in the department of draftsmen's geometry of the Moscow Aviation Institute, saw the plaids, realized the need for mufflers, and acted. She bought a quantity of shawls, cut each into eight sections, stitched the edges of each section, and there were the mufflers. She sold her production at 100 per cent profit and made many Soviet citizens happy. Her business grew, and in three years she found herself the owner of several machines and the employer of her parents, her neighbors, and others. Conducting the business from her home, she shipped her production to the black markets of a number of cities all over the Soviet Union.[41]

VI

Legal loopholes demand, of course, a consummate art of manipulating documents, to be obtained from all the proper Soviet offices, with all their paraphernalia of seals and signatures. A private entrepreneur was presented by a Moscow journalist as employing eight bookkeepers and three lawyers to safeguard his affairs with necessary documentation, so that "any prosecutor, any expert can be convinced that Iksov did not pilfer, did not steal, but obtained everything by virtuous labor." Iksov owned a dacha, and for "each nail" in it he had a document stating "where it was bought, for how much, from whom." There was a notarized document proving that he had purchased a caracul coat for his daughter with the proceeds of a bet he had won. (The journalist hinted, however, that Iksov had paid the "bettor" a bribe to swear out that document falsely.) Iksov's son, a student at an institute, was similarly protected by a file of documents testifying to the legitimacy of his high style of living. Other documents in Papa Iksov's files showed that his chauffeur, his watchman, his man-cook, and two other servants were not any illegal hired help but distant relatives of either Iksov or his wife, all pensioned off by the state, and all residing with the Iksovs legally. Yes, citizens complained about the Iksovs' riches. Yes, each month two or three demands of investigation of the family's wealth were received by the authorities. But the Iksovs did not worry. They had those documents, a separate set of them for each member of the family, all safe in a fireproof vault.[42]

Some of the New Class are not afraid to flaunt the Party by faking their precious documentation. Members of a ring in Moscow collected from the state's treasury, by presenting fraudulent expense receipts, the difference between the low prices they paid thieves and other "left-side" operators for stolen gasoline and the higher prices usually charged by the state's own gasoline stations. How to convince the state that they had indeed bought from the state's stations at those higher prices? Very simply: the ring got in touch with another ring which sold blank letterheads and bills illegally printed in the state's own printing shops by certain money-hungry printers. The gasoline ring filled in the handy blanks with the fraudulent receipts, and pocketed its profit (minus the price the ring paid for those forged blanks).[43]

Forged season passes for soccer games were uncovered by the Moscow police and this led to the exposure of a number of highly skilled printers in the capital as manufacturers of a wide variety of illegal letterheads, which were sold to private entrepreneurs at sizable profits. Among others, the staff of The Red Proletarian printing plant were implicated.[44] At Ufa, a printer was so clever in forging Soviet state papers that his customers said smugly, as they compared an original with the printer's effort: "These are as alike as two drops of water! St. Nicholas the Miracle Worker himself won't be able to tell them apart!"[45]

For some letterheads a citizen does not even have to apply to an illegal printer: certain kinds of bills of lading and other blanks are on sale in Soviet stationery stores as openly and legitimately as they are in stores all over the world, and at least on one occasion a representative of the Moscow police protested against this practice as smacking of too much freedom.[46] And it is a simple matter to fake a seal without which no Soviet bill or any other document is valid: one sly criminal used an ordinary 50-kopek coin, the side that bears the official Soviet state emblem, to "certify" his fraudulent papers. He merely inked that side, applied it to the document at hand—and presto, it was legal. All manner and rank of Soviet officials held and examined such documents and saw the "seal," but "found nothing suspicious" in it.[47]

Some lax servants of the Soviet state are simply ill-trained or unobservant or both. Others, however, are by now in the pay of private entrepreneurs turned forgers, of slick traders and sly traitors, far more than in the pay of the Party.

VII

Of course, in every society—and not alone in the Soviet Union —there will be some who will try to feather their own nests at the expense of the state or of others. There is, for instance, wide-spread tax evasion in America and Western Europe. Everywhere there is price-fixing of bids for government contracts; there are enormous swindles in the government highway contracts; there are the scandals involving, say, supermarket employees stealing from the stores and short-changing customers, and all of these too can be considered flaws of the capitalistic system no less than individual faults.

And yet, the essence of the cheating and the thievery that goes on in the Soviet Union is different. There are two main elements of difference.

First, for whatever reasons of personal greed the Soviet individuals commit those economic crimes, in toto the crimes represent disaffection from the regime which, ideologically and politically, proclaims itself—and tries to act as—the only owner of all enterprise and the only employer of all men and women in the realm. Thus the individuals' economic transgressions defy the regime itself (much more than any such misdeeds defy the state in the West).

Secondly, the Moscow regime has long ago declared that there now exists and will continue to exist the new Soviet man, completely reformed and transformed from the pre-revolutionary pattern, a faithful adherent to Marxism-Leninism and to its practical consequences. (No such mass-produced virtue is claimed for the non-Soviet world by any non-Soviet ideologues.) But the stark reality of the Soviet 1960s, nearly a half-century after the Bolshevik revolution, shows no such miraculous transformation. Man's economic sins in the Soviet Union, increasing rather than decreasing, prove this amply.

CHAPTER XIV

The Jewish Issue

ONE IMPORTANT AND much discussed concomitant of the official Soviet campaign against the nation's illegal capitalism is the Jewish issue. So many members of the managerial-technical elite charged with this transgression are Jews that some Western observers view the campaign as more anti-Semitic than anti-capitalistic.

The Jewish issue in the Soviet's underground capitalism first came to the surface as the result of names and statistics. Foreign correspondents in Moscow and other experts on things Soviet, mostly those scholars who made their headquarters at the various Sovietological centers abroad, began to notice the frequency of Jewish-sounding names in the lists of Soviet men and women arrested, tried, and sentenced on charges of economic corruption. From the latter 1950s on they started to keep score.

The figures are impressive; they are unmistakable, coming as they do from official Soviet sources, which seem to take a kind of malicious satisfaction in hunting out the Jewish origin of the defendants. If a defendant's surname is not indicative enough of his Jewish blood, the Soviet prosecutors and journalists make a point of publicizing also his (or her) first name and patronymic, thus establishing beyond doubt that the target is a Jew. Sometimes the only clue is a patronymic, but it is a revealing one.

In general, the ratio of Jews in this roll call of victims is about 60 per cent. But occasionally it rises to as high as 78 per cent, as happened in the case—tried in Moscow in the winter of 1963–64—of the illegal traffic in knitted-goods produced by mental patients, where 18 of the 23 defendants were Jews.[1] In the Ukraine, however,* the over-all percentage of Jews doomed to execution in

---

* For a variety of historical reasons, both long past and quite recent (down to the region's Nazi occupation in World War II), anti-Semitism in the Ukraine is noticeably stronger than in other parts of the U.S.S.R.

economic trials is about 80 per cent: in the two-year period of
1961–63 they numbered 37 among the 46 persons sentenced to
death (fifteen trials in eight cities).[2]

Nationally, in death sentences for economic misdeeds, the proportion of Jews stays firmly at that 60 per cent mark. Thus, in
June 1962 it was estimated that, in the first year since the Soviet
reintroduction of capital punishment for economic crimes (May
5, 1961), at least 26 of the 41 persons drawing this sentence were
Jews. This constituted 63 per cent of the total, "whereas Jews
represent only 1 per cent of the Soviet population."[3] By April
1964 the count showed that Jews numbered "60 per cent of the
160 persons executed for economic crimes since 1961."[4] A London observer commented: "The consistency of the high national
percentage of Jews sentenced to death, which varies only a degree
above or below 60 per cent as trial follows trial, must lead to
the conclusion that this is a deliberate matter of policy."[5]

It was certainly a matter of deliberate anti-Semitic policy to
spell out Jewish names and patronymics with such gleeful care.
And there could be no mistaking the intent of Khrushchev's Party
and government in announcing time and again that the entrepreneurs did their illegal business in synagogues among other handy
places. When the Party's newspaper in Lvov (in Western
Ukraine) charged that the city's "synagogue is the focal point of
large-scale speculation," it accused "atheist as well as religious
Jews, inveterate speculators all, . . . bound together by one urge—
the insatiable thirst for money and its illegal acquisition," of using
the house of worship as "the locale for their activities."[6] The
atheist Jews were denounced for their alleged hypocrisy in resort-
ing to the synagogue as their business shelter. Religious Jews were
mocked for their refusal to sign protocols of their interrogation on
a Saturday.[7] Religious leaders, including rabbis, were pilloried
and sentenced for the economic illegality ascribed to them.

By the spring of 1963 the campaign was in full cry, and uncensored reports, brought from the Soviet Union by returning foreign
tourists, diplomats, businessmen, and correspondents, painted this
unlovely picture:

> In some areas of the Soviet Union large numbers of Jews have
> been taken in for questioning; many are detained in prison awaiting
> interrogation or trial; informers are again active among them;
> children in schools are said to be encouraged to report on any
> expensive purchases their parents may have made, and many Jews

have been intensively questioned on their income-returns over the past ten years and on their standard of living. If explanations are "unsatisfactory," there are confiscations of possessions and the people concerned count themselves fortunate if they escape prosecution. Some have gone to lengths of destroying luxury goods like crystal decanters or silver . . .[8]

Protests from abroad were not long in coming. In June 1962, a petition signed by 223 prominent Americans, and sent to Anatoly F. Dobrynin, Soviet ambassador in Washington, urged the Soviet government to repeal capital punishment for economic crimes. Unless the death penalty was abandoned, the world would be led to believe that in the Soviet Union "property rights are to be guarded more than human rights." One of the six originators of the petition was Dr. Linus C. Pauling, Nobel Prize–winning scientist, well known for his pro-Soviet sympathies. His cosigners included a number of Americans similarly connected in the past with various pro-Soviet causes and committees.[9]

I I

In early February 1963 the nonagenarian Lord Bertrand Russell paused long enough in his denunciations of Western armed-might policies to voice once more his dismay at the news of discriminatory capital punishment for Soviet Jews convicted of economic lawbreaking and "the official encouragement of anti-Semitism, which apparently takes place" in the Soviet Union.

He had begun to express his disquiet at this phenomenon early in 1962 by sending a telegram of protest addressed to Khrushchev and signed jointly by himself, François Mauriac, and Martin Buber. Evidently there had been no reply, for through 1962 he continued to write letters to Khrushchev on this and other subjects.

Finally, in a brief but strong letter of February 2, 1963, he again wrote how "deeply perturbed" he was "at the death sentences passed on Jews in the Soviet Union" and the general policy of Moscow's official anti-Semitism. He pleaded:

You of course know that I am a friend of your country, and that I have a friendly attitude towards your personal efforts directed to peaceful coexistence, efforts which I have publicly supported. I appeal to you for an amnesty, proceeding from humane considerations and our joint interests, which consist in peaceful relations between East and West.

To this, Khrushchev did finally reply, in a letter several times longer than Lord Russell's plea. Moreover, he gave both letters, Lord Russell's and his own, the widest publicity possible in the Soviet Union, even though the British philosopher had previously mentioned that he was writing "in a private capacity," thus possibly suggesting that the matter could be settled without necessarily publicizing it.

In his answer, dated February 21, and published on the front pages of *Pravda* and *Izvestiya* for March 1, 1963, and broadcast on the Moscow radio at the same time,[10] Khrushchev vehemently denied that there was any anti-Semitism, official or unofficial, in the Soviet Union. He proclaimed that "the very nature of our multinational socialist State precludes the possibility of such a policy." He reminded Lord Russell that the Soviet constitution itself stipulated the equality of all citizens of the U.S.S.R. "irrespective of their nationality and race." He quoted from the constitution's appropriate clause: "Any advocacy of racial or national exclusiveness or hatred or contempt is punishable by law."

Khrushchev blamed "bourgeois propaganda [which] often resorts to slander and falsification in order to vilify our Socialist system and our morals," and has thus invented the anti-Jewish bias, which in actuality does not at all exist in the Soviet campaign against the country's illegal capitalism. Facts "easily refuted" this bourgeois falsehood, he said.

> It is not difficult to find proof, even in the records of trials published in newspapers, that among those punished for what is called "economic crimes," including those sentenced to capital punishment, there are Russians and Jews, Georgians and Ukrainians, Belorussians and people of other nationalities. . . . these court verdicts are directed not against any particular nationality, but against crimes, against their carriers, irrespective of their nationality.

He did not discuss outright the question of the high percentage of Jews among those arrested and sentenced. He did refer to it obliquely by saying that the problem of "which nationality has more or fewer criminals of any kind at one time or another is a social question and not a question of nationality."

But this did contain the implication that the Jews of the Soviet Union may be involved in economic transgressions against Socialism and Communism for reasons of social status, that the causation here is one of certain developments within the New Class itself.

III

What indeed was the social position of the Soviet Jew? Was he discriminated against socially and economically because he was a Jew? Western critics said that, yes, he was—that he was often prevented from rising to the New Class, that he was barred from certain special kinds of higher education as a route to the New Class or, once in the New Class, from coveted fields and strata within the New Class.

Khrushchev, particularly in his reply to Lord Russell, seemed to suggest that if there was any emphasis on Jews as targets of Soviet justice battling economic transgression it was because Jews, socially but not as a nationality, more than other groups broke the laws of Socialism.

Yet, to the Western accusations that the Soviets practiced socio-economic and educational discriminations against the Jews, Soviet officials abroad and in Moscow replied that there were no such practices in fact. On October 3, 1962, Georgi M. Korni-yenko, counselor of the Soviet embassy in Washington, wrote to a protesting Jewish group in New York that Jews in the Soviet Union numbered 2,268,000 or 1.1 per cent of the population, yet Jewish students were 3.2 per cent of the total undergraduate enrollment in the Soviet institutions of higher learning. He went on to claim that Jews also constituted 15.7 per cent of all the doctors in the Soviet Union, as well as 10.4 per cent of lawyers, 8.5 per cent of all the writers and journalists, and 7 per cent of actors, artists, musicians, sculptors and other men and women of the arts.[11] In April 1964 an American correspondent in Moscow was told that Jews made up 10 per cent of the Soviet Union's scientific personnel, 13 per cent of the artists, 14 per cent of the writers, and 23 per cent of the composers.[12]

Note, however, two curious and significant omissions: neither the foreign service nor the armed establishment of the Soviet Union was mentioned. The truth is that Jews have been rigorously excluded from the Soviet diplomatic field ever since the middle and late 1930s and from the top ranks of the armed forces since the Second World War. This part of the anti-Jewish policy, begun by Stalin, was certainly continued by Khrushchev, and is still in effect in these post-Khrushchevian times.

Even before the dismissal of Maxim Litvinov, a Jew, from his long-time post of Commissar of Foreign Affairs in May 1939 (as Stalin's preliminary offering to Hitler on the eve of the Nazi-

Soviet pact of a few months later), Jews were systematically removed from that department. Very few Jews remained by early 1940. "I was one of the last Jews in the Soviet diplomatic service," a high member of the Soviet embassy staff in Rome told me after his defection and arrival in New York in the summer of 1940. He had defected, he said, because Stalin was recalling him to Moscow with the clear intention of liquidating him physically.

In World War II very few Soviet generals and admirals and no marshals were of Jewish origin. In 1964, to an American journalist in Moscow, a Communist scientist who was a Jew "named a Jewish general who was twice a Hero of the Soviet Union, and another one who was a Jewish general and a member of the Supreme Soviet." And "although 110 Jews have been named Heroes of the Soviet Union during the war,"[13] this was a small recognition indeed compared with that in the early times of the Soviet regime—with the high rank and highest praise accorded those Jewish associates of Lev Trotsky who helped him to win the civil war of 1917–21 in which he was the Red warlord.

In Khrushchev's time Jews did not come back to the Soviet diplomatic service, but they were indeed gradually returned to the military establishment. This last was for a unique reason, which had nothing to do with any essential change in the Party's attitude toward Jews. It involved the radical transformation of war technology in the new nuclear and rocket era. The reason is still valid in these post-Khrushchevian days, of course. The Soviet armed forces needed atomic physicists, astrophysicists, aerodynamics specialists, nuclear chemists, linear programmists, and other higher mathematicians. There is a considerable incidence of Jews among such urgently needed brains. This is how Jews have been re-entering the Soviet military establishment at its newest version and its highest ranks, in its laboratories and on its launching sites rather than on parade grounds, but coming back nevertheless and with much awe and prestige surrounding them.

But in the high industrial command Khrushchev still tried to keep the Jews down. True, in July 1962, the elevation of Veniamin E. Dymshits, a Jew, to the important positions of Chairman of the Council of National Economy and Deputy Premier in the Soviet government was announced. But, as rightly remarked at the time, this was "in part intended to lull Western opinion" into thinking that surely a power which "raises a Jew to so high a post could not itself be guilty of hostility to Jews."[14] Since 1962 there has been little evidence that Dymshits is indeed a man with much say in his country's industrial policy, his high positions notwithstanding.

In the latest weighty discussion of planning and profit for Soviet industry, Professor Yevsei Liberman, a Jew, is considered the brightest light of wisdom, squarely in the center of the national stage. But he is a rare exception, which only proves the rule of the absence of Jews from this field. And from a careful reading of the current Soviet sources we can glean the indisputable fact that few Jews occupy commanding positions as industrial managers. They are submanagers, chief bookkeepers, engineers, governmental corporation lawyers, but are not members of the top strata of the Soviet manufacturing and selling world. In hiring, in promotion, in being sent abroad on missions, they are often shunted aside because they are Jews. Anatol Mikhelson, a Soviet engineer who defected to the West in 1956, said to me on this subject: "We Soviet Jews are not so readily sent abroad by our Communist employers." He was the logical choice to be sent, by the Moscow factory where he was employed, to Poland to examine a certain new German machine and to report on it. But at the very last possible moment he was kept home, and another engineer, less qualified but a non-Jew, was sent instead. Mikhelson's superior, also a Jew, confided to Mikhelson sadly that "your Jewishness is against you."

We know how few Jewish scientists are sent abroad on missions or given permission to go abroad. The great Lev Landau, the Nobel Prize winner, certainly fared better under Khrushchev than he did under Stalin, who once, in the 1930s, even jailed him and nearly killed him on the preposterous charge of being a Nazi spy. But did Khrushchev in all his benevolence allow Landau to go to foreign lands? Not at all. Was Iosif Shklovsky, the internationally celebrated astrophysicist, permitted to visit in the West? Not to our knowledge. And although Khrushchev is on his throne no more, his successors have not materially altered his policy in this respect at least.

True, Brezhnev and Kosygin do use such Jewish scientists as Landau and Liberman to answer the indignant outcry of American Jews against the persecution of their coreligionists in the Soviet Union. This is indeed clever of Khrushchev's heirs; unlike their garrulous predecessor, they stay in the shadows and order their subordinate elite to speak for the Party's cause.

Thus it was that on May 31, 1965, both Lev Landau and Yevsei Liberman signed a letter to *The New York Times,* published on June 2. Voicing their protest against the circulation in the West of "all kinds of fabrications on the position of the Jews in the U.S.S.R.," the two scholars repeated the standard Party thesis that there is no national persecution of any minority or group in the Soviet Union: "The Jews of the U.S.S.R., as the other national minorities, are inseparable from all Soviet multi-national people. They enjoy all social benefits in an equal degree, and participate in all economic, political and cultural life of the country."

They were answered in the same newspaper on June 21 by Saul Bellow, Richard Hofstadter and two other American professors (letter to the editor dated June 17). The rebuttal stated that "discrimination against Jews has not disappeared" with Stalin's death; that job opportunities are still not equal for Soviet Jews; that the Soviet government, even in these post-Khrushchev days, still inflicts upon the Jews of that nation "the deprivation of cultural and religious rights which all other similar groups enjoy and without which the survival of the Jewish community is impossible."

It was generally held in the West that neither Landau nor Liberman put his distinguished name to that letter of his own free will. Comment was made especially about Landau's personal freedom as a Soviet citizen, most particularly of his freedom of movement, of going abroad to foreign universities and laboratories and international conferences, invitations to which the world-famous physicist-mathematician certainly does not lack.

I V

On a rare occasion a high Soviet official may inadvertently admit anti-Jewish discrimination, as did Yekaterina Furtseva, who until late October 1961 was the only woman member of the Party's Presidium, when she declared: "The [Soviet] government found in some departments a heavy concentration of Jewish people, upwards of 50 per cent of the staff. Steps were taken to transfer them to other enterprises . . ." She hastened to add that on such transfer these Soviet Jews were given "equally good positions without jeopardizing their rights."[15] Still the odor of discrimination hung heavily over Furtseva's statement, and Leonid Ilyichev, the well-known Soviet propagandist, tried to explain it away:

In her interview she meant that if at some time there had taken place changes in office personnel, these changes were dictated by the economic needs of the country and under no circumstances were aimed at any discrimination of persons of any nationality. . . . Never at any time during the Soviet power have there been any quotas for Jews or persons of other nationalities, and there are not now.

Which explanation really explained nothing. As one American commentator observed, Yekaterina Furtseva "spoke not of an oversaturation of specialists but an oversaturation of Jews."[16]

Another smoke screen with which Soviet chiefs like to becloud the argument is their insistence on the fact that there is anti-Semitism in the West, including the United States. But two wrongs do not make a right. Besides, the Jews in the West and all those who help them to fight discrimination do precisely that: fight discrimination. The Jews of the Soviet Union have to accept their plight in silence.

Indeed, to cite as one instance the barring of American Jews from some higher strata of American economics,

> discriminatory hiring practices in American corporations have ex-
> cluded numerous Jews from top executive positions. Jews constitute
> less than one half of one per cent of the total executive personnel in
> leading American industrial companies, although they are 8 per
> cent of the college-trained population from which the managerial
> staffs are chosen. . . . However, two mitigating circumstances are
> present here that cannot be found in the Soviet Union. In the
> United States Jews can fight back; they can publicly demand their
> equality of opportunity; they can expose the evil and exert pressure
> for its elimination. Here, too, Jews can organize their own corpora-
> tions, even buy up the discriminating corporations, and have their
> own outlets for their executive talents and energy. In the Soviet
> Union this is impossible. There is no private enterprise affording an
> escape, and there is no possibility of contending with the discrimi-
> natory authority, which is the state.[17]

Plainly, the Soviet state—the Communist Party—needs at all times a convenient scapegoat for its failures, just as the tsars and dukes and landlords did before it. Anti-Semitism is an old Russian and Ukrainian tradition, and an ancient phenomenon gen-erally in Eastern Europe; in more recent and tragic times it served the purpose of its practitioners even farther west, in Hitler's Germany.

V

There is hardly any economic sin against the Party and the state that the Soviet Union's Jews have not been blamed and punished for. Most especially, however, the Jews of the Soviet Union are accused of black-market foreign-currency and gold-trading activities.

But accusations of this kind did not originate in the Soviet Union. The widespread East European image of Jews as bankers, as money dealers, as experts on gold, silver, and paper bills dates back several centuries. There is some validity to this view, of course. In the darkest days of the Middle Ages, amid persecutions and sudden massacres of the ghetto denizens by governments and mobs alike, Jews had to be ready to flee on a moment's notice, at the very first sign of menace. In the flight they could carry with them only a minimum of their belongings. They early learned to have with them valuables that were most compact and portable, that could be concealed on their persons most quickly and easily. These were gold coins and ingots, jewels, and in time also tightly rolled money bills. Non-Jews when similarly endangered or simply pressed by other troubles knew where to find sage advice and quick money or jewels.

The spate of charges by the Soviet government against Jews about their supposed or actual part in black-bourse activities reached a high point in 1960. The month of May was notable. Early in May 1960 Khrushchev's government announced that all Soviet money would lose a zero on January 1, 1961. This meant all the Soviet currency in private hands had to be surrendered to the government in exchange for new money, at the rate of 100 to 10. Many persons did not at all relish the idea of bringing their rolls and stacks to the state banks. Embarrassing questions were inevitably in the offing; an accounting of the money's origin would have to be given to the government men. In the same month of May 1960 the American U-2 was shot down, the Summit Conference in Paris was wrecked by Khrushchev, and war clouds seemed to threaten. In a panic many Soviet Russians sought security by converting their paper rubles into gold coins, jewels, and foreign currency. That is how so many arrests of black-exchange dealers, so many of them Jews, suddenly flared up all over the land.[18]

Another reason why numerous Jews have found themselves in violation of Soviet laws relating to private economic transactions has been that traditionally in Russia, old and new, these people have always constituted a considerable part of the middle echelons of trade and, particularly in Soviet times, of industrial management. This fact, in the opinion of some well-qualified observers of the Soviet scene, makes the Jews "more vulnerable to prosecution than higher officials who, though they may be profiting more, are better protected."[19]

And it is so easy for Soviet prosecutors and judges to pretend their righteous Marxism and yet engage in an anti-Semitic vendetta to their hearts' content—easy to accuse the Jews above all of thwarting the Soviet government's (and ostensibly the people's) will to Socialism and Communism, because of the Jews' undoubted socioeconomic devotion to capitalism, their historically proven commercial ability, even if Karl Marx himself and many of Lenin's (if not Stalin's) associates were of Jewish origin.

V I

There is no denying the historic fact of a sizable proportion of Jewish participants in the early stages of the Russian Revolution. The explanations for this are at least two. There was, for one, the tsars' stupidity in erecting for the Jews in the old empire so many unjust, unfair restrictions on their education and socioeconomic welfare. Young Jews in their protest joined with Lenin and other non-Jewish revolutionaries in the underground plotting and in the final seizure of power. There were also the young Jews' general intellectual curiosity, idealism, heightened desire for action—any action that promised social justice for all.

But that early explosion of revolutionary or Soviet activity on the part of Russian Jews soon cooled. Stalin helped to cool it, of course, by his hatred of Trotsky and of all intellectuals, particularly Jewish intellectuals. The Stalinist trail of purges led from Trotsky in the 1920s to the "plot" of Jewish doctors in early 1953. Khrushchev participated in the Stalin-era purges and he continued them in his own time, even if they became less bloody. Essentially, the peasant in Khrushchev, suspicious of all intellectuals and other city slickers and particularly of *Jewish* intellectuals, followed the path of Stalin the seminarist.

But even without the Stalinist purges and Khrushchev's milder continuation of them, many Jews in Russia would have gotten off the Communist "locomotive of history" (to employ the Party's old favorite expression). Most Jews of the Soviet Union need Socialism-en-route-to-Communism as much as "a fish needs an umbrella" (to quote a whispered quip of anti-Soviet jokesters). The Jews are a rational, pragmatic people. Their long and bitter history has taught them to be practical—and sardonic. They are quick to see when something idealistic or pseudoidealistic turns sour and gory and economically and socially impractical, as Russia's effort to achieve Communism has proved to be. That is why they feel no moral compulsion to support the Party's policy, particularly in the country's economics. So, if any of the economic-transgression charges against them as a group (more than any other group in the Soviet Union) are valid, the Jews involved in illegal "firms" and "rings" do not really feel guilty. They see the Russian attempt at Communism as (to use its definition by a gifted English writer) "a simple failure of the human reason."[20]

I said they are sardonic about it, and this is particularly true when we examine the origin of the many anti-Soviet anecdotes current in Eastern Europe. Many of these are plainly of Jewish genesis, born in the peculiarly Jewish sense of humor, and some, clearly, are mere modern versions of ancient ghetto jokes through which the Jews laughed not alone at their enemies and tormentors but at themselves as well.

Highly modern and illustrative is this story:

Three Jewish fathers meet in a Vienna café. One comes from Moscow, the second from Warsaw, and the third from Tel Aviv. They boast of their sons, of course (a continuation of that old Jewish jest about "my son the doctor").

"My son in Moscow is building Communism," says the first oldster. "He is a very important nuclear physicist, he is!"

"In Warsaw we cannot as yet say we are already building Communism," the second one chimes in. "We are building Socialism nevertheless. My son is helping to build it by holding a high post as a rocket-and-missile engineer."

"In Tel Aviv my son is a very successful factory manager," the third Jew beams.

The two others turn to him. "But what is he building there— Socialism or Communism?

The third man is indignant. "In his own country? Is he crazy?"

CHAPTER XV

Home on the Steppe

ONE OF THE surest signs of the embourgeoisement of the new Soviet society is its enthusiastic drive toward individual real-estate ownership. Great is the passion of the New Class, both technocrat and bureaucrat, for a house and a lot all its own. With a quiet and persistent frenzy it fills the house with all sorts of *kulturny* oddments of furniture, furnishings, and scarce household gadgets; and the lot with a garage and a fruit and berry orchard.

To be sure, the Party cadres feel impelled by their professions of Marxist principles to disapprove this penchant for private property; and as bureaucrats they occasionally have to dam as well as damn the rush to home ownership. For this reason they are somewhat more vulnerable than the technocrats are to the shame of being found indulging a bourgeois desire for property; and so they do it much less frequently than the others.

One phenomenon that spurs the longing is the Party's failure to build enough new housing for the populace. While in Western Europe, housing space in 1964 was "a sanitary norm of some 9 cubic meters per dweller," the Soviet inhabitant had "approximately half that space." The state-financed residential construction declined from 8.3 billion rubles in 1959 to 7.7 in 1962, and an American expert observed in 1964 that "the promise for substantial improvement seems dim."[1]

Another reason for the private-home yen is the Party's fight against that yen. There is no blinking this fact of human nature: the more a fruit is forbidden, the sharper is man's appetite for it. The draconian Soviet decree on the subject permits no private ownership of any land, be it a miserable lot under a pitiful hovel. Anyone in the Soviet Union who uses any land is the state's usufructuary, or tenant.[2] It is true that, while all the soil in the nation belongs to the state, the house above the ground may be individually owned. But the law allows private home building and owning to the extent of no more than a five-room house per family, with a total living space not exceeding (since 1958) sixty square meters.[3]

On the lower strata of Russia's present-day society the result is a rash of little jerry-built houses dotting the fringes of Soviet cities with no regard for any planned streets or plazas. Often they do not have either regular sewage disposal or running water. At times there is not even electricity.[4] Not only do the lower classes live in such houses themselves, but often they let roomers in. Some owners move out, rent these humble abodes to others yet poorer than themselves, and become absentee landlords.

But there is nothing ramshackle about many other privately built and personally owned houses and dachas in the Soviet Union. A typical target of the Communist antiproperty campaign is a well-constructed and amply appointed private house, on a neat street or in an attractive grove on a pleasant hill. Most such houses are built singly, a good distance from one another. Others line up together, in a community all their own. Such "a kingdom of private enterprisers" is reported by an indignant correspondent from a new industrial town in the Kemerovo Region in Western Siberia:

> Solid-looking, thoroughly built houses-cottages, some two-storied, their roofs of slate or even iron. Each has its own steam heating, also verandas, with or without mansard attics, with barns made of slag-blocks, and basements of reinforced concrete. As we pass, people are on guard as they stare at us from their windows with curiosity, and angry watchdog barking sounds . . . [5]

Watchdogs as an inevitable feature of such new non-Soviet house ownership upset Communist propagandists no less than those high fences around the dachas or cottages, the scarce, high-quality materials out of which the houses are built, and the quick tempo with which this housing usually rises. The West Siberian correspondent is bitter about "this 'private sector' as it has risen despite all the projects" sponsored or permitted by the Soviet authority, "and in record-breaking short spans of time." And the gall of these private builder-owners in using the latest "industrial methods of basic blocks and panels made of reinforced concrete, slag-blocks, rails, girders, and prefabricated materials," which official Soviet state building often lacks but which these smooth "privateers" manage to obtain somehow!

I I

Watchdogs and high fences are not only physical phenomena. They are also striking symbols of the distaste for the life around them that the intellectuals, the professionals, and other middle- and upper-class men and women feel as they travel up the socio-economic ladder in the Soviet Union and begin to satisfy their craving for privacy.

Anatol Mikhelson, the engineer-defector quoted in the preceding chapter, said to me: "You can stand some lies and privations and chaos if there are just a few of them. Not that you make your terms with them, no, you simply cringe before them, and that is how you live. But when there are not just a few of them, but many—when the whole life is full of them—then it is utterly impossible to live in such a country. And that is how you decide to leave." But if you cannot leave, you fence yourself in, you become what the Russians call *vnutrenniy emigrant*, that is, an inner *émigré*. Your watchdog and high fence around your house and orchard, should you be lucky or smart enough to own such, help you to become and stay an inner *émigré*.

A judge in Kazan, a faithful Communist, was indignant in print about a neighbor of his, a decent, hard-working veteran, respected not alone for his honesty and skill at his plant job, but also for the wounds and medals he had received in World War II. But now behold this man Pavel—he was toiling and scrimping to build a house of his own. The judge argued with him that it would be easy for Pavel to get a fairly good apartment from the plant "where they respect and value him." No, Pavel countered, he wanted a house: "I want a house of my own. Do you understand, *my own* . . ." And when finally he gathered enough rubles, and the new large, strong-walled house was ready, its shutters big and with iron bolts, there was a wooden sign on the gate, with the picture of a dog's head and the words: "Ferocious dog in the yard!"[6]

The wife of a military officer, living in a large 80-apartment building in Cheliabinsk, wrote to a Moscow editor: "Ours is a good flat, but all the time I daydream about a house of our own, any kind, but our own, with a high fence. To go away, to take our children with us, to fence ourselves away from everybody and everything in the world, not to hear and see anything whatever."[7]

It is in such moods that members of the New Class have been building those private houses for themselves in increasing numbers and with higher and yet higher walls around their spacious dachas. They mean to shut themselves off from the lowly, smelly, noisy mob. In a village for well-to-do writers outside Moscow, a visiting Britisher found that the largest of the dachas were occupied by the wealthiest of the group, most likely (he surmised) playwrights and film makers. He noted: "One could clearly spend all one's time in one's dacha and quite forget the outside world. Some obviously did this . . ."[8]

Injuries to curious passersby or mischievous trespassers, caused by bad-tempered watchdogs, are repeatedly making Soviet press headlines. In Kiev a scientist, "set on the safeguarding of his suburban property, and dubious of ferocity of chained dogs," daringly acquired a bear instead, and "let him run along a wire."[9]

Elsewhere, in addition to using dogs, owners "go as far as electrifying their wire fences."[10] They plant mines under their apple trees,[11] but at least one such owner, a metallurgical engineer of Magnitogorsk, forgot the location of his mine and inadvertently blew himself up; "curious neighbors . . . were eyewitnesses of a tragic picture"—there was the engineer-homeowner "lying on the ground with a bloody head."[12] Similarly, a military engineer with the rank of major decided to safeguard his brand-new Moskvich car by fastening to the garage door an ingenious detonating device (*adskaya mashina*, or "hellish machine," as the Russians call it). He had the nerve of having it rigged up in the state shops, apparently at the state's expense. Once, however, in his impatience to get his precious car out, the major forgot to use the safety catch—and was himself caught in an explosion. He recovered after some surgery, but when fellow Communists asked him about the ethics of his device he replied: "I don't see anything unseemly in it. But I guess it would be safer for me to use an animal trap instead."[13]

More often, as they patrol their orchards and other property with guns in their hands, they shoot and kill others. The victims are usually boys and youths, occasionally a girl, at times adults.[14]

III

Dexterity of truly novel types distinguishes some such home-owning efforts.

In the Moscow Region, an executive, employed in the state's trading apparatus and placed in charge of building materials, used the singular advantage of his position to erect, not just one house for himself and his family, but two. The second, of brick, stood near by and had two rooms and a bathroom, and below this additional house a reinforced-concrete bomb shelter (rarer in the Soviet Union than it is even in the United States) was concealed. Both houses were filled with expensive furniture. There was also a car in a newly constructed brick garage.[15]

One large two-story dacha at Kuntsevo, near Moscow, bought for 28,000 rubles by a senior salesman in a food store, was found by the investigating authorities to have even a swimming pool—an unheard-of luxury for the Soviet middle-rank elite.[16] A coal-mine manager in the Ukraine, having gone on two foreign missions totaling more than a year's duration, brought back from his travels "an irresistible thirst for material welfare and comfort." So he used the state's carpenters and cabinetmakers to change a simple one-story house into a two-story villa for himself, all "in a Western manner," filling it with furniture custom-built in accordance with the blueprints of his own drafting and, apparently, also of Western style.[17]

In Moscow a senior engineer in charge of a large powerhouse used his foremen and workers to build his dacha by giving a whole team of them leaves from their jobs without pay, and then paying them out of his own mysterious pocket at higher rates than their powerhouse wages—plus food and drink. The "lovers of the long ruble" (the Russian phrase that serves as an equivalent of the American "chasers after the easy dollar") fell in with the engineer's offer most enthusiastically. The group was carefully chosen: "it was not a simply team, but a complex one," its members representing all the fine crafts needed to build the engineer's elaborate dacha. When finished, this turned out to have not only two surface levels, but also one subterranean, secret story, and, in addition, five glassed-in terraces.[18]

Near Moscow, a former *zootekhnik* (zoological technician) developed a thriving mail-order business of medicinal herbs, which he obtained in the Soviet Far East, and which he sold to many influential persons all over the country. His mansion was also his business headquarters. The gate to the house was "armored," the large yard held "hothouses, nurseries, pumps, electric motors, a water-tower (built of steel), motorcycles, a garage, a gasoline-filled cistern," and of course two cars.[19]

Such new landed gentry reveal full-blown neofeudal habits: in Dnepropetrovsk in the Ukraine, the local authorities obligated the work crew of a factory to sweep a certain street, "and, at that, precisely those blocks which are built up with private houses." The workers sent in a lament: "So what happens? The factory crew, mostly women, do not go home after their shift but, armed with brooms and shovels, work on the street, while the house owners stand there and smile."[20] A man in Tashkent built two separate houses for his two wives and bought a third house for his mistress and then, to show his social conscience, built for the city a cemetery, and over its gate erected a sign, reading simply "Davydov," this being his own name. But, said the police, the money for all this was not his—he was charged with its theft from the state.[21]

IV

Two interrelated problems bother the Party faithful as they try to beat down the rising wave of hunger for real estate: How do the malefactors manage to circumvent the law? And where and how do they get the building materials to raise their unclean edifices—materials so precious, so scarce in the Soviet Union, *defitsitnyie* as the peculiar Soviet word has it (from the Latin word *deficit*, "it is lacking")? A few cases will give the reader the extent of variety of the puzzlement.

In the North Caucasian mineral spa of Yessentuki a member of the new enterprising elite had a house built for him in strict accordance with the Soviet law on the touchy subject. Also quite legally he erected a bathhouse right next to his abode. But not at all legally he made it a public bath, charging a fee to citizens wishing to keep clean. And there were many such eager citizens in the area, not known for either its private bathrooms or its public baths. In a short time the profit was sizable enough to allow the entrepreneur to construct one more house in his courtyard and to add a few rooms to his original house. A Party functionary writing on these peccadilloes wondered angrily: "Is he planning to build a laundry, thus to create a bath-laundry combine as a complete cycle?"

The Party functionary also noted that the transgressor managed to register his illegal bathhouse with the local Soviet taxing authority somehow, thus invoking undeserved legality for his profitable enterprise. Was there collusion and corruption? Possibly. The functionary exclaimed: "Thieves and grabbers live not on a desert island. Soviet people are all around them. Many state institutions and offices are inevitably on their path. But at times you are puzzled how all this can happen. How is it that scoundrels succeed in fooling honest people so easily?"

The fact is, of course, that those honest Soviet bystanders are not so honest, and not bystanders at all, but participants in the unholy scheme in one way and another. Take another case cited by the same indignant Party functionary:

In the famous Black Sea resort city of Sochi, three friends came together to start a large-scale illegal enterprise. As if to prove that Russia was indeed a harmonious union of nations, the three were a Russian, a Ukrainian, and an Armenian. Forming a building cooperative, they erected a big three-story apartment house—for their own private profit, naturally. They were most adroit in obtaining bricks, cement, steel, gas pipes, and high-quality glass at wholesale prices from mysterious sources. Not so secret was the origin of the transport they used: "a whole hundred trucks, belonging to sundry [state] organizations, were kept busy in moving . . . the building materials so scarce and valuable" in the Soviet Union.

From the same state building concerns, at whatever illegal price, the dexterous trio secured also their cement mixers, a lifting crane, and even a few searchlights for night work. They found, however, that they could not hire their own carpenters and cabinetmakers. "But here, too," the Party functionary said, seething with ire, "the contractors did not fall flat on their faces in the mud. With no trouble or mishap all their woodwork was done, at nominal charge, by state factories."

What sort of "contract" did the state factories sign with these bold entrepreneurs? The Party functionary called for a thorough investigation. But what good would such calls do? He reveals that all over the nation "honest Soviet people in good time signal to the authorities about the wheeler-dealers' dark activities," but that this valiant informing yields absolutely no results; in the local or regional state offices, to which they are sent, these reports "gather dust for months, with no action taken on them." Such cases have been observed in regions as far distant from one another as those of Volgograd (formerly Stalingrad), Kaliningrad (formerly Königsberg), Stavropol (in the North Caucasus), and Astrakhan (on the Volga).

Somebody covers up for somebody. At best, the police and the prosecutors are just too negligent. They accept too easily the slick operators' alibis. "And these wheeler-dealers can indeed duck and swim! They obtain and present fictitious certificates, they formalize their mansions and dachas as belonging to their relatives, they show the cost of their building lower than it actually is." Thus they keep within the law. "We must not let them fool us," the Party functionary cries in despair, "we must stop these thieves, we must confiscate from them everything that they have stolen from the people!"[22]

And still the mad carousel of trickery and theft whirls on. Again and again it is noted that some building materials and services come to builders quite legitimately, within norms and through documents set and signed by proper authorities. But often authorities authorize, or wink at, things either only partly legal or not at all legal. In Rostov on the Don, the state's water-and-sewage engineers built waterworks for private homeowners, using state-owned pipes and other equipment and contributing their own state-paid time to such projects, but pocketed the proceeds for themselves instead of turning them over to the state's treasury. The head manager and the chief engineer of the organization "were well aware of these machinations," but not only did they fail "to pull the thieves and bribe-takers back—at times they helped in this lawlessness."[23]

The private builders' cement and slate, brick and flooring wood "do not fall from heaven." Often, these are "nomad" supplies: they "migrate" from one state building site to another until they are conveniently lost—that is, till the private builders get them via bribery or outright theft. Truck drivers employed by the state have developed a "leftist" (the Russian term for "illegal") sideline of their own by selling state-owned materials to such builders or simply accepting payments for delivering that which is stolen by others. A West Siberian correspondent notes that "a thief does not have to climb stealthily over a fence or break a lock" in order to get such materials. They are, "in the main, lying scattered under an open sky, guarded by no one." All a private builder has to do is "find a 'leftist' chauffeur and take whatever he needs!"[24]

Certain building materials are in an extremely short supply in the Soviet Union. Among them is roof slate. One of the few legitimate ways in which a Soviet private-home builder may obtain such slate is to apply to a slate-making plant for permission to pay for, and cart away, a quantity of condemned slate. The slate is condemned because it does not come up to official standards of perfection, which happen to be uncommonly—and unnecessarily—high. The slate thus discarded is actually very good and thoroughly usable.

Or, speaking of yet more expensive and scarce roof sheeting, do you need rubberoid? Rolls after rolls of rubberoid disappeared en route from its Krasnodar factory to its legitimate customers— the state organizations in charge of state building sites. A number of officials were involved in the illegal sale of this costly material to private builders. The staff lawyer of the Krasnodar plant tried an ingenious excuse: "The rolls . . . melted away because of the unfavorable climate."[25]

A clearer key to the mystery of just where and how private builders obtain scarce heavy equipment is in such exposés as the one of Engineer Shilov in Moscow. He was caught red-handed on a major square of the Red capital as, in the thick crowd of passersby, he casually met Supply Manager Kondratenko and was about to accept a bribe from him. The bribe was payment for delivery to unauthorized persons of bulldozers and lifting cranes, belonging to the Council of People's Economy. From this engineer and this supply manager the police path led to a number of their accomplices, other Moscow and provincial engineers and managers, who were at once arrested.

Below these, a number of plain transport workers were discovered in the plot, for the engineers and managers had never failed to give them a share (even if modest) of the bribes received.

Above them, was a go-between, one Petrushansky, a man who held several fictitious state jobs but whose entire working day was spent in arranging illegal bulldozer deals and other chicanery. In his busy travels he ranged as far afield as Uzbekistan in Soviet Central Asia. When questioned by a Moscow prosecutor he is reported to have replied: "By my nature I am a *biznesmen*. In fact, this is my nickname among my acquaintances—Misha the *biznesmen*. Of course, I don't work for a mere thank-you."[26]

(Incidentally but importantly, while the Communist hierarchy and its press have consistently tried to make the word *biznesmen* a word of opprobrium, the cynical elite have apparently come to be proud of it, as something to be admired rather than hated and cursed.)

V

In August 1962 the Party finally cracked down on real-estate owners by issuing state decrees which, on the one hand, provided for confiscation, with no compensation, of houses, dachas, and other buildings "built or bought with nontoiling profits," and, on the other, encouraged legitimate individual and cooperative building of homes with the state's help. In cases where offending citizens were found guilty or were at least suspected of stealing state funds and state materials to build their ample houses, such ill-gotten properties were to be confiscated and turned into kindergartens or other state institutions.[27]

But early in 1964 two local law-enforcement officials in Krasnoyarsk made a complaint that is typical for many Soviet communities: "We meet often in the municipal committee which judges cases of confiscation of houses built or bought with non-toiling income. . . . One of us sighed: 'It is so very useless.' " The trouble is that the victims appeal their cases, from one court to another, through the labyrinth of Soviet officialdom they know so well—and meantime, for months and sometimes years, they remain in their houses "pending the appeal."[28]

There was indeed a special committee formed by the city Soviet in Ashkhabad to investigate illegal deals in real estate. But it had strict instructions from above to act only after it received a complaint, never to initiate any investigation. The result was that from August 1962 to March 1963 it presented to the proper authorities just two confiscation recommendations. The complainant in one case concluded: "Taking advantage of such abetting, certain persons continue to transact their dark business. They get rich at the expense of the toilers and of the state. They infect unstable citizens with the spirit of illegal enrichment."[29]

They think up all sorts of dodges. They build those perfectly legal five-room houses, to each of which, again quite lawfully, they add a veranda but illegally turn it into a sixth room by glassing it in. Typically, the illegal owner of a house had the foresight to register it as the property of his sister, an invalid entitled to such homeownership.[30]

Some of the elite are careful enough to build their illegally gained houses away from the geographic points where they hold their posts or are otherwise known. This is done, of course, not only to escape early detection and punishment, but also with an eye on eventual retirement—to make the sunset years peaceful no less than prosperous, to safeguard the stealers from future retributions. Thus collective farm managers have been found the proud possessors of comfortably appointed houses, built with the farms' funds and materials, not in nearby villages but in towns quite a distance away.[31]

Thus the New Class finds loopholes. It bribes prosecutors and confiscators, it runs circles around the Party and its real-estate regulations—and continues to live high on the hog in this most Socialist of all the Socialist societies marching toward Communism.

CHAPTER XVI

The Cherry Orchard and the New Ax

WHEN CORNERED BY Soviet investigators, the erring elite sometimes have the nerve to laugh right into their tormentors' faces.
The Fedechkin family were supposed to live on the modest earnings of their son, who managed a section of a Moscow store. Yet
the family, in addition to their "separate three-room apartment in
Moscow" (considered a rather extraordinary comfort in view of
its three rooms and its separateness), had also a dacha near
Moscow, which the authorities indignantly described as "a shack-
castle"—that is, a fine house officially played down by the
family in their statements as a mere shack. And where did the
Fedechkins get the money to buy such a costly castle? Mamma
Fedechkin sneered her answer: "I sold a piglet and bought this
dacha!" In other words, put *that* into your high and mighty
Communist pipe and smoke it.[1]

Bitter helplessness at the gall of the home-owning transgressors
was evident in two other official reports. "Black-marketeering?
No. Nikolai Vasilyevich sits in our editorial office and argues that
he is an honest and decent man." How did he and his wife build
their house? Proudly he says that both of them economize: "We
don't drink vodka, we don't go to the theater."[2] Another man, an
engineer, also spoke of economizing—he refused to belong to
the state-run trade-union in his area, so that he could save the
cost of membership dues and use the money for his truck-garden
expenses.[3] And they tell these bold-faced lies about their incomes
and economies calmly, often with a show of outraged virtue
which the Party's propagandists find difficult to combat.

When *Pravda* in January 1962 published a particularly vitriolic
attack on those of the elite who build their own mansions, often
at the state's expense rather than their own, several such members
of the privileged class wrote their indignant protests.[4] Some did it

anonymously, but others did not fear declaring their names and positions. From the industrial town of Novotroitsk, in the Urals, four managers and engineers of the metallurgical works responded to the personal chiding they had gotten. They wrote back to *Pravda:* "Why do you call us names? What is so bad about our separate houses? What kind of moral damage and unproductive spending of spiritual and physical wealth are you talking about?" The four writers charged the author of the original attack with "lack of objectivity"; they listed their industrial achievements and other merits. *Pravda,* rather feebly, replied: "Well, no one denies these merits." But it argued that the elite should not "live in such an aloof way and demonstrate their lack of modesty" before the mass of workers to whom they—the engineers, managers, and other leaders—were supposed to show an example of democracy, of devotion to Soviet ideals of fairness and eventual equality.

Local Party chieftains kowtow to this mansion mania of the engineering and managerial brass, or so the lower-echelon Party faithful complain in their letters to *Pravda.* From Vyazma in the Smolensk Region a Communist zealot reported:

> In our city the building of separate houses for leading personnel has gone into high gear. They keep on building them. When I informed the Smolensk Regional Committee of the Party about this, at first I did not even get an answer. I wrote again. This time the chairman of the Regional Committee visited Vyazma. So what? He went away, and everything remained with no changes.

From the town of Amvrosiyevka, in the Donetsk Region, a Party snooper wrote: "The root of evil, in my opinion, can be traced in many local cases to the complacent attitude [of the Party officials] to the lovers of this separate living in the quiet behind the high fences." The Party officials simply "wave the workers' complaints away." Even the local Party press chooses to ignore such complaints from informers. A Party "activist" in Tashkent wrote to that city's *Pravda Vostoka* (Truth of the East) about the separate houses, complete "with automobile garages and those proverbial fences," built for themselves by the engineers and managers in charge of canal works. He wrote no fewer than three times, but not a line of his reporting was printed, much less acted upon. He did not even receive any answer or acknowledgment from those Party editors of Tashkent.

If homeownership is investigated and private houses are confiscated, it is mostly store managers and store salesmen who figure

in the accusations and the confiscation proceedings. Plant managers and engineers are so charged and punished rather less frequently. They can generally prove that their legitimate income, in
salaries but particularly in bonuses, are large enough for them to
afford their own houses, dachas, garages, and gardens.

If a civil airline pilot, or a professor, or a writer owns a dacha
worth 6,500 rubles, this is considered by the Soviet government
quite legitimate and above suspicion. But if a certain dacha has
been owned (ever since 1959, when he bought it from a pilot) by
a mere operator in a Moscow shoeshop getting some 70 rubles a
month, then it is an entirely different story. Where did he get all
that money for buying and maintaining such a house? At that,
filling it with French and Chinese porcelain, most of it collectors'
items, also with a piano, rugs, a costly refrigerator and an expensive television set? And building a garage near the house for a
costly Volga car? And where did all those rubles to finance the
shoe worker's annual trips to resorts come from? How could he
afford to pay for the grandiose parties at the dacha?

The suspect, one M. Kh. Shraiman, replied to all these questions by a mild assertion that he "had saved up" all this money,
presumably from his earnings. The police could not readily prove
that he had either stolen it all or had been black-marketing.

But the informers insist that it is not really necessary to prove
the new elite's guilt. If there is no law covering this particular
situation, there should be one. The burden of the proof ought to
be on the Shraimans, not on the state. It is not the Party and the
state that should prove that Shraiman had stolen the price of his
house and its contents and that consequently his property should
be confiscated. It devolves on each and every Shraiman to convince the authorities that his money and his property are perfectly
legitimate.[5]

But it is surely different when a suspect or a culprit is a man
of academe. Sometimes the Party finds itself entirely too be-
witched by the charm and glibness of academicians as they
illegally reach out for more and more private property. At the University of Kazan a high official, a *prorektor*, or in our terms, a
vice-president, was widely respected not alone as an academic
person but also for his decorations won in World War II battles.
"He was trusted," a district Party secretary exploded in due time,
"but behind the façade of a man mentally well-developed and
politically intelligent we failed to notice how the worminess of
love for property had gotten into him and was ruining him. Let us

admit that we were surprised when we received information that Zakirov in a dishonest way had built himself two dachas." The academician kept on "denying everything."

A Party functionary who was called upon to look into the matter, not only neglected to do his duty, but even tried to help the property-mad academician. He "believed the *prorektor's* word of honor . . . he approached this case with lack of his own principle, but with blind faith in the infallibility of this highly placed Communist."

Trust those academicians, yes, but don't overdo your faith in them, the author of the exposé admonished his fellow Party secretaries. "Trust them, yet investigate them!"[6]

I I

Renting of private property in the Soviet Union takes many wondrous forms. In a dacha area near Moscow a New Class landlord let two small rooms in his house to a woman tenant. His charge was 350 rubles for the summer season—and he added an extra 50 rubles for the use of "this path to the gate." His injunction was: "You are to walk along this path only, and not an inch to either side of it. Else I will throw you out . . ."[7]

If a private houseowner in the Soviet Union rents out any part of his property, the law says such rent can be no more than 20 per cent above the rates charged by the state for its rented property. Yet cases are numerous where private landlords charge three times as much, and the law-enforcement officials have a hard time catching the violators and proving their greed.

Rent gouging is rampant at Yalta, Sochi, and other magnetic resorts. Tourists and vacationists without *putyovki*, or state-assigned accommodations in the state resthouses, are at the mercy of the "sharks," the owners of private homes along the Black Sea shores. In the Crimea, to beat the law imposing the five-room limit per family, the homeowners "produce heated verandas, usually capacious summer kitchens, and inhabitable barns," all rentable, too.[8] Persons living in the resorts' communal apartments also rent out to rest-seekers "rooms, corners, and cots, thus making a profit 10 to 15 times the amount they pay as their apartment rent."[9] In 1962, "nearly 10 million rubles, in a most conservative estimate, came into the hands of those who rent out cots."[10]

An illegitimate hotel or other room-renting business is some-

times established in a large city. In Moscow the Yutkin family
were caught using their apartment as "a singular hotel" for tran-
sients. Periodic police raids flushed out as many as ten illegitimate
tenants, that is, men and women who lacked lawful permits to
stay in Moscow but whom the Yutkins sheltered for a price. Also
in Moscow a certain I. Burkutsky engaged in a similar profitable
philanthropy to what the police terms as "incidental persons."
The Yutkins were deported from Moscow, with strict prohibition
of any return to the capital. Burkutsky was put on a warning.
Next time he dares to break this law, he too will be deported.[11]

I I I

Many of these middle-class homeowners have been rapidly
moving up the socioeconomic ladder into the nation's higher
strata precisely through their real estate, in the following way:
The state has permitted and even encouraged Soviet citizens to
use suburban land for orchards or summer rest, and certain citizens have transformed such land into sources of private profit by
marketing produce on a large scale, by renting and even selling
summer houses for personal enrichment. Thus have their capital
and their social status grown.

It is forbidden in the Soviet Union to engage men and women
for private employment, but there is one loophole at least: you
can legally hire a woman servant, provided you call her not a
servant but "a domestic worker." Many New Class members hire
such women—and employ them as farm hands in their private
orchards, much of whose produce is then offered for sale to the
public. Some such employers are bold enough to send these
women (and sometimes even men hired by them as gardeners) to
the public market to hawk the fruit and the vegetables of their
harvest.

The new orchard cultivators were early and late hemmed in by
special Party and state restrictions, but ever and again they were
able to circumvent the unfriendly law. Thus, in 1952, the Soviet
government prohibited the erection of any structure on orchard
and garden plots within a 50-kilometer zone around Moscow itself. The Party did not want a *petit bourgeois* group to arise with
their houses, barns, and sheds too close to the Red capital. But
citizens insist that the law really specifies 10 kilometers instead of
50, and so they build up the orchard plots of which they are the
users. For proof they usually refer to a book on the subject of

land use in cities and near cities, issued in 1962 by the State Publishing House of Juridical Literature, which, through an error (possibly inadvertent, possibly not), stipulates 10, instead of 50, lawful kilometers.[12]

The law says that land of collective and state farms cannot be touched for any private purpose whatever, except the use of small plots for farmers' own needs. But managers, middlemen, and wheeler-dealers buzz around any loophole they can find in the law to divide sizable stretches of kolkhoz and sovkhoz land into private gardens for themselves—and for others who legally have very little, if anything, to do with the given farm properly.

In Volgograd the manager of a suburban state farm was approached by the manager of a building trust. In exchange for lumber needed for the house which he wanted to build for himself, the farm manager gave the trust manager "a thriving garden," which the latter promptly divided among his submanagers and engineers: thirteen trees to one, eight to another, seven and six to yet others. An *Izvestiya* correspondent complained: "Thus, with the aid of mutual bribery, in essence a purchase-and-sale of state land was committed."[13] In Lipetsk a similar transaction took place, when an apple orchard belonging to a collective farm near that city was sold in separate plots, not only to the nearby factories and cooperative organizations, but also to several scores of private suburbanites. The city authorities officially approved the deal on the grounds that the fast-growing Lipetsk was already engulfing the kolkhoz anyway, so why not make its garden "non-state-property." The buyers were quick about their purchase: they began to build houses on their plots, "started to surround the plots with fences and barbed wire; and doghouses also appeared."[14]

Where a suburban property is at first "a collective garden," it does not long remain such a cooperative. It is soon divided into "individual pieces," and there is presently "the ferocious growl of newly purchased sheep dogs."[15] Sometimes the "cooperative" garden has one great fence around it, but inside there are dozens of other fences crisscrossing the grounds, dividing the area into individual domains. "But instead of summer dachas, enormous houses are being built. After all, no one controls this. 'I have obtained land—I am building whatever I wish.' . . . 'What's so unusual about it? Am I alone in this?'" Desperately a Party fanatic cries out to the authorities: "Lower the boom on them!"[16]

The Party tries to swing its ax on this new cherry orchard of the new bourgeoisie. But the Party is having a hard time. For the new bourgeois has his own ax to grind—and use. Some of the neobourgeoisie of the Soviet Union are so bold in building their dachas amid the fruit trees and berry patches that they even, calmly, as their due, request the aid of their acquaintances and associates—various officials in charge of permits—to give illegal leave and state funds for such private housing. The associates of one such nervy manipulator knew they were asked to act against the Soviet law, but did his bidding nevertheless, later helplessly explaining: "We respected him very much and did not wish to turn him down."[17]

One faithful Communist appeared heartbroken about transgressions of his real-estate–loving friends and associates. He deplored this latest Soviet phenomenon wherein "a patch of land, received [for use] in a collective garden, aroused in these people private owner instincts." Yet his sorrow was not of the angry kind that the Party wanted of him. He continued to "rub shoulders" with them at those Soviet offices and jobs he shared with them; "he warmly shook their hands, beamed his amiable smiles at them, never shamed anyone, never said to anyone: 'Listen, what are you doing?'" Above all, he never rose indignantly at any public meetings to denounce these "privateers" of Soviet real estate.[18]

Do not retreat, the Party urges its faithful. Give them a battle. In the name of Marx show them who the real boss is—the Party with its stubborn edict. Else, the garden plot may yet become a far more dangerous plot.

IV

The faithful respond. Typically, as part of a deliberate campaign ordered from above, an indignant case study of the orchard activity is presented by a Soviet woman journalist.[19] A young physician is picked by her as one of the targets of the campaign. He has done nothing illegal; he was not charged with any transgression; but he was chosen as a fairly representative middle-class professional to be castigated and to be won over. He was selected possibly because in the countryside where he tilled his plot he had become known as a vacillating individual who was ready to cease being an individualist; who could be shamed and reformed.

It all began for this young Moscow doctor, Dmitry Nikolayevich, employed by the state in a neighborhood clinic, when he was told by his wife that her father's factory had given the father, for use, a garden plot in the capital's environs—as it gave such plots to many others of its workers.

By now there are several thousands of such small plots ringing Moscow. Many of them form regular summer settlements; some have become year-round residences. The theory is that workers and white-collar employees of the city's factories and offices get the use of such plots so that their diets would be supplemented by the vegetables and fruit of their own gardens, also for their summer rest and relaxation. By accepting the use of the plot, the physician's father-in-law found himself a member of a cooperative society, with bylaws that defined it as "a collective gardening effort."

But of course there was no collectivism in that effort whatever. The area's old groves were chopped down and the tree stumps were removed by each family separately. Strawberry patches and sundry vegetables were planted on each plot individually. Fences went up; behind them, family huts were built far from one another. Each "cooperative member" and his family were thus in fact individual gardeners from the very start.

Dmitry Nikolayevich and his young wife went on their weekends to help the old man. Soon Dmitry had to postpone, then give up, his plans of winning a higher medical degree for which he had already done some study and passed a few examinations. "No time to study any more," he sighed. "Saturdays, after work, I hurry to the country—to dig those rows, to help the carpenters. My father-in-law cannot do much by himself; he is ailing."

In melancholy fact, the father-in-law had heart trouble. His doctors told him to take it easy on his days off. They forbade him any and all exertion—outside his factory job, that is. "But stronger than the physicians' arguments was the drawing power of 'one's own' land and 'personal' economy," the journalist moralized. "The sick man, no longer young, spent whole days digging drainage ditches; pushing wheelbarrows of fertilizer; fainting time and again right there, between those vegetable rows; but, on regaining consciousness, once more picking up his shovel and hammer."

Finally, in the fall of 1958, this old proletarian, this long-time Communist gone land-greedy, dropped dead—right onto "his" earth, which he had just finished enriching with manure. Dmitry had to take over.

All around him other men and women of the younger generation—engineers, scientists, managers and other middle-class professionals—were taking over such plots from the proletarian
hands of their parents and parents-in-law. By 1962 each plot was
well cultivated, securely fenced in, and solidly built up. The initial
modest hut of the Sunday diggers and planters had become a
sprawling house encrusted with all sorts of annexes. A well was
dug. There was still no inside plumbing, but the garden path to
the privy was paved. Some of the annexes were let to summer
tenants, at stiff rents.

But for Dmitry at least there were drawbacks, too. He worked
on his plot harder and yet harder; he spent on the improvements
so much money that he could not buy a new suit for himself for
quite a while. And one ill-fated Sunday evening, when, fatigued
and sleepy, he was hurrying from the plot back to the city, he was
run over by a car and was laid up with brain concussion and a
broken leg. "Now I am asking myself: in the name of what is all
this? for whom?"

But often there is no failure and no regret. Some middle-class
produce-raising families have waxed prosperous and happy. They
have become smug and selfish. Or so the Soviet government
charges. As already mentioned, such families sell their produce at
high profits on private markets (legally permitted in the Soviet
Union). Others say that they sell "only from time to time," when
they need money badly. Both categories protest that they are no
black-marketeers nor any other kind of profiteer. And why should
I be ashamed of bringing my harvest to the stalls, even Dmitry
argued. Look, he said, at the many others who are doing this:
"engineers who live behind the adjacent fences, and even the
domestic worker [servant] of a certain very well-known professor."

It is true, Dmitry concedes, that some of those plot tillers have
become too proprietary about their gardens and orchards. The
lady journalist bolsters this argument by presenting the case of
her own neighbor—a retired test pilot. He bought an enormous
beast of a wolf dog to guard his domains from intruders. One day,
as he and his wife (a woman no longer in her prime) bent their
backs over their spades, a goat wandered into their garden
through a hole in the fence. Behind the goat a scared boy sneaked
in, trying to get his family's animal out of the privileged place.
The dog howled at the interlopers, straining at his chain. The ex-

pilot leaped forward. Grabbing the boy, the man flung him bodily
against the fence. The man's face was livid with rage.

Alarmed by such non-Communist behavior, some faithful in
the area summoned a meeting of the gardeners. They proposed
taking down the fences. They moved that all the gardens, houses,
wells, and fruit trees be made one huge collective farm where
people would toil together, sharing their produce. But the others
would not hear of it. "Burn it!" they exploded at the meeting.
"We'd rather burn everything! So that nobody would get it!"

Dmitry Nikolayevich wavered. Should he, too, join the Communists who insisted on collectivization? He tried to argue on
their side. To the stubborn individualists he quoted Friedrich
Engels on the sins of love of property. "But they only laugh in my
face," he lamented to the lady writer.

The comrade lady sadly comments that to many a Soviet citizen such "high sounding" words as Dmitry tried to quote "always
seem funny." Such words "do not have any relation to one's own
private little affairs." Indeed,

> what worth are these phrases, unrelated to his own personal con-
> cerns and little worries, but side by side with this real phenomenon
> of his own plot of land, this sharply felt matter of one's own ditch
> behind the fence, this asphalt-paved path to his own privy? . . . This
> is real, this can be touched and felt with one's hands, and it is
> precious also because it can become a durable guaranty of some
> more future prosperity, such as one's own car . . . and you can
> never tell what else may yet be installed on one's own land.[20]

V

When in their heartbreak and fury the pressed orchard tillers
cry out that they would burn their homes and huts amid the trees
and the berries rather than give them up, some of them really
mean it. Anyway, if they don't burn the homes, they chop down
the trees.

In Ashkhabad V. V. Morozov and his wife Lydia Morozova, a
professional couple (the woman was a university *dotsent*), had to
give up their house and garden, since they were being transferred
to Voronezh. They tried to sell their house at a certain price, but
somehow could not. Their neighbors later claimed that they had
asked too much. From the subsequent newspaper accounts it was
not clear to whom or to what state organization the couple had to

abandon the house and the garden. In any case, both the husband and the wife were fighting-mad as they were leaving. With cold fury, systematically, methodically, they chopped down every tree, every grapevine, right at the roots.[21]

Many stubborn suburbanites disregard the Party's appeals and injunctions to leave their property behind as gifts to the state when they move. A little boy is quoted: "We lived at Pushkino, near Moscow. We had a small dacha there. When we received an apartment in the city we were supposed to hand the dacha over to the state. But my parents said: 'Let them look for fools somewhere else!' We sold the dacha, got the money, and moved." And who are the parents? Papa is a *dotsent*; Mamma is a laboratory technician. They were read the riot act by a well-known *Pravda* writer: "You are accused of crippling your little son Garrik. . . . You have mangled his soul, you imbue him with bourgeois views . . ."[22]

When a Soviet newspaper publishes an attack on this love of private property, there is always a wave of readers' letters protesting the attack. The newspaper then proceeds to publish, not the letters themselves, but a sneering summary of them, with plenty of editorial comment to show how low these readers have fallen. In a typical summary of this kind the gleeful editorial remark is made that the bitterest protesters prefer to remain anonymous.[23] As if this did not prove that there is no real freedom of public opinion in the Soviet Union, and that the letter writers simply fear what the government may do to them should their identities become known! Some not only omit their names or sign with names not their own, but disguise their handwriting, "in order to surround their identities with an impenetrable mystery," as the official summary acidly describes this effort. Some take care to drop their letters into mailboxes in neighborhoods far away from their own. This is also used by the official summarizers of the protests as one more proof of the letter writers' "cowardice." (Yet we do know how often Soviet protesters are not afraid to identify themselves.)

The gist of the protest nevertheless comes out, despite the rather pointed synopsizing by the Kremlin's journalists and editors. The main thesis of the Party, that personal property is allowed in the Soviet Union, but that the Party leaders "will never permit it to grow ugly into private property," is answered by the protesting property owners with the assertion that there can be no true line of demarcation between the two: "Personal property and private property are one and the same." The overwhelming feeling in the land is (and justly) that the Party leadership has never succeeded in drawing a clear enough frontier between the two kinds of property. And no matter how hard the Party propagandists hit, the property owners' protest does not subside.

The protesters keep on firing back. The Soviet journalists involved in this antiproperty campaign are charged by the protesters with inciting people to hatred of their fellow citizens. The protesters point out that they own their houses and orchards quite legally, but that, after reading the attacks, "the populace point their fingers at our lots, and say, 'Here are the new landed gentry.'"

Yes, the Party and its Soviet government reluctantly admit: The ownership of such houses, orchards, and truck gardens is legal. But it is what the owners do with the yield of that property that is so very wrong. Still the orchard owners fight on. A Moscow vegetable-and-fruit grower wrote to one of the chief Party campaigners: "If only you would be more practical and not just a brave hack of a writer, you would find in these cucumbers, these cabbages and potatoes, a great deal of down-to-earth wisdom and common sense for yourself, too . . . What, then, do you advise— that I raise a ton of cherries and hand it over as a free treat for everyone in my shop?" Precisely, replies the Party's righteous preacher, I do so advise. Silly of you, counters the orchard-owning protester. "You won't build Communism with such a formula . . . There is no reason why an individual should work for the collective, with the collective as his guests. There will be just too many such guests."

An *Izvestiya* writer exclaims: "But in our society, the material thing does not dominate man; man is above the material thing."[24] Another Communist journalist pleads: "We are not hypocrites and not ascetics. We wish everyone to have a good apartment, handsome clothes, graceful furniture, just as it is said in the Party program. But we want our youth to walk toward it by the same honest path that their fathers used. So there won't be any backstairs way to it."[25]

The skeptical answer seems to come up in one mighty chorus, addressed from all those new cherry orchards to all those Party axwielders:

Oh yeah?

CHAPTER XVII

~~~~~~~~~~~~~~~~~~~~~~~~~~~~

The Struggle up the Stairs

"IF AND WHEN the Party and the Komsomol call such people [to duty], will these people be able to part with the goods they have accumulated?"

The implied answer to this worried query is "No." The question is asked by a zealous Communist, who, in signing her name to her public complaint about laggards and deviators, proudly explains that she is a textile worker and a deputy in the Supreme Soviet of the Russian Soviet Federated Socialist Republic. The complaint concerns a couple of her acquaintance. Both man and wife are workers; they study in the evening, hoping to become engineers.

> They are well thought of at their jobs: they are valued for their skill, exemplary behavior, honesty. He is a young Communist; she is a Komsomol member.
>
> They have arranged their time schedule extremely tightly. And yet, each free Sunday these young people take a walk through . . . antique stores.
>
> No, they are not at all collectors; they are not lovers of old things. It is simply that they walk around full of admiration: "Look how those people lived! Oh, if only we had that much money . . ."
>
> Their small, sunlit room seems to have come down from a picture in an advertisement in the magazine *New Merchandise*. Elegant modern furniture, a tall candelabra, an antique vase "just for style," fashionable window blinds . . . They keep on purchasing from month to month, out of each pay. Persistently they hunt up one new thing after another, squeezing out of their close-packed schedule free time for such searching.
>
> And at times, in the evening, they daydream: "When both of us become engineers, how much will we be getting? . . ."[1]

The zealous woman Communist observed the couple for months and finally could hold herself no longer. She upbraided them to their faces for the pettiness of their ambitions. "The couple were offended. What was so bad in their desire to earn more, to dress well, to live among beautiful things? We spoke different languages. They were preoccupied with their personal welfare. I wanted for them toil, high and tense; life, bold and bright, full of search, achievements and victories, so that a song could later be composed about them." An orthodox Communist song, that is. "You are robbing yourselves," the complainant harangued the two future engineers prematurely playing their New Class roles. "Don't you notice that in your chase after prosperity you are losing something immeasurably more important? Can one be happy living for oneself only . . . ?"

And this is where the alarmed question comes in, Will they respond to the Party's call in an emergency? The negative answer to it is quite clear and, to the Party hierarchy, most disturbing.

The Soviet revolution, its propagandists insist, was carried out "so that work, instead of being a curse, would become man's greatest happiness."[2] Of course, as Khrushchev in his revision of the austere Lenin and the slave-driving Stalin tried to promise, work would lead to goulash and ballet and other satisfactions for both the masses and the classes. But, propagandists remind the people, one's personal welfare should not be achieved at the expense of, or even separately from, the welfare of fellow humans. In Soviet reality, however, a great many individuals strive only for their own property and prosperity. The revolution, they feel, whatever its initial aim, has come to mean for each Soviet inhabitant this narrow, selfish possession and enjoyment of material goods.

Of course, some citizens, when pressed for an answer to the question "What was the revolution for?" would be too shrewdly cautious—too "politically literate"—to be frank. They would give the proper, pious, official Communist reply about the splendid values of the future Communist society. But down deep in their hearts and thoughts they would be motivated by their own personal interests only. The revolution was carried out "so that I would be able to acquire a serving table," a well-polished, modish piece of furniture to which these days many Soviet citizens aspire; "so that I would live peacefully and comfortably."[3]

I I

To reach a higher station a citizen needs education. And that is what education in the Soviet Union is for—not to help the new and supposedly wonderful state and society, but to help oneself, to lift oneself out of the mire and misery of lower-class life, to struggle—or, more rarely, sprint—up those social stairs.

In the room of a young coal-mine engine driver in the Donets Basin a group of his friends and workmates gathered for a snack and a talk. The discussion veered to that favorite Russian theme, "What is happiness?" Someone unfolded a newspaper with an article containing a letter on this subject, from an engineer to a miner. A girl present at the reading sighed:

"Remarkable how he discourses about himself and people, but after all, he is already an engineer. He has found his happiness. But what are we to do? Must we also wait for our full maturity?"

She said this with such melancholy that the host became upset. His feeling was ambivalent. On the one hand, he was deeply sorry for her. On the other, he wanted "to lash out at her." He said that such young persons as this girl were well-nigh stupid. "They don't even cherish their own youth. Tell them to cherish their youth, but they would sacrifice their youth, all of it, just to jump over a few steps leading upward. So that they could close their eyes for a trice, open them, and presto, find that they are engineers."

But what for? What is their motive? "Do you think they envy [the engineers'] knowledge? Lies!" What then is it that attracts such lower-rung Soviet youths? Nothing but "the engineer's clean work and decent salary, his 'intellectual' apartment"—that is, an apartment of some comforts and conveniences usually achieved by Soviet intellectuals.

The host spelled out his indignation, but one of his male guests objected quietly: "Well, now, no one would decline all this."

Yet another young engine driver hotly sided with the host: "I won't deny it. Only I understand it like this: The apartment, the conveniences, and all the other goodness—it is fine when it comes by itself, well, automatically. You work, but you don't think of all those goodies, yet they come to you just the same—because you have deserved them. But if you bend your back all your life merely for the sake of some junk—to hell with it. For me the important thing is not what to accumulate but how to live."[4]

Brave words, indeed, but plainly a minority opinion among the Soviet masses. The majority feels that it is not enough to live honestly, and that surely it is preposterous to devote all of one's time to Communist ideals—to be an activist for the Party. "To know how to live" (*umet' zhit'*), a favorite expression of Soviet citizens "on the make," means to achieve status, a comfortable home, a car, and other tangible and selfish things. "I want to live the way the doctors of sciences do," a film-projector operator insisted as he kept on demanding from the state, his employer, a new and better apartment.[5]

A widespread feeling, this. Khrushchev did not like it, and his political heirs who displaced him may also dislike it, but Mao Tse-tung is right in his discovery that the post-Stalin Russia has gone bourgeois.

III

Rare is a young Soviet inhabitant who accepts his low position in the current version of Soviet society, who is not trying his desperate best to struggle up the stairs. In no modern nation do we find such acute embarrassment among the lower classes over their humble status as in the Soviet Union today. No one is truly proud of going through the school of hard knocks and a university of adversity. Practically every young Ivan and Natasha wants to be a graduate of a four- or five-year institute, with a diploma entitling its holder to all the prestige and privileges thereof, plus more of those rubles, of course.

You would think that in a country where a certain political party holds a monopoly of power young men and women would want to become political chiefs, Communist Party functionaries. Not so. The target, the ideal, is to be an engineer, a doctor, a scientist, a professor, or—the sweetest of all dreams—an academician. And in a sense the Party itself is responsible for such strivings. For it is the Party that, without realizing the full import of its own doings, has for years built up science and technology as the twin goddesses for the old and the young to worship.

The change in the ambitions of the nation's young was gradual yet clear for anyone with perception to see. In 1934 Ivan Makaryev, a Communist writer (who was soon to begin an eighteen-year term in a North Siberian concentration camp as one of Stalin's purgees), wrote to Maxim Gorky:

> A new generation is growing up, and it begins with technology, with the precise sciences. We have recently gathered school children of various ages and talked with them. Among other questions we asked: "What profession do you have in mind for yourself? What will you be doing two years from now?"
>
> Sixteen years ago each one of us—fifteen-year-olds then—gave to such a question one and the same answer: I will be a Commu-

nist, I will be defending the October Revolution. At that time, I remember, we would have jeered at anyone who would have said that he wanted to be a physician or an engineer. But now a twelve-year-old girl gets up to respond to this very question, calmly and confidently: "On finishing the nine-year-school I will go to college, I want to be an electrical engineer." A boy says he wishes to specialize in reinforced concrete. Another girl chooses radiotechnology. And so on, all forty of them, with no exceptions.[6]

In 1934 many such youngsters were motivated by their desire not only to improve their own personal status but also to serve the new Soviet state. By 1964 very little idealism was left. Personal reasons only or mainly governed the children and youths in the age brackets of, say, twelve to twenty-five in their intense drive to get an education. They wanted to give orders, not to accept and suffer them. Typical was a twenty-five-year-old worker, at last in his fifth year of correspondence courses at a technical institute, who was bluntly candid about his persistence: "I am studying only because I don't want to be walking around in dirt and swinging a sledge hammer forever." This is everybody's and anybody's reason for studying; it's all students' reason, he said, and don't let anyone tell you differently—"I declare this authoritatively. . . . I am tired of being shoved around, of being assigned dirty work. So much easier to command others."[7]

From time to time the Party is aghast at such sentiments. It deplores this wholesale infatuation with status; it takes practical measures. In its school reform of 1958 it decreed manual labor and the learning of crafts for elementary and high-school students as part of their curricula, to be interlarded with their books. It ordered more "practice," that is, work with their hands, for college students too. Most importantly, it introduced a two-year gap between high-school graduation and college entrance, to be filled with labor in factories and fields for youths and girls, lest they grow up too snobbish, too divorced from their parents' habits of honest, callus-raising toil.

By such measures the Party has in recent years denied college education to thousands upon thousands of "unfit" high-school graduates, mostly the offspring of the lower classes. Many more were stopped at the completion of the eighth grade, at the age of fourteen or fifteen, to be diverted from then on to inferior manual-trade schools and thus to second- or third-class citizenship for life.

The Party tries propaganda as well as legislation. It trumpets the glories of proletarian or farm labor; it urges the young to stay in their parents' factories or villages, to be the replacement that is so urgently needed in those lower strata of Soviet life and economy as their patriotic duty, as their Komsomol pledge. It tries to misrepresent such strata as not low at all, but high in purpose and merit and surely earning for their crews a tremendous sense of moral satisfaction.

Far more frequently and raucously, the Party denounces the lack of pride in honest, horny-handed toil—the gold rush of the lower classes toward diplomas for their children. It hurls thunder and lightning at those young who have neither ability nor true desire to study hard and successfully enough to be engineers and other professionals, who want status with no sweat of any kind, be it physical or intellectual.

> The petty man does not wish to work. He wants to "look well." He wants to gain an appearance, to pull the wool over our eyes by some diploma stolen from society by his five-year-long warming of an institute bench. . . . The ethic of the little men of low minds and high voices is based on their insurmountable thirst to "look decent" at any price, even the most rotten price. They have not a whit of human dignity. They have not the least conception of human pride, the least understanding of their own pitiful and ridiculous appearance.[8]

The Soviet propagandist calls such aberrantly ambitious youths and their parents "homespun aristocrats." He holds that parents are sometimes even more guilty than their young. They, of lower origins themselves, are surprised and indignant when a few of their boys and girls happen to wish such lower life work as their own destiny.

They are horrified when a rare boy wants to be a crane operator or a locksmith; when an occasional girl tries to be a seamstress or a saleswoman. And so the son is made to choose an institute against his will. The very thought of an institute "repels him" because "he wants to be a chauffeur." Not if Papa and Mamma can help it. For "Papa and Mamma are already infected by their own ethic." They will not tolerate "an unclean profession" under their roof. "And so the boy is harnessed and led like a horse on which a bet is made. They lead him to an institute. No matter what institute. So long as it is an institute."

It is such parents who are responsible for the prevalent view which makes the Soviet society of today into a kind of Noah's Ark separated into "seven pairs of 'clean' and seven pairs of 'unclean' professions." It is they who "bend their filthiest efforts to maintain their 'theory' of division of labor." It is they who are boorish to waiters and arrogant to taxi drivers; who mistreat scrubwomen and salesgirls. "Why do we have so few young talented tailors, to be artists of our attire?" Because of these new Soviet snobs who have made such essentially worthwhile professions a subject of sneer and derision, who insist that their children be naught but engineers.[9]

I V

Many are the cases cited in the daily Soviet press, of this inordinate parental drive.

A boy takes an institute entrance examination but fails. He wants to join his chums who plan to be factory workers. "But Mamma ordered me not to. She said they were not my equals, and that tending a lathe was not a proper occupation for an intelligent man. She wanted me to become an artist."[10]

A girl is asked by a teacher: "Have you already chosen, Galia?" The high-school senior "laughs as if she had not a care in the world" and replies: "I chose nothing. It's simply that Mamma came and filed an application for me to study for a draftsman-designer [of machinery]. She says it's better anyway than being a seamstress."[11] But another girl, one of the star pupils of her class, is even more practical as she daydreams: "How I would like to get married after I am through with school! But married not to someone plain, of course, but to a real money-earner, so that I could live like a queen. *Akh*, how fine that would be!"[12] And this girl's mother, too, is the inspiration.

The mother of a Soviet medical student meets one of her son's former high-school friends. She tells the young man the latest news of her son: "Lyonechka is now in Moscow, finishing his medical course. And you, Sashen'ka? Still an engine driver?" She asks this gently, pityingly. The young engine driver is greatly disturbed by her question and her tone. Later, telling of it with much anger to his friends, coal-mine engine drivers like himself, he bangs his enormous fist on the table: "Yes, I have been an engine driver, I will remain an engine driver, and I will order my children also to be engine drivers. I love this work, you understand! When I am on a leave, I become bored within a week, I get sluggish. But when back on the job, I mount my electric engine and I whiz through the mine, all my melancholy vanishes as if by magic . . . I love my work, I love miners."[13]

But will he indeed order his children, when they grow up, to be engine drivers? Despite all the official glorification of the heavy toil of the simple man, the lower classes of the Soviet Union again and again want their children to move up, not to stay at their parents' humble stations. A passenger on a train talks to a woman porter. He tells her that he is a worker—has toiled hard as a miner and a fitter. He has his calloused hands to show to the woman as his proof. He asks her: "Aren't you sick and tired of working? You ride and ride these trains. You have to take care of the toilets, and cater to capricious passengers." He suggests marriage, not too subtly: "I alone will work, and you will have everything. . . . You will stay home and rest." He thoughtfully selects their children's future: "The son will be an engineer; the daughter, a physician." He asks: "Aren't these dreams good?" She agrees: "Pretty good." Then she adds: "Let your son be a worker." He is startled. "A worker? No-o-o . . ." And he takes his calloused hand away from her.[14]

The Soviet young themselves do not want to stay in the society's basement if they happen to be born that low. Their fathers' muscle is no ideal to them. The industrial district Party secretary of Sverdlovsk complained about the "unpleasant" results of a questionnaire among the working-class teen-agers of the city of Nizhni Tagil in his bailiwick. He wondered aloud: "Why is it that so few youngsters want to be like their fathers?" He answered his own plaintive question: "Not because their fathers are bad, not at all. No, there are among them [the fathers] real heroes worthy of emulation. The trouble is that fathers pay little heed to their children, and do not open up before them the beauty and romance of their own toil."[15] In the Kuznetsk Basin, in Siberia, the same dismal situation prevails: young children "have very little knowledge of the Basin's best toilers." A child here and there "will name one or two such names" of the well-known workers. "And yet these boys and girls are our replacement. It is they who are to continue the glorious worker-class traditions."[16]

The fathers do not inspire their offspring, but the Soviet school is also held at fault:

From the first grade on, some teachers keep on telling the children: "To become an engineer or a flyer, you must study well, you must study much." But seldom can be heard: "To become a good lathe hand, you must also study well and much." And why not relate during the lessons about those lathe hands and milling-machine operators of nationwide renown—those talented men possessing a profound knowledge of physics, chemistry, and mathematics.[17]

The school is blamed because it does little or nothing to dispel the notion of "many young workers . . . that science is needed only by future engineers, and not at all by [the future] lathe hands, fitters, and electricians."[18]

There is a widespread indifference to the study of some exact sciences as well as of history and geography on the part of those youngsters who know they will not make college and a middle-class career. One such seventeen-year-old was quoted: "It is necessary to know only that which I will find applicable. And the rest—what for?"[19]

The awareness that institute entrance and eventual graduation into the higher class is forbidden fruit fills some Soviet youths with bitter resentment. They become Russia's angry young men. One such worker, on meeting an old schoolmate who has become an engineer, looks at Peter with "bad-tempered eyes" and thinks: "Aristocrats, intelligentsia, higher society. Where then is equality? Why could Pet'ka go on with his studies and be an engineer while I, a working stiff, am without education?"[20]

Why unequal salaries, why more and better conveniences and comforts for some and hardly any for others? "I come from work, but there is no place for me to rest . . . I am a labor-union member and pay my dues, but there is no help for me . . . Where then is equality? Some live, others exist . . ."[21] And: "It would be more just for everyone to receive the same pay—the cabinet-maker and the professor, the engineer and the worker."[22]

Soviet propaganda promises pie bye and bye here on earth. "After all, come Communism, we will all be engineers."[23] More and more "the essential difference between mental and menial labor is disappearing," and—under Communism—will melt away altogether.[24] So runs the Party's radiant tranquilizer.

But hollow laughter or quiet smirks of the populace high and low greet these assertions.

V

Aversion to physical labor is downright remarkable in the Soviet Union. If any trait or feeling is common to all classes, this is it. Sometimes you cannot say for sure who hates menial toil more: those who are cursed with it for their lifetime, or those who (thanks to the law of 1958) have had to put in a mere token amount of it en route to their higher stations in Soviet society.

Many young men and women of the higher classes, in fact, find loopholes to stay away from dirty work altogether, to go directly to institutes and universities from their high-school years, and on to their elite careers. Those who cannot escape even a minimum of work duty make no secret of their dislike for calluses. "At work they feel they are temporary guests only, show a frivolous attitude to labor, shy away from 'black-handed toil,' and wait impatiently for the time when 'all this' will finally end and they can go to college."[25]

Old-timers who profess to love menial labor are astonished that some youths assigned to them as apprentices quit after a mere day of work, saying: "It's dirty here—so much machine oil . . ." An old-timer describes his subsequent chance meeting with one such deserter:

"Where do you work now?"

"I am only a watchman. But on the other hand, I have to work at it two years only, and then I get my diploma."

In other words, the high-school graduate's required two years of "practical labor" have to be fulfilled somehow, and it better be done at a clean, though lowly, job as a watchman than as a dirty, even if more worthwhile, machinist's helper. The old-timer is indignant:

> So that is how it is! He needs not knowledge but a diploma. He does not value his future profession, just as he did not value his rank as a worker. He has become a watchman, don't you see, which is an old man's work. He does not mind, so long as that [two-year] phase is recorded, entitling him to college entrance. Formally he does everything correctly, and his diploma will be a correct one. But in substance we have somehow lost that fellow, and I don't believe that in time as an engineer he will ever be of any real use. He cannot become a good leader of a working collective when he shies away from physical labor and schemes to sneak into a plant without soiling his hands with that machine oil.[26]

A graduate of ten grades bitterly resents the law which says that, despite his high-school diploma (in Russian, *attestat zrelosti* —"certificate of maturity"), he has to do those two required years of "dirty, uninteresting work" before he can apply to college.* "And I will be paid for it a mere sixty rubles [per month]. Sixty rubles! And what can I do with these? Go with my friends to a restaurant just twice." The worst part of it all is the menial character of his job as a painter-plasterer's apprentice. "But I want to do intellectual work. There is some such at this factory, right? Any way of life, and ours—the Socialist way—in particular, should have its aristocrats of spirit. Or don't you recognize the intellect either?" he questions his fellow workers half plaintively, half mockingly.[27]

Looking for an easier job, a muscle-bound young man speeds from factory to factory, earning from their mates such partly derisive, partly indulgent names as *letun* ("flyer") and *begun* or *begunok* ("cross-country runner," or "race horse"). The flighty youths alibi themselves with such sayings as "Fish seek deeper spots, men look for better places" and "I do not intend to be a Hero of Socialist Labor."[28] Among other common comebacks made by the shirkers of dirty, heavy toil are:

"Only horses work"; or "Even horses die of work."[29]

"Only donkeys work"; or "Let the bear work—he has four paws."[30]

"I am not a tractor to work so hard"; or "Let the tractor work, it is made of iron."[31]

"Let the fool work, but the wise man will survive anyway."[32]

"Let the uncle take the journey." (The equivalent of the American "Let George do it.")[33]

"Work is not a wolf, it won't run off into a forest."[34]

"Work is not a flock of pigeons, it won't fly off in all directions."[35]

V I

But nowhere in the Soviet Union is life of labor as dismal and degrading as in the countryside. Or so holds the current Soviet belief, both urban and rural. Being a villager is the lowest form of Soviet existence. The very word *derevnia* ("village") is a curse. "How can we be indifferent," an irate Soviet journalist exclaims, "observing as we do those frequent scenes in our streets where some pimply youth taunts a policeman as 'village'? Truly one must have the iron self-control of our policemen not to deal with

---

* The law was considerably softened, if not entirely abandoned, a few months after Khrushchev's downfall, by the new and milder college entrance regulations of March 1965. One more evidence of the Party's retreat.

these 'enlightened personalities' as they deserve."[36] A Russian writer in New York, who studies the Soviet press well, notes in it frequent evidences of scorn of kolkhoz peasants by the young people of present-day Russia: "The kolkhoz peasant is [to the Soviet youth] a personification of the provincial simpleton."[37] Young men and women content to live in Soviet villages, or just arriving in cities to try urban careers, are held to be ignorant and naïve. The word *serost'*, for "grayness" or "colorlessness," is often—and with utter derision—used for them.[38]

In the cities of the Soviet Union not infrequently

> it happens that one hears from a person who is inadvertently pushed in a [crowded] trolley car: "Where do you think you are? At your kolkhoz?" For such people, you see, a kolkhoz man or woman is a lower being, not worthy of attention and respect.[39]

In a regional maternity hospital two new mothers struck up a friendship—until one of them waxed enthusiastic about her life and work on a collective farm. Later she recalled:

> I was so carried away by my own tale that it wasn't at once that I noticed [the other woman's] haughty glance . . . ". . . Oh, you are only a kolkhoz woman . . ." she drawled, almost with pity. She then caught herself and said, as if trying to console me: "Well, what can one do about it? Not everybody is apt at studies . . . My own mother is a plain kolkhoz woman. Everyone cannot be educated. Someone has to dig around in the manure."[40]

Peasants are sometimes gleeful or puzzled when they see high-school graduates toil by their side "in the manure."[41] What indeed was your education for? This is exactly the soul-searching question the young villagers ask themselves. As these eighteen-year-old lads and girls "kept on laboriously chipping the frozen manure and sorting potatoes in the bins, they thought their melancholy thoughts" about all those wonderful things they had learned in their ten- or eleven-year schools: the heroes and heroines of the ancient Slavic epos, the history of Tamerlane's invasions, or the intricacies of botany's teaching on the Ranunculaceae, the crowfoot family, or Newton's binomial . . . "What did we have to learn all this for? To throw a healthy potato to the right, and a moldy one to the left? One can do this without knowing even the alphabet. And will such toil be our destiny all life long?"[42]

Manure as a bugaboo is mentioned repeatedly, in a host of such accounts from all over the Soviet empire. It has by now become the hateful symbol of this village hopelessness. A young man asks: "To cart cow dung around—is this why I finished the ten-year school?"[43] A peasant woman angrily rebuked her mother, a poultry caretaker, for chiding the family's young daughter about her idleness: "Why are you picking on the girl? She has her own worries. She is a person of books. All our lives her father and I have worked like the devil. Let at least our daughter see the world. Are we making it possible for her to study only that she would be cleaning those poultry coops?"[44]

When Soviet girls are told that kolkhoz swineherd girls are paid the rather high (for the Soviet Union) wages of 150 rubles a month, one girl speaks for many as she explodes: "Be it even a thousand, what use would it be? Some joy—to wither your whole life away at a kolkhoz!"[45] A village boy planning to strike out for the city replied to someone who tried to dissuade him: "Only the ungifted and the ne'er-do-wells remain in this hole."[46] Another sneered when kolkhoz life was suggested to him: "You think I am a fool?"[47] When three girls, each sixteen years old, came to a pig farm as volunteers the farm manager was astounded: "I've been working here so many years, but this is the first time that they came [to the pigsties] of their own free will."[48] More often a girl will run off to the city, "to get any job—to tend a furnace, for instance." One such ex-kolkhoz girl "lived in a cellar, next to the boiler, in dampness, with no daylight, but in the city! . . ."[49]

But many an ex-villager will use such a terrible city job and lodging as a temporary stage only. If the young had enough spunk to flee from the country mire, they won't be stuck next to a furnace for long. They will perform miracles to get a good education and thus a better city station in life. It is true that if they don't make a university or a technical college, they seem to be thrown back as they accept the lowest possible training—that leading to an agricultural degree. An American scholar visiting the Soviet Union in May 1963 reported that agricultural training in that country "is downgraded or, at best, is used in lieu of general education." So said Theodore W. Sudia, an assistant professor of plant pathology and physiology at the University of Minnesota, as he elaborated:

> Since agriculture is considered to be a low status occupation in the Soviet Union, this program has not attracted large numbers of capable students who elected it as their first choice. . . . University training has the highest status among prospective students in the Soviet Union and the competition for places in the university is

most intense. Agricultural training, on the other hand, is a low status program which has a great many students in it because it is the only program open to them.[50]

Some become agronomists because they really want such professions and such rural lives. And quite a few of these live to become disillusioned. "In my institute [days] I was an idealist," one such agronomist confesses, "but speaking plainly, I was a fool. I came here thinking to move mountains. But the mountains turned out to be too steep for me!"[51]

Many finish those agricultural courses but don't go to the village at all, or, once there, quickly desert. They cling to their agricultural diplomas nevertheless, because it is an education anyway, even if they don't use it in any manner whatever—except as a thing of status, of course.

The statistics of such diploma-owning deserters from the villages and their vocations is, as we know from the daily Soviet press, truly overwhelming. When pressed too hard by the authorities to return, an agronomist will exclaim: "I am ready to return my diploma, but I will not go to the village."[52] All the desperate propaganda in the press, in the novels and stories, in the theater and other media, do not seem to make the slightest dent. Stop idealizing kolkhoz life, Soviet cynics hurl back at the propagandists.

Oh the rustic idiocy of it! The younger among Moscow's literati boldly parade their "lordly attitude . . . toward the rural theme." One of them said to an older novelist: "Why do you keep on writing on the rural theme? After all, this is not fashionable. Today's literary idol is the intellectual hero."[53] To an idealist who volunteered to work in the wilderness of Soviet Bashkiria, an urban friend wrote: "What unholy spirit has chased you to borrow trouble in that far-off land neglected by nature itself? Duty? Eh, don't even recall . . . such highfalutin words. Let them resound in official holiday orations only."[54]

CHAPTER XVIII

And the Caste Came Back

BY NOW IT IS HARDLY A SECRET that, while denouncing any and all class structures and divisions in general, but in the capitalistic world especially, the Soviets have been guilty of the same sin at home. What is not commonly realized outside the Soviet Union is the extent to which this class separateness, this status feeling based on one's socioeconomic position, has come to pervade all fields of Soviet life. Indeed, with much astonishment, foreign observers reach the conclusion that the Soviet chasms between class and class are greater, sharper, in fact and in feeling, than such phenomena are in the non-Soviet world. The Second World War, with its mobility, brought this to foreign attention more readily and clearly than it could be recognized earlier. Two accounts are particularly worthy of citation here:

In 1944–45 a Polish woman named Lida, who was married to a Hungarian, happened to be in a Hungarian village when the victorious Russian troops swept in. In the chaos and misery that followed, Lida supplied whatever stability and understanding could be had in the vortex. For she spoke some Russian and so served as an interpreter, mediator, and, on occasion, rescuer. With her keen ear and eye she perceived, among other things, this extreme class pride and pretense among the Russians. Every officer and soldier of those Soviet regiments said that before the war he had been either "an engineer or director of a factory, or a professor." With well-placed irony she wrote:

> In Russia, land of peasants and workers, there do not seem to be
> any peasants or workers at all. Of all the hundreds I got to know
> during those months spent under the Red Army, I only met one or
> two drivers or mechanics and not a single peasant. The corn in
> Russia seems to grow by itself, and the factories to run without
> workmen, being manned exclusively by directors.

She and the other West Europeans who met these Red pretenders were skeptical. They shook their heads in disbelief: "An engineer? A culinary professor? A mathematician? Director of the Odessa opera? Well, I wonder." They wondered why these modern Russians were ashamed to admit the undubitable fact that they came from, and after the war would return to, their humble jobs at factories and on the collective farms.

An added tragicomic touch was in the effort of these West Europeans, caught in the Red zone of occupation, to court favor with the conquering horde by passing themselves off as lowly farmers or honest proletarians, which, of course, most of them were not. The result was

> the paradoxical situation that we were always trying to persuade the Russians that we were a sort of peasant, or at any rate working class, and would proudly exhibit our carefully neglected fingers and the blisters that we were at such pains to renew; while they took as much trouble and used the same ingenuity in trying to persuade us that they were soloists in the Leningrad opera, brothers-in-law of some marshal, or directors of a factory. It was all very strange.[1]

The strangeness of it increased when the conquering soldiers and their reluctant hosts in Hungary compared factory wages West and East. These Soviet warriors did some peculiar bragging:

> It seems that in Russia there is an enormous discrepancy between the different rates of pay. The difference between the earnings of an engineer and an ordinary laborer is reminiscent of the times when the Pyramids were being built. Or perhaps those soldiers were lying, just trying to boast of the huge income of an engineer or factory director in the Soviet Union. Yet, many other Russians had also boasted about that. They did not seem to realize what bad propaganda that was for their system. Why, I wondered, didn't they call themselves the land of high officials and technicians instead of workers and peasants?[2]

Back in Moscow, in the very heart of this strange nation and its curious system, another foreign woman—an American—noticed the same phenomenon but in a somewhat different form. Here, for ten months in 1945–46, Mrs. Brooks Atkinson, the wife of a *New York Times* drama critic and war correspondent, found that a Russian could not shamelessly lie that he was of a class to which he did not actually belong. But as in Hungary, so in Moscow, he was exceedingly class-conscious and, in the same uneasy way, most unflattering to his country and its regime.

After noting the extreme manifestations of wealth and poverty in this "Socialist" land, the American went on:

> I have never known a society where such innumerable strata of rank exist. Everybody is fanatically aware of his own place in his own class and is intent on impressing the fellow just a little lower down the ladder. There's no use beating about the bush. Russians are arrogant to one another and oftener than not downright mean. Take the small world of an office. Among the employees, the secretary is top dog and is usually unspeakably arrogant to the others of the staff. . . . But the couriers, who are next below, receive this meekly enough. They have their chance to be arrogant to the porters and chambermaids.

Where does it stop? Where is the rock bottom? The American visitor did not know "whom the porters and the maids find to snub, but they surely find somebody." (My guess is that they tyrannize over their families, particularly those members who are fresh arrivals from the village, or who are either too young, too old, or too ill and feeble to work and contribute.)

Mrs. Atkinson generalized that "the least bit of authority makes a Russian incredibly overbearing," and went on to give chapter and verse out of her own experience:

> Russians with whom I was well acquainted astonished and abashed me by their attitude toward those who were in their employ or who were, for the moment, under their direction. Women who spoke to me in the modulated and gentle tones of ladies would turn on a waiter or a maid and give out like a virago. A domestic servant who is unlucky enough to be employed by a Russian is sure to be ground into the dirt. In this country [the United States] anybody who spoke to an employee as the Russians do would soon be the bewildered possessor of a black eye or a bloody nose. Employees in Russia expect to be treated with superciliousness and brutality.

Then followed a most particularly enlightening illustration:

> I took Lydia Vyschinskaya, our courier, to a concert one night. Lydia knows more about music than I do and she makes a very pleasant companion to boot. Sitting next to us was a Russian woman we both knew, and she was embarrassed and outraged at the fact that I had Lydia with me. (A courier!) She was distinctly uncomfortable and embraced the first opportunity to detach herself from us and get with people of her own class.

The worst of it all was that, while Mrs. Atkinson took the incident as something both comic and absurd, "Lydia, although a little crushed by the snubbing she received from this regal lady, nevertheless meekly seemed to feel that it was the normal course of events and that nothing else was to be expected."

Any excuse for such conduct? A very tenuous one: Russians appear to behave so boorishly as a kind of self-defense. "If you don't treat a waiter or a porter like a dog, he thinks you are a fool and begins to treat you like one." And yet there is a hope: Western residents in Moscow, if they had wisdom and patience enough, gradually taught their Russian servants to respond to decency with decency as these natives proceeded to "enjoy the dignity accorded them" by their employers.[3]

I I

Over the years, but particularly since the Second World War, evidence of social gaps has come to light in the cases where the various Soviet classes have met—and clashed—in marital unions. Indeed, many tragedies of love and marriage have been caused by this new class feeling and caste fear in the land supposedly made safe for equality by Marx and Lenin.

A young woman worker became a chemistry student at the Novocherkassk Polytechnic Institute. She met a young man who appeared to be far more polished than she ever hoped to be, and whose friends were "future actors, future artists, and future diplomats." They criticized "old music" and "photographlike paintings"; they "searched new forms of art"—they were intellectual snobs. The young man introduced the young woman worker-student to "his circle," but had first warned her not to talk of her working-class antecedents. "A simple worker," he mused, "this is so prosaic."[4]

Another young man discarded his early love and became engaged to another girl. A friend of his was surprised. "But you did love Inna!"

"Yes, I loved her, I don't deny this . . . But I am almost an engineer, while she is an ordinary salesgirl . . . My future wife is about to get her engineering diploma. In our incomes we will be well fixed."

"But do you love her?"

"I view life soberly, without sentimentalities. Accordingly I chose that which suits me best—that which has good prospects."[5]

Sometimes it is the parents or other relatives who either interfere with the budding romance of "the unequals" or even break up a marriage.

A young candidate of the technical sciences started a veritable campaign against his brother's bride. He chided the brother: "Whom did you marry? Where were your eyes? She has no diploma, and no one can really live without it. Leave her before it is too late!" He made life hell on earth when she with her husband and their baby came to live in his parental home, which the caste-conscious candidate of the sciences also shared.[6]

If the family does accept the mesalliance, they still cause trouble when they clumsily try to elevate the low-class stranger. For instance: Two lovers were happy until they became officially engaged. Then the young man's parents "categorically refused to accept a waitress as a member of their family." They issued the ukase: "Bring home anyone except a waitress!" So she quit her job, where she had been so well-adjusted and happy, to take up clerking (considered more genteel), where she promptly found herself horribly unhappy. She was now "irritable," and "a morose wrinkle furrowed her forehead." For she no longer dealt with people, whom she liked, but with "little papers and more of those little papers," which she did not like.[7]

The family of a retired colonel received their daughter's husband at first quite well, but soon it began to irk them that the new son-in-law was uneducated. The young man complained: "They are intellectuals, don't you see, but I am a worker, not equal to them. So they are now busily destroying our young marriage." The new relatives tried to involve him in things of the spirit. Their conversations "irritated him, particularly when they talked of some book that interested them." He did not like books. He did not want to study in the evening. Instead he played a horn in an amateurs' band and loved to march in funeral processions, blowing with all his might. His young Katia blushed with shame each time she saw and heard him in such a public exhibition. Finally she said: "I can't bear it any more. Leave us, you are not our equal."[8]

In a Poltava Region village the relatives of a local male teacher decided that it was most embarrassing that his wife was well known in the kolkhoz as its hard-working swineherd. They were influential relatives, and by pull and pressure they obtained her appointment as the village Club of Culture leader. The club at once deteriorated. Neither lectures nor concerts graced its boards. It was not the woman's fault, said an indignant correspondent. "She is conscientious and industrious. It is simply that she does not fit the job. Her education stopped at a low point, she has

never participated in any [culture] groups, and she lacks organizing abilities. She herself understands all this, but, despite herself,
is silent." Her husband and father-in-law are quoted: "We have
taken you away from your pigs, we have made a person out of
you, so just accept the money and keep mum. We will see to it
that you remain in charge of the club."[9]

When a woman, married to a higher-status man, insists on
doing a lowly job, the man's superiors are aghast. A naval officer's wife was a skilled automobile mechanic and chauffeur. She
asked her husband's commander for a job in the naval shops. He
was dismayed. "Just think what people will say: the husband is a
senior officer, and the wife is a chauffeur. Don't you understand
that you will embarrass your husband!" She was offered an office
job instead, but she declined.[10]

I I I

But it is rare that a Soviet citizen protests against somebody's
effort to deprive him of a low-status job, to give him a higher
occupation. The reverse is far more common: everyone is trying
to pull himself up by his bootstraps, to be—by hook or crook—at
the next stage of society, whether or not the arrival at that next
stage is genuinely earned.

The young men and women of the Soviet Union may hold
lowly technical positions for a long time without any likelihood of
promotion if only because the level of their education is too far
below their ambition. Continuing or not continuing their studies
to achieve the desired higher status, some invent short cuts at
least via phraseology: an engineer-designer once complained that
his subordinates refused to call themselves by their proper name
of draftsmen. The word "draftsman," he pointed out, practically
disappeared from everyday Soviet life. "Nearly everyone who can
hold a drawing pen in his hand is called a designer."[11]

Above all, however, everybody seems to call himself an engineer. Men and women with no engineering diplomas or any pertinent technical education promote themselves, arbitrarily, to this
socially (and sometimes materially) desirable status. At the Scientific Research Institute of Rural Construction, situated near
Moscow, the former assistant hotel manager pops up as "the
senior engineer of the technical-economic research sector." A
woman, whose chief schooling in the past was in bookkeeping,
finds herself in the same Institute as "the senior scientific col-

laborator on problems of reinforced concrete." Other newly ele-
vated engineers and "scientific collaborators" of the same staff
turn out to be former ship's mechanics and pilots, an ex-telephone
operator, some railroad engine repairmen and a railroad traffic
expert, and even an erstwhile restaurant cook (male)![12] At
Makhachkala, in Daghestan (North Caucasus), "the majority of
senior engineers arriving from other regions to serve in the construction and electrification industries have an education that
stopped at six or seven grades."[13]

Early in 1963 the number of engineers in the Soviet Union was
estimated at close to 1,500,000,[14] but just how many of these
were possessors of real training and true diplomas and how many
were indifferently self-taught or even crassly self-styled? The
answer at the time was: "Only 38 per cent of all the engineering
jobs in the R.S.F.S.R. are occupied by persons with higher education. Nearly two thirds of the country's engineers are not at all
engineers."[15]

IV

Even as a Soviet man or woman achieves a middle- or upper-
class station there is still a higher rung to be gained, and thus,
somebody's grip to be removed from your neck. There is still the
salary to be improved before your new status is indeed secure—
en route to yet higher station. Your college education does not
put you higher on the social ladder if your salary somehow happens to be low.

When the manager of a Soviet state supply depot in the city of
Gorky called a woman buyer on his staff into his office and began
to upbraid her, she objected to his rudeness. He became yet
angrier: "How can you argue with me when all you are worth is
seventy rubles a month?" She started to cry as she spoke about
her higher education and her human dignity.

And so he had to explain to her that "in nature a certain ladder
exists, upon which some people stand higher and others lower,
and with each new step people get larger salaries and with these—
you know what?—yes, dignity." And so, who has more dignity,
the likes of him or the likes of her? "Who should learn from
whom?"

She tried to say through her sobs that her manager was a fool.
She attempted to say this in the form of an old Russian folk
saying, but he interrupted her with an admonition that "this folk

saying is not a Soviet one, that for a long time now we have no fools and cannot have any," and therefore he ordered her to leave his office.[16]

Yet, on the whole, education does mean better wages for the diploma holder and thus a higher social standing. The lower classes of the Soviet Union are firmly convinced that at the end of the diploma's rainbow there is indeed a pot of rubles as well as society's respect. And real class struggle comes to the Soviet Union when those with diplomas feel that the recognition of such degrees is not expressed in material-enough terms.

Young engineers frequently complain that not always do they find true use and recognition of their diplomas and talents. At certain plants young graduates of engineering schools are used as mere technicians, as supply managers, as clerks, but not as engineers. Some suffer this demeaning fate the three years which officially they must serve at their assigned jobs, working off their debt to the state for their education. Some even get used to the routine and security of their unimaginative toil so much that they remain at those plants for a long time beyond the prescribed three years.

But others protest this awful waste of their long years of engineering training. They say how miserable they feel when they meet their luckier classmates who are employed properly and who talk of exciting laboratories and experiments of their jobs—that is, talk on these wonderful themes among themselves, but when they turn to their "overlooked" fellow graduates, "they can talk with me about football only."

As a matter of sad fact, even for their jobs as minor technicians, supply supervisors, and routine plant clerks, these young engineers are ill prepared. For their training was far more complex and precious; they were to be engineers—only to be underused, "devalued" as engineers. What a tough end to their ardent dreams, what stupid irony! And why isn't Soviet government doing something about it?[17]

Thus, young Soviet engineers are often restless and even bitter. "The young specialist is dissatisfied," an older engineer warns his fellow countrymen. "This must put us on guard." He goes on to tell how awkward he feels when a young engineer on his staff comes to him with the request: "Transfer me"—that is, from one department to another; usually, from a direct contact with machinery and workers to the peace and quiet of one of the plant's offices. The older engineer also tells how much more his day is

THE NEW CLASS DIVIDED

spoiled when one of his young charges, an engineer just beginning his career at the plant, asks him: "Let me go"—that is, give him his discharge from the plant altogether. The young man, you see, is completely disappointed.

One reason for the young engineers' restiveness is the reluctance of their superiors to give them interesting, independent, challenging work. "The engineer begs to be entrusted with work that is more complex [than what he is doing], but the answer is: 'Don't be in a hurry. Every fruit has its season. You must ripen first.' And so the man 'ripens' a year, 'ripens' another year, and then quits the plant." Another weighty reason is housing—the lack of it. There are not even enough dormitories for young engineers. Separate rooms ensuring privacy are still scarcer. Apartments for young engineers are indeed a rarity. "Newlyweds obtain rooms after considerable troublesome red tape."[18]

But the validity of such reasons is denied by some of the young people's superiors. More typically than any sympathy for young engineers there is impatience and resentment on the part of the higher authority when it runs head-on into the youth's rising expectations. It's just too bad about so many young Soviet engineers, the higher-up man says, that they do not want to work right next to the machines and furnaces, that they long and scheme for clean office jobs. "I think that the institutes are to blame in this respect," one such superior pontificates. "They don't prepare young specialists psychologically for toil in the thick of production." As students these young people do all sorts of things except labor with their hands and tools. But this they must certainly and uncomplainingly "do at the very beginning of their engineering biographies."[19]

Persistently, stubbornly, young engineers disagree. Said an engineer in Soviet Karelia, with complete candor: "My diploma works for me. It is enough for me to come to work on time and wait for the quitting whistle." He had some ten or twelve workers under him, but hardly talked to them, and wrote out their assignments only once a month.[20] Another engineer, sent to a small provincial factory, refused even to come to his office. When pressed, he said scornfully: "I was trained to be the captain of an ocean liner, but your little no-good factory is only a barge."[21]

Young degree-holders are told to learn engineering by firsthand experience, but they say they are insulted: "I, a candidate of the sciences, join a mine staff?"[22] As already indicated, they do not want jobs in the mines or the plants, but positions in research offices, planning and designing bureaus, and clean, high-prestige laboratories. "They shy away from production and gravitate to places that are less 'dusty' and, in their opinion, quieter and more promising."[23] Out of fourteen engineers who in 1961 came to a Yaroslavl plant to labor with machines and workers, by January 1963 one half managed to find themselves cleaner and less hectic jobs in the plant's offices, away from the lathes and the crew. By that time also the 1962 graduates became frequent visitors and inquirers at the plant's offices and laboratories.[24] Nobody, it seemed, wished to stay even a short time at the lower and dirtier notches of the Soviet totem pole. At Cheliabinsk, a plant producing road-building machinery reported that fewer than 20 per cent of its engineering staff stayed at the lower posts with the actual production, and "the plant's chief engineer sadly admits that practically every engineer" down below wants to get out of the shops and "dreams of going away to be the chief designer and the chief technologist"—that is, to clean, neat, high-shelf jobs in the *bil'ding* (the new Russian borrowing of the English "building"), which is the plant's office.[25]

The engineer expects as his right a higher place in today's Soviet society—better living conditions and more respect from the very date of the issuance of his diploma. He kicks up a fuss when his sometimes inflated expectations are not immediately fulfilled. In his student days he was not a spoiled brat. For five or even six long years at the institute he and perhaps a young wife lived a most Spartan life. They worked hard, ate little, asked no favors, and bought their textbooks and their modest clothing with their own earnings. "But perhaps because their student years were not at all easy, this concept . . . had already then gradually formed in his mental make-up that with the engineer's diploma there should come to him all the goodies at once."[26] The hard work of those five long years was behind; now the engineer should have his ample compensation. Everything should be served to him on a silver platter.

The Komsomol accusers condemn this claim as "a concept that is half childish, half petty." But young engineers dissent. They feel that through their long-drawn-out study and privations they did indeed earn their place on the higher ladder of Soviet society. They want better housing, fatter and sweeter food, and other emoluments. They look down on people and things below them because they are sincerely convinced they are now entitled to this position and to this viewpoint.

V

The caste is solidified by parents who have arrived, not alone through their position and pull that give the children preferred education and privileged jobs, but also through one of the most un-Marxian features of Soviet life: the right to inherit the parents' property. From time to time the faithful in the Soviet flock protest against the nation's inheritance law as too permissive, as leading to the perpetuation of the idle part of the new elite.

One such protester reminds his fellow citizens of the basic Soviet precept, "whoever does not work, he should not eat." This, he says, stems from the basic Socialist precept, "From everyone according to his ability, to everyone according to his work." He poses the indignant question:

> How, then, do these commandments manage to coexist with the situation wherein, upon their parents' death, the children inherit everything that their father or mother received from the state for their toil (everything, including author's rights for valuable scientific works, inventions, artistic creations, etc.)? Through this, the children, quite often already of age, receive that which has not been earned by them, and which really does not belong to them.

Because they are of age, these adult heirs, who can and should make their own living, are not ethically entitled to their late parents' bounty. The Communist zealot sees "tremendous moral harm" in certain consequences of the inheritance law: "Such children know, while their parents are still alive, that they do not have to worry about their future, that there is 'a reserve' made ready by Papa and Mamma." And there is one more bad feature of it all:

> Frequently, unclean persons fawn upon such future inheritors. These persons' influence has a clearly negative effect on the moral development of the heir. And we do not have to be reminded of the numerous instances when around the inheritance there emerges a dirty wave of litigation, court cases, and at times even criminal actions.

The protester demands an immediate drastic revision of the inheritance law that would give the children no more than a part of their parents' estate, a modest stipend until the children are through with their schooling. The rest should revert to the state, so that "the outdated principle of inheritance" would no longer "create conditions for the appearance of new and yet newer parasites, idlers, hooligans, and drunkards."[27]

But such protesting puritans are, on the whole, few and far between. This and other Soviet inequality is generally given the popular nod. Fame and position, inherited or not, are accepted by the nonfamous and nonpositioned as something to cater to, even to worship, in a spirit not at all democratic or otherwise fitting the brave new world of Sovietism.

The student son of a celebrated Soviet aircraft designer received his first assignment as a plant trainee (within his college program). The father saw him off rather modestly; he toasted him with a single glass of champagne at the railroad station, just before the lad's train pulled out, and he gave a few sparse points of fatherly advice.

Not so spartan was the reception awaiting the celebrity's son at the other end of the railroad journey. Bowing and scraping, the plant's administration announced a much-higher-than-usual rate of pay for the youth's labors while training. Instead of housing him in a common dormitory, they gave the youth a separate room with all "high-life" comforts. The training schedule itself was arranged in as light a manner as possible.

But the father, on his very first visit to the son, was not at all pleased. Holding severe views on the upbringing of the young, he was so angered by this pampering "that he nearly had a heart failure." He took measures, with telling results. "That very day the son moved to a common dormitory, received from its superintendent a set of bed linen that had been laundered many times, and returned to the cashier all the money issued to him by those servile lickspittles." Thus the aircraft designer "taught an excellent, unforgettable lesson not only to his son, but . . . to the lickspittles too, and to the son's comrades, and to the parents of an entirely different school of thought"—the parents who like to say: "We have worked hard, let our children live better than we did."[28]

But mostly, as already mentioned, it is parents who take the lead in seeking privileges and comforts. It is the parents who often push their unwilling and incapable sons and daughters into and through institutes. And if the son manages to stay in his institute the five or six stipulated years and finally grasps that precious diploma, Papa and Mamma will see to it that he is not sent away by the state authorities to work off his debt to the state for three long years in some faraway and godawful province.

The fond parents want their darlings to remain amid the bright lights and good comforts of "centers," as large Soviet cities are called caressingly. "Papa has enough contacts, and Mamma enough voice to keep the young *baccalaureus* at home. In such cases they proclaim their kiddie short of full value [to the state], sick, subject to paroxysms, married—anything at all, so long as he is not sent away."[29]

The official Soviet propaganda line presents such doting parents as the lowest of the low: "The dull inhabitant humiliates himself, spits at his own horrible face, bows low, crawls on his belly, only to save from attack his exclusiveness, his supernoble origin." But the Communist Party is strong and hits hard, particularly in its latest measures against "the idlers." The parents are outwitted. "Papa does not after all have enough contacts to appoint his kiddie engineer-in-chief, and Mamma lacks sufficient voice to place her baby as manager."

So they try again. They invent part-time jobs, sinecures, fictitious positions for their children. "But this, too, does not always work out." And so, as the very last resort, the newly graduated engineer is given a job "not according to his specialty, his profession, his wish even," but to hide him somewhere, somehow— "until everything settles down."

And so engineers take other jobs, just so they can stay in parental homes. Some of these jobs are startlingly menial—the very thing the families originally strove hard to avoid as they pushed their darlings into institutes. But now an engineer waits on tables! Still the family can boast that it has a son who is officially an engineer. "Most likely, at an aunt's birthday party Papa brags of his son the engineer, and the auntie is much pleased that she, too, is related. . . . How humiliating all this. . . . And an engineer may be needed in some or other far-off places . . ."[30]

V I

And then, again, even when an engineer or other technician accepts a position that he does not exactly like, he will find ways in which to express his dissatisfaction while holding that job and doing his duty. Nor is this protest quiet and barely noticed. To the contrary, it may turn out to be bold and loud, for everyone to see, and for the Party to be shocked by it.

Technicians' open opposition at times takes forms quite unusual for a totalitarian society. Among them we note a contemptuous refusal to accept the state's medals. A well-publicized case occurred at Volgograd, where three junior technicians acting as foremen at the building of that city's giant power dam declined the medals awarded to them by the Soviet government, two "For Labor Valor," and one "For Labor Excellence."

All three had deliberately failed to warn the Party and the government functionaries in charge of the medal distribution. They had purposefully left the functionaries in complete ignorance of their intention not to come to the solemn ceremony in the Palace of Culture and not to offer any excuses for their non-acceptance. They had apparently wished to make a public demonstration of their refusal. The Party men running the Palace ceremony were visibly embarrassed when silence greeted their announcement of the three names, when none of the three men came forth to be pinned and congratulated.

The Party men stammered: "What happened? Are they ill?" No, all three came to work the next day, all three hale and hearty but sullen and even angry. They were asked: "Why didn't you come to the Palace of Culture?" The three scornful answers were: "There was nothing for me to do there." "That medal is not enough for me, give it to somebody else." "I expected more than that medal."

The first reaction of the Party men in the area was, "We will yet talk them into accepting their medals." But higher Party authority pronounced its stern judgment: Don't waste your time on these "capricious" men who "spit in the collective's face."

And so the local Soviet propagandists were at once given instructions to denounce the trio publicly, to compose a list of their demerits, to say that they really did not deserve those medals in the first place—it was all a mistake to award them such honors, for they had, long before, "become too cocky and too proud," had developed much earlier a "snobbish attitude to the collective."[31]

VII

Snobbishness is the sin often and shrilly ascribed by the Party to the scientific, engineering and managerial elite, as this elite becomes more and more conscious of its education and worth. In 1963 in the universities and colleges of a number of Soviet cities (Ufa, Omsk, Ivanovo, Vladivostok, Kazan, and Gorky) a survey by the Ministry of Higher and Secondary-Special Education of the

R.S.F.S.R. found among students "young persons with unstable ideas," some of whom "acquire a lordly and scornful attitude toward those around them, are dissatisfied with everything, grumble about everything . . ."[32] Two years after his graduation from an institute an engineer is described as having purposely sharpened his formerly soft and round features: he has succeeded "in giving his face a slightly arrogant, subtle expression with the help of an eye squint and a skeptical half smile." Even his posture and walk were now "an obvious imitation of manners observed by him in foreigners: he usually stood with legs wide apart and arms folded on his chest, and he walked with a loose-jointed gait."[33] In short, he wanted everyone to know he was now of a higher stratum. Two other engineers, man and wife, are depicted as living amid comforts, music, and flowers, in "a beautiful, aromatic world" all their own, both "elegant and absolutely calm" —and calmly indifferent to human unhappiness right next door.[34]

The new elite has status. The new elite insists on more and more kudos and comforts. Status as enjoyed and yet more demanded takes many significant forms. Status is a many-headed hydra and a many-splendored siren. Status is placing your children in the few select schools in Moscow, Kiev, Gorky and other cities where instruction is solely or mainly in English, French, and other foreign languages. Rules for acceptance are vague, the admission quota is "many times smaller than the number of applicants," and the result is the popular (and correct) rumor that "these schools are for the 'privileged.' "[35] A typical first grade will take sixty boys and girls out of some two hundred applicants, and so, naturally, the academicians, scientists, engineers and other elite papas and mammas engage in pull and intrigue to get ahead of one another.[36] And once a professor's spoiled brat is in such a school he may poison his teachers' days by disobedience and some such remarks as "For me the only authorities are members of the Academy of Sciences."[37]

Status is bringing a cowboy suit for your girl from your foreign mission, and the suit's winning the first prize (naturally) at a school carnival while scores of other "girls and boys, having themselves rigged up their primitive makeshift outfits, were offended in their best aspirations."[38] Status is also pre-empting the new and splendid Pioneer Palace, in Moscow's Lenin Hills, the University's neighborhood, "for whiz-kids only," so that "not so-gifted, but a lively and knowledge-hungry urchin" cannot get into any of the hobby groups of the Palace.[39]

Status is also building a complex of the new buildings for the Kirghiz Academy of Sciences with needless luxury: bas-reliefs of majolica on the walls inside and outside; other walls, columns, and pillars resplendent with marble and brass facings; oak panels in libraries and studies; furniture of rare and costly woods; chandeliers of bronze and crystal; and, last but not least, pools and fountains. Two Soviet finance officers, having recited this remarkable guidebook description, gently protested: "We . . . respect science and scientists not less than do those who planned the above mentioned project. And we are convinced that the scientists will understand us when we say: Really, comrades, marble walls and fountains will not after all help you in your work!"[40]

Status is a variegated wonder. "There are among us unfortunately," a Soviet journalist sighs, "some scientists who, before they even begin their work, surround themselves by a whole legion of assistants, laboratory aides, helpers, and statisticians."[41]

Also status is when, at a research institute, all the junior assistants must register the exact time of their arrival at and departure from the day's work, but not the holders of the degrees of doctor and candidate of sciences. These are exempt—they have "arrived" once and for all.[42]

Status is to consider a vacation at a seashore resort, instead of any inland trip or rest, as much of "an element of *bon ton* as coming to a solemn evening celebration in a snow-white shirt or wearing the Bologna raincoat in rainy weather."[43]

Status for a manager is to ignore the greetings of his subordinates[44] or to appear among his subordinates so infrequently that they mistake him for a visiting official.[45]

And status (the Party continues its charge) for a woman physician, head of the staff, is to force a middle-aged orderly, also a woman, to her knees, and thus to beg the chief's favor in granting the orderly a decent place to live.[46] Status for a plant manager is to eat in the plant's dining room, while everyone is quiet because the manager is eating. Thus, such a manager acts as if he were saying that "here I am now, within your sight, doing the same thing you are doing, but God save you from being a nuisance to me, by making noise, talking among yourselves, or approaching me with some question. I am dining."[47]

The Party, of course, may exaggerate the elite's snobbishness grossly. Yet there is no denying the fact that some of the Party's anguish is real; that the professional elite indeed feels superior and does not exactly conceal this. The professional elite did not, for instance, wait for Khrushchev's downfall to express its contempt for the uncouthness of Nikita Sergeyevich and to hold his crudity as a symbol of the Party. Indeed, despite the avoidance of the subject in the Soviet press, an increasingly large part of the Soviet intelligentsia learned—and did not like—the fact of Khrushchev's rude behavior in Paris in May 1960 and his shoe-banging at the United Nations in New York in October 1960. The professional elite's mildest term of scorn for him was *kukuruznik* ("corny guy")—to suggest his crudity rather than to allude to his onetime campaign to force Soviet peasants to raise more and better corn. The more forcefully derogatory *svinopas* ("swineherd") was also used. In Russian, this conveys far more disdain than its English counterpart. (A woman swineherd once complained that in a Ukrainian town any state employee found guilty of theft is punished by being sent to a pig farm. "It seems that in their eyes this is the highest penalty there can be. Such 'aristocratism' appears to us laughable, absurd, and insulting.") [48]

The Soviet press, with much indignation at engineers, scientists, managers, and students, reveals that their favorite term in scoffing at the uneducated, particularly if these happen to be Party activists, is *plebei* ("plebeians," or "plebes"). [49] Party zealots who willingly go off to distant provinces to dig or build new Socialist projects are called *plebei i psikhi* ("plebeians and psychos"). [50] Another denigrating term for the lower-class Party fanatics or gullibles is *pigmei* ("pigmies"). [51]

When Party men complain of managers' highhanded behavior, the managers hit back at the complainants' "lack of culture." In the Virgin Land area, the wife of a state farm manager, herself holding the job as her husband's personnel inspector, filed this countercomplaint: "We ask to punish him [a Party man representing the regional headquarters of trade unions] for his lack of tactfulness, his rudeness and ignorance. In the presence of workers, and using a sharp tone of voice, he chided the manager. He showed an absolute ignorance of both grammar and syntax." [52]

Yes, we are indeed the new breed of Soviet snob, admits a young physician. But, don't you see, we can't help it: "In each of us, to one extent or another, there sits the snob who forces us to look at everything around us with a wee bit of superiority." It is all in the nature of things human. [53]

CHAPTER XIX

The Technocrats and the Arts

IN THE ELITE'S EYES the Party is "plebeian" in many ways and for many reasons; among other things there is its notable lack of sensitivity to the finer things of life. At certain times the Party's official attitude toward modern art is regarded as particularly indicative of its uncouthness and ignorance. And the professional elite, in its own opinion, is that much better, finer, higher than the Party hierarchy, if only because, among other things, the elite understands modern art, while the hierarchy does not, yet dares (spasmodically) to fight against it.

Within the professional elite itself we find gradations and nuances in this matter of attitude to modern art. There is no doubt that Soviet scientists, accustomed to experimentation in their fields, are on the whole more receptive than other members of the intelligentsia to Western experimentation in the arts. Engineers follow close on the scientists' heels. One of the first visitors to the Soviet Union to notice this was Dr. Richard B. K. Mc-Lanathan, an authority on modern American art who in the summer of 1959 was curator of painting and sculpture at the American exhibition at Sokolniki in Moscow. Khrushchev, dropping in at the exhibit, got into a lively argument with Dr. Mc-Lanathan on the merits of abstract art, and various other Soviet viewers offered the curator their dissenting views, but, Dr. Mc-Lanathan tells me, remarkably sympathetic appraisals of latter-day experiments in art came from Soviet scientists and engineers, particularly young ones, who happened to be in the attending throngs.[1] These are the prosperous groups who support native experimenters. It is estimated that between 100 and 400 Soviet artists "continue to work in modern manners," despite the Party's ferocious campaign against such experimentation.[2]

The campaign reached its peak in December 1962, when Khrush-chev summoned to a glass-walled reception palace in Moscow's Lenin Hills a group of top-ranking writers, painters, and sculptors to harangue them on their sins. Courageously they talked back, and the argument stormed for five hours. One of the most inter-esting points of the debate was the answer given by Ernst Neiz-vestny, the well-known abstract sculptor, to Khrushchev's abuse of him: "You may not like my work, Comrade Khrushchev, but it has the warm admiration of such eminent Soviet scientists as Kapitsa and Landau." Khrushchev countered with scorn: "That's not why we admire Kapitsa and Landau."[3] Apparently he did not realize how much beside the point his answer was.

Unafraid, important physicists and chemists came out publicly in support of the experimenting artists. Two Nobel Prize–winning scientists, Igor Tamm and Nikolai Semyonov, lent their enormous prestige to the cause of the persecuted by signing the letter of seventeen outstanding Russian artists and men of laboratories addressed to Khrushchev personally. Khrushchev's ideological hatchet man Leonid Ilyichev complained about this in a speech wherein he quoted the seventeen as asking Nikita Sergeyevich "to stop the swing in the representational arts to past methods which are alien to the whole spirit of our times."[4]

An American art critic later confirmed that Soviet physicists were indeed among Neizvestny's "most influential supporters," and that this support stemmed from the physicists' interest "in the theoretical connection between abstract art and science."[5] That the scientists' support was decisive, prevailing over the Party's attack, may be seen from the fact that a year after the celebrated Neizvestny-Khrushchev debate, the sculptor received commis-sions to do the busts of Landau, Mstislav Keldysh (president of the Academy of Sciences), and Mikhail Lavrentyev (head of the Science City of Novosibirsk).[6]

The Party appeared to accept this defeat: the three commis-sions came to the sculptor from the Soviet government, from its Ministry of Culture, which is run by the Party (as is every min-istry in Moscow). In December 1962 Khrushchev speaking for the Party had denounced Neizvestny for his "revolting concoc-tions." In late November 1963 Khrushchev and the Party were silent as the nation's money went to the sculptor for the busts of three of Russia's most outstanding scientists. *The New York Times* commented:

Among the most important supporters and patrons of Soviet abstract artists have been affluent members of the scientific elite. Men who in their laboratories and studies wrestle with the intricacies of relativity theory, the indeterminacy principle and quantum mechanics could hardly be satisfied in their moments of leisure with the starkly representational figures of heroic workers and peasants which dominate the products of orthodox Socialist realism.

In the Stalin era, scientists with complex artistic tastes were wisely discreet. In the Khrushchev era, this latest evidence suggests, they have been able to exercise an important and useful corrective influence against the reactionaries in art who look nostalgically back to the "good old days" before 1953.[7]

I I

Scientists appreciate also the subtlest of modern Russian poetry. "In my experience," said Anna Akhmatova, one of the greatest modern Russian poets, in the spring of 1962, "scientists are the most sophisticated, sensitive readers of poetry today . . ."[8] The reason is the same as already noted for modern painting and sculpture: scientists and engineers like modern poetry precisely because it is so experimental and unconventional.

During his Paris visit in 1962 the controversial Soviet poet Andrei Voznesensky was asked: "Your poetry is not easy to understand at first sight, yet you are published in editions of 50,000 to 120,000 copies. Who are your readers?" Voznesensky was quoted as replying:

In today's world, in which Sputniks and other extremely complex machines are constructed, there are a vast number of people interested in such things. The people who especially like modern poetry are the young physicists, the young scientists, men who, while they appear very uncomplicated and ordinary, do complex things and are complex people. Thus they don't want overly simple poetry, just as they are not interested in primitive tools.[9]

On second thought, Voznesensky added that physicists and other scientists were not his only admirers. "Just recently I gave a poetry recital in a factory before simple workers, without higher education. They reacted the same way."

He explained why new Russians, particularly those with higher technical education, liked his poetry: "Poetry must not be completely understandable; it isn't, any more than the mists of Paris or the rustling of leaves are. Poetry, like natural phenomena, creates not only thoughts but also feelings. Certain poetic thoughts are not wholly subject to reason." A higher technical education, he implied, made the new young Russian not only erudite but also sensitive to fantasy and obscure imagery.

Two years later, in October 1964, the Moscow magazine *Molodaya gvardiya* (Young Guard) published Voznesensky's long poem "Oza," and this at once became the rage among the sophisticated Soviet readers, "notably the younger scientific people who constitute an elite that is unquestionably the most refined and independent in the Soviet Union."[10] The poet opens his narrative by saying that it is really a notebook found on the night table in a hotel room at Dubna, the Soviet atomic research center. It is primarily a love poem, but one that is wonderfully shot through with musings on the impact of technology on human emotions—and the grip of bureaucracy over an individual. The poet sings of Dubna and his friends the scientists—"the gods" —who work in its laboratories. But he also brings in a woman who stands by a cyclotron, who "listens, fully magnetized." Here mechanization is fused with mysticism, laboratory with love, all to the heated and delighted response of Voznesensky's readers, the multitude of Russia's new engineers, physicists, chemists, and mathematicians.[11]

Some Soviet mathematicians appear to be fascinated by poetry because the latest machines and methods of programming may be applied to the art and science of verse-making. Cybernetics itself may be of use in poetry. No less a celebrity of Soviet mathematics than Academician Andrei N. Kolmogorov pointed this out in a special report on the subject. Employing statistical methods of the theory of probability, he attempted to penetrate the basic essence of the musical and rhythmical structure of verse. He took several Russian poets as his examples, and "in each poet he discovered . . . that which is in harmony with mathematical laws and can be analyzed accordingly."[12]

Humorously describing himself as "one of the most passionate cyberneticists there are," Kolmogorov nevertheless warned against those even more fanatical advocates of computers who proposed to use electronic machines in music composition. This, he chided, was "an example of a simplified approach to cybernetics."[13] A computer, he said, will not produce a Bach or a Tschaikowsky. But, contrary to the Party's will, Kolmogorov has indeed done much to encourage modern experimentation in Russian poetry.

III

Here, too, the Party retreats not without a struggle. True, the official arbiters of Soviet literature and art do admit that an "intellectually developed man . . . has the right to demand from modern literature generally and from poetry in particular a high intellectual level." As an example of a modern intellectual who has the right to demand higher levels from the letters, the arbiters respectfully name the Soviet physicist. Still, "poetry is not physics," and poetry cannot claim the same daring in experimentation that physics can. The experimenter and the innovator in arts has no right to seek just for the sake of seeking. Even the technical progress of man has a social meaning, and the poet and the artist must put "the social moment," that is a political message acceptable to the Party, into his experimentation.[14] In short (says the Party) any experimentation in the Soviet Union should stay within the limits decreed by the Party.

A comparison of abstraction in modern science with abstraction in modern art was made by a Soviet critic Vladimir Turbin in his 1961 book on aesthetics, *Comrade Time and Comrade Art*. He implied that both abstractions were equally necessary and triumphant. But a high official of the Soviet artists' union, a functionary doing Khrushchev's bidding, denounced this concept as a "particularly harmful viewpoint."[15]

Indeed, at times the infatuation with the arts-and-machines connection is carried too far. A cybernetics enthusiast declared to Ehrenburg: "Some twenty or thirty years from now thinking machines will be correcting errors in books written by humans." But Ehrenburg had his doubts even though he agreed up to a point:

> I concede willingly that in the not too distant future machines will replace not alone hacks but also popularizers and imitators. And yet man will have to correct the production of the most perfect of machines—after all, it may happen that something taken by a machine as "a machine" may turn out to be a find, a discovery, the beginning of a creative process.[16]

The conformists among writers and artists, as well as the Party hierarchy whose orders the conformists carry out so ardently, are quite upset by the kinship attributed by some to scientists on the one hand and artistic experimenters on the other. There is no resemblance whatever, they insist, between a scientific experiment of any kind and a literary-artistic experiment of any sort. One literary henchman of Khrushchev's entourage wrote:

> Literary polishing, the laboratory working-over of our performance —our creative process, our artistic means with which we are able to express these new times and new feelings—are unlike the work of a scientist or an engineer-designer. Our experiment is narrow; it can and should remain on our desks.

The bootlicker approvingly quoted another servile Soviet poet, who, at a public discussion of Khrushchev's campaign against artist-experimenters, declared that if such experimenters indeed wanted to establish a kinship with scientists they should do as scientists do: refrain from exhibiting their experiments to the public eye, but show only the finished product—". . . when a scientist or an inventor performs his experiment, he shows the people nothing unless he completes it" successfully. "This is how our literati should behave in the process of their innovating searches."[17]

Attempts on the part of abstractionist artists to bolster themselves by this talk of modern science were particularly decried. "Of course," sneered a corresponding member of the Soviet Academy of Arts, "such references to science are laughable. They are sheer cheating."[18] Another toady insisted that true scientists laughed at the abstractionists' claim of the novelty for their "mathematical models as materialized and graphic incarnations" of higher geometry. Nothing new there, the sycophant declared: to real scientists such models reflecting mathematics had been known "already for three hundred years."[19]

The conformists and conventionalists are pained by the argument that the experimenters in arts should be given leeway, and even respect and homage, because they represent the new era of technology. One conservative Soviet artist called this argument nothing less than "slander upon Soviet art which our enemies love to use"—slander, that is, upon the Soviet art of official, traditional Socialist realism. Indignantly he charged: "They repeat in all sorts of ways one and the same thing: that Soviet artists fail to comprehend the sweep, the speeds, rhythms, forms, colors, and images of the twentieth century—the century of atomic energy, cybernetics, and outer-space flights." He thundered: "Yes, Soviet artists have never tried and do not try now to depict technology as such; do not attempt to show that which science has just discovered . . . They are interested first of all in the modern man who has mastered the mighty forces of science and technology."[20] In sum, man readily recognizable by the onlooker, and not his machine distorted by the artist in his endeavor to express the machine's motion and color, should be the proper subject of the loyal Soviet artist.

Servile third-rate novelists and short-story writers hastened to join the howling pack. "We long so much for something abstract in art," the wife and friends of a famous engineer are represented as saying by a loyal Soviet writer, Valeria Gerasimova, in a story lampooning the new Russian intelligentsia infatuated with the West. But the engineer is finally outraged by the "harmfulness" of this milieu and of the views of the people in it. With the help of a sturdy-souled woman doctor he returns to the verity and virtue of Soviet patriotism and Socialist realism.[21]

If a Soviet engineer is depicted in a 1960–63 Russian novel as aloof, arrogant, disliking his fellow humans, then he can be suspected of applauding abstract art among other sins. This is the charge advanced by Nikolai Shamota, a high Party authority on Ukrainian fiction, an ardent advocate of Socialist realism and an enemy of anything new in Soviet letters. Shamota spotted an engineer, a negative personality, in a novel by Boris Polevoy, and denounced the fictional character's desire "to spread his wings . . . a pretense to occupy a special place in society." The official critic declared that, should this character by some chance "become disappointed in his profession" of engineering, and should he try his wings in art, "abstractionism would be most becoming to him."[22]

I V

Not that Polevoy, the creator of the character, himself tried to connect the engineer's unlovely characteristics with abstractionism. In fact, when other Soviet fictioneers write about science and the arts, whatever interest they depict as felt by their scientists and technologists in things artistic and experimental turns out to be a positive phenomenon. Such interest is treated by better Soviet authors with warmth and sympathy.

At the very least, there is a kind of humor without bite; there is understanding of young rebels by such Soviet authors. Young scientists in Daniil Granin's novel *I Go Against the Storm*, in their general policy of trying to show that "they liked everything that was officially denounced," valiantly and happily defended expressionism in art, although "not one of them knew really what this was."[23]

Also in Granin's novel a young scientist joins a crowd of Moscow exhibitgoers arguing in front of abstractionist Polish paintings. He is on the side of abstractionists; he declares that "realism is outdated." When his opponents demand his explanation of these circles and blots, "he of course replied that they mean nothing; that it was necessary for a person to grow up until an understanding of modern art is reached." He asked: Can you convey music by words? Can you explain colors to a blind person? He said: "This kind of painting mirrors new physics—in atomics there is no difference whatever between a chair and a stool. The world has become richer, more complex."

The author observed that the young scientist "argued with these troglodytes scandalously and pleasurably." As the young man and his girl companion left the exhibit, the girl timidly confessed that she understood nothing in this abstract chaos of "circles and washed-out lines." Whereupon the young scientist admitted: "Me too. It's delirium!"

"Why then did you defend them?"

"Rebellion! Why are they being suppressed? Let me reach my own conclusion."[24]

In other words, if anyone is to decide that abstractionism is nonsense, let there be no binding Party directive on it. Let young scientists themselves figure out the whole matter for themselves. But meanwhile, while thus deciding, the scientists will back the abstractionists if only because these painters are rebelling, experimenting, seeking.

V

Is it a mere coincidence that some of today's nonconformist Soviet writers have backgrounds of science and technology? Aleksandr Solzhenitsyn came into literature of protest not only as a former inmate of a Soviet concentration camp but also as a long-time teacher of physics. Viktor Nekrasov, whose pro-American writings and anti-secret police sallies caused Khrushchev's personal ire, is a graduate architect. Andrei Voznesensky had studied architecture for years and seriously, missing it as a lifetime career almost on an impulse, and still deriving some of his unruly poetic images from his knowledge of the precise sciences. Aleksandr Yesenin-Volpin, the son of the great poet Sergei Yesenin (who

committed suicide in 1925), and himself a poet, works as a
logician on the staff of an institute within the network of the
Academy of Sciences.

Yesenin-Volpin's daring is particularly noteworthy. Now 41 years
old, he has a record of unique imprisonment: for his anti-Soviet
verse, which had been smuggled out to the West and printed
there, Khrushchev's government condemned him to a mental in-
stitution (such as described by Valery Tarsis in *Ward No. 7*).
Eventually released and restored to his scientific job, he defied
Khrushchev's heirs. On December 5, 1965, he led 200 students in
an anti-Party demonstration in Pushkin Square, in the heart of
Moscow. He and his young friends were protesting the recent arrest
of two Soviet writers, Andrei Sinyavsky and Yuli Daniel. These
two were accused by the secret police of writing anti-Soviet prose,
Sinyavsky under the pseudonym of Abram Tertz (*The Trial Begins*
and other works), Daniel signing his short stories as Nikolai
Arzhak. Smuggled out, their writings had for years been published
in the West, much to the Party's consternation.

Once more Yesenin-Volpin was detained, and again released,
this time with the policemen's threat that his academic superiors
at the institute would be notified of his "antisocial behavior." The
dialogue between the police and the poet-scientist during his
December 1965 detention was significant. The police asked him
to explain the poster, which he had carried during the demonstration, and which demanded a public trial for the two writers—
out of "respect for the Constitution." He countered: "Is it wrong
to demand respect for the Constitution?" The police insisted: "Are
you directing your demand at the Soviet rulers?" Said the poet-
logician: "That is your suggestion. If you feel they need this advice,
let them have it."[25]

CHAPTER XX

~~~~~~~~~~~~~~~~~~~~~~~~~~~~~

How Marxist the Mood?

PERHAPS THE SCIENTIFIC-TECHNICAL ELITE object only to the bluntness and primitiveness with which the Party tries to make them believe its dogma? Perhaps the elite really believe in Marx but in their own, more profound and intellectual way? Even if the elite change the Party dogma (as Professor Tokaty-Tokaev insisted to me), is the changed dogma still not Marxism?

My answer is, No. In my view of them, most technocrats of the Soviet Union do not really believe in Marx. True, they take their time summoning courage to speak out against the ponderous naïveté and deadliness of Marx. But gradually they do speak out, and more of this is inevitably coming. Let us briefly consider the opposition's past and present:

At the dawn of the Soviet regime it was fairly common for dissenting Russian intellectuals to make flip or tart remarks about Marx and Marxism. If they erred, it was on the side of caution; they indulged in this criticism of the new state religion in private only. Very few dared to air their opposition or doubts in public. The secret police were strong, and they showed no mercy.

Among the bold handful, Academician Ivan Pavlov spoke up with particular verve. At one point in the very beginning of the 1920s he dared a political preface to an otherwise nonpolitical lecture with which he opened a course he gave to Communist students in Moscow. The lecture apparently was never printed in any book or journal nor fully reported to the press. But it must have attracted considerable attention, for Nikolai Bukharin, then the high priest of Soviet Marxism, directed an eloquent attack against its prefatory part. He said that Pavlov had criticized him personally and not Marxism alone.

Using a stenographic record of Pavlov's anti-Marxist sally, Bukharin argued with the great Russian physiologist (winner of a

Nobel Prize as far back as 1904). In the process, Bukharin *nolens volens* revealed at least part of Pavlov's trenchant text.

And here, as quoted in Bukharin's countercastigation,[1] is what Pavlov thundered:

> Dogmatism of Marxism or of the Communist Party is sheer dogmatism because they, the Communists, have decided that such is the truth. They wish to know nothing more. They constantly labor one and the same point. But if you regard learning the way you really should, if you become acquainted with science thoroughly, then, despite your being Communists, worker-students, and so on, you will nevertheless recognize that Marxism and Communism are not an absolute truth, that they are one of [many] theories which perhaps contain a part of the truth but, then again, may hold no truth at all. And then you will look at the whole of life from a free viewpoint, and not from such an enslaved one.

Bukharin exclaimed: "Professor Pavlov protests against the destruction of cultural and scientific values by the Communist ignoramuses. 'Don't tackle that which you don't comprehend' —such is the basic preachment of our critic." Did Pavlov say that the Marxists of Russia are not scientific because they are so prejudiced, so partial? Ah, Bukharin replied, but "the impartiality of science in Professor Pavlov's sense is a myth." He and the other Communists declared themselves to be far truer representatives of the new epoch than any scientists of Pavlov's Olympus could be:

> Our time needs not any mythmaking but a dauntless, brave understanding of reality. Not a saccharine self-solace and not ostrichlike habits [of burying one's head in the sand], but "a physical strength of thought" and steel-like will power are necessary to pass triumphantly, even if with hundreds of wound marks on the body, through this historic stretch of torturous but great times wherein we live.

One wonders what Bukharin would have said in late 1923, when he wrote these fiery lines, had he known that in the next fifteen years his fellow Marxist, Joseph Stalin, was to take him and the entire Communist Party (not less than all of the Russian nation) through torturous times, indeed; that late in that period his, Bukharin's, personal steely will power was to be sorely tested in prison and courtroom, all under the aegis and excuse of Marxism; and that, finally in 1938, he, the erstwhile chief shaman of the Marxist-Leninist cult, was to be done to death by the cult's inevitable inheritor Stalin.

Did Bukharin die still convinced that Pavlov was wrong and he right, just because his executioners called themselves Marxists?

II

Ivan Pavlov died two years before Nikolai Bukharin was shot in the name of Marxism. Before going, Pavlov had the satisfaction of seeing much of his prediction come true. The rise of Stalin's despotism in the late 1920s and the purges of the early and middle 1930s were witnessed by Pavlov, and he could have truly felt that the worker-students he had addressed early in this Soviet era were by now sadder and wiser.

But for at least ten years before his own death in 1936 Pavlov said hardly anything political—at least, not in public. Not that he was afraid for himself; his worldwide fame was too powerful a deterrent even for Stalin's police to act against him. Most likely he simply did not want to bother. And he was getting old and tired even if not afraid.

Others, however, did fear. Thus, all through the Stalinist dark ages and well into the Khrushchevian period, hardly any Russian scientist, engineer, or other intellectual mounted a platform to question the country's official faith. It was only in 1962 that sly manifestations of heresy began to appear in Soviet print—that the guarded sortie against Party dogmatists by Academician Kapitsa, with its unkind words for the dogmatists' misuse of dialectical materialism, was printed in *Ekonomicheskaya gazeta*. (See Chapter III, above.)

That article of March 1962, mild though it may seem to some uninitiated Westerners, had the effect of a bombshell in Soviet science and politics. Encouraged by this success, Russian scientists shifted their target from the Marxists to Marxism itself.[2] The argument presently was that Karl Marx and Friedrich Engels may have been all right for their time, and perhaps for a few decades thereafter, but surely not for this modern era with its astonishing discoveries. Soviet biologists, in particular, opened a blunt attack against Marxism-Engelsism in biology. In June 1962 Professor Viktor M. Zhdanov, head of the Institute of Virology at the Academy of Sciences, publicly pointed out that Engels as a writer on biology was outdated. Engels wrote his *Dialectics of Nature* "nearly a century ago," Zhdanov said, when he "generalized the knowledge accumulated by the science of his time." In the life-times of Marx and Engels "the existence of viruses and nucleic acids was unknown"; hence the regrettable lacunae and errors in those saints' teachings. "Science," Professor Zhdanov pointed out most logically, "constantly encounters phenomena which in the view of the preceding decades would have seemed incredible. That is why it is science . . ."[3]

The heresy spread. In 1963 an American economist visiting in the Soviet Union was asked by some Russian economists: "Are you a Marxian or an anti-Marxian?" The visitor replied: "Nei-ther. I am a post-Marxian."

His Soviet hosts chuckled appreciatively. And in their chuckle there was more than a shade of a hint that they, too, were post-Marxian, perhaps well beyond Liberman's revisions of the faith; and that all reality in their country of the great experiment was post-Marxian, if indeed it had ever been truly Marxian.

No longer did all Soviet professors genuflect at every mention of Marx and Marxism. Some academicians in power even dared to refuse to award prizes to works on the sacred dogma. In Mos-cow, professional propagandists complained that scientists in charge of prize-awarding committees did not consider them scholars and all too frequently deprived them of academic kudos.

A group of the Party's top-notch Marxists calling themselves "philosophers" made a public protest against the Lenin Prize Committee, which did not include a single Marxist entry in the category of finalists one recent year. The propagandists recalled the committee's yet graver sin: "Surprising indeed is the fact that the prize named after V. I. Lenin, the great Marxist philosopher, in all the committee's existence has not been awarded to a single work on Marxist philosophy." Beware, Comrade Committeemen, of your "dangerous tendency"—your "underevaluation of the Marxist-Leninist science."[4]

Similarly, the committee declined to honor with a Lenin prize a biographical novel by Galina Serebriakova dedicated to Marx's life, and an *Izvestiya* writer praised the committee's decision for its "wisdom and insistence on high standards."[5] And about the same time the Institute of Marxism-Leninism complained that the nation's Highest Certification Commission used a mere techni-cality to table indefinitely the Institute's request that one of its top-bracket staff men be granted a doctorate for editing the fourth volume of *Capital*.[6]

III

It is apparently no longer physically dangerous to express misgivings about Marx in the Soviet Union. But even though the Communist Party less often uses the police as its ultimate argument, it is a stubborn retreat that the Marxists are beating, and the younger generation of the scientific-engineering elite is their special concern.

As in the armed forces, so in civilian school halls, listeners do not actually listen to their Marxist preachers. Instead, the young folk catch up with their extracurricular reading (including spy thrillers and Western novels), or their gossip (sometimes above the whisper decibel), or even their naps (with an occasional loud snore). Some who tutor to augment the government stipends use the time to correct their charges' papers while the Party pastors drone. Thus are doctrine-doubters also doctrine-dodgers.

Not all of it is a matter of silent indifference, passive resistance, and artful dodging. There is, increasingly, active defiance. The Party knows this only too well. The Party sounds an alarm. Hear ye, heed ye, and take measures, Comrades: Soviet students ask searching and embarrassing questions nowadays; "they pose before these instructors some anxious problems of our modern times," but the Party's preachers are ignorant and clumsy—and the inquiring young "receive no answer" to their challenge. The Leningrad Party Committee secretary is upset; in the name of the Party she proclaims:

> . . . the cause of ideas suffers no vacuum; should we slacken our Communist influence upon these minds and hearts, then foreign catchers of souls will attempt to occupy these heights. In our work with the young we have no right to smooth the sharp corners and to silence difficult questions.[7]

So many of these young ones no longer obediently echo the old Communist slogans. They raise their voices in what has come to be known in the Soviet Union as "snorting skepticism." They hoot at their leaders' "dry-as-dust babbling." At an institute, to the propagandist presiding over a dispute on the theme "Communism and I," a note was handed from the audience: "I want to interrupt you. Who needs your primitive philosophy interlarded with little quotations—your examples so distant from real life?"[8]

And so the leaders stutter and retreat; break off arguments, or attempt to prevent genuine disputes at the least indication that such honest-to-goodness discussions may flare up. For they know their own inadequacy—and the paucity of the dogma they represent.

"Why is it that some Komsomol leaders at times do not dare to get into arguments at the factory, in the institute, in a school, on the street?" a first secretary of the Party in Krasnodar (North Caucasus) asked brokenheartedly. He answered his own question with unexpected frankness: "This is because some leaders' intellectual horizon is as yet very limited. It is hard to convince people by general slogans. In order to argue you must know a lot." Thus admitting the ignorance of his propagandists, the first secretary of Krasnodar had the gall or stupidity or both to call upon scientists (of all people!) among other "helpful . . . elder comrades" to train these Komsomol simpletons to argue on behalf of Communism more effectively than they have been doing.[9]

The highest Party authorities sometimes admit how successful the opposition is and what feeble showing the Party propagandist makes by comparison. In December 1962 Sergei Pavlov* himself, first secretary of the Komsomol, voiced the Kremlin's alarm:[10]

Let us give serious thought again and again to the question why it is that many Komsomol leaders, dexterous with directives, are afraid to debate at a workers' dormitory or at a students' evening affair, and quite often retreat before demagogues and skeptics.

Of course, in the eyes of Communist hierarchs, anyone who bests their propagandists in an argument is "a demagogue." The cussword "skeptic" is franker and truer: it is applied to those oppositionists who dare to question the Party line in the least.

But why do the Party and Komsomol propagandists retreat? Sergei Pavlov gives his answer:

This apparently comes from their lack of inner confidence in their own strength, and from their ignorance as to how and of what to try to convince others, also from the poverty of their tongue and thought. During a debate some "orator" [of the opposition] pours right and left his metaphors, images, and rhetorical questions, and cites historical parallels. And then our secretary or instructor comes out to argue against him, and what happens? His ideas are correct, but his tongue is like a heavy log, it hardly turns. And in his long-chewed phrases you will hear such dense formalism that it nauseates you to listen to him.

* Fortunately, no relation to the great Ivan Pavlov.

At this point Pavlov apparently decided that he confessed the Komsomol's weakness a bit too much. He tried to soften his admission of defeat: "Do we have many such functionaries? Perhaps not. Perhaps there are just a few such ones. But we live in an epoch when there should be none such!"

But slightly more than a year later, in March 1964, Comrade Pavlov had to confirm again that there were more than "just a few such ones." He shook his furious finger:

> Unfortunately Komsomol staff personnel often do not consider it as their duty to carry on man-to-man discussions with our youth on the most actual, sharp problems, and at times simply fear such conversations because they don't feel prepared for them. They cannot argue and convince; they lack erudition and political knowledge.[11]

The epoch had by then advanced by some fifteen months, yet, despite all the proddings from Pavlov and other higher powers, the lower-strata propagandists were as ignorant and stagnant as ever.

I V

The epoch is indeed significant, whether the Communist leaders realize this or not. Many Komsomol propagandists of the 1960s are so unlike their fiery predecessors of the 1920s and '30s, who believed in their cause fanatically, who were not afraid to charge into a battle of words, to repress angrily the doubters and opponents—by summoning the secret police if need be. The current activists too may be angry, but they seem to be helpless in their ire.

Aleksandr Chervonny, a fifth-year engineering student who had to put in a period of "practice" (undergraduate internship or apprenticeship) in a mine, dismayed his Communist associates: "He grumbles, he is dissatisfied with everything. In the mine during his practice he, don't you see, has never met any real Soviet people. He praises those who crawl on their bellies before Western bourgeois culture. Chervonny will soon be graduated from his institute. What, then, will he be teaching people [those who will be subordinate to him]?" The most disquieting feature of it all, to Communist functionaries, was the lack of any opposition to Chervonny at the Sverdlovsk Mining Institute, in the Urals, where he was studying and where he spread his pro-Western views. "And nobody in that higher school fights back against his rotten views, nobody summons courage enough to condemn his trickery, to help Chervonny find himself."[12]

Sadly the Communist secretaries and propagandists admit their own failure: "Quite often aggressiveness and sharpness are absent from ideological work."[13] A Leningrad propagandist confessed: "We ourselves devastate and ruin Komsomol meetings, depriving them of any political and intellectual enthusiasm. For instance, we summon young engineers to Komsomol meetings and nag them . . . Our agitation has so much dyed-in-the-wool naggingness that nausea comes to our soul."[14]

Aggressiveness and sharpness rise from the audience, challenging the Party leadership, which in its middle and lower echelons appears so surprisingly lost or listless.

A Western exchange student described three cases of open defiance of Party directives at the University of Moscow. In one case, at the general meeting of the Komsomol organization of the University, a long and passionate debate flared up from the floor. Many students demanded changes in the Komsomol structure. They turned down the plan of activities for the academic year sent from above; they wanted to draw up a plan of their own. The secretary insisted on the official plan, a vote was taken, and his proposal was defeated. Days later the protesters were severely reprimanded, and six of the more articulate disappeared—apparently expelled from the University, if not worse.

In the second case the authorities wanted the students themselves to punish a recalcitrant classmate for, among other sins, "listening to foreign broadcasts, rarely attending meetings," and otherwise "neglecting his Komsomol duties." But when the comrades' court was convened to deal with the student, the tables were turned: the authorities were criticized instead. At long last, after a great deal of verbal fireworks, the panic-stricken chairman persuaded the meeting to reprimand the student. The Westerner noted: "Recalling the results of the general Komsomol meeting and the subsequent disappearance of certain students, those present agreed to this compromise."

The third outburst at the University was caused by a lecture on Socialist realism in Soviet literature. The orthodox lecturer was heard "with the greatest indifference," but in the ensuing debate "a student of chemistry routed the lecturer completely," and others joined in to attack the propagandist on the platform. Not a single student got up to defend the lecturer. "The lecturer did not reply," but during the entire onslaught he kept on writing something—most likely, the students grimly jested, "the names and surnames of those who had taken the floor."

The Westerner pointed out that most of the students who led all three of these attacks were studying natural sciences. He elaborated:

> Chemists and mathematicians, botanists and zoologists—these are the active people in the University. They are the most intelligent among the students. Their interest in public, political, and literary life is all the greater because they devote their free time to it. They are interested in literature in particular . . . because they consider it one of the necessities of life.[15]

Another Western (American) exchange student, who spent a year at the University of Moscow, told me that the physical-science majors he had met there were by far more alert and critical of the regime than social-science students. Among the latter, young historians were the worst conformists—veritable rubber stamps of all the official Soviet propaganda. Physical-science students were aware of the difference and proud of their own critical attitude. One of them, a major in physics, once said to my informant: "We are much more pragmatic and rational than those would-be historians." And in fact, they knew much more history and literature than the so-called liberal-arts or social-science majors.

Not infrequently, loyal propagandists discover in gloom that the opponents win chiefly through their superior education. In the Kostroma Region in Central Russia a staff propagandist (full-time, professional) heard to his horror that a young engineer at a local metallurgical plant was "an ideological opponent" of the Party; that he dared to criticize the plant's Komsomol and bosses as being "not up to snuff"; and that he bolstered his "deviations" from the Party line by "quoting from classical literature most fluently." The most disturbing feature, to the propagandist, was the fact that the young engineer, in his opposition talk, showed himself so "well-shod" with an education resulting in those effective quotations, so effective that the local Party wheel horses who tried to refute him had to retreat in a kind of embarrassed fright. And the staff propagandist himself somehow failed even to get the name of the nervy engineer, much less to travel to the plant, in order personally "to listen and to argue," not only to vanquish the opponent, but "in such skirmishes to test one's own arsenal of ideas and ability as a fighter."[16] Ah, melancholy times, indeed, my comrades! This would have been impossible in Stalin's era.

V

A Komsomol youth asked a Komsomol girl on the eve of her brief trip to Western Europe: "Bring me a shirt from Brussels and another from Sweden, also a portrait, not of Karl Marx, but of some foreign writer, and the more fashionable the better."[17]

But at times an ingenious gambit of the students is to attack Marxism while holding high Karl Marx's image, while declaring tongue in cheek that they are better Marxists than their teachers. As witness this case:

In Ulyanovsk, formerly Simbirsk, Lenin's birthplace on the Volga shores, a propaganda talk was being given to senior students of chemistry and biology of the local Pedagogic Institute. The propagandist, whose official title was "assistant of the cathedra of philosophy and political economy," declared that "capitalism prevents people from developing many-sidedly and harmoniously." Suddenly, from the third row of students' seats came the loud voice: "Not true!"

The propagandist recognized the voice: "Ah, it's you. Again an opinion of your own? You wish to correct Marxism-Leninism? . . . You, young man, are defending capitalism."

This was not the first clash of the two men. The student was "a picking one"—a nagger. "His bearing was entirely too independent, he was bold in his judgments, he liked to pose sharp questions." On one occasion, speaking of the student to an administrative superior, the propagandist insisted: "This son of a bitch should be handed over for a trial." The propagandist was flabbergasted when he heard that the young critic had just been accepted into the Party. He roared: "On what basis?" But the young man continued with his objections and questions claiming them as his true-red Marxist right. For his nerve he was neither arrested and tried nor thrown out of the Party.[18]

The young intellectuals fling at their Marxist shepherds some irrefutable facts of Soviet life: corruption, inequality, injustice. They are tired of the pious Communist cant, and they say so. They point to the gap between the proclamation and the practice. They refuse to blame only Stalin for Stalinism—they accuse the Party and its present leaders as well as its long-deceased evil genius.

This, then, is the sort of argument and protest with which the young opponents badger their teachers and preachers. This is their triumph, their pride, as they boast about the hard time they gave a Party instructor at the University of Rostov on the Don: "At her very first lecture on the history of the Party we floored her with our questions."[19]

A Party secretary observed: "Today's youth is certainly different from those . . . of ten or fifteen years back. They have a different level of knowledge, a different view of the world. They don't like trite and outdated forms of political work."[20]

V I

From time to time desperate steps are taken by the Party.

Beginning with the 1963–64 academic year, a new propaganda course was introduced in all the colleges and universities of the Soviet Union. Called "Fundamentals of Scientific Communism," it was established as an ironbound requirement for all students. It was something less than successful. Even after the introduction of "Fundamentals," Soviet press reports were gloomy. Correspondents complained about the dullness of the courses and about the mocking indifference of those compelled to attend them. The scientific-engineering students were particularly frank about their boredom and contempt.

In engineering institutes the nonpropagandist faculty often sided with students by rejecting the very idea of including Marxism in their curriculum. The year before "Fundamentals" were brought in, a *Pravda* correspondent was shocked by the professors of the Volgograd Medical Institute, because, in examining students on general biology, they "did not demand of them any knowledge of the declarations of the Party's Program on the tasks of biology under modern circumstances." A Party commission investigating ideological propaganda in the Volgograd Institute of Municipal Engineers had to argue long and hard—and apparently fruitlessly—with some instructors that they should really put Communist propaganda in their technical courses.[21] After "Fundamentals" came, one engineering institute in Voronezh would not establish a propaganda department despite all the directives from above. At another engineering institute in the same city a propaganda department was indeed organized, but "it was with difficulty that it enrolled thirty-two students, and by the year's end this number melted like spring snow." A correspondent asked:

"Why?" All the students answered: "Boring." And so the department was closed, without any visible "worry from the Voronezh Region Committee of Komsomol."[22] Needless to say, professors and students worried even less.

Some professors dare to oppose the Party by recommending for an assistantship or other promotion one student rather than another despite the protégé's greater laxness as a Marxist. Academician Igor Tamm has not been afraid to fight it out with Party stalwarts, usually with success. His clever argument is that his candidates were "not lacking in political consciousness," but that they were merely too "absorbed in scientific research" to bother with Party activity. He has reminisced proudly: "In one such case I successfully won the acceptance of a needed man only by taking most extraordinary measures."[23] Chances are that the measures consisted of the academician's going over the heads of Party officials to Khrushchev himself or at least to Khrushchev's immediate entourage.

VII

Late in 1964, a University of Moscow professor proposed boldly and publicly that propaganda courses be further curtailed in all the universities and colleges where scientists and engineers are trained. He argued that "despite all the curtailments" of such courses, "hundreds of 'untouchable' hours immutably remain in the curriculum of any and all higher schools."[24]

He was at once attacked by some loyal Marxists, yet in early 1965 Pravda ran an article which clearly implied that all was not well with such courses on Marxism. In fact, the article proposed changing such studies by reintroducing political science where Marxism for so long ruled supreme in the Soviet curricula. In June 1965 Pravda followed up the suggestion by printing a summary of the many readers' letters received in the wake of the original proposal. The consensus was in favor of broadening the narrow "scientific Communism" into a richer comparative study of sources, including "foreign literature."[25]

And what sort of foreign literature should it be? It is to include the latest proponents of West European and American philosophy, sociology, and logic—surely of later vintage than the ones served to Soviet students by Marxist propagandists. Already in 1961 an instructor at the Herzen Pedagogic Institute, one of the Soviet Union's best-known teachers' colleges, declared that "wrong are those teachers who proceed as if the Marxist philosophy has already given its answers to all the problems of man's social and even personal life." Marxism may be valuable, the Soviet instructor continued, but it should not base itself on outdated arguments and superannuated examples.

> . . . contemporary bourgeois philosophy changes constantly as it takes into account both the accomplishments of science and the transformations in the world. The ideas of [Bertrand] Russell, [Alfred North] Whitehead, [Jean Paul] Sartre, [Ludwig] Wittgenstein, [Karl] Jaspers, and others have acquired wide currency in the bourgeois world. But how many of our students know the essence of these philosophers' views, and know how to criticize them?

The author pretends that his main concern is to arm his country's youth as they are faced with the need to demolish Western thought. He points to the increasing number and frequency of East-West contacts "between people of different lands, cultures, and professions." He asserts that "in order the better to fight the ideological foe, it is necessary to know him better."[26] But as the Soviet student gets to know the best of Western philosophy better than he knows it now, will he not succumb to that best?

To what extent is the Western influence already at work upon Soviet Marxism, softening or even negating it? Mikhail Suslov, the watchdog-in-chief of Kremlin ideology, once deplored the fact that "in the current circumstances [that is, with the policy of coexistence with the West] the influence of bourgeois propaganda seeps through to us in many ways: through the press, radio, and all kinds of delegations and tourists." He blamed the rising intransigence of the Soviet young on this bourgeois influx of ideas.[27] At a high-level Communist conference in Kiev, a loyal Communist artist spelled it out in detail:

> With each year our cultural ties with the peoples of foreign countries widen and grow. A lively exchange of delegations, latest books, periodic press and exhibits takes place. This is good. However, the bad feature is that, in the process of implementing such useful measures, strange ideas, hostile to us, penetrate. As a rule, exhibits from capitalistic countries are accompanied by a large number of guides, who distribute various literature, prospectuses, magazines, catalogues. In their explanations we can often find propaganda of movements strange to us—formalistic, abstractionist, of the proverbial "freedom of creativeness," "capitalistic

prosperity," and so on. But our reviews of such publications and exhibits are extremely few in number, and they are frequently too diplomatic, they lack principle and a fighting, aggressive spirit.[28]

Unfortunately, another Soviet propagandist notes, it is the Soviet government itself that "officially" helps "the penetration of our life by bourgeois morality, through the films we buy, through the books we publish," imported from the West in the course of peaceful exchange. There is a hint of a complaint that such purchases and publications are unnecessarily numerous: "We buy in the West many films, good as well as mediocre. Almost all these films enjoy popularity in our country." But the Soviet viewers and readers of the Western imports simply "don't understand the social subtext" of the films and the books the way the Party wants them to "understand"—critically, anticapitalistically.[29]

The Party calls upon the nation, particularly the New Class that loves these Western gifts so much, to resist their influence. "You will see foreign films. You will read a Western author's book. One or another of your acquaintances has heard a foreign broadcast, has met with foreign tourists." That is almost permissible from the official Soviet standpoint. For "these contacts and meetings bring much that is useful; they satisfy a natural curiosity." But, in Karl Marx's and Vladimir Lenin's holy names, please "don't be simpletons, don't take everything at its face value, as our enemies wish [us to do]; don't permit this oozing through, into our midst, of the falsehoods of their bourgeois world view, of their moral decay, their cynicism . . ."[30]

Sadly the propagandists agree that "bourgeois ideology, as the oldest, is most durable and is more easily absorbed" than the Communist idea.[31] Suslov feels that it is not enough to explain the success of non-Soviet concepts among Russian students by either survival of Russia's own prerevolutionary capitalist memories or the inadequacy of Soviet ideological indoctrination. He stresses the harmful essence of the foreign import.[32] Another Soviet propagandist echoed this doleful observation when he wrote that "it was not at all necessary to be born across the ocean to fall under the influence of ideology foreign to us, of bourgeois morals."[33] A student could stay all his formative years in Moscow or Leningrad, Minsk or Omsk, and still discover all those bad foreign books.

Here is the case of young Stanislav Zhukov, taken in hand by the Moscow police, apparently for his "antisocial behavior." The police reported that "Zhukov read much but unselectively, absorbing and applying to our life uncritically many postulates of utopian Socialists, of Western philosophers, among them those of idealistic movements." The reporting policeman declared that after a few conversations he was able to convince Zhukov how wrong he, Zhukov, was with all his pro-Westernism.[34] But one wonders.

A propagandist attached to the Odessa conservatory (young Soviet music students also need Marxist indoctrination!) was handed an anonymous note at the end of one of his seminars on historical materialism. The note jeered at the propagandist for spending the five years of the course "on whipping the opportunists of the past," on this uninteresting going-over of "the battles, buried decades ago, with all those Prudhonists, Blanquists, and anarchists."[35] It was quite clear that the author of the note knew those old Socialist and anarchist writings quite well, but that he did not feel they were so important to current Soviet reality as, let us say, the problem of excessive Soviet bureaucracy was.

In other words, many bright young students, engineers, and other intellectuals know Western ideology, old and new, much better than the propagandists do. In their thinking and discussions they make better use of it. Of course, at examinations they serve back to those propagandist teachers whatever rot-by-rote they are supposed to remember from their teachers, but they laugh to themselves as they do this.

For them, a species of post-Marxism is the ideology in season.

CHAPTER XXI

But What Do They Believe In?

IF NOT MARX, what do the new Russian intellectuals believe in?

We must first of all make one important reservation: there are in the Soviet Union intellectuals who are indeed sincerely convinced Marxists. But, unlike the early phase of the Soviet era, this is not their time in history. They are not the main factor in the nation's life. They are comparatively few in number and their influence is nearly nil.

They are a separate caste: not technicians or executives, they are the ecclesiastics, the clerics of the new state religion, and only a few outside scholars would grant them the cover name they relish—philosophers. Among such generous Westerners is Professor Lewis S. Feuer, of the University of California, who a few years ago took some time off to visit the Soviet Union in order "to engage in discussions with its philosophers, sociologists, and students."

In his subsequent report[1] Professor Feuer sounded an optimistic note, saying that scientific realism, existentialism, and pragmatism were beginning to attract the younger of this group. These discover and enjoy Bertrand Russell, Jean Paul Sartre, Nikolai Berdyayev, Sigmund Freud, and John Dewey. But the discouraging element is that, despite such widening of their horizons, the young Communist priests still intone the names of the fathers of their stifling church: "All the varieties of dialectical materialism in the Soviet Union fasten on different texts of Marx, Engels, and Lenin for their support."

The nonpriestly part of the Communist apparatus—the Party officials actually running the state, members of the governmental civil-service network high and low—only say they believe in Marx and Lenin. They are not true believers, they are only "Communist conformists," wrote an astute American observer after several years in Moscow. "Ideology among them is dead; at best, it is like Latin, a language in which to communicate to the select. There is no question now that, both within the country and without, the Russian Communists' job is to pursue not Marxism or Communism but Soviet national power and interests."[2]

That much for the priests and for the political bosses. What about the subject of this book, the scientific-engineering and managerial elite? As they, with an increasing candor, reject Marxism, what do they profess? Do they have a definite body of beliefs, a set of ethics or a social conscience or a religion of their own, different enough from the tenets of Marxism to be a good antidote to Marxism?

I I

We have already noted the Western rain upon the native seed. We may now definitely affirm that pro-Westernism is a prevalent part of this elite's new credo.

Quite often young Soviet engineers and scientists speak of freedom—"freedom of my soul, freedom not to agree, freedom to be sad," as one of them put it,[3] and they think of the West when they talk this way.

Freedom can be a many-sided, rainbow-hued thing—even the right of a Russian scholar to turn into a Western playboy for the nonce. A Soviet physicist of great fame, apparently barred by the Soviet government from trips to foreign lands, was both courageous and sarcastic as he asked an academician, a loyal Party man whom Khrushchev sent abroad to sundry conferences quite often: "Tell me, will a time come some day when everyone of us would have the freedom to go to Paris and visit the night clubs of Montmartre?"[4]

The West means freedom, an antithesis of this Soviet version of "Kafka's world," as one young Moscow intellectual put it to a Western visitor. The young intellectuals' interest in the West is their quietly smoldering rebellion. They dress in Western-style clothes, they study Western languages and read all the Western literature they can lay their hands on, in "a personal form of protest," to show their Kafkaesque jailers and tormentors just how these Soviet youths "really feel."[5] When they trust a Western visitor they open before him all their thirst for the land of his origin. Here, for instance, was a young couple in post-Stalinist

Moscow, both studying for the doctorate of the sciences and both members of the Komsomol. "They were passionately interested in the West . . . their curiosity about the West insatiable. They could have gone on for hours asking me questions about its material and intellectual side. . . . They made me tell them about my travels in Mexico or Equatorial Africa, the United States, Spain or Denmark. These unknown worlds fascinated them."[6]

The feeling for freedom is intertwined here with the desire for the exotic and the wish for material goods. For despite the decided improvement of the general tone and color of life in the Soviet Union since Joseph Stalin's death, the Russian student's or engineer's existence in that country is still rather on the drab side. The Kazakhstan-Siberian Virgin Land horizon does not offer any real lure. But foreign lands do—yet travel to non-Soviet destinations is severely restricted by Soviet passport regulations. So, when a young Russian scientist, engineer, technician, or manager is ordered by his superiors to go on a foreign mission, all his relatives burst with pride and all his friends turn green with envy. The attraction of such a mission is also in the foreign clothes, shoes, luggage, phonograph records, and even television sets and refrigerators—so poor in quality and small in quantity in the Soviet Union—which the emissary can buy abroad and send home or bring with him at the mission's end.[7]

III

Admiring the West, yearning for a closer contact with the West both physical and spiritual, the scientific-engineering and managerial groups may be considered as the peaceful part of the present-day Soviet elite. Pacifism, conscious or not, is an unmistakably important ingredient of this elite's philosophy.

Of course, there is no organized antigovernment movement of such pacifist committees or clubs in the Soviet Union as dot the Western scene. The existent "peace" groups in the Soviet Union are those formed by the Party and the government to denounce the "warmongers" of the West and to laud as genuinely peaceful any and all policies of the Soviet government and the Communist Party—no matter how essentially aggressive they may be.

There are, to be sure, some native religious pacifist groupings in Russia, Jehovah's Witnesses and some other, smaller sects of conscientious objectors. These are persecuted and prosecuted by the government. Their men's conscientious objection to military duty is not at all respected. The men are treated as deserters and traitors and taken to jail.

But such religious nonconformists are neither numerous nor influential. Their non-Soviet pacifism makes little dent on the population at large for two main reasons. First, this pacifism is religious in a country where the millions of younger inhabitants are either atheists or agnostics while the older men and women, even if believers, stick with the established orthodox faiths, not with the sects. The second reason is that, in Russia, Jehovah's Witnesses and sundry pacifist sects are isolated unskilled workers and lower-middle-class artisans, not too adept and successful at proselytizing. Their influence is thus quite limited.

The middle- and upper-class Soviet elite, when antiwar, seems to be unorganized. But being higher up in social scale and most articulate, it wields considerable influence even when it acts individually.

Sometimes, however, their influence is felt through official Soviet organizations that were not at all meant to be pacifist by the Communist creators and bosses of such committees. From the defector Boris Antonovsky, a former Soviet industrial manager now living and working in Washington, I gathered that vital among such channels of influence is a little-publicized network of consulting offices, manned by scientists and other experts, attached to the Party's Central Committee and constantly deferred to by the Presidium and the Secretariat. He elaborated in his recent talk with me:

"The world at large is unaware of the very existence of this network, of these offices and their personnel. Yet, these experts number hundreds and thousands of men. They are experts on every conceivable subject: science, technology, all kinds of economics, and even arts and literature. Most of them are full-time employees, others are outside consultants called in for specific short-term tasks. Most of them—perhaps all of them—are Party members. But above all they are practical men, technicians. Since Stalin's death they are pretty daring in disregarding the Party's dogma, dialectics, directives or what-have-you, when their own common sense, but particularly their technical know-how, tells them that Party directives are impractical or even harmful."

This is where the Liberman Reform of unchaining the factory manager from the Plan and bringing him closer to the customer's need and the factory's profit was born and fostered. And yes, this is where one of the chief influences to pull back from the Cuban confrontation in October 1962 had its origin.

This last came out in my conversation with another Soviet defector whom I met in New York, and whom I shall call here Ivan Doloshenko. One of the youngest intellectual defectors in recent years, this man was only twenty-four when he crossed over to us in a West European city. The son of a scientist, he won an engineer's diploma at the age of twenty-two, and had already held an important and interesting scientific-research position in a large institute of the Academy of Sciences when he decided to defect. To my question he said:

"Yes, scientists and engineers are more genuinely for peace with the West. The problem of Cuba is a good example. They don't want the Cuban adventure begun by Khrushchev and Company to go too far toward the brink of a war, but the Party apparatus takes this risk. Scientists and engineers do exert a restraining pressure in this matter."

He cited his own experience in the Soviet Union. "I saw this in the Soviet Union in April 1961, during the crisis briefly caused by your Bay of Pigs invasion. There was danger of a Soviet-American war then, you will recall. And scientists and engineers of my acquaintance in the Soviet Union clearly showed that they—far more than the Party apparatus—wanted no war. In the October–November 1962 crisis, too, scientists and engineers in the Soviet Union may well have exerted a similar restraining influence."

A third defector, who at one time as a young Soviet rocket specialist reported to Stalin himself and was now teaching aeronautics and space technology in a London college of advanced technology (Professor Tokaty-Tokaev, already quoted in Chapter X), spoke to me about some of the methods used in the latter-day scientific advising in Moscow. The time of our conversation was spring of 1963. Claiming some special knowledge of what was then happening in the Soviet capital, and using a rather cautious language, the defector related to me that "on one recent occasion, Soviet scientists, although representing a minority opinion at a certain high-level Soviet meeting, compelled the majority to change the resolution of the meeting to one in their own rather peaceful spirit, instead of the original, aggressive one."

He continued:

"The original resolution would have followed the orthodox Marxist doctrine; it would have meant aggressiveness. But the scientists proved at that conference, with facts, that the time for such an aggressive resolution was long past. They convinced the nonscientific majority, and so carried the day."

I V

On the levels below such top brackets, the restraining pacifist role of the professional elite is less direct, but more widespread and more cogent, if you will. Sometimes it is even more apparent than the influence of the high scientific advisers to the Party—if one may judge from the complaints of the faithful in the Party press.

Hardly noticed by the Western press, there is in Soviet journals the official Party lament that such young and youngish Russian poets as Bulat Okudzhava refuse, in their public appearances, to recite any poems of condemnation of "Yankee imperialists" in Vietnam, the Congo, and Latin America.

In fact, Okudzhava, the forty-year-old darling of Soviet youth, has not written any such anti-Yankee poems and firmly declines to write them. Instead, this World War II veteran of the Soviet Army has written a number of pacifist poems wherein he bluntly rejects and ridicules *any* kind of war and *all* the world's armies. Mihajlo Mihajlov, the young Yugoslav literary critic who on his 1964 visit to the Soviet Union, wrote in his *Moscow Summer*: "Undoubtedly, Okudzhava's songs alarm all those who love the marching step and military music. 'A lot of fools are still going to enjoy lively soldier songs,' Okudzhava sings. He has written many songs about war and the Army. But his attitude toward war must repel overpatriotic spirits . . ."[8]

Note the words "sings" and "songs." Okudzhava indeed sings his poems rather than declaims them. He is a minstrel, a balladeer, accompanying himself on a guitar. The Soviet authorities try to discourage his platform performances, and they limit or ban his records; but Russian students make tapes of his songs by the thousand, and these travel all over the Soviet Union to great and avid acclaim.

Other poets and fiction writers have been attacked for their pacifism. The poet Ye. Khramov was singled out because in his poem "The Victors," which he had recited at a public meeting in Saratov on the Volga, Russian war veterans were represented as low-life characters who could be "bought for vodka and a salami sandwich."[9] Novelists and short-story authors have been publicly chided for their call to peace. A particularly virulent campaign was unleashed in the early 1960s against certain film makers for their insistence that any war is horror.

In June 1963 the Party chief of Soviet military propaganda, General Aleksei Yepishev, addressed the plenary session of the Party's Central Committee with severe strictures against the pacifist and defeatist trend "in certain literary works and films wherein heroes thrash around in fear of death."[10] On February 7, 1964, writers, artists, and film makers were summoned by the Ministry of Defense and the chief military propaganda office to a special meeting in a military club to hear the riot act. The main reprimand was delivered by Marshal Rodion Malinovsky. "Yes," he admitted, "war is cruel, inhuman, destructive." But—"We do not have the right to transfer Remarque's ideas mechanically to our creative arts and to deprive them of the genuine heroism inherent in our lives."[11]

But Soviet fiction writers continued in their lackadaisical attitude or, more often, persisted in their half-concealed pacifism. In early March 1965, at a major Moscow conference of writers in the Russian Soviet Federated Socialist Republic, Leonid S. Sobolev chided his colleagues: "I can't understand how this has come about, but for a long time now we haven't seen books about the present-day Soviet army, about our navy, about the modern Soviet man under arms." He urged fellow writers to tackle this "decisively necessary" task at once—"to penetrate into the most interesting, and, for literature, absolutely new, inner world of the men to whom the Fatherland entrusted our most perfect, most formidable, and technically most complex weapons."[12]

Nor were Russia's artists spared. In January 1963 a Party faithful accused "certain teachers" in Soviet state art schools of telling the students not to choose "military-patriotic themes" for their final graduation time paintings and sculptures (the so-called diploma projects). He declared that such instructors say to the students who insist on military-glory subjects that "the war ended a long time ago, so why do you want this?"[13]

Nearly one year later an official of Komsomol's Central Committee upbraided the members of two "artistic-technical councils," one in Moscow, the other in Kiev, for discouraging the production of more war toys. These advisers used their positions in the Soviet ministries of education to veto the manufacture, in one case, of a war game full of "automatic riflemen, machinegunners, and grenade throwers," and, in the other instance, of "an automatic gun made of plastic."

The advisers explained their prohibition of this war-toy production by a pious reference to the official we-are-for-peace policy of the Soviet government; increased war-toy manufacture, they said, "goes counter to the tasks of bringing up our children in the spirit of the peaceful policy of our state." In short, some Soviet citizens take the Kremlin's sham protestations of pacifism seriously! Of course, the Party does not like such literal-minded application of its slogans. The Komsomol official, censuring the anti-war-toy advisers argued: Even when deprived of manufactured war toys, Soviet children make their own sabers and guns out of whatever material they can find; they play with such makeshift weapons and "do not at all turn into haters of mankind and into cannibals." The Komsomol official felt that the advisers were guilty of a wrong kind of pacifism—"Toys that help to foster the feeling of courage, ingenuity, and daring are very much needed by the children."[14]

V

Less often, the elite's pro-Westernism is coupled with compassion for the Soviet downtrodden. Such was the case of Lev Predtechevsky, a specialist in naval radar, whom I have already quoted in another connection (see Chapter X, above, on the military). When I met and talked with him in Munich in the spring of 1963, it became clear to me that here was an idealist who had left the Soviet Union mainly because he had developed a social conscience—he had become an anti-Communist idealist. He fled in 1957 not only because he had seen, on earlier trips to Western Europe, some of the goodness of the West, but also because he had grown convinced of the essential social evils of the Soviet system.

The son of a peasant family of the Yaroslavl Region, on the upper Volga, Predtechevsky saw some of his uncles sent to Siberian concentration camps during the Stalinist purges. "My father too would surely have been arrested," he remarked, "except that he had powerful friends in Moscow. Even this would not have saved him; but the war came, and Father was killed at the front. Mother too was a war victim. She was being evacuated when her train was bombed by Nazi planes, and she died of wounds soon after."

In part because of his parents' war record, but in greater part because of his own ability and determination, Lev got more and better schooling than is given an average boy of his social stratum. He early became interested in geodesy and its military applications. He worked hard and was presently ascending the Soviet ladder of success as a young military scientist.

"But," he related, "when I reached the middle strata of the Soviet privileged I began to think of others. Not until then, mind you. I had until then been too preoccupied with my studies and my struggle up that ladder. Till that point I had had time and thought for my books and instruments only. But now I was successful and, for a young man in my position, quite well off—and I began to feel guilty.

"Suddenly I began to notice that others around me, in the Soviet Union, were suffering from privations and injustice. I wanted to leave such a country that would allow such inequalities and cruelties."

He was by then being sent abroad on all sorts of geodetic and radar missions. His trips contributed to his feeling and his decision. "I saw the many-faceted life in the West, and I wanted that life for Russia—for myself, if Russia could not or would not have it."

Predtechevsky, of course, realized that in that variety of Western life "not everything was good." Certain phenomena in the West, he held, "were worse than what the Soviet regime had." But, despite such worse features, and surely in much that was better than in the Soviet Union, he perceived the Western man—in his variety—as a much freer and happier man than the Soviet man amid his monotony and injustice. "Above all, the Western man had freedom," Predtechevsky said to me.

I asked: "But can a Soviet man come to the same conclusion, about the superiority of the Western variety over the Soviet monotony and so on, without seeing for himself the Western reality as you did?"

Predtechevsky thought a moment, then replied: "Hardly. Besides, even if an average Russian, plucked from the masses, so to speak, does happen to witness such Western reality, can he endure such an experience, such firsthand revelation? I don't think he can. I think he will break under the impact of such an experience. They say about a hare grown to maturity in captivity that, should you suddenly release him, he will start to run but will immediately drop dead of heart failure. Freedom will be too much of a shock for him."

(Compare Oleg Penkovsky's essentially optimistic belief in his people's future freedom as in his *Papers* he, like Lev Predtechevsky, voices his conviction that the Communist regime is undemocratic.)

VI

Last and least there is an occasional member of the scientific-technical elite whose code includes belief in God. I say "least" advisedly. Already in the middle 1950s, after his two years as the American chaplain in Moscow, Father Georges Bissonnette remarked to me that, in whatever else the Communists had failed, in one field they did win a victory: they had succeeded in making the majority of Russians atheistic.[15]

This is true of Russian youth, and even of the men and women in their forties and fifties. It is particularly valid of the Soviet Union's scientists and engineers. Religious men and women—that is, those who believe in God and wish to attend church—are extremely rare among Soviet scientists and engineers. One thing Soviet savants and technicians are sincerely puzzled about is the religious belief of some of the Western—particularly American and British—scientists and engineers they meet. The usual question, offered with no Party strings attached, is this: "How can you, an intelligent scientist, a smart and practical engineer, believe in such superstitions as God and church?"

Once in a while the Soviet press irately reveals that a young engineer or scientist would tolerantly let his elderly mother or old grandma take his newborn baby to be baptized in a church. A Moscow researcher, a Komsomol member on the staff of a scientific institute, shrugged his shoulders when questioned by the authorities: "Yes, I baptized my child. What is so special about it, and what harm has it done? . . . It's just a folkway."[16]

From time to time a Russian *émigré* in Western Europe reports in great wonder that a Soviet scientist or engineer finds his way to, say, the Russian church on Rue Daru in Paris, or to the Notre Dame, there to make the sign of the cross even if furtively, and, what's more, to kneel and pray behind a shield of trusted friends.[17] But these are, decidedly, exceptions.

The most unusual representative of this tiny group of Russia's scientific-technical elite is Oleg Lenchevsky, who in fact defected from Russia chiefly because he believed in God. A top-level specialist on salt-water conversion, he defected while on a mission in London, in 1961. Next summer, in his fourth letter to Khrushchev imploring him to allow Lenchevsky's family to leave Moscow to rejoin their husband and father abroad, the scientist wrote: "One can only lose, not gain, when one leaves one's country and I believe that everyone knows this in advance."

He had not left because of any desire to improve his material welfare. "My material situation at home was steadily getting better. I had recently been given gratis an excellent flat in a new block; I had written my doctor's dissertation. My prospects in my scientific work were most attractive." He tried to assure Khrushchev that he was grateful to his country for giving him his education and his career. "I owe everything to my country and I am *incapable* of betraying it," he wrote in the summer of 1962. By leaving Russia he was not turning against it—he was voicing his opposition to everything for what the Communist Party stood. And he placed God above all in his remarkable credo:

> . . . I am equally *incapable* of:
> pretending to be an atheist while believing in God;
> regarding world Communist revolution and unappeasable class war as inevitable, when I see that the minds of ordinary people here [in England] are open to reformist ideas and the trade unions are all-powerful, while in our own country we have seen the rise and growth in strength of our own unprecedented new ruling class;
> believing genuine peaceful coexistence to be possible side by side with most ruthless ideological warfare and isolation;
> expecting complete and universal disarmament while giving our blessings to "just" wars;
> approving of generous aid to other countries while a great many of our own people cannot yet eat their fill;
> assuming that the consequences of the cult of Stalin's personality have been liquidated in our country while the omnipotent and omnipresent apparatus of Terror and mind-control created by Stalin is preserved. . . .[18]

Where did Lenchevsky get his ideas? His father, a doctor who was killed during the Russian civil war of 1917–21, was not even a memory to him, but the faint legend in his mother's sad tales. The mother, a dentist in a Soviet lumber camp, had brought him up. She was a strong personality with an intense religious feeling. But this did not prevent Oleg from becoming a scientist and a Party member. Still, it may have been her latent religious influence that finally prompted him to defect during his mission in England.

Not that he found in the West a complete answer to his inner political and spiritual needs. In 1961 he said that "capitalism has more sores than a dog has fleas." Nor would he deny whatever good may have been produced in Russia. In 1962 he wrote: "I am as far as ever from condemning wholesale all things Soviet as I am from praising indiscriminately all things foreign."

But from the very beginning of his Western stay he acknowledged how helpful—albeit unwittingly—the West had been in opening his eyes, in making up his mind, by just being itself, the free and generous West. In Russia, for years, he had tried to discipline his religious thoughts and feelings out of his consciousness. Now, in Britain, this Western freedom drew him to church irresistibly. The Western man's liberty to think and talk was, in his growing conviction, producing a better atmosphere for meeting the problems of the atomic age than any political or intellectual climate that the Soviet regime could offer. Thus came his realization that he could not bear returning to the Soviet Union, to its suppression of truth, to its use and praise of lies.

When I met him in the spring of 1963 in Holland (where he had shortly before moved to take a job at an important laboratory), Lenchevsky told me that he did not consider himself typical of the Soviet intelligentsia, particularly of its scientific part. I agreed with him insofar as his rebellion against the Communist Party was not that of a scientist or an engineer specifically but was motivated largely by his deep religious feeling.

In nonreligious matters, Lenchevsky's revolt seemed to me, as he talked about it that evening in Amsterdam, fairly representative of a decent, clear-thinking Russian intellectual's disapproval of the Party—except that whereas the vast majority of intellectuals were disapproving because the Party was antihuman, Lenchevsky was the rare modern Russian who said: "Antihuman *and* anti-God."

CHAPTER XXII

~~~~~~~~~~~~~~~~~~~~~~~~~~~~~~~

The Good Erosion

WHAT NOW IS the verdict?

Sufficient evidence has been presented in this book to show that, in spite of the nearly half century's experiment by Russian dogmatists and politicians, no new ideal Soviet man has evolved or is evolving as claimed by the regime. Instead, a definite class society is in being and is further developing, with sharp and growing cleavages between the menial and the mental workers, between the have-nots and the haves; with a never-ceasing contrast in the promise and the performance, in the ideal and the real.

It is a greedy, truculent society, not at all infused with any such spirit or action of social justice as is officially preached and pretended. Men and women fight up the stairs grubbily and often desperately, but very few of them aim at a high or even middle place in the Party hierarchy. No, the ablest or simply the most ambitious in the vast populace want to be engineers, scientists, managers, doctors—professionals of technology and science, not of Party dogma and rule.

Science is the new goddess of Soviet society. That little black skullcap worn by elderly academicians in Russia is among the highest status symbols of the nation. It now receives more respect and awe than ever before in Russian history. And certainly it is a greater mark of prestige than the academic gown-and-mortarboard in the Western world.

Engineers are highly regarded in all parts of Europe, but in Russia they are especially favored. The status of the Soviet engineer is more meaningful than is that of his counterpart in the United States. The largest part of the Soviet intelligentisa, the engineers are steadily growing both in numbers and in social weight. Managers are envied, if only because of their constantly increasing independence—and the chance they have to enrich themselves legally or, more often, illegally through corruption and "left-hand" enterprise.

But one can hardly say that there is a dynamite charge hidden in the edifice. It is erosion, not explosion, that we discern.

At the apex of the Soviet state and society the Party still stands —but, at best, it stands still. It is there not by the will of the people, but by a chain of historical accidents and aberrations beginning with Lenin[1]—through deceit and naked force. This is the force that is now being slowly (and sometimes not so slowly) eroded.

Enough proof has been collected in the foregoing chapters, I think, to demonstrate one of my main premises that increasingly the Party needs the professional elite far more than the elite needs the Party. The complex technological nature of this age is, of course, the prime reason for this change. But the Party's spiritual poverty and emotional instability are also among the causes.

The Party hierarchs may claim that the Party is ever flexible and never wrong as it adapts itself to the changing times. They may insist on credit for themselves as they court and use the professional personnel of the new era. They say that the Party, far from standing still, rides ahead to its Leninist goals in this new space-age vehicle of progress and power. Yet, there is evidence that the Party is not so foolish as to believe its own claim. The more perceptive among the hierarchs realize the dangers of riding the technological tiger.

In truth, in these mid-1960s the Party retreats far more definitely and clearly than it either advances or stands still. The Party has by now fully conceded the defeat of its dogma and policy on cybernetics; defeat by the scientists and engineers who believed in, and brought into Russian reality, the pragmatic wonders of linear programming, of computers.

The Party has fought a long and bloody battle against modern genetics. Once the post-Stalinist retreat in this field started, the Party was stubbornly slow in admitting the fact of its retreat. But from mid-October 1964 on, with Khrushchev gone, the Party was in complete rout here, too.

In medical research, more than three years ago the Party hierarchs made the reluctant admission that they had no right to dictate to scientists any decisions whatever. An important about-face, this, with far-reaching consequences for so many fields in science and technology other than that of medical investigation and progress.

The Party still attacks the nation's industrial and commercial managers for their independence bordering on impudence; it accuses the managers of corruption and sundry crimes—yet, through the now officially blessed Liberman Plan and its variations and expansion, the Party gives and proposes to give the managers far more power than they have ever had, and clearly non-Party power this is, too. In the just words of Professor Jeremy R. Azrael, "ideological agnosticism" of the technical intelligentsia, "the tendency to denigrate the role of ideology" has recently spread not only among managers and other economic personnel, but also among Party officials.[2] Thus the manager infects the Party official stationed to watch the manager's ideological obedience. Infects and diminishes! The prospect of the manager's further enhancement at the expense of the Party's prestige and strength is not to be doubted.[3]

If you cannot fight them, join them. And so the Party joins to its apparatus the engineers as well as managers and other technicians, making them into Party secretaries and other functionaries, in the process hoping thus to reinforce and reinsure the Party. Some Western observers think that the device indeed works. But in fact the engineers and other technicians are either cynical or sly, either self-serving or patently much more proud of their professional competence than of their Party status. They either neglect their Party duties or use their new Party posts to advance the good of their industry, of their profession, and not of the Party. The hierarchs take umbrage or even fright; they dismiss whole batches of such Party functionaries and recruit others, more docile or loyal, they hope, but out of the same professional technical strata. The result in the long run, however, is the same. The new functionaries serve themselves and their part of the New Class, not the Party.

There is a steady retreat before the elite's spirit of friendly inquiry about the West and its values. True, as they concede and retreat, the Party bosses do not at all share the elite's sympathy for the West.

The Party admits its own cultural inferiority as at last, on dismissing Khrushchev, it rebukes him for his crudity in exactly the way the former dictator was for so long criticized *sotto voce* by Russia's more sensitive intellectuals.

Quite often the Party cadres do have the same yen as the professional elite for property and the incidental but important privacy this property (particularly real estate) gives the Soviet man. But they cannot indulge this yen as readily as the professional personnel can. The Party bosses use state property, but less often do they own houses. So their enjoyment of state-owned villas is in essence ephemeral. Scientists, engineers, and managers (as well as professors, writers, artists, and actors) can far more easily prove the legitimacy of their high incomes making the erection of their own dachas legal and otherwise proper. Thus, in the matter of actual ownership of property, the scientific-technical, managerial, and other professional strata are accumulating such tangible assets much more extensively and rapidly than the other part of the New Class—the Party personnel—can or does.

I I

It is this possession of economic assets that makes the professional elite no longer the Party's helot, but actually a countervailing force—and potentially a competitor of the Party, a contender for control of the nation, even if their own new role is imperceptible to so many members of the scientific-technical-managerial elite.

Certain Western experts on things Soviet define this professonal part of the New Class as "the middle leadership"—to distinguish it from the Party's elite, from the Presidium and its top leadership. In this last differentiation I see a certain portent. No middle leader is content to be a junior partner of the higher leader for long. Human nature is to want to be the man at the top. The inexorable rule of human history is that once a group, a class, gains economic and technical power it inevitably reaches for political power as well—both to safeguard its newly won socio-economic advantages, and to extend them, too.

But does it mean that the managers, say, can or may take over politically just because the Liberman Reform gives them more administrative leeway? Does it mean that managers, engineers, and scientists would eventually move to political heights simply because there are all those small cases of their petty insubordination, of their nagging defiance of Party hacks? After all, their contrariness *is* petty, nagging, and mostly on the state's middle or even lower levels. It seems to have little to do with the higher levels of power where real decisions of policy are made and where the Party still reigns supreme and where scientists, engineers, and managers as yet appear to be wholly under the Party's thumb.

My answer to these arguments is that the Liberman idea of

profit may indeed be regarded by the Party (and even by some Western analysts) as strictly peripheral, but, in its far-reaching essence, it is symbolic of deeper reforms yet to come—deeper and more basic, so basic that they may yet abolish Marxism in Russia.

And my answer also is that in its lower and higher echelons the professional elite is far more interconnected than it may appear to the naked eye. Pressures from the lower echelons do reach upper ones, even in a totalitarian society. There is no such sociopolitical vacuum below the Kremlin heights as some Western Sovietologists sometimes briefly and erroneously describe and contemptuously dismiss. Nor is there such a foolproof control of the Party-decreed rigid structure of, say, the Academy of Sciences or sundry professional technical societies as some Western experts hopelessly concede to the Kremlin.

There is no such airtight compartmentalization of Soviet science and technology, no such inner Iron Curtains between one field of research and another, as some Western observers claim to see as one more tool of Party control over the professional elite. The experience of Siberia's Science City in collecting and integrating so many divergent institutes and laboratories in one place; the role of computers in cutting across disciplines, in bringing together physicists, biologists, economists, linguists in common projects—all this is sufficient proof that Russia's science and engineering cannot be so readily or lastingly thwarted by the Party hierarchs from free and easy cross-fertilization and thus from one more step to independence and political influence.

I I I

Indeed, we cannot ever emphasize enough the implacable fact that life is stronger than dogma; that humans can and do break through artificial barriers; that they can and do live outside the rigid structures their moral or intellectual inferiors erect.

The Soviet state is not necessarily cast in concrete and fixed forever—so long as its society is in flux and the professional elite throws a long and meaningful shadow before it. So many Western observers suffer from the hardening of categories; they are hypnotized by the mere fact of endurance, for nearly a half century, of the top institutions of the Party's power: the Central Committee, and, above it, importantly, the Presidium and the Secretariat.

Certainly these three Party bodies are strong and may yet last for a time, but for how long or short a time no one can tell. Yes, there is no closing our eyes to the absence from them of true scientists, true engineers, true managers. But from the defectors interviewed by me and from other stray indications, we know that there is that little-publicized but highly significant network of consulting offices, manned by scientists and other experts, attached to the Party's Central Committee and constantly deferred to by the Presidium and the Secretariat. The policies, domestic and especially foreign, that the Presidium and the Secretariat decree are increasingly influenced by the experts—by the scientists, engineers, and other technicians.

From more than one source we gather that Khrushchev's retreat from the Cuban brink of World War III in the fall of 1962 was in no small measure due to the advice—nay, the pressure—of these experts. For Russia's scientists and engineers, on the whole, unlike Russia's Party bosses, do not hate the West. On the contrary, they admire the West, particularly America. They don't want to conquer the world; they want to see the world—as travelers, not as hated conquerors. They know the potential of American scientific and technical genius far better than a Party leader knows it or can ever know it. They are aware of the fact that America is not licked yet and is far from being licked. Above all, they know that even if America should be destroyed in World War III, Russia would not survive it either. Which means they themselves will not survive.

Some Soviet scientists and engineers may, indeed, be idealistic enough to care about the world's survival. But many of them care about themselves and their families only. Whatever the reason, the point is they *are* on the side of the angels—on the side of peace.

The Party's hierarchs, especially in times of crisis, ask these experts' advice for one reason only: they are experts, they have the complex know-how of this space-age day. But in the experts' own opinion they are not only experts; they are also honest, and this is because they are scientists. In the fall of 1963, at the Pugwash Conference held at Dubrovnik in Yugoslavia, between sessions a Soviet scientist had a private conversation with an American journalist. He was Academician Lev Andreyevich Artsimovich, the well-known atomic physicist.

The American asked: "What qualifications do you think scientists have for forming judgments on political matters?"

The Soviet scientist replied: "We have one or two good features. We have a comparatively high degree of honesty. That comes from our scientific style of thinking, which is carried on without reference to the opinions of other men. And we are comparatively independent, which also comes from our scientific training. We direct our thought to the problem we are working on. We are not easily distracted—comparatively, I mean. . . . I think we are better educated than politicians."

He gave numerous examples out of philosophy, history and geography proving that scientists knew more about all these than most politicians. That is why, expert and honest, these "voluntary advisers to our political leaders" (as the Soviet atomist described himself and his colleagues) are highly valued and are listened to in Moscow. For, Academician Artsimovich insisted, "we know better than anyone else what there is to be concerned about . . ." The net result? "There has been a sudden surge for us to levels of high importance."[4]

And, in their honesty, they tell the Kremlin the truth, despite the instinctive fear the Communist leaders have of this truth, any truth.

I V

Fearlessness is the new quality of so many younger Soviet scientists, engineers, and other technicians. Their elders, with the exception of the few Kapitsas, Bergs, and Parins, cannot quite understand this freedom from fear. In the best Soviet novel on the life of scientists, an old professor "still cannot unbend himself to a straight position" even as he is told by the Party superiors that he can indeed be freer than before. "Strange, but now that nothing was hampering him he began to feel certain fetters within himself. The young ones . . . could not comprehend this feeling: they never experienced his fears, no one of them had worked in those years when one had to keep silence, when often it was impossible to utter one's thoughts, when the result of scientific discussion was predetermined by some directive or other, when he . . . feared to reply to his foreign colleagues' letters . . ." Now all this seemed funny to the young ones, but he, the old professor, had "felt it on his hide." Such things "do not pass without a trace," and "fear has eaten into him, has permeated his brain." But the young ones were truly free of all this. "They thought freely and mockingly, and he envied them—envied not their youth, but the fact that this present time has come too late for him."[5]

My friend Leon Herman, of the Legislative Reference Service at the Library of Congress, tells me that on his recent trips to the Soviet Union he noticed precisely this uncomfortable feeling on the part of some older Soviet academicians as they viewed the young ones and their freedom. He reports the frowning and squirming of an elderly economist he visited in Moscow. The old scholar in fact tried (unsuccessfully) to shush his daughter and son-in-law in some of their bold remarks in front of visiting Americans. "They were too critical of Soviet ways, too admiring of the West," Mr. Herman recalls. "The academician could not get used to the idea that such remarks would now go unpunished by the authorities. He was not sure that the old times would not come back and careless remarks of the 'free' era would not be dragged forth in the purges of the future."

The young ones, and increasingly many of their elders, have the supreme conviction that Stalinism cannot come back; nay, that Marxism is passing or already passé (many of them almost openly acknowledge themselves to be "post-Marxian"); that fear is out of place and will not return.

But do they have a sense of mission, a feeling that they, the professional elite, hold the answer to the world's problems where the Stalinists and the Khrushchevists failed so abysmally? Yes, says one Soviet engineer, "science and technology create the face of the current epoch. Increasingly they influence the tastes, the mores, the behavior of man." Two Moscow instructors of technology wondered: In this statement did he include in science also "the sum total of . . . man's socioeconomic knowledge?" Not at all, they said in answer to their own question; the proud engineer "has in mind the precise, natural, technical sciences only."[6] Thus the Party's pretension to "scientific" Marxism is swept away by the engineer, at least implicitly.

Daniil Granin's young physicists make the half-humorous, half-serious suggestion that geniuses of science should be venerated in the Soviet Union to the point where their portraits would be carried on the streets and plazas at May Day demonstrations and other Soviet parades,[7] side by side, apparently, with the portraits of Party leaders, if not to the exclusion of the latter.

And typical is the attitude of a young laboratory assistant at a Moscow research institute of electronics: "In his eyes physicists and computer-programmists were the real people, the elite of the twentieth century. The rest were lined below, down a descending line. He of course counted himself also among the elite."[8]

V

Snobbishness is the sin often and shrilly ascribed by the Party to the scientific, engineering and managerial elite, as this elite becomes more and more conscious of its education and worth. We know that much of the elite has a great deal of self-esteem. Will this characteristic (call it self-esteem or call it snobbishness) come to ugly selfishness if ever the scientists and technicians achieve power?

Are they at all humanitarian? As yet we do not have enough conclusive evidence on that. They hold no discernible unified philosophy or even a system of ethics—as a group. Some, as we have noticed, are sympathetic to literary and artistic experiments. They seem to want the same freedom for writers and artists to experiment which by now the scientists have in their laboratories. This much makes some of this elite humanitarian. In my chapter on the real beliefs of scientists and engineers I dwelt on the religious experience of Oleg Lenchevsky and the "repentant-nobleman" concern of Lev Predtechevsky for the underdog. These two points are also indications of humanitarianism. But Lenchevsky's belief in God is not typical for the scientific-technical elite of Russia today. Most of them are atheists, or at least agnostics. Down deep inside their hearts and minds they scorn Karl Marx, but in one thing they do agree with him—they, too, say and are convinced that religion is the opium of the masses. (But since they do not really believe in Communism, their slogan seems to be also that Communism is the myopia of the asses.)

It is different with Predtechevsky's feeling of guilt before the deprived. Surely most of the elite believe in materialism, but they are not dialectical materialists. They are individualistic materialists. They are hard-working, but cynical. They are industrious, but they are selfish wire-pullers and "long-ruble" chasers, too. And yet, there is a streak of old-fashioned Russian intellectual concern for the less privileged in them as well.

Here is where the likening of Soviet intellectuals today to German intellectuals of Nazi times (quoted in Chapter II) is wrong. Here is where some good heritage of tsarist times comes in; German intellectuals had no such tradition of indignation at oppression as old Russia's intellectuals had. It was old Russia's

intellectuals who led the peasantry and other lower classes in their
century-long opposition to the tsars.

Before 1917 and its revolution the old-time scientists such as
Dmitry Mendeleyev and Ilya Mechnikov did not think of themselves as a group to be pampered or catered to by the ruling class
of that day, by the Tsar's high-ranking nobles who ran the old
Russian state. Those scientists thought of the people as a whole
—including the country's lower classes then deprived of some
basic human rights. And that was so because the scientists of that
period belonged to the intelligentsia as a whole—intelligentsia
with a strong tradition of heartbreak for the people and service
to the people. The Mendeleyevs and the Mechnikovs just naturally
partook of that tradition, not setting themselves off from the rest
of Russian intelligentsia.

The situation is now different in that science and technology in
the 1960s are far more important than they were in 1900 or
1860. Granted that scientists and engineers are a much more
definite and separate class in the Soviet Union than they were in
old Russia. True, there is less of humanitarian spirit in Soviet
intellectuals than in their predecessors. Every man is for himself
in today's Russia. Every class is for itself, too. This is because the
Soviet era took its early but awful moral toll of the intellectuals
it found in Russia. After 1917 the Communists crushed Russia's
intellectuals (as they crushed or entrapped all other classes); and
for some forty years the remnants of the old intelligentsia, as well
as the new, Soviet-reared technicians and other educated experts,
seemed totally obedient to the new rulers and oppressors.

Many even praised the grossest of injustices committed by the
Soviet regime—so terrorized were they. But the spark of their
opposition to the butchers continued to smolder despite all the
purges, and now the old-Russian intellectual tradition of unrest,
of opposition, of pro-Westernism is once more alive.

Even the old-Russian willingness to risk one's privileges, if not
liberty and life, is beginning to reassert itself among some intellectuals—scientists, engineers, and managers. In this respect,
Soviet intellectuals today are as different from the German intellectuals so subservient during the Nazi regime as their predecessors—old tsarist intellectuals—were different from the Kaiser's
doctors, lawyers, engineers, professors, and other "middle leaders."

Much of the old noble tradition of concern for the less fortunate, of course, needs to be rebuilt. And it may be rebuilt. Or, if

already reappearing, it may be strengthened. Wistfully, openly, the new Soviet intellectuals make an appeal to one another to learn from the old-Russian intelligentsia. We read in *Literaturnaya gazeta*: "Here were [men and women] who knew how to do this splendidly, to live with the people and among the people: the old-Russian intelligentsia. Here is where some of us could learn attentiveness to people, also modesty, also that genuine, profound democratism!"[9]

At the very least, the elite's protest against the Party's arbitrariness and injustice may serve as a human and humane example to others. Yes, the new scientific-engineering elite in the Soviet Union may well be demanding and gaining rights only or mainly for themselves. But in doing so, in raising their voice, they may well be setting a precedent for other, lower classes in that country—for the general run of Russian humanity.

VI

The Party is retreating high and low. The Party knows it is behind the new times and cannot catch up. To what extent Party secretaries realize their own backwardness, or, to use a Soviet expression, "nonsynchronization with the times," may be seen from a striking bit of talk by a fictional Communist functionary in one of Aleksandr Solzhenitsyn's short stories. There, a Party City Committee secretary indulges in verbal self-flagellation as he recalls his experience of witnessing the examination of a nineteen-year-old student graduating from a provincial technical school. The erudition of the youth astonished and awed the Party secretary:

> . . . I was simply envious! . . . I sat there, and found myself upset. Think I: what about me, I have been footslogging on this earth all of fifty years—and what specialty do I have? Is it a specialty that in the past I have tended a factory lathe? But all those lathes have long since been thrown out as obsolete. Is it a specialty that I know the Party's history and Marxist dialectics? But everybody should know this. We don't hold any privilege by such knowledge. Enough! The time has come that no one should be a Party functionary without having a true specialty.

The true specialty now was not Marxist theorizing but scientific and engineering knowledge. The Party secretary soberly emphasized this as he recalled that when he, at some past time, had worked in a factory, "just such youths ran all the affairs at my plant." He now knew that he, the Party boss without any special technical knowledge of his own, "could not impart to such a young man any instructions on how to increase the plant's productivity." In fact, had he been younger, he—this not-so-proud Party secretary—would have gone back to school, "to an evening technical school."[10]

Some will say, however, that as the Party retreats, the young technician would not always move into the political void; he would not deign to be interested. A Soviet mathematician and a French biologist, both young, met at a French exhibit in Moscow and became trusting friends, periodic visitors in each other's homes in Russia and France, and frequent correspondents. In one of his letters the Russian wrote: "I must tell you that all of us here are convinced that the world's future no longer depends on political systems but on science and technology. In this is the essence of the evolution, and in this respect we are ahead of you." And in another letter: "Do understand me that politics here instersts hardly anyone. Not a single wise and self-respecting man will call himself a Communist. Communism is slowly being gotten out of our beings. . . ."[11] And no other politics (it is implied) is replacing it.

We find an echo of this in Viktor Nekrasov's statement about another young Russian: "Here, for instance, is a physicist, and a good physicist, who in addition is excited about Heinrich Boell [a modern West German fiction writer popular in the U.S.S.R.], frequents Richter's recitals and Mexican exhibits, but God save him from politics; the farther away from politics, the better he feels—'Leave me out of it, it's a dark business . . .' "

Other Soviet young people, however, combine politics with whatever else occupies them, be it science or art or both. This, in Nekrasov's view, "is a more complex and more earnest category of youth. They live through tortures as they think and talk of the latest revelations of Stalinist atrocities. These say bluntly: 'We want to know the truth . . .' These will have the most difficult time of all."[12] An eventual, inevitable disillusionment with the Party itself for such young scientists, engineers, other professionals, and students en route to their professions is hinted by Nekrasov—a political activity of some sort is implied, quite likely of a non-Communist kind, I will add.

VII

Is there any likelihood that the Soviet Union's new scientific-technical personnel will not be able to achieve any role of its own in that country's politics, vis-à-vis the traditional Party leadership, if only because this personnel is not truly united within itself? Recall what C. P. Snow has said and written on the basic difference between scientists and engineers in Western countries. In my conversation with Lord Snow in his London home on March 31, 1963, I posed this question: "Do you see a similar split between Soviet scientists and engineers as well?"

His answer was that, from his long-time acquaintance with Soviet Russians of the corresponding strata, he saw no such phenomenon in that country; that in his opinion scientists and engineers were not so different from one another in the Soviet Union as they were in the West. He reasoned: Soviet scientists tend to be practical adapters as well as pure researchers and experimenters, men who apply their theories in practice more habitually and consistently than do their colleagues in the West. When I mentioned Academician Peter Kapitsa, Lord Snow agreed readily: "Yes, this is a very good example." He went on to say that, most importantly, Soviet engineers are not as narrowly trained—just for engineering—as Western ones are. They are trained to look into the essence of science even as they are prepared to apply it for the practical glory of Soviet industrialization.

My late good friend Konstantin Solntsev, one of the best-educated and most perceptive minds of the Russian migration in Paris and New York, held the same view on the closeness of the Russian engineer to the Russian scientist. Solntsev wrote: "The Russian engineer is not merely a master of his applied, narrow specialty—he is also a theoretician. He is an accomplished professor, of broad erudition, ready at any moment to deliver a college course of mathematics or physics or chemistry."[13]

In a way, this idea of C. P. Snow and Konstantin Solntsev coincides with the official Soviet stand on the problem. There is no such problem in their nation, the Soviets say. This pronouncement is made with a particular emphasis whenever Soviet critics discuss the novels of the American writer Mitchell Wilson, little known in his own country but greatly trumpeted in numerous Soviet translations, repeated editions, and fulsome reviews. The critics in Moscow are particularly fascinated by "the obstacles faced by Wilson's scientist-heroes" in America, and, among these handicaps, "all attributed to capitalist maladjustment," they note "the competing demands of theoretical and applied science" in America, something, they say, that is totally and happily absent from the Soviet scene.[14] One Soviet critic wrote: "For a Soviet reader (and more so for a Soviet scientist) who is used to seeing the cooperation of science and industry—one of the most important conditions for the development of both—it is strange to see this."[15]

But Professor Deming Brown, a discerning American observer of the Soviet scene, doubts that all is well in the Soviet Union in this respect among others. He does see "a continuing conflict between theoretical and applied science," and he points out that this is precisely one of the reasons "why Wilson's novels are so popular in Russia." He explains, correctly, that "the Soviet reader does not view with pitying detachment the troubles of the American scientist fighting to capture his own individual vision of the truth. The reader's own experience has taught him to recognize these troubles, and to feel a close sense of identification with them."[16]

Professor Brown makes it clear, however, that if theoreticians and practitioners in Soviet science and technology do clash, it is not so much among themselves, as with the bureaucrats interfering with them, bossing them, or trying to boss them. And whatever there is of that other conflict, of the struggle between scientists and engineers, on the whole it is a smaller, less significant rift than we may find in the West; and certainly smaller and less important than is the Soviet dichotomy already present or now developing between that country's scientific-technical personnel on the one side and the Party's top rulers on the other.

Lord Snow is quite right in what he says on the absence of a chasm of any appreciable depth between scientists and engineers in the Soviet Union. The official Soviet line is right, too: there is really no such problem. But there may be this other, greater problem of a more vital split, which of course is hardly mentioned by the Soviets.

VIII

Mao Tse-tung is not that shy. He does speak, loudly, of the Soviet state going to the bourgeois dogs by its leadership's default, by the awful anti-Marxist sin of the Kremlin in letting the Soviet bourgeois take over. For once, Mao is right—except, of course, in holding that Khrushchev could, or his heirs can, prevent the inevitable.

That it is inevitable Mao could learn from the grand old historian of the inevitable, Arnold Toynbee, who in an interview has spoken of the imminent victory over the Soviet Union's Communist Party by "a professional class of people with special knowledge"—by scientists, engineers, and other technicians. "Power in the world today," remarked Toynbee, "means good scientists and technicians."[17] That the process is developing also in the East European satellite lands (if not in China as yet) is observed by that astute foreign correspondent, Max Frankel, of *The New York Times*, when he quotes a Hungarian teacher: "Even ambitious people realize you don't have to join the Party now to make something of yourself." The same writer notes the same irresistible phenomenon in East Germany:

> . . . unorthodox economists and young plant managers are being called upon to put the East German house in order, to take over where the older politicians and ideologists have failed. Here, as elsewhere in Communist Europe, the old Marxist texts are being tossed away. . . . A dispersal of power and an increasing reliance upon experts will continue to erode the prescribed leadership of the Communist Party in every field. Conspicuous Party control over the police, information and cultural affairs is disguising this subsurface shift. . . . [18]

In the eyes of the young economists, plant managers, scientists, and technicians everywhere in East Europe, but especially in the Soviet Union, the Party politicians have failed not only generally, by mismanaging the countries' economics and politics, but also specifically, by not giving the professional elite the share of welfare the elite feels it deserves. As the chief engineer of the Kuibyshev ball-bearings plant said to the Party officials when he was caught stealing at the plant: "Are you being serious? I have taken from the state less than I have given to the state . . ."[19]

On all sides we are told the indubitable fact that the Soviet technical elite has positions, prosperity, prestige. These men and women have an investment in the Soviet system. We are asked: Why should they turn against it? But that is just it: they have an investment, and they feel that they do not get a fair share for their investment, that the Party takes undue credit—and cash—for the work they, the technicians, have done. The technicians view themselves as the real producers and the Party hacks as drones.

I X

How close is the world to a rule of the Soviet Union by a technocracy that would be at least non-Communist if not anti-Communist?

Now that Nikita Khrushchev is gone and Leonid Brezhnev and Aleksei Kosygin are the two new bosses of the Soviet Union, some sanguine commentators say that the day of technocracy has already arrived.

Indeed, Khrushchev had no higher education, and hardly any middle schooling either; but Brezhnev is an engineer by training and Kosygin is an economist-manager as well as an engineer by his past schooling and experience. In his interview with James Reston of *The New York Times* on December 6, 1965, Kosygin said proudly: "I am not only the president of the Council of Ministers, but I am an engineer. As an engineer, I am never absolutely satisfied with the state of our economy and our science."[20]

However, Brezhnev and Kosygin (and their chief aide Nikolai Podgorny) are of the technical elite on the surface only; they are Party politicians rather than technicians, and in this sense they are in Khrushchev's own image; they are the direct-line inheritors of the Lenin-Stalin mantle, more than they can or do represent any real, deep-going change from the Party pattern. It was Khrushchev himself who designated Brezhnev and Kosygin as his heirs. From Khrushchev's standpoint their only fault was and is that they had a premature idea of succeeding him. Otherwise, they are his own men of course.

Yes, indeed, 'way back in 1935, at the age of twenty-nine, Brezhnev was graduated from an engineering institute, gaining his diploma of a metallurgist. But as an engineer he practiced just two years, no more. At the age of thirty-one he went into Party politics, became a full-time Party official, and ever since then—all these twenty-eight years (he is fifty-nine now)—he has been a Party functionary, a Party walking-talking delegate, not an engineer.

Kosygin is in his early sixties. As a young man in his twenties he was a self-made economist specializing in the field of consumers' cooperatives. In his thirties he switched to textiles, in which field he was graduated from a technical institute. For some three years he held jobs as a foreman, then a manager, in spinning mills, but, like Brezhnev, very early he went into professional Party work, and that is where he has been all these years since 1938—in a long chain of Party jobs.

So, neither Brezhnev nor Kosygin is a genuine engineer, economist, or manager. They are not considered as such by the vast majority of Russia's scientific-technical-managerial elite. They are considered *apparatchiki*—that is, part and parcel of the Communist Party apparatus, with much of that mossback traditionalism of the Communist Party, with much of that blood-purge guilt and concentration-camp responsibility which go with the Party and its apparatus.

Real scientists, engineers, and managers may be—many of them—Communist Party members, but they are this reluctantly, mechanically, automatically. As much as they can, they disassociate themselves from the *apparatchiki*, from the Party professionals, from the men and women who have the Stalin-time blood on their hands. And conversely, genuine Communists seldom make the real scientific-managerial elite.

True, Brezhnev and Kosygin are different from Khrushchev in some respects at least. They are different if only because at the beginning of their careers they had some engineering and managerial training, which such old Party chiefs as Khrushchev never had.

There is something sober and practical about them and their habits of thought and action—more so than was in Khrushchev. They are less flamboyant and colorful, yes, but also less impulsive and irritable; more humdrum, yes, but more dependable, perhaps, insofar as further reforms of Russian life and politics are concerned, insofar as further improvement of coexistence with the West is involved.

In this sense, Brezhnev and Kosygin may indeed represent a good transition en route to such a rule by the true scientists, engineers, and managers as I envisage for the future of the Soviet Union.

In sum, the Brezhnevs and the Kosygins are not as yet the wave of the future. But they are a step forward on the way to the better future, and as such, even if cautiously, we should give them the benefit of our doubt—even if they do not represent a power of their own but are a façade for some other and as yet unknown groups and cliques; even if those other forces lurk somewhere behind them in the back of the Soviet stage; even if the Brezhnevs and the Kosygins do not last long.

The very fact of their appearance in the center of the Soviet political stage, for whatever short period of time this may turn out to be, is a good sign for the future. For it may prove to be one more of the very first outward signs of the good erosion now in progress in the Soviet Unoin—erosion of the Communist Party and its power, the power that on the whole has been so bloody, so reactionary, so unscientific, and so much opposed to the best there is in human nature.

NOTES

Russian-language newspapers and magazines cited in these notes are, unless otherwise stated, published in Moscow. For other publications, the city of publication is indicated the first time, but not necessarily subsequently.

In the transliteration of Russian names and words in these notes, palatalization (softening) of consonants is uniformly indicated by the insertion of an apostrophe after such consonants; in the text this is done only occasionally. Oleg Pen'kovsky's name, for instance, is used in the text without the apostrophe between "n" and "k"; similarly, Michael Ol'shansky is mentioned and quoted in the text without the apostrophe between "l" and "s." This is because in Western sources both names (and others like them) appear with the proper palatalization omitted, the apostrophe apparently being too bothersome for the Western readers' eyes.

In transliteration I prefer to use *y* chiefly to indicate the hard *ee* sound (the Russian letter *yerry*); but I also employ *y* as part of my indication of *ya, yi, yo*, etc., instead of *ia, io*, and so on, which I use only in such words as have become relatively familiar to the English reader in *ia*, etc. spelling. I also use *y* for the short *ee* (*ee kratkoye*), preferring it to the second *i* in what some transliterators of the Russian give us as *ii*. But, in a number of cases—particularly in proper names or well-known adjectives— I prefer just one *y* to either *iy* or *ii* (such as: *russky* instead of either *russkiy* or *russkii*).

In the names of newspapers, and titles of books and articles, the Russians capitalize the first letter of the first word only. I have followed this custom in citing Russian sources both in the text and in these notes.

PREFACE

1. Letter from Professor Joseph A. Raffaele to Albert Parry, May 11, 1961.
2. Conversations with Dr. Raffaele during my visit with him at his home in mid-June 1961. His *Labor Leadership in Italy and Denmark* (Madison: University of Wisconsin Press, 1962), indicates the impressive contribution he would have made to our understanding of the role of labor-and-elite relationship in the Soviet Union if he had not been frustrated in his investigations there.
3. John A. Osmundsen, "U. S. Scientist Back from Soviet Tells of Laboratory Work There," *The New York Times*, March 7, 1959.
4. Transcript of Barghoorn's news conference, *The New York Times*, November 18, 1963.
5. Typical is I. Kon, "Burzhuaznaya sotsiologiya na sluzhbe imperializma" [Bourgeois sociology in the service of imperialism], *Krasnaya zvezda* [Red Star (the official daily newspaper of the Soviet armed forces)], December 23, 1964. The author of this article is identified in the by-line as "professor, doctor of the philosophical sciences."
6. George Fischer, *Science and Politics; the New Sociology in the Soviet Union* (Ithaca, N. Y.: Cornell University Center for International Studies, 1964), *passim*; Anatoly Nikul'kov, "V razvedke—sotsiologi" [Sociologists are reconnoitering], *Literaturnaya gazeta*, March 2, 1965; and unsigned, "Nad chem rabotayut sotsiologi" [What the sociologists are working on], *Trud* [Labor], June 5, 1965.
7. Yu. Filonovich, "Nado li vynosit' sor iz izby?" [Is it necessary to carry trash out of the hut?], *Izvestiya*, [News] March 30, 1962.
8. Arkady Raikin, "Tainstva smekha" [Mysteries of laughter], *Izvestiya*, April 13, 1965.

CHAPTER I

The Problem and the Premise

1. Harry Schwartz, "Ranks of Science Double in Soviet," *The New York Times*, March 14, 1965.
2. L. I. Brezhnev, "Velikaya pobeda sovetskogo naroda" [The great victory of the Soviet people], *Pravda*, [Truth] May 9, 1965. This speech was delivered at the Moscow celebration of the twentieth anniversary of the end of World War II.
3. A. Rumiantsev, "Partiya i intelligentsiya" [The Party and the intelligentsia], *Pravda*, February 21, 1965.
4. Moshe Decter, "Profile of a Soviet Prisoner," *The New Leader* (New York), April 1, 1963, p. 16.
5. Z. Nemtsova, "Prinimayushchim estafetu" [To those who relay the message], *Izvestiya*, March 24, 1963.
6. For the best modern exposition of Saint-Simon's life and philosophy, see Frank E. Manuel, *The New World of Henri Saint-Simon* (Cambridge, Mass.: Harvard University Press, 1956).
7. For a thoughtful discussion of this side of Wells, see W. Warren

NOTES   319

Wagar, H. G. *Wells and the World State* (New Haven: Yale University Press, 1961), pp. 96, 165–166, 178, 211–212, 219, 220.

8. Max Nomad, *Rebels and Renegades* (New York: The Macmillan Company, 1932), pp. 206–208, 213, 239.

9. Unsigned, *"Makhayevshchina"* [Makhayevism] *Bol'shaya sovetskaya entsiklopediya* [Great Soviet Encyclopedia], 2d ed. (Moscow, 1954), Vol. 26, p. 544.

10. Rumiantsev, *Pravda*, February 21, 1965.

11. Daniel Bell, "The Dispossessed—1962," *Columbia University Forum*, Vol. V, No. 4 (Fall 1962), pp. 5–6.

12. *Ibid.*, p. 12. This article, with minor stylistic changes, is included by Professor Bell in the anthology, which he edited, *The Radical Right* (Garden City, N. Y.: Doubleday and Company, 1963).

13. Herbert McClosky and John E. Turner, *The Soviet Dictatorship* (New York: McGraw-Hill Book Company, 1960), pp. 591–592.

14. Leonard S. Silk, *The Research Revolution* (New York: McGraw-Hill Book Company, 1960), p. 207.

15. "Changing Russia?" (a survey by six staff members after a trip to the Soviet Union), *The Economist* (London), June 1, 1963, p. 893.

16. Vsevolod Kochetov, *Brat'ya Yershovy* [The Yershov brothers] (Moscow: Molodaya Gvardiya [Young Guard, publishing house of the Central Committee of the Communist Youth League], 1959), pp. 85, 298, 410. This novel, by an antithaw writer and editor, is generally known in the Soviet Union as the Party's official answer to Vladimir Dudintsev's 1956 novel, *Ne khlebom yedinym* [Not by bread alone], wherein a persecuted engineer-inventor defies, and finally triumphs over, a Party bureaucrat.

17. Daniil Granin, *Idu na grozu* [I go against the storm] (Moscow and Leningrad: Sovetsky Pisatel' [Soviet Writer publishing house], 1963), p. 151.

18. Mikhail Alekseyev, "Svet dalekoi zvezdy—Novaya povest' Aleksandra Chaikovskogo" [The light of a far-off star—Alexander Chaikovsky's new novelette], *Pravda*, January 28, 1963.

19. Alexander Chaikovsky, "Svet dalekoi zvezdy," *Oktiabr'*, November 1962, pp. 73–74, 76, 93, 100.

CHAPTER II

The Case Against

1. Speech in the village of Obnova, May 18, 1962, *Pravda*, May 19, and *Izvestiya*, May 20, 1962.

2. F. Konstantinov, "Istiny i zabluzhdeniya Erika Fromma" [Erich Fromm's verities and delusions], *Literaturnaya gazeta*, October 24, 1964.

3. Mihajlo Mihajlov, *Moscow Summer* (New York: Farrar, Straus and Giroux, a *New Leader* Book, 1965), pp. 145–146.

4. Carl E. Hartbower, *Technical and Sociological Observations on My Trip to the Soviet Union* (Cambridge, Mass.: Manufacturing Laboratories, Inc., Research Division, 1961; mimeographed and privately distributed), p. 76.

5. *Ibid.*, p. 17.

6. *Ibid.*, pp. 17, 76. *Cf.* the "deep enthusiasm for Communism" encountered by Dr. Konrad B. Krauskopf of Stanford University among the Russian geologists who were his hosts in the Soviet Union and described by him in "Russia a 'Land of the Free'?" in Harry G. Shaffer, ed., *The Soviet System*

in Theory and Practice (New York: Appleton-Century-Crofts, 1965), pp. 337–342.

7. Richard Pipes, "Russia's Exigent Intellectuals, a Eulogy and a Warning," *Encounter* (London), January 1964, p. 81.

8. See, in particular, Nicholas DeWitt, "The Politics of Soviet Science: Is the Soviet Scientist a Policymaker?" a paper presented at the Fifth-eighth Annual Meeting of the American Political Science Association, Washington, D. C., September 7, 1962, pp. 8–10 and especially the concluding paragraph on p. 14.

9. Philip E. Mosely, "Soviet Myths and Realities," *Foreign Affairs* (New York), April 1961, p. 349.

10. *Ibid.*, pp. 350–351.

11. *Ibid.*, pp. 351–352.

12. *Ibid.*, pp. 352–353.

13. Letter from Professor Mosely to Albert Parry, December 21, 1960, and several subsequent conversations on the same subject in 1961–65.

14. TASS dispatch of December 5, 1957, quoted in *Soviet World Outlook* (Washington: Department of State, 1959), p. 169.

15. Yu. Denike, "Kriticheskaya problema sovetskogo obshchestva" [The critical problem of Soviet society], *Sotsialistichesky vestnik* [Socialist herald] (New York), July-August 1962, p. 94.

16. W. S. Woytinsky, *Stormy Passage: A Personal History Through Two Russian Revolutions to Democracy and Freedom—1905–1960* (New York: Vanguard Press, 1961), p. 137.

17. C. P. Snow, *Science and Government* (Cambridge, Mass.: Harvard University Press, 1961), pp. 80–81.

18. C. P. Snow, *The New Men* (New York: Charles Scribner's Sons, 1955), p. 176.

19. Hartbower, p. 14. The Soviet candidate degree is slightly higher in academic and social value than our master's degree; it is a little below our doctorate. The Soviet doctorate is harder to get than our Ph.D. The average age at which a Russian reaches his candidate status is about thirty; the average age of a freshly fledged doctor of sciences in the U.S.S.R. is fifty.

20. Granin, *Idu na grozu*, p. 138.

21. See my Chapter I.

22. John O'Hara, *From the Terrace* (New York: Bantam Books, 1960), p. 965.

23. Albert Wohlstetter, "Scientists, Seers and Strategy," *Foreign Affairs*, April 1963, p. 471.

24. Albert Wohlstetter, "Scientists as Seers" (letter to the editor), *The New York Times*, April 11, 1963.

25. S. N., "Chto s nei stalos' " [What has become of it], *Novoye russkoye slovo* [New Russian Word] (New York), February 19, 1963.

26. Allen Kassof, "The Administered Society: Totalitarianism Without Terror," *World Politics* (Princeton University), Vol. XVI, No. 4 (July 1964), p. 575.

CHAPTER III

Peter Kapitsa: Symbol of Resistance

1. An official Soviet biography of Peter Kapitsa is in *Biografichesky slovar' deyatelei yestestvoznaniya i tekhniki* [Biographical dictionary of leaders of natural science and technology] (Moscow: State Scientific Publishing House

of the Great Soviet Encyclopedia, 1958), Vol. 1, p. 394. This contains a
brief bibliography of his earlier official Soviet biographies, also in Russian. A
more recent source is Yevgeny Dobrovol'sky, "Stranitsy iz zhizni uchyonogo"
[Pages out of the scientist's life], *Literaturnaya gazeta*, August 27, 1963.
Most important are pages and paragraphs on Kapitsa in S. Timoshenko, *Vospomi-
naniya* [Reminiscences], (Paris: Society of the Alumni of the St. Petersburg
Polytechnic Institute, 1963), pp. 214–215, 256–257, 268, 315; also Academician Lev Landau, "Derzat' rozhdennyi—k 70-letiyu akademika P. L. Kapitsy"
[Born to dare—On the 70th birthday of Academician P. L. Kapitsa], *Komsomol'skaya pravda*, July 8, 1964; and Yu. N. Khlopov, "Fizik shirokogo di-
apazona" [The wide-range physicist], *Sovetskaya Rossiya*, December 22, 1964.
Somewhat autobiographical is P. L. Kapitsa, *Zhizn' dlia nauki* [Living for
science] (Moscow: Znaniye [Knowledge] publishing house, 1964). Quite revealing is the interview granted by Kapitsa to Ye. Grigoryants, "Chelovek
v mire informatsii" [Man in the world of data], *Komsomol'skaya pravda*, September 2, 1965.

In English, the reader is referred to "Academician Peter Kapitza Honored
With Title of Hero of Socialist Labor," *Information Bulletin*, Soviet Embassy
in Washington, D. C., May 22, 1945, p. 5 (includes comment by Oleg
Pisarzhevsky, "one of Kapitza's assistants," who also discussed Kapitza's work
in another article, "Discoveries in Super-Fluidity," *Information Bulletin*, Sep-
tember 11, 1945, pp. 5–6); also to Richard E. Lauterbach, "Russia's Kapitza,"
Science Illustrated (New York), March 1948, pp. 24–25 and 105; and (un-
signed) "Russian Atom Scientist," *Science News Letter* (Washington, D. C.),
September 3, 1949, p. 149. On Kapitsa's arrest see Boris I. Nicolaevsky,
"Soviet Science and the Purges," *The New Leader*, December 14, 1946, p. 10.
I corresponded with Mr. Nicolaevsky, a knowledgeable Russian Socialist
émigré then residing in New York, and have gratefully used the information
he kindly shared with me for my own writings. (See Albert Parry, "Peter
Kapitza and the H-Bomb," *New York Herald Tribune*, August 21, 1953; and
"The Russian Who Talks Back to Khrushchev," *Science Digest* (New York),
June 1963, pp. 45–51. This last article is used for a part of the text of my
present chapter.) In a class by itself, a curious source is A. M. Biew, *Kapitsa,
the Story of the British-Trained Scientist Who Invented the Russian Hydrogen Bomb*, translated from the German by James Cleugh (London: Frederick
Muller Ltd., 1956). It smacks of fiction, although it does contain elements
of authenticity. Other, briefer sources are introduced in some of the notes
below.

  2. Dobrovol'sky, *op. cit.*
  3. Timoshenko, pp. 214–215.
  4. *Ibid.*, p. 256.
  5. Aleksei Krylov, born in 1863, died in 1945. See the numerous articles in
the Soviet press in mid-August 1963 commemorating the centenary of his
birth, particularly M. Lavrentyev and P. Favorov, "Osnovopolozhnik kora-
bel'noi nauki" [Founder of the shipbuilding science], *Pravda*, August 15,
1963, and V. Gubarev, "Lotsman golubykh dorog" [Pilot of azure-blue
routes], *Komsomol'skaya pravda*, August 15, 1963. A comprehensive biographical entry on Krylov is in *Biografichesky slovar' deyatelei yestestvoznaniya i
tekhniki*, Vol. 1, pp. 462–464.
  6. Timoshenko, p. 267.
  7. Letter from Boris Nicolaevsky to Albert Parry of December 16, 1949.
  8. Timoshenko, pp. 256–257. The extent to which Timoshenko disliked
Kapitsa may be judged from Timoshenko's recollections of Kapitsa's "inde-
cent behavior" at a dinner at Trinity College where the two Russians shared
the meal with a large group of British scholars. Kapitsa "talked Russian
loudly, making various remarks about those present." Later, Kapitsa invited

his Russian guest for a walk in a small garden at the College. "He orated loudly all this time, and as we were leaving he remarked that this was 'a garden of silence,' and that talking was not permitted there."

9. Timoshenko, p. 268.
10. *Ibid.*, pp. 268, 315.
11. Landau, *op. cit.*
12. Norbert Wiener, *I Am a Mathematician*, (Garden City, N. Y.: Doubleday and Company, 1956), p. 155.
13. Lauterbach, p. 24. Nicolaevsky, in his December 1949 letter to me, warned that Lauterbach's writings should be used with caution: "Lauterbach's information is incorrect, as is much else in his articles." By this, most likely, Nicolaevsky meant that Lauterbach (at least in the 1940s) was too pro-Soviet to be trusted as a reporter.
14. M. Mihajlov, *Moscow Summer*, p. 97.
15. Ilya Ehrenburg, "Lyudi, gody, zhizn'" [People, years, life], *Novy mir* [New World], March 1965, pp. 109–110.
16. P. Kapitsa, "Teoriya, eksperiment, praktika" [Theory, experiment, practice], *Ekonomicheskaya gazeta*, March 26, 1962, p. 10.
17. Harry Schwartz, "Physicist in Soviet Says Regime Gets in Way of Research," *The New York Times*, April 25, 1965.
18. P. Kapitsa, "*Lomonosov i mirovaya nauka*" [Lomonosov and world science], *Sovetskaya Rossiya*, April 15, 1965.
19. Unsigned, "Kapitsa, Soviet Physicist, Is Going to Copenhagen," *The New York Times*, May 23, 1965; and TASS dispatch on the same subject from Copenhagen of May 25, published in a number of Soviet newspapers on May 26, 1965.

CHAPTER IV

The Soviet Battle over Einstein

1. Philipp Frank, *Einstein, His Life and Times* (New York: Alfred A. Knopf, 1947), p. 149.
2. *Ibid.*, pp. 145–146, 256–260.
3. *Ibid.*, pp. 261–262.
4. B. M. Kedrov, "Lenin v bor'be za materializm v fizike" [Lenin in the struggle for materialism in physics], *Ogoniok* [Little Flame] January 22, 1949, pp. 20–21.
5. Yu. Zaretsky, "Leninskoi mysli polyot" [Flight of Lenin's thought], *Izvestiya*, April 20, 1963.
6. Ehrenburg, "Lyudi, gody, zhizn'," *Novy mir*, February 1965, pp. 20–24, and March 1965, p. 90.
7. S. I. Vavilov, A. N. Frumkin, A. F. Ioffe, and N. N. Semyonov, "About Certain Fallacies of Professor Albert Einstein," *The New Times* (English-language edition of *Novoye vremia*; Moscow), November 26, 1947. Reprinted, with Dr. Einstein's reply, in *Bulletin of the Atomic Scientists* (Chicago), February 1948; also in Otto Nathan and Heinz Norden, editors, *Einstein on Peace* (New York: Simon and Schuster, 1960), Chapter 13, "The Need for a Supranational Organization," pp. 400–457. See also Mikhail Koriakov, "Listki iz bloknota—Al'bert Einshtein i Akademiya nauk SSSR" [Leaves from a notebook—Albert Einstein and the Academy of Sciences of the U.S.S.R.], *Novoye russkoye slovo*, April 18, 1965.

8. *Bulletin of the Atomic Scientists*, February 1948.

9. Ehrenburg, "Lyudi, gody, zhizn'," *Novy mir*, February 1965, p. 24.

10. Antonina Vallentin, *The Drama of Albert Einstein* (Garden City, N. Y.: Doubleday and Company, 1954), p. 283.

11. Unsigned, "Nauchnoye naslediye Einshteina" [Einstein's scientific heritage], *Izvestiya*, April 18, 1965.

CHAPTER V

Computers and Politics

1. André Marie Ampère, French physicist and mathematician, used the term "cybernetics" two years before he died, in his *Essais sur la philosophie des sciences* (Paris, 1834), to indicate "the science of ruling a state." In this he apparently followed ancient Greek philosophers (particularly Plato), who derived the word from the Greek for "ship pilot," or "steersman." See G. Onanyan "Strannyie sovpadeniya" [Strange coincidences], *Literaturnaya gazeta*, December 14, 1963; also Jack P. Hailman, "Cybernetics," in "Queries and Answers," *The New York Times Book Review*, May 30, 1965, p. 23.

2. Miron Petrovsky, "Khochu smotret' i videt'" [I want to look and see], *Literaturnaya gazeta*, June 12, 1962.

3. Ehrenburg, "Lyudi, gody, zhizn'," *Novy mir*, February 1965, p. 15.

4. Irina Radunskaya, "Tri eskiza k portretu" [Three sketches for a portrait], *Literaturnaya gazeta*, November 16, 1963.

5. In his article "Pobedy 'elektronnykh ekonomistov'" [Victories of "electronic economists"], *Komsomol'skaya pravda*, July 7, 1962, Professor Kantorovich states that American scientists came to the same methods "only ten years later," that is, by 1949.

6. N. Voloshin, V. Mash, and others, "Kibernetika i milliony" [Cybernetics and millions], *Komsomol'skaya pravda*, April 24, 1965.

7. I am indebted to Professor Warren B. Walsh for an opportunity to consult his 35-page mimeographed manuscript entitled "Some Notes on Mathematics and Mathematicians in the Soviet Union, a Preliminary Study," written in 1959. *Cf.* Wiener's own remarks on his relations with Kolmogorov in *I Am a Mathematician*, pp. 145, 261–262, 325.

8. A. Stroilo, "Po-moyemu, nichego strashnogo" [In my opinion, nothing frightful], *Literaturnaya gazeta*, June 30, 1962.

9. Voloshin, Mash, and others, *op. cit.* For an excellent Western review of Soviet computer philosophy and development see Loren R. Graham, "Cybernetics in the Soviet Union," *Survey* (London), July 1964 (issue entitled "Report on Soviet Science"), pp. 3–18. (The "Report on Soviet Science" is also available in book form as *The State of Soviet Science*, edited by the *Survey* editors and published by the M. I. T. Press in Cambridge, Mass. in 1965.)

10. Maurice Hindus, *House Without a Roof* (New York: Doubleday and Company, 1961), pp. 547–548 and 550.

11. Saul Kravetz, "Mathematics," *McGraw-Hill Encyclopedia of Russia and the Soviet Union* (New York: McGraw-Hill Book Company, 1961), p. 340.

12. Unsigned, "Novyie gorizonty nauki" [New horizons of science], *Pravda*, July 1, 1962.

13. I. Sabel'nikov, *"Elektronnyie lotsmany"* [Electronic pilots], *Komsomol'-skaya pravda*, November 2, 1963.

14. Interview with Sobolev, "Kazhdyi uchyonyi—propagandist nauki" [Each scientist is a propagandist of science], *Sovetskaya Rossiya*, July 5, 1962.

15. Interview with Dr. Donald F. Hornig and others, "Innovation in the Soviet Union," *International Science and Technology* (New York), February 1965, p. 51. One member of the delegation, IBM's chief scientist Dr. E. R. Piore, estimated that "computer technology in the Soviet Union is five years behind Western developments but this gap can be overcome whenever that country's national goals dictate such a move." See "Russian Computer Technology Viewed by IBM Chief Scientist," *IBM News* (Armonk, N. Y.), July 10, 1965, p. 7.

16. V. Lagutkin, "Ekonomika i upravleniye proizvodstvom" [Economics and production management], *Sovetskaya Rossiya*, May 16, 1965.

17. M. Sulim, "Vychislitel'nyie mashiny i avtomatizatsiya upravleniya" [Computers and automation of operations], *Pravda*, May 19, 1963.

18. A. Rusakov, M. Mariyan, S. Zinovyeva, and others, "Sovety dast mashina" [The machine will give advice], *Komsomol'skaya pravda*, September 11, 1963.

19. S. Sobolev, "Poeziya matematiki" [Poetry of mathematics], *Literaturnaya gazeta*, December 14, 1961. For an official Soviet biography of Sergei Sobolev see *Biografichesky slovar' deyatelei yestestvoznaniya i tekhniki*, Vol. 2, pp. 230–231.

20. Sobolev, "Poeziya matematiki."

21. Interview with Academician V. M. Glushkov, "Kibernetika v spetsovke" [Cybernetics in overalls], *Komsomol'skaya pravda*, April 3, 1965.

22. V. V. Parin, "Avtoritet faktov" [The authority of facts], *Literaturnaya gazeta*, February 24, 1962.

23. Interview with Academician Berg, "Kibernetika i filosofiya" [Cybernetics and philosophy], *Pravda*, June 8, 1962.

24. Ilya Vekua, "Nyet uchyonykh bez uchenikov" [There can be no scientists without students], *Izvestiya*, June 8, 1962.

25. S. Sholokhov, "Istorikam pomogayet mashina" [Historians are being helped by a machine], *Pravda*, June 13, 1962. On life and work at Novosibirsk, see Albert Parry, "Akademgorodok, That Science City in Siberia," *Industrial Research* (Beverly Shores, Ind.), December 1963, pp. 30–34.

26. S. L. Sobolev, "Uchit' myslit'" [Let's teach them to think], *Literaturnaya gazeta*, June 26, 1962. See also Theodore Shabad, "Soviet Educator Urges Stress on Individuality," dispatch from Moscow, *The New York Times*, June 27, 1962.

CHAPTER VI

Retreat and Attack: Genes and Grain

1. A typical attack was a four-hour symposium of sixteen prominent scientists gathered to recite and condemn Lysenko's biological heresies. A trenchant summary of the round table discussion filled nearly one quarter of *Literaturnaya gazeta* for November 24, 1964. A comprehensive review of the 1964–65 anti-Lysenko measures is in G. Z., "Lysenkovskaya epopeya" [The Lysenko epopee], *Novoye russkoye slovo*, March 19, 1965.

2. Dispatch from Moscow, May 24, 1965, by Theodore Shabad, "New

Soviet Genetics Journal Presses Anti-Lysenko Reform," *The New York Times*, May 26, 1965.

3. Conway Zirkle, ed., *Death of a Science in Russia—The Fate of Genetics as Described in Pravda and Elsewhere* (Philadelphia: University of Pennsylvania Press, 1949), p. 25.

4. Julian Huxley, *Soviet Genetics and World Science—Lysenko and the Meaning of Heredity* (London: Chatto and Windus, 1949), pp. 182–185.

5. *Ibid.*, p. 184.

6. *Ibid.*, p. 183.

7. *Ibid.*, p. 185.

8. Zirkle, p. 33.

9. Albert Parry, *Russia's Rockets and Missiles*, (Garden City, New York: Doubleday & Company, (1960), p. 63 (part of the chapter "Russian Technical Genius: Facts"). *Cf.* Zirkle, *passim*, and Huxley, *passim*, and the numerous sources they cite; also David Joravsky, *Soviet Marxism and Natural Science, 1917–1932* (New York: Columbia University Press, 1961), Chapter 19, "The Crisis in Biology," pp. 296–310; D. Joravsky, "Soviet Marxism and Biology," *Natural Law Forum* (Notre Dame, Indiana), Vol. 8 (1963), pp. 35–50; and David Joravsky, "Lysenko's Maize," *Survey*, July 1964, pp. 91–99. The very latest source on the Soviet massacre of Russia's Mendelians in the 1930s and '40s is A. Ivanov, "Biologiya i ideologicheskaya bor'ba" [Biology and ideological struggle], *Novy zhurnal* [New Review] (New York), No. 74 (December 1963), which on pp. 260–261 supplies names of victims additional to the ones mentioned in my text.

10. Ivanov, *op. cit.* pp. 264–265.

11. Ivanov, otherwise a most reliable source, misspells this name as Kupriyevich.

12. Drs. Heinrich E. Schulz and Stephen S. Taylor, eds., *Who's Who in the USSR, 1961–1962* (New York: Scarecrow Press, 1962), p. 464.

13. See above, my Chapter IX.

14. *Pravda* and *Izvestiya*, March 11, 1962.

15. T. D. Lysenko, "Teoreticheskiye osnovy napravlennogo izmeneniya nasledstvennosti sel'skokhoziaistvennykh rasteniy [Theoretical principles of controlled changes of heredity in agricultural plants], *Pravda* and *Izvestiya*, January 29, 1963.

16. M. A. Ol'shansky, "Protiv falsifikatsii v biologicheskoi nauke" [Against falsification in the biological science], *Sel'skaya zhizn'* [Rural Life], August 18, 1963; digested in *Pravda*, August 21.

17. M. Ol'shansky, "Biologicheskaya nauka i sel'skokhoziaistvennoye proizvodstvo" [Biological science and agricultural production], *Kommunist*, March 1963, pp. 14–26.

18. Zh. Medvedev and V. Kirpichnikov, "Perspektivy sovetskoi genetiki" [Prospects of Soviet genetics], *Neva* (Moscow and Leningrad), March 1963, pp. 165–175.

19. Ivanov, "Biologiya i ideologicheskaya bor'ba," pp. 253–254. For the text of the resolution see *Pravda* for January 25, 1963. For English-language accounts of Lysenkoism in 1963 see *The New York Times* of April 13 and 18, August 25, and September 6, among others.

20. Huxley, p. 182.

21. Zirkle, pp. 26–28.

22. Unsigned dispatch from Moscow, November 25, 1964, "Lysenko Disputed at Own Institute," *The New York Times*, November 27, 1964; and Ya. Gordinsky, "Fakty protiv domyslov" [Facts versus false claims], *Komsomol'skaya pravda*, November 29, 1964.

23. Semyon Novikov, "Korni" [Roots], *Literaturnaya gazeta*, August 24, 1961.

24. Nikita Khrushchev's closing speech at the plenary session of the Party's Central Committee on December 13, 1963, *Pravda*, December 15, 1963. See also Theodore Shabad, "A Commuter Gets Khrushchev's Aid," dispatch from Moscow, *The New York Times*, December 22, 1963.

25. At this time, in early 1962, a Russian *émigré* journalist in New York quoted Khrushchev's hypocritical announcement, "Science is a noble and majestic phenomenon; Soviet people are imbued with respect for science, they bend their knees before it," then commented: "Precisely the ignoramuses of Khrushchev's type 'bend their knees' before science—bend their knees as if before an idol, demanding from it the impossible. And if they do not get what they demand, then, like Khrushchev, they will cover it with abuse." The author goes on to explain Khrushchev's attack on the Soviet agronomists by his ire at their inability to give him high harvests on the exhausted soil tilled by oppressed, listless peasants. Yuri Mishalov, "Krutoi pod'yem . . . ili?" [A steep rise . . . or?], *Novoye russkoye slovo*, January 13, 1962.

26. Unsigned, "Akademiya sel'skokhoziaistvennaya imeni Timiryazeva" [The Timiryazev agricultural academy], *Bol'shaya sovetskaya entsiklopediya*, Vol. 1 (Moscow, 1949), p. 584.

27. "Propashnaya sistema—put' k izobiliyu" [The arable system is the path to abundance], *Sovetskaya Rossiya*, January 27, 1962.

28. For an official Soviet biography of Vilyams before the denunciation, see *Biografichesky slovar' deyatelei yestestvoznaniya i tekhniki*, Vol. 1 (1958), pp. 165–167.

29. N. Novak-Deker, "The Reorganization in Soviet Agriculture," *Bulletin* of the Institute for the Study of the USSR (Munich), April 1962, pp. 29–35.

30. I. S. Malyshev, ed., *Sel'skoye khoziaistvo SSR, statistichesky sbornik* [Agriculture of the U.S.S.R., statistical anthology] (Moscow: Council of Ministers of the U.S.S.R., 1960), pp. 334–336.

31. Theodore Shabad, "Khrushchev Gives Plan to Ease Vegetable and Potato Shortage," dispatch from Moscow, *The New York Times*, August 12, 1964.

32. Aleksander Kutt, "Soviet Crop Data Disputed," *The New York Times*, August 13, 1964. See also the official Soviet (and most ineffective) answer, to Mr. Kutt's figures and arguments, in the letter by Samuil Kolesnev, member of the Lenin Academy of Agriculture in Moscow, entitled "Russia's Farm Production—Role of Private Plots in Total Output Declared Exaggerated," *The New York Times*, November 25, 1964.

CHAPTER VII

A Deep Bow to Economists

1. In particular see a firsthand account of Mikhail Larin's articles on German planning and their effect on Lenin and the beginnings of Soviet planning in S. I. Liberman, *Dela i lyudi* [Affairs and people] (New York: New Democracy Books, 1944), pp. 45–47; English translation, *Building Lenin's Russia* (Chicago, University of Chicago Press, 1945), pp. 21–23.

For the native Russian genesis of Soviet planning, see Prof. Vasily I. Grinevetsky's *Poslevoyennyie perspektivy russkoi promyshlennosti* [Postwar prospects of Russian industry], first published in 1919, and appearing in its second edition in 1922 on Lenin's order. Had he lived beyond 1919 (when he died of spotted typhus), Prof. Grinevetsky might have achieved a high post in Soviet state service despite his strong anti-Communist views—so great was Lenin's interest in Grinevetsky's ideas on planning. Grinevetsky's formal training and active teaching had been in technology rather than economics. For refreshing my memory of Grinevetsky's curious role in Soviet planning I am indebted to my friend Prof. Nicholas V. Pervushin, of McGill University, and his remarks on this subject in the course of his paper "Contemporary Russia: the Weight of Tradition" delivered at Princeton University on December 3, 1965.

2. On the connection between the clumsiness of the Plan and the remedies proposed by Liberman see V. Belkin and I. Birman, "Samostoyatel'nost' predpriyatiya i ekonomicheskiye stimuly" [Independence of enterprise and economic stimuli], *Izvestiya*, December 4, 1964; S. N., "Sdvig poseriyozneye" [A rather more serious shift], *Novoye russkoye slovo*, March 15, 1965; Ya. Kabkov, "Tovarooborot, magazin, pokupatel'" [Merchandise turnover, store, buyer], *Izvestiya*, June 8, 1965; unsigned, "Russia, Borrowing from the Capitalists," *Time*, February 12, 1965, pp. 23–29; Edward Crankshaw, "Russia Discovers the Customer Is Always Right," *The New York Times Magazine*, March 28, 1965, pp. 26–27 ff.; Harry Schwartz, "The Kremlin and the Consumer—a New Program," "The News of the Week in Review," *The New York Times*, April 25, 1965; Robert Minton, "Why Russia Is Flirting with Profits," *Think* (Armonk, N. Y.), May-June 1965, pp. 6–10; and Theodore Shabad, "Soviet Planning Assailed as Curb" (dispatch from Moscow), *The New York Times*, June 2, 1965.

3. N. Petrov, "Ne dlia pokupatelia, a dlia . . . plana" [Not for the customer, but for . . . the plan], *Pravda*, December 22, 1964.

4. *Time*, February 12, 1965; also short stray items in the Soviet press, too numerous to cite here.

5. Ye. Liberman, "Plan, pribyl', premiya" [Plan, profit, bonus], *Pravda*, September 9, 1962.

6. Marshall I. Goldman, "Economic Controversy in the Soviet Union," *Foreign Affairs*, April 1963, p. 498. This able article presents a concise and penetrating summary of the debate around Liberman's ideas and cites most important Soviet articles pro and con.

7. Vero Roberti, "Fear Returns," *Atlas, the Magazine of the World Press* (New York), May 1963, p. 277. (Originally published in *Corriere della Sera*, Milan.)

8. See *Pravda* for September 14, 16, 17 and 21, and October 7, 12 and 19, 1962 as a fair sample of this discussion of the Liberman plan. Other bibliography (*Ekonomicheskaya gazeta*, November 3 and 10, 1962; *Planovoye khoziaistvo*, March 1963; and so on) is cited in Alec Nove, "Revamping the Economy," *Problems of Communism* (Washington, D. C.), January-February 1963, pp. 10–16; Harry G. Shaffer, "What Price Economic Reforms? Ills and Remedies," *Problems of Communism*, May-June 1963, pp. 18–32; and Alfred Zauberman, "Liberman's Rules of the Game for Soviet Industry," *Slavic Review* (Seattle), December 1963, pp. 734–744.

9. Theodore Shabad, "Workers' Watch Ordered in Soviet," dispatch from Moscow, *The New York Times*, November 29, 1962.

10. P. Volin, "Poka eksperiment . . ." [An experiment so far . . .], *Literaturnaya gazeta*, July 4, 1964.

11. *Ibid*.

12. Harry Schwartz, "Soviet Joins Other Red Lands In Trying Capitalistic Devices," *The New York Times*, May 24, 1964.

13. Editorial note at the end of K. Pogodin, "Firma rabotayet po-novomu" [The firm works in a new way], *Pravda*, January 13, 1965; Theodore Shabad, "Demand to Guide 400 Soviet Plants," dispatch from Moscow, *The New*

York Times, January 14, 1965; "Russia's Consumers Win a Round," an editorial, The New York Times, January 19, 1965.

14. L. Pekarsky and S. Anufriyenko, "Kryl'ya eksperimenta" [The wings of the experiment], Komsomol'skaya pravda, June 3, 1965.

15. Theodore Shabad, "Profit-Plan Test Hailed by Soviet," dispatch from Moscow, The New York Times, May 28, 1965.

16. Pravda (and all other Soviet newspapers) for October 1, 1965, and a few days after.

17. Ray Wicker, "Marxists, Inc.; Eastern Europe's Reds Adopt Capitalist Ideas To Pep Up Economies," dispatch from Budapest, The Wall Street Journal, April 3, 1964.

18. Academician V. Trapeznikov, "Za gibkoye ekonomicheskoye upravleniye predpriyatiyami" [For a flexible economic management of enterprises], Pravda, August 17, 1964.

19. Wicker, dispatch from Budapest, The Wall Street Journal, April 3, 1964.

20. Yu. Mushkaterov, "Kto otkryl yashchik Pandory?" [Who opened Pandora's box?], Sovetskaya Rossiya, April 10, 1965.

21. V. Azar, "G-n Sul'tsberger 'otkryvayet Ameriku' " [Mr. Sulzberger "discovers America"], Krasnaya zvezda, June 9, 1965.

CHAPTER VIII

Hail the Healer

1. For the factual side of this episode, see—in addition to Page 2 of Pravda for August 1, 1962—Theodore Shabad, "Soviet Party Bars Interference In Conflicts on Scientific Issues," dispatch from Moscow, The New York Times, August 2, 1962. For an earlier background of the Kachugin case see Academician A. Bakulev and others, "O lzhenovatorakh v meditsine" [About pseudo innovators in medicine], Pravda, April 20, 1960.

2. V. Bondarenko, "Dogovorilis' do . . . zdravogo smysla" [They talked themselves into . . . common sense], Novoye russkoye slovo, August 31, 1962.

3. Quoted and ably analyzed in A. Natov, "Nachalo perestroiki rukovodstva sel'skim khoziaistvom" [Beginning of reconstruction of the agricultural leadership], Novoye russkoye slovo, April 12, 1963.

4. Report of the United States Public Health Mission to the Union of Soviet Socialist Republics, August 13 to September 14, 1957, Public Health Service Publication No. 649 (Washington: U. S. Department of Health, Education, and Welfare, 1959), p. 60.

5. Associated Press dispatch from Moscow, "Soviets Pamper Researchers," The Christian Science Monitor (Boston), April 15, 1964.

6. S. Antonov, "Nochnoi vyzov" [A night call], Izvestiya, April 12, 1964.

7. M. Barsukova and Ye. Rozanova, "Riaska" [Weeds on stagnant water], Izvestiya, June 19, 1964.

8. Unsigned, "Podvezite vracha" [Give the doctor a ride], Sovetskaya Rossiya, June 21, 1964.

9. Khrushchev's report to the Supreme Soviet of the U.S.S.R. at its session of July 13, 1964, Pravda, July 14. For the background of the status of the Soviet medical profession see Mark G. Field, Doctor and Patient in Soviet Russia (Cambridge, Mass., Harvard University Press, 1957).

10. For a typical story see Anatoly Agranovsky, "Otkrytiye doktora Fyo-dorova" [Doctor Fyodorov's discovery], *Izvestiya*, April 29, 1965.

11. Gay Talese, "Wanted: Spouses," *The New York Times Magazine*, November 13, 1960, p. 133; and UPI dispatch from Washington, "$186,000 Prestige Poll Ranks Low in Congress," *The New York Times*, March 5, 1965.

12. S. Mardashev, "Biologiya i meditsina" [Biology and medicine], *Pravda*, June 11, 1965.

13. Valery Tarsis, "Palata No. 7" [Ward Number 7], *Grani* [Borders] (Frankfurt on Main), January 1965, pp. 20–21. Available in English as *Ward 7; an autobiographical novel*, translated by Katya Brown (New York: E. P. Dutton and Co., 1965).

14. V. Zukhar' and I. Pushkina. "Novaya nauka—kosmicheskaya psikholo-giya" [A new science: space psychology], *Literaturnaya gazeta*, October 13, 1964.

CHAPTER IX

Anonymity for Rocket-Men

1. See announcements from the Presidium of the Supreme Soviet of the U.S.S.R. in Moscow newspapers, April 29, 1963.

2. N. S. Khrushchev, "Polneye ispol'zovat' vozmozhnosti rosta proizvodstva v kazhdom kolkhoze i sovkhoze" [You must increasingly use opportunities to raise productivity on each collective and state farm], *Pravda*, August 3, 1962.

3. *Soviet World Outlook: A Handbook of Communist Statements* (Washington: Department of State, 1959), pp. 169–170.

4. *Ibid.*, p. 170.

5. Yuri Gagarin and his fellow cosmonauts, "Veter oktiabria veyet nad planetoi" [October wind wafts over the planet], *Pravda*, November 7, 1962.

6. N. Denisov and S. Borzenko, "K zvyozdam" [Toward the stars], *Pravda*, July 8, 1961.

7. Ya. Kirillov, "Kuznetsy groma" [Blacksmiths of thunder], *Komsomol'-skaya pravda*, August 20, 1961.

8. John Scott, *The Soviet Economic Offensive: A Report on Ruble Diplomacy to the Publisher of Time* (New York: Time, Inc., 1961; limited circulation), p. 39.

On Scott's mention of trips abroad for rocket specialists let me note here that apparently some such experts can indeed be sent on missions to foreign countries, but still without having their identities divulged. According to Oleg Pen'kovsky's papers (which I accept as authentic), the Party uses certain precautions as it sends such men on foreign assignments. On p. 181 of *The Penkovskiy Papers* (Garden City, New York: Doubleday & Company, 1965), under the date of May 16, 1961, we read: "As a rule, Soviet scientists, engineers, and technicians who work directly in the production of missiles and missile armament are not allowed to go abroad. But lately, because these scientists must know something about U. S. missiles and about those of other countries, they have been given permission to travel abroad, provided they have not participated in any production work connected with the Soviet missile program for the past two years—and, of course, only if they have been carefully checked. The Central Committee CPSU exercises extreme caution in this matter. It is very careful about letting these people go abroad. These people are high-ranking scientific and specialist personnel of the Central Committee CPSU. The two-year waiting period was established because it was figured that during the two years the techniques would advance to the point where what was known to these people two years before would have lost its importance. Therefore, if they defected to the West, they would not be able to talk about these techniques in such detail as they could have done two years earlier; and they would not know about the latest innovations."

9. Anatoly Agranovsky, "Kolumby" [The Columbuses], *Izvestiya*, April 12, 1962.

10. B. Krayevsky, "Razgovor s fizikom" [Conversation with a physicist], *Literaturnaya gazeta*, August 10, 1961.

11. Report of speeches, "Slovo razvedchikov budushchego" [Word from the scouts of the future], *Trud*, April 27, 1963.

12. Col. Ye. Petrov, "Kosmonavty" [Cosmonauts], *Krasnaya zvezda*, February 15, 1962.

13. *Ibid.*

14. Lieut. Col. N. Mel'nikov, "Start dan!" [He is off!], *Krasnaya zvezda*, June 15, 1963.

15. V. Peskov, "Zvyozdy kosmodroma" [Stars of the cosmodrome], *Komsomol'skaya pravda*, June 19, 1963.

16. Vladimir Orlov, "Tvortsy kosmicheskikh korablei" [Creators of space ships], *Pravda*, August 27, 1961.

17. Gagarin and others, *op. cit.*

18. For typical examples of such noncommittals and generalities, see Chief Designer's article "Pervootkryvateli zvyozdnykh trass" [First discoverers of starry routes], *Izvestiya*, December 31, 1961, taken by that newspaper from the January 1962 issue of *Aviatsiya i kosmonavtika*; also interviews with the Chief Designer following the double orbiting of Valentina Tereshkova and Valery Bykovsky in June 1963—G. Ostroumov, "Vperedi—luna" [Ahead is the moon], *Izvestiya*, June 23, 1963; and N. Denisov, "Na puti k glubinam vselennoi" [En route to the depths of the universe], *Pravda*, June 23, 1963.

19. Theodore Shabad, "Talk in Moscow Names 2 as Top Space Planners," *The New York Times*, November 12, 1963.

20. *Biografichesky slovar' deyatelei yestestvoznaniya i tekhniki*, Vol. 1, pp. 246, 445; also *Who's Who in the U.S.S.R.*, 1961–1962, pp. 245, 385; also Shabad, dispatch in *The New York Times*, November 12, 1963.

21. Obituaries in the Soviet press in mid-January 1966 and *The New York Times*, January 17, 1966.

CHAPTER X

The Rise of the Military Engineer

1. Col. V. Larionov and Engineer Col. V. Vaneyev, "Strategiya i kibernetika" [Strategy and cybernetics], *Krasnaya zvezda*, July 3, 1962.

2. Albert Parry, *Russia's Rockets and Missiles*, p. 126, quoting G. A. Tokaev, *Soviet Imperialism* (London: Gerald Duckword and Co., 1954), p. 51.

3. Parry, *Russia's Rockets and Missiles*, pp. 126, 184.

4. Lieut. Col. Ye. Smotritsky, "Svetlyie dali" [Bright perspectives], *Krasnaya zvezda*, June 20, 1961.

5. Khrushchev himself, on May 4, "in an expansive mood at a Czech Embassy reception, dropped a tidbit" of this news of elevation of rocket forces. See David Wise and Thomas B. Ross, *The U-2 Affair* (New York:

Random House, 1962), p. 69. Incidentally but importantly, this reorganization is still not too clearly understood in the West. The new and separate branch of rocket troops embraces strategic or long-range missiles only. In addition, tactical rocket arms with and without nuclear arms are given to the Soviet land forces, the navy, the air force, and the antiaircraft troops. According to Sergei S. Varentsov, chief marshal of the artillery, rocket units "are now the principal strength of the land troops." S. Varentsov, "Obobshchat' i vnedriat' opyt peredovykh raketnykh chastei" [We must use as a model and firmly introduce the experience of our leading rocket units], *Kommunist vooruzhyonnykh sil* [The Communist of the Armed Forces (official organ of the Main Political Office of the Soviet military)], November 1962, p. 27.

6. S. S. Biryuzov, "Povyshat' rol' inzhenera v voinskom vospitanii" [We must enhance the engineer's role in military upbringing], *Krasnaya zvezda*, May 21, 1961.

7. Severyn Bialer, "The Men Who Run Russia's Armed Forces," *The New York Times Magazine*, February 21, 1965, p. 50, citing Western estimates of the size of the Soviet military establishment.

8. Lieut. Gen. I. Kuzovkov and others, "Yeshchyo raz o 'chistykh' inzhenerakh" [Once more about "pure" engineers], *Krasnaya zvezda*, March 9, 1965.

9. Marshal R. Malinovsky, "Nadezhnyi strazh otchizny" [Fatherland's reliable sentinel], *Pravda*, February 23, 1965.

10. Unsigned, "Formirovat' nauchnoye mirovozzreniye" [To form a scientific view of the world], *Krasnaya zvezda*, June 15, 1965.

11. Speech by Marshal Malinovsky at the All-Army Conference on Ideological Problems, *Krasnaya zvezda*, October 25, 1962.

12. Maj. Gen. D. Reshetov, acting chief of propaganda and agitation in the Main Political Office of the Soviet Army and Navy, "Vyshe uroven' marksistsko-leninskoi podgotovki ofitserov" [The level of Marxist-Leninist preparation of officers must be raised], *Kommunist vooruzhyonnykh sil*, October 1962, pp. 22–25.

13. Unsigned, "O vospitanii rukovodiashchikh voyennykh kadrov" [On the upbringing of the leading military personnel], *Krasnaya zvezda*, May 24, 1963.

14. Col. V. Tumanov and Lieut. Col. I. Prazdnikov, "Nasha obshchaya zadacha" [Our common task], *Krasnaya zvezda*, October 24, 1962.

15. Maj. Gen. V. Buyanov, "Otkuda berutsia obyvateli?" [Whence come petty men?], *Krasnaya zvezda*, September 7, 1963.

16. Lieut. Col. P. Yarovoy, "A na bumage vsyo krasivo" [But on paper everything is beautiful], *Krasnaya zvezda*, June 1, 1963.

17. Col. K. Prokofyev, "A pervoistochniki prochitat' ne uspel . . ." [As for original sources, he did not manage to read them . . .], *Krasnaya zvezda*, January 18, 1964.

18. Col. S. Isachenko, "Seminar venchayet delo" [The seminar crowns the work], *Krasnaya zvezda*, April 1, 1964.

19. Capt. N. Boikov, "Pod muzykal'noye soprovozhdeniye" [With musical accompaniment], *Krasnaya zvezda*, November 13, 1962.

20. *Ibid.*

21. *Ibid.*

22. Major I. Britchenko, "Kogda tsvetyot cheremukha" [In cherry-blossom time], *Krasnaya zvezda*, June 2, 1965.

23. Lieut. A. Tertichny, "Samyi nadezhnyi put'" [The most reliable path], *Krasnaya zvezda*, January 17, 1964.

24. Lieut. Gen. Ye. Mal'tsev, "Nastupayushchiy front" [A front on the offensive], *Krasnaya zvezda*, May 22, 1963. *Cf.* Lieut. Col. N. Stasenko, "Skol'zheniye po poverkhnosti" [Skimming the surface], *Krasnaya zvezda*,

October 9, 1965; and Senior Lieut. B. Koshkin, "Mezhdunarodnoi teme—vnimaniye" [Let's pay attention to the international theme], *Krasnaya zvezda*, January 13, 1966.

25. Col. V. Komissarov, "Tvoi luchshiye gody" [Your best years], *Krasnaya zvezda*, May 20, 1964.

26. Col. A. Podcherniayev, "Soobshcha, kollektivno" [All together, collectively], *Krasnaya zvezda*, December 15, 1964.

27. Unsigned editorial, "Partiynaya printsipial'nost'" [Upholding Party principles], *Krasnaya zvezda*, January 8, 1965.

28. Lieut. Col. A. Goliakov and Major A. Malykh, "Zhivaya serdtsevina ideologicheskoi raboty" [The living core of ideological work], *Krasnaya zvezda*, May 28, 1963.

29. Col. A. Nedosugov, "Na boyevom napravlenii ideologochiskogo fronta" [In the fighting direction of the ideological front], *Krasnaya zvezda*, January 29, 1963.

30. Col. Gen. S. Vasyagin, "Partiynyie organizatsii i polevaya vyuchka voisk" (Party organizations and field training of troops), *Krasnaya zvezda*, May 18, 1965.

31. Col. L. Oshurkov, "Politrabotnik u raket" [The political worker at the rockets], *Krasnaya zvezda*, September 1, 1964.

32. Lieut. Col. L. Bublik, "V nebe i na zemle" [In the sky and on the ground], *Krasnaya zvezda*, July 16, 1964.

33. Col. B. Sobolev and Major V. Pivovarov, "Ruka ob ruku" [Hand in hand], *Krasnaya zvezda*, February 7, 1964.

34. Col. G. Khetagurov, "Dusha partiynoi raboty" [The soul of Party work], *Krasnaya zvezda*, March 4, 1962.

35. Lieut. Capt. M. Mayenkov, "S komandirskogo mostika" [From the commander's bridge], *Krasnaya zvezda*, June 6, 1965.

36. Engineer Lieut. M. Lysenko, "Chto dlia nas glavnoye?" [What must come first for us?], *Krasnaya zvezda*, March 26, 1961.

37. Engineer Lieut. V. Kopeikin, "Ya—za opredeleniye granits" [I am for drawing limits], *Krasnaya zvezda*, April 19, 1961.

38. Col. D. Levchenkov, "Komandir i novaya tekhnika" [The commander and new technology], *Krasnaya zvezda*, December 10, 1960.

39. Engineer Lieut. Col. V. Gerasimov, "Trebovatel'nost' i avtoritet" [Demanding (of obedience and efficiency from subordinates) and authority], *Krasnaya zvezda*, April 19, 1961. The articles by Lysenko, Kopeikin, and Gerasimov, are part of the symposium "Inzhener i voinskoye vospitaniye" [The engineer and military upbringing].

40. Col. Yu. Artamoshkin, "Koeffitsiyent poleznogo deistviya" [Coefficient of useful action], *Krasnaya zvezda*, January 29, 1964.

41. Col. M. Makoveyev and Lieut. Col. L. Kotenev, "Tishina i sekundy" [Stillness and seconds], *Krasnaya zvezda*, October 26, 1962.

42. Unsigned editorial, "Politrabotnikam—prochnyie voyenno-tekhnicheskiye znaniya" [Political workers must have solid military-technical knowledge], *Krasnaya zvezda*, June 2, 1965.

43. Lieut. Gen. S. Chubaryov, "Kogda raschyot na boyevom dezhurstve" [When the crew is on its fighting watch], *Krasnaya zvezda*, June 23, 1965.

44. Col. P. Sidorenkov, "A ved' reservy yest'" [But we do have reserves], *Krasnaya zvezda*, May 16, 1963.

45. Lieut. Col. I. Litvinov, "Dva podkhoda" [Two approaches], *Krasnaya zvezda*, May 30, 1962.

46. Capt. V. Rastorguyev, "Politrabotnik uchitsia zaochno" [A political worker takes a correspondence course], *Krasnaya zvezda*, June 22, 1965.

47. Maj. Gen. I. Ovcharenko, "Delo, kotoromu sluzhish'" [The cause which you serve], *Krasnaya zvezda*, June 17, 1965.

48. Capt. Yu. Kvitko, " 'Khvatit boltat'! Razoidis'!" [Enough babbling! Break it up!"], *Krasnaya zvezda*, November 22, 1964.

49. The first official Soviet revelation of Pen'kovsky's arrest was made on December 12, 1962. From then on, but particularly in May 1963, during the trial, the Pen'kovsky case was fully covered by the world's press. Some of the best reporting of the trial was by Seymour Topping, a Moscow correspondent for *The New York Times*. The reader is referred to his dispatches in that newspaper for May 1963. The Soviet coverage of the trial is to be found in *Izvestiya, Pravda*, and other leading Moscow newspapers for that period. Latest and by far not least is *The Penkovskiy Papers* (Garden City, New York: Doubleday & Company, 1965), translated by Peter Deriabin (himself a defector from the Soviet military intelligence), introduction and commentary by Frank Gibney, foreword by Edward Crankshaw.

50. Interview with Chief Military Prosecutor Lieut. Gen. A. G. Gorny, "Khvost staroi lisy" [The tail of the old fox], *Izvestiya*, May 30, 1963. Also, Lieut. Gen. V. Borisoglebsky, "Pervaya zapoved': bditel'nost'!" [The first commandment: watchfulness!], *Krasnaya zvezda*, June 14, 1963.

51. John N. Hazard, *The Soviet System of Government* (Chicago:ʻUniversity of Chicago Press, 1957), pp. 196–197.

CHAPTER XI

The Civilian Technician: Coercion and Courtship

1. Report from a plenary session of the Moscow Committee, "Povyshat' rol' nauki v razvitii proizvodstva" [We must enchance the role of science in the development of industry], *Pravda*, May 18, 1962. Cf. the flat statement in "Kommunisty nauchnogo instituta" [The Communists of a scientific institute], leading editorial in *Pravda*, July 14, 1965: "The Party Organizations of institutes, not connected with industry directly, have no right to control the work of the [institutes'] administration." For quite a contrary view of the Party's power over the academic community see Hans Kuebler, "Exchange Scientist in Leningrad," *Survey*, July 1964, pp. 67–68.

2. Text of the speech of N. M. Gribachev is in *Literaturnaya gazeta, Komsomol'skaya pravda*, and other Moscow newspapers for October 28, 1961.

3. M. Zhuravleva, secretary of the Komsomol's national Central Committee, "Dveri vuza raspakhnuty v zhizn' " [The doors of higher schools are flung open into life], *Komsomol'skaya pravda*, May 10, 1961.

4. L. Shinkarev, "Tropicheskiy zagar" [Tropical tan], *Izvestiya*, July 16, 1961.

5. A. Kirilenko, first secretary of the Sverdlovsk Regional Party Committee, "Tvortsy tekhnicheskogo progressa" [Creators of technical progress], *Izvestiya*, November 30, 1960.

6. V. Markelov, "Ob 'okhvate' i razgovorakh po dusham" [About "involvement" and man-to-man talks], *Sovetskaya Rossiya*, May 8, 1963. Cf. Jeremy R. Azrael, "Politics and Management," *Survey*, October 1963, p. 99: ". . . judging from personal observations and from a not inconsiderable amount of evidence found in Soviet sources, the modal attitudes and values of the Soviet technical intelligentsia as a group are relatively non-ideological if not apolitical, relatively pragmatic if not technocratic."

7. N. Sidorov, "Dolg odin—byt' chelovekom" [One duty only—to be human], *Komsomol'skaya pravda*, January 29, 1963.

8. A. Lazarev, "Otvet pered sovest'yu" [Answer to one's conscience], *Komsomol'skaya pravda*, January 11, 1963.

9. V. Kokashinsky, "Stavka na doveriye" [Betting on trust], *Komsomol'skaya pravda*, July 4, 1963.

10. Aleksandr Mikhalevich, "Dela dostoiny slov vysokikh" [Deeds are worthy of lofty words], *Komsomol'skaya pravda*, June 20, 1962.

11. Nataliya Pritvits, "Vyigrysh sopernikov" [Competitors' winning], *Sovetskaya Rossiya*, June 24, 1964.

12. Vasily Azhayev, *Daleko ot Moskvy* [Far from Moscow] (Moscow: State Publishing House of Fine Literature, 1961), pp. 199–200. This superloyal Stalinist novel was first written and published in 1946–48. The engineer, quoted above, is made by the author to brand his non-Party (if not anti-Party) behavior "a light-minded attitude." In the novel the engineer, on reaching what is described as maturity, finally joins the Party.

13. R. Zaitsev, "Stremis' v geroi!" [Strive to be a hero!], *Komsomol'skaya pravda*, January 5, 1964.

14. Vl. Dobrovol'sky, "Trus na sluzhbe" [A coward in service], *Komsomol'skaya pravda*, December 16, 1962.

15. D. Volkogonov, "Pust' ne dremlet sovest' " [Let your conscience not be asleep], *Komsomol'skaya pravda*, January 5, 1963.

16. Lazarev, "Otvet pered sovest'yu."

17. Academician Aksel' Berg, "Soyuz chisla i mysli" [Union of number and thought], *Izvestiya*, October 6, 1961.

18. John A. Armstrong, *Ideology, Politics, and Government in the Soviet Union* (New York: Frederick A. Praeger, 1962; paperback), p. 53.

19. A. Bogachuk, "Kadrovaya 'kadril' " [A "quadrille" of cadres], *Komsomol'skaya pravda*, November 17, 1963.

20. D. Kaunov, "Organizator ty khoroshiy, a znatok li dela?" [You are a good organizer, but are you an expert?], *Sovetskaya Rossiya*, December 13, 1963.

21. P. Tumilovich, "Chuzhaya nosha" [Somebody else's burden], *Sovetskaya Rossiya*, June 28, 1964.

22. The figures quoted below this point, and until the next note, come from Solomon Schwartz, "K sotziologii Kompartii" [Speaking of the sociology of the Communist Party], *Sotsialistichesky vestnik* (New York), January-February 1963, pp. 9–11. He bases them on a number of official Soviet sources.

23. To see how smoothly the Party transformed engineers into Party functionaries in those days, read the novel by that unregenerate Stalinist, Vsevolod Kochetov, *Sekretar' obkoma* [Secretary of Regional Committee] (Moscow: Molodaya Gvardiya publishing house, 1962). The hero of this story, Vasily Denisov, was an engineer by education who in the 1930s was drafted into professional Party work and indeed became a loyal Communist functionary. Nothing was left of his engineering, and the Party was safe. For a cogent analysis of the novel and its main character, see Vera Aleksandrova, "Sekret uspekha Kochetova" [The secret of Kochetov's success], *Novoye russkoye slovo*, February 18, 1962.

24. M. Pimenov, "Glavnoye zveno" [The main link], *Pravda*, January 14, 1962.

25. Schwartz, *op cit.*, p. 9.

26. I. Gotsiridze, "K rukovodstvu prikhodiat inzhenery" [Engineers come to leadership], *Partiynaya zhizn'* [Party Life], second issue for January 1963, p. 33.

27. "Doklad tovarishcha L. N. Yefremova" [Report by Comrade L. N. Yefremov], *Sovetskaya Rossiya*, March 12, 1963.

28. Unsigned, "A teper'—tselaya armiya" [And now—a whole army], *Sovetskaya Rossiya*, July 30, 1963.

29. Prof. Azrael in his already cited article "Politics and Management" (*Survey*, October 1963), gave an excellent analysis of the November 1962 move, correctly predicting its eventual abandonment, and noting: "Even so, however, it will have contributed to the further 'managerialization' of Soviet politics and will have complicated for the Party the task of preventing the erosion of Communist ideology." (See in particular page 101.)

30. L. Karpinsky, "Proraby budushchego" [The foremen of the future], *Komsomol'skaya pravda*, June 6, 1963.

31. G. Yakovlev, "Raz'yezdy 'nalegke' " [Traveling "lightly"], *Komsomol'skaya pravda*, July 12, 1962.

32. A. Saakyan, "Lish' by kreslo ne pustovalo . . ." [So long as the armchair is not empty . . .], *Komsomol'skaya pravda*, April 4, 1963.

33. Galina Nikolayeva, *Bitva v puti* [A battle along the way], (Moscow: *Sovetsky pisatel'* publishing house, 1960), p. 266. I quote from the 1960 edition, because I happen to have no earlier one at hand. Originally the novel was published in 1957.

34. B. Finiasov, "Bogatyri pod nagruzkoi" [Giants under a load], *Izvestiya*, April 7, 1963.

35. I. Borisova, secretary of the Gorky City Committee of Komsomol, "Komitet za partoi" [The Committee is studying], *Komsomol'skaya pravda*, March 1, 1963.

36. *Ibid.*

37. Schwartz, *op. cit.* The italics in the quoted matter are Mr. Schwartz's.

38. V. Petrykin, "Obshchestvennyie nachala v ideologicheskoi rabote" [Basing ideological work on society's own initiative], *Pravda*, May 10, 1963.

39. M. Stepichev and M. Korolyov, "Krepkiye zven'ya" [Solid links], *Pravda*, December 13, 1965.

CHAPTER XII

The Managerial Evolution

1. David Granik, *Management of the Industrial Firm in the U.S.S.R.* (New York: Columbia University Press, 1954), and *The Red Executive* (Garden City, N. Y.: Doubleday and Company, 1960); Joseph S. Berliner, *Factory and Manager in the U.S.S.R.* (Cambridge, Mass.: Harvard University Press, 1957), and "The Situation of Plant Managers," in Alex Inkeles and Kent Geiger, editors, *Soviet Society: A Book of Readings* (Boston: Houghton Mifflin Company, 1961), pp. 361–381, an excerpt from Dr. Berliner's 1959 writings. For a glimpse of a more modern, more daring manager see the already cited Azrael, "Politics and Management," *Survey*, October 1963, particularly pp. 99–100.

2. G. Popov, "Kommunisty" [Communists], *Pravda*, August 11, 1964.

3. Report of the conference of local Party functionaries of the Russian Socialist Federated Soviet Republic, "Uluchshat' partiynoye rukovodstvo predpriyatiyami i stroikami" [Party guidance of plants and construction projects must be improved], *Pravda*, July 31, 1962.

4. A. Durnov, V. Tsarev, and others, "Plan—zakon zhizni zavoda" [Plan is the law of the plant's life], *Pravda*, May 23, 1963.

5. Ye. Syrtsov, "Sovest' snabzhentsa" [The conscience of a supply man], *Sovetskaya Rossiya*, January 18, 1963.

6. G. Somov, *"Lichnyie ubezhdeniya"* [Personal convictions], *Trud*, May 29, 1963.

7. N. Globa, "Komissiya za komissiyei" [One commission after another], *Sovetskaya Rossiya*, May 11, 1963.

8. A. Romanov, "Perestroika k nam ne otnositsia?—Zabluzhdeniye" [Reconstruction does not mean us?—You are mistaken], *Sovetskaya Rossiya*, March 1, 1963.

9. I. Skiba, first secretary of the Syktyvkar Party Committee, "I trebovat', i ubezhdat' " [Both to demand and to convince], *Sovetskaya Rossiya*, July 20, 1962.

10. V. Boyev, "Ofitsial'naya versiya" [Official version], *Trud*, January 31, 1961.

11. I. Agafonov, "Zhdi menia, Natasha!" [Wait for me, Natasha!], *Komsomol'skaya pravda*, October 2, 1962.

12. Yu. Kotliarov, " 'Milyi' byurokrat" [Darling bureaucrat], *Komsomol'skaya pravda*, October 30, 1963.

13. S. Etkalo and P. Karkokha, "Pochemu direktor ne prishyol v nash tsekh" [Why the manager did not come to our shop], *Pravda*, May 12, 1963.

14. M. Burenkov and A. Klimenkov, "Krusheniye" [Crash], *Izvestiya*, May 14, 1963. *Cf.* I. Zenin, "Pochemu rabochiy ukhodit s sobraniya" [Why the worker leaves the meeting], *Trud*, October 30, 1964.

15. Ye. Borodin, "Kritika? Zapreshchayu!" [Criticism? I forbid!], *Sovetskaya Rossiya*, December 15, 1962.

16. A. Klimenkov and others, "Nazovite vashikh pomoshchnikov" [Name your assistants], *Izvestiya*, January 23, 1964.

17. A. Bogma, "Ne oberegat' ot kritiki, a ispravliat' nedostatki" [Not to shield from criticism, but to correct failings], *Pravda*, March 20, 1964.

18. Ilya Omelichkin, "Skazaniye o levoi noge" [The tale of the left leg], *Trud*, January 23, 1963.

19. D. Ivanchenko, "S molchalivogo soglasiya zavkoma" [With the tacit agreement of the plant committee], *Trud*, January 9, 1963.

20. I. Astov, "Vse vrut kalendari" [All calendars lie], *Trud*, December 9, 1962.

21. I. Osinovsky, "Nakazaniye . . . bezdel'yem" [Punishment . . . through idleness], *Trud*, February 24, 1961.

22. Ivanchenko, *op. cit.* See also the official text of the decree "Polozheniye o pravakh fabrichnogo, zavodskogo, mestnogo komiteta professional'nogo soyuza [Statute on the rights of the factory, plant, and local committee of a trade union], *Trud*, July 16, 1958. An admirably complete and concise summary of post-1956 Soviet legislation on the rights of trade unions is in Albert Boiter, "When the Kettle Boils Over . . . ," *Problems of Communism* (Washington), January-February 1964, pp. 33–34. (Boiter's article is a study of the Soviet workers' riots in 1962–63, particularly at Novocherkassk in the summer of 1962.) For the January 1965 measures against arbitrary managers in their relations to workers, see the unsigned editorial "Na strazhe trudovogo zakonodatel'stva" [Safeguarding labor laws], *Trud*, January 26, 1965.

23. S. Grigor'yev, "Anatoly Ivanovich zakusil udila" [Anatoly Ivanovich bit the bridle], *Trud*, May 11, 1963.

24. F. Kuznetsov, "Ssadina na serdtse" [A bruise upon a heart], *Sovetskaya Rossiya*, June 2, 1963. But there is also the view of the higher Party authorities that the middle-echelon Party functionaries are simply afraid to replace old-timer managers with "young and capable cadres" even when the latter are available. See I. Lukin, "Rukovoditel' i kollektiv" [Leader and the collective], *Pravda*, January 27, 1965.

25. D. Zaslavsky, "Potomok Prishibeyeva" [Prishibeyev's descendant], *Pravda*, August 5, 1962.

26. V. Logvinov, "O ryzhikh koshkakh i razdutom samolyubii" [About red cats and inflated self-love], *Komsomol'skaya pravda*, March 30, 1965. Complaints on managers' extraordinary rudeness are constant. Typical is A. Polkanov, "Ravneniye na vremia!" [Keep up with the times!], *Komsomol'skaya pravda*, May 13, 1965.

27. V. Demchenko, "Chtoby v samoye 'yablochko' . . ." (To hit right that little "apple" . . .), *Sovetskaya Rossiya*, October 12, 1963.

28. N. Kanishchev, "Ogradit' ot kritiki—isportit' cheloveka" [To shield from criticism is to spoil a man], *Sovetskaya Rossiya*, July 28, 1963.

29. E. Parkhomovsky, "Dobrota na postnom masle" [Kindness based on vegetable oil], *Izvestiya*, December 15, 1962.

30. A. Bogma, "Zazhimshchikov kritiki—k strogomu otvetu!" [Repressors of criticism must be hauled on the carpet!], *Pravda*, July 22, 1963.

31. Report by S. P. Pavlov, first secretary of the Komsomol Central Committee, at the 14th Congress of Komsomol in Moscow, *Izvestiya*, April 17, 1962.

32. Osinovsky, *op. cit.*

33. Yu. Zubrilin, "Kto zhe otstal?" [Who, then, has lagged behind?], *Sovetskaya Rossiya*, November 27, 1962.

34. V. Komov and V. Yelyutin, "Ekzamen na chestnost'" [An examination in honesty], *Izvestiya*, June 11, 1961.

35. Mariya Baranova, "Printsipial'nost' poshla mne vo vred" [Standing up for principle did me harm], *Sovetskaya Rossiya*, February 1, 1964.

36. Yu. Novikov and A. Podol'sky, "Printsipial'nost' vo vred ne poidyot" [Standing up for principle won't cause harm], *Sovetskaya Rossiya*, March 12, 1964.

37. R. Myaskov, "Gorlovaya nadbavka" [Overusing one's throat], *Sovetskaya Rossiya*, August 9, 1963.

38. A. Orlov, "Dvoye u rulia" [Two at the wheel], *Sovetskaya Rossiya*, April 16, 1963.

39. Aleksandr Mikhalevich, "Izmeniat'sia!" [They must change!], *Literaturnaya gazeta*, April 18, 1963.

40. R. Sabirov, "Ochkovtirateli 'kombiniruyut'" [Schemers "make combinations"], *Pravda*, November 30, 1962.

41. T. Avaliani, "Pobedit printsipial'nost!" [Standing up for principle will triumph!], *Sovetskaya Rossiya*, May 31, 1963.

42. A. Osipov, B. Porfir'yev, and V. Verbikov, "Pena" [Foam], *Sovetskaya Rossiya*, March 29, 1963.

43. N. Ilyinsky, "Besprintsipnost'" [Lack of principle], *Pravda*, January 22, 1963.

44. S. Gus'kov, "Besprintsipnost' k dobru ne privodit" [Lack of principle leads to no good], *Sovetskaya Rossiya*, September 19, 1962.

45. M. Kruglova, "Makar'yevskiy vel'mozha" [The grandee of Makar'yevsk], *Trud*, January 24, 1963.

46. V. Yakhnevich, "Chtoby uiti ot kritiki" [In order to walk away from criticism], *Pravda*, February 27, 1960.

47. P. Il'yashenko, "Snova Verchenko . . ." [Again Verchenko . . .], *Literaturnaya gazeta*, November 30, 1961.

48. Unsigned, "Kogda nyet argumentov" [When they lack arguments], *Izvestiya*, June 16, 1964.

49. V. Molchanov, "Stengazeta v . . . seife" [A wall newspaper in . . . a safe], *Pravda*, April 19, 1963.

50. I. Kir'yanov, "Zazhimshchiki kritiki ne unimayutsia . . ." [Repressors of criticism do not subside . . .], *Pravda*, June 28, 1961.

51. Boiter, "When the Kettle Boils Over . . . ," p. 33.

52. *Pravda*, August 9, 1962, quoted by Boiter, pp. 38–39. Boiter also cites secret decrees of the Party and the government of August 9 and 10, 1962, which chided the managers on their mistreatment of workers.

CHAPTER XIII

Underground Capitalism

1. Theodore Shabad, "Soviet Notes Rise in Some Crimes," dispatch from Moscow, *The New York Times*, July 3, 1964, quoting figures given by V. I. Laputin, an official of the Party's Central Committee, in the Moscow legal journal *Sovetskoye gosudarstvo i pravo* [Soviet State and Law].

2. Unsigned, "Reshitel'no presekat' zloupotrebleniya v torgovle" [Law-breaking in commerce must be stopped decisively], *Pravda*, March 29, 1963.

3. Yelena Kononenko, "Chervotochina" [Worminess], *Pravda*, July 27, 1962.

4. Yu. Dmitriyev and A. Yevgen'yev, " 'Firma' terpit krakh" [The "firm" suffers a crash], *Trud*, May 26, 1963.

5. Albert Parry, "Private Enterprise in Russia," *New York Herald Tribune*, September 4, 1953.

6. For a typical American reaction to such repressive measures and an official Soviet alibi of them, see letters to the editor of *The New York Times*: Rev. George B. Ford, Henry P. Van Dusen, and Simon Greenberg, "Soviet Penalty Protested," May 27, 1962; Boris Nikiforov, "Economic Crimes in Russia," July 20, 1962; and Nathan Berman, "Crimes Against Property," September 7, 1962. For a later view and summary see George Feifer, "Russia Shoots Its Business Crooks," *The New York Times Magazine*, May 2, 1965.

7. N. Vorob'yov and V. Zhuravsky, "Ruka khapugi" [The bribe-taker's hand], *Pravda*, March 23, 1962; and N. Vorob'yov, "Po zaslugam!" [Serves them right!], *Pravda*, August 9, 1963.

8. A. Romanov and Yu. Feofanov, "Za tyulevoi zanaveskoi" [Behind the tulle curtain], *Izvestiya*, November 26, 1961; and unsigned, "Zasluzhennaya kara" [Deserved punishment], *Izvestiya*, July 22, 1962. See also Theodore Shabad, "Soviet Accuses 50 Kirghiz Aides," dispatch from Moscow, *The New York Times*, January 16, 1962; and unsigned, "Soviet to Shoot 4 Plant Officials," dispatch from Moscow, *The New York Times*, July 22, 1962.

9. Unsigned dispatch from Moscow, "Soviet Trade Aide to Die For Embezzling $62,000," *The New York Times*, October 4, 1962.

10. Yu. Dmitriyev and A. Yevgen'yev, " 'Firma' terpit krakh" [The "firm" suffers a crash], *Trud*, May 25 and 26, 1963; and Yu. Vasil'yev and V. Nikolayev, "Vrach ili 'kompanyon' " [Physician or "partner"?], *Trud*, September 15, 1963.

11. A. Matov, "Chto skryvalos' za vyveskoi" [What was concealed behind the sign], *Trud*, January 15, 1963.

12. Yu. Feofanov, "Voram poshchady ne budet" [There will be no mercy for thieves], *Izvestiya*, October 20, 1963; and Yu. Dmitriyev and D. Yegorov, "Rasplata" [Payment for crime], *Trud*, February 27, 1964.

13. Val. Gol'tsev, "Krakh korolia gubnoi pomady" [Downfall of the lipstick king], *Izvestiya*, December 2, 1961; also Theodore Shabad, "Soviet to Execute 'Lipstick King' for Private Use of State's Plant," dispatch from Moscow, *The New York Times*, March 4, 1962.

14. V. Sapozhnikov, " 'Korol' taigi" [The "king" of the taiga], *Literaturnaya gazeta*, May 6, 1965.

15. For the Rokotov case I used the following sources: three articles by I. Shatunovsky in *Komsomol'skaya pravda*—"Sterviatniki" [Vultures], May 19, 1961, "Sterviatniki derzhat otvet" [Vultures have to answer], June 10, 1961, and "Svideteli byvayut raznyie" [Witnesses can be a varied lot], June 11, 1961; two articles by N. Dobrovitsky and V. Segalov in *Trud*—"Kosoi Yan i drugiye [Yan the Cross-Eyed and others], June 10, 1961, and "Kosoi Yan i drugiye poluchili po zaslugam" [Yan the Cross-Eyed and others got what they deserved], June 16, 1961; also D. Zarapin and K. Raspevin, "Pered otvetom" [They have to answer], *Pravda*, June 10, 1961; A. Ivanov and Yu. Feofanov, "Na zhestkoi skamye" [On the hard bench], *Izvestiya*, June 10, 1961; the TASS communiqué on the original sentences, "V moskovskom gorodskom sude" [In the Moscow city court], *Pravda*, June 16, 1961; A. Ivanov, "Konets 'chernoi birzhi' " [The end of "the black bourse"], *Izvestiya*, June 16, 1961; the official communiqué about the revised sentences, "V Verkhovnom sude RSFSR" [In the Supreme Court of the R.S.F.S.R.], *Krasnaya zvezda*, July 21, 1961; the Reuters dispatch from London, "Soviet Executes Two For Currency Dealings," *The New York Times*, July 27, 1961; T. Troyanov, "Rasstrel valyutchikov" [Shooting of currency dealers], *Novoye russkoye slovo*, August 4, 1961, and Iv. Demidov, "O dele Rokotova i Faibishenko" [On the Rokotov-Faibishenko case], *Novoye russkoye slovo*, August 12, 1961.

16. Theodore Shabad, "Soviet Sentences Five to Death And Jails 13 for Speculation," dispatch from Moscow, *The New York Times*, June 26, 1962, quoting *Sovetskaya Belorussiya*.

17. K. Raspevin and A. Rudzinskas, "Za barkhatnymi gardinami . . ." [Behind the velvet curtains . . .], *Pravda*, January 31, 1962; V. Lebedev, "Parazity" [Parasites], *Trud*, January 31, 1962; and unsigned, "Zakorenelyie prestupniki nakazany" [Incorrigible criminals are punished], *Pravda*, February 12, 1962.

18. A. Navozov, "Konets 'korolia' chernogo rynka" [The end of the "king" of the black market], *Pravda*, September 5, 1963.

19. Unsigned dispatch from Moscow, "Soviet to Execute 6 As Speculators," *The New York Times*, October 24, 1962.

20. P. D'yachkov, "Nakazaniye neotvratimo" [Punishment is inescapable], *Trud*, January 22, 1965.

21. Theodore Shabad, "More Jews Put on Trial in Soviet," dispatch from Moscow, *The New York Times*, October 11, 1962.

22. S. Rozhdestvensky, "U sovetskikh sobstvennaya gordost' " [Soviet people have a pride all their own], *Novoye russkoye slovo*, September 20, 1964, quoting from the newspaper *Zaria vostoka* [Dawn of the East], published in Tbilisi, Soviet Georgia.

23. V. Kondakov, "Sarancha v Zapoliar'ye" [Locusts beyond the Arctic Circle], *Komsomol'skaya pravda*, December 7, 1961.

24. A. Kanayev and V. Prokudovich, "Lovkachi" [Wheeler-dealers], *Izvestiya*, October 18, 1960.

25. Georgiy Radov, "Na 'levoi' dorozhke" [On the little "leftist" path], *Literaturnaya gazeta*, July 27, 1963.

26. G. Volkov, "Pravdu v glaza" [Telling the truth outright], *Izvestiya*, May 16, 1961.

27. G. Kochergin, "Lipkiye ruki" [Sticky hands], *Komsomol'skaya pravda*, May 18, 1961.

28. S. Kutarov, " 'Neuyazvimyi' Albegov" [The "invulnerable" Albegov], *Pravda*, March 2, 1963.

29. M. Bekhalo and A. Pasechnik, "Ukrali traktor" [They stole a tractor], *Sovetskaya Rossiya*, April 29, 1962.

30. Mariya Zakharova, "Ne v bumazhke delo . . ." [That little paper is not the main thing . . .], *Komsomol'skaya pravda*, March 20, 1963.

31. V. Shustikov, "Chelovek ostalsia odin" [The man remained alone], *Izvestiya*, January 11, 1961; and F. Ganichev, "Gorst' gvozdei" [A handful of nails], *Izvestiya*, February 10, 1962.

32. Eh. Cherepakhova, " 'Chuzhoi' " ["Stranger"], *Literaturnaya gazeta*, February 12, 1963.

33. I. Shatunovsky, "Inzhener v livreye" [Engineer in a lackey's uniform], *Komsomol'skaya pravda*, June 6, 1962.

34. Ed. Elyashev, "Vosstaniye v serdtse" [The heart's revolt], *Komsomol'-skaya pravda*, October 28, 1964.

35. A. Zhigaryov and R. Papikyan, "Prestupleniya moglo i ne byt'!" [The crime could have been avoided!], *Trud*, November 19, 1961.

36. Yekaterina Lopatina, " 'Svoya' korova" [A cow of "one's own"], *Literaturnaya gazeta*, September 7, 1963.

37. V. Lukovenko, "Chuzhaya ten' " [A strange shadow], *Sovetskaya Rossiya*, May 12, 1962.

38. Vasily Ardamatsky, " 'Advokaty' " ["Advocates"], *Literaturnaya gazeta*, January 5, 1963.

39. A. Lavrov, "Protiv tuneyadstva" [Against parasitism], *Literaturnaya gazeta*, September 27, 1960.

40. V. Varavka, "Plyushevyie rukavchiki" [Little gloves made of velvet], *Sovetskaya Rossiya*, November 21, 1963.

41. A. Sukontsev and I. Shatunovsky, "Chastnik na defitsite" [The private trader atop a scarcity], *Krokodil*, June 10, 1961.

42. Boris Privalov, "Razgovor s nepoimannym vorom" [Conversation with a thief who is not caught], *Literaturnaya gazeta*, November 16, 1961.

43. Yu. Mikhailov, "Po podlozhnym kvitantsiyam" [On the basis of forged receipts], *Trud*, July 24, 1963.

44. L. L'vov and S. Fainshtein, "Fint na tribunakh" [Crookedness in the stands], *Komsomol'skaya pravda*, November 18, 1962; and David Miller, "A Paunchy Soccer Fan Upsets Red Apple Cart," *New York Herald Tribune*, November 19, 1962.

45. N. Vorob'yov and A. Romashov, "Za kruzhku piva" [For a mug of beer], *Pravda*, August 30, 1962.

46. N. Blinov, "Raznotsvetnyie fal'shivki" [Multicolored false documents], *Sovetskaya Rossiya*, August 13, 1963.

47. I. Shatunovsky, "Razini s pechatiami" [Simpletons with seals], *Pravda*, October 18, 1964.

CHAPTER XIV

The Jewish Issue

1. George Feifer, "Russia Has 'Socialist Crime,' Too," *The New York Times Magazine*, April 5, 1964, p. 111.

2. Moshe Decter, "The Lvov Case, A Self-Portrait of Soviet Anti-Semitism," reprint from *Midstream*, A Quarterly Jewish Review (New York), June 1963, p. 5.

3. Peter Kihss, "Americans Ask Soviet to Halt Executions in Economic Crimes," *The New York Times*, June 24, 1962.

4. Feifer, "Russia Has 'Socialist Crime,' Too," 111–112.

5. Unsigned, "Economic Offences, Social Repercussions on Jewish Population," *Jews in Eastern Europe* (London), May 1963, p. 27.

6. Decter, "The Lvov Case," p. 4, quoting *L'vovskaya pravda*, February 16, 1962, and subsequent issues covering "the Lvov Case."

7. Unsigned dispatch from Moscow, "Soviet Dooms Head of Currency Ring," *The New York Times*, December 14, 1961.

8. "Economic Offences," *Jews in Eastern Europe*, May 1963, p. 27.

9. Kihss, *op. cit.*

10. "Obmen pis'mami mezhdu B. Rasselom i N. S. Khrushchevym" [Exchange of letters between B. Russell and N. S. Khrushchev], *Pravda*, March 1, 1963; and for English texts and acute analysis of both letters, see unsigned, "Khrushchev-Russell Correspondence," *Jews in Eastern Europe*, May 1963, pp. 20–26.

11. Unsigned, "Embassy Denies Discrimination," addendum to Theodore Shabad dispatch from Moscow, "More Jews Put on Trial in Soviet," *The New York Times*, October 11, 1962.

12. Paul Wohl, "Special Problems of Soviet Jews," *The Christian Science Monitor*, April 4, 1964. For other statistics on the same theme, see Harry Schwartz, "Soviet Cites Data on Jewish Gains," *The New York Times*, May 13, 1962; and editorial, "Jews in the Soviet Union," *The New York Times*, May 14, 1962.

13. Wohl, *op. cit.*

14. Eric Goldhagen, "A Russian Exception" (letter to the editor), *The New York Times*, July 21, 1962.

15. B. Z. Goldberg, *The Jewish Problem in the Soviet Union, Analysis and Solution* (New York: Crown Publishers, 1961), p. 323.

16. *Ibid.*, p. 324.

17. *Ibid.*, pp. 322–323.

18. N. Gradoboyev, "Epilog protsessa 'podpol'nykh millionerov' v Vil'nyuse" [The epilogue of the court case of "the underground millionaires" in Vilnyus], *Novoye russkoye slovo*, August 17, 1962.

19. Feifer, "Russia Has 'Socialist Crime,' Too," p. 112.

20. Lawrence Durrell, *Mountolive* (New York: E. P. Dutton and Co., 1959), p. 70.

CHAPTER XV

Home on the Steppe

1. John P. Hardt, *The Future Role of the Soviet Central Planner*, a paper read at Saint Anthony's College, Oxford, England, on May 25, 1964 (published by the Research Analysis Corporation, McLean, Virginia, in 1964; limited circulation), pp. 18 and 31, quoting *Narodnoye khoziaistvo SSSR v 1962 godu* [National economy of the U.S.S.R. in 1962], p. 434.

2. T. M. Davletshin, "The Soviet Land Tenure Laws," *Bulletin* of the Institute for the Study of the U.S.S.R. (Munich), December 1963, pp. 5–16.

3. D. Todesas, "Dokhodnyie doma" [Profitable houses], *Izvestiya*, July 18, 1961.

4. N. Gradoboyev, "Problema zhilploshchadi" [The problem of living space], *Novoye russkoye slovo*, April 11, 1962.

5. Yu. Kotliarov, "Lipoi shito, aktom kryto" [Made through fraud, camouflaged by documents], *Komsomol'skaya pravda*, May 26, 1963.

6. V. Kulikov. "Syn ushyol iz domu . . ." [The son has left home . . .], *Izvestiya*, February 22, 1962.

7. V. Beloborodov, "Prospekt i tropinka" [The avenue and the little path], *Sovetskaya Rossiya*, April 7, 1962.

8. Stanley Mitchell, "Impressions of Russia," *New Left Review* (London), January-February 1963, p. 54.

9. A. Ivashchenko, "Za gorst' vishen . . ." [For a handful of cherries . . .], *Komsomol'skaya pravda*, September 8, 1963.

10. *Ibid.*

11. A. Vasinsky, "Schastye s chyornogo khoda" [Back-door happiness], *Izvestiya*, November 25, 1962.

12. F. Pivovarov and A. Adzhubey, "Podorvalsia na sobstvennoi mine" [Blown up by his own mine], *Izvestiya*, September 8, 1961.

13. Lieut. Col. Ye. Smotritsky, "Pochemu krichali galki?" [Why did the jackdaws cry out?], *Krasnaya zvezda*, October 31, 1964.

14. Vera Tkachenko, "Gnilyie korni" [Rotten roots], *Trud*, February 13, 1962; and A. Ivashchenko, "Pro yabloko i chuzhoi sad" [About an apple and somebody else's orchard], *Komsomol'skaya pravda*, December 21, 1963. For an eyewitness account of a court case stemming from such a slaying, see Jeremy R. Azrael, "Murder Trial in Moscow," *The Atlantic* (Boston), May 1962, pp. 63–69.

15. V. Tikunov, "Dolg kazhdogo iz nas" [Duty of everyone of us], *Izvestiya*, April 28, 1963.

16. Yu. Solov'yov and Viktor Cherniavsky. " 'Prodala porosyonka—kupila dachu' " ["I sold a piglet and bought a dacha"], *Sovetskaya Rossiya*, April 27, 1963.

17. Yekaterina Lopatina, "Malek na orbite" [A little fish in orbit], *Literaturnaya gazeta*, December 1, 1964.

18. Interview with N. T. Sizov, chief of the Office of Guarding Social Order in Moscow, "Sornuyu travu s polia von!" [Let's weed out the field!], *Izvestiya*, April 26, 1963; also N. Vorob'yov and V. Zhuravsky, "Treugolka i shliapy" [A tri-cornered hat and (other) hats], *Pravda*, May 16, 1963. The Russian word *shliapy* ["hats"] is often used colloquially to indicate men with sloppy, neglectful, naïve ways of discharging their duties. In the *Pravda* article above quoted, the word is used to criticize those superiors or associates of Engineer Dubrovich who did nothing to expose him on his route to his illegal wealth.

19. A. Gorokhov and Yu. Doinikov, "Seraya plesen' " [Gray mold], *Sovetskaya Rossiya*, July 12, 1962.

20. Ivanova, Ponomaryova, and others, "Galochka vinovata" [That little check mark is responsible], *Izvestiya*, June 7, 1964.

21. N. Mironov, "Glavnoye—profilaktika" [Prophylaxis is the main thing], *Izvestiya*, June 2, 1963.

22. V. Blinov, "Khapug i tuneyadtsev—na chistuyu vodu!" [Let's expose the grabbers and the parasites!], *Pravda*, April 27, 1963.

23. V. Ponedel'nik, "Oblaskannyie likhoimtsy" [Petted money-grabbers], *Izvestiya*, July 7, 1961.

24. Kotliarov, *op. cit.*

25. Yu. Alekseyev, "Sukhoi bassein" [The dry basin], *Sovetskaya Rossiya*, July 30, 1964.

26. Yu. Dodolev, "Bul'dozer za vziatku" [A bulldozer for a bribe], *Komsomol'skaya pravda*, May 9, 1963.

27. Unsigned dispatch from Moscow, "New Soviet Decree To Allow Seizure Of Grafters' Homes," *The New York Times*, July 31, 1962; text of the confiscation degree for the Russian Republic in *Sovetskaya Rossiya*, August 1, 1962 (each of the fifteen constituent republics of the U.S.S.R. was to issue

its own confiscation decree); text of the all-Union Party and government decree of assistance in legitimate individual and cooperative building is in *Pravda*, August 7, 1962.

28. M. Chyorny and M. Ivanov, "'Tuneyadets v labirinte" [A parasite in a labyrinth], *Sovetskaya Rossiya*, January 4, 1964.

29. P. Esenov, "Popustitel'stvo khapugam" [Abetting the grabbers], *Pravda*, March 25, 1963.

30. Tikunov, *op. cit.*

31. Unsigned, "'Glaz na Arzamas' " ["His eye toward Arzamas"], *Pravda*, August 30, 1962.

CHAPTER XVI

The Cherry Orchard and the New Ax

1. Yu. Solov'yov and V. Cherniavsky. "Prodala porosyonka—kupila dachu,' " *Sovetskaya Rossiya*, April 27, 1963.

2. I. Shatunovsky, "Zolotoye yaichko" [The little golden egg], *Komsomol'-skaya pravda*, September 23, 1960.

3. I. Shatunovsky, "Sem' tomov naglosti" [Seven volumes of gall], *Pravda*, May 24, 1964.

4. An editorial survey of readers' letters, "Pochta Pravdy—'khutoriane' " [*Pravda's* mail—"the separate settlers"], *Pravda*, May 18, 1962.

5. A. Khodanov. "V chuzhom karmane" [In a stranger's pocket], *Komsomol'skaya pravda*, May 5, 1963.

6. G. Safin, "Chestnost' i pravdivost' " [Honesty and truthfulness], *Sovetskaya Rossiya*, January 24, 1963.

7. Yu. Yur'yev, "Na chistuyu vodu" [Let's expose them], *Trud*, June 5, 1963.

8. V. Moskalyov and G. Yakovlev, "Akuly zhivut na beregu" [Sharks live on the shore], *Komsomol'skaya pravda*, July 1, 1962.

9. Unsigned, "Del'tsy i tuneyadtsy v kurortnykh gorodakh" [Wheeler-dealers and parasites in the resort cities], *Pravda*, August 3, 1963.

10. A. Beruchan, "Oprava zhemchuzhiny Chernomor'ya" [The mounting of a Black Sea shore pearl], *Izvestiya*, June 20, 1963.

11. G. Bessonov, "Rvachi" [Grabbers], *Sovetskaya Rossiya*, February 22, 1963.

12. S. Bystrov, "Kniga s seryoznymi oshibkami" [A book with serious errors], *Izvestiya*, June 6, 1962.

13. V. Rostovshchikov, "Kak delili sad" [How they divided the orchard], *Izvestiya*, May 31, 1962.

14. V. Komov, "Optom i v roznitsu" [Wholesale and retail], *Izvestiya*, September 30, 1961. For other cases of similar nature see also interview with P. Usikov, "Priusadebnyie uchastki v sovkhozakh" [Private plots on state farms], *Sovetskaya Rossiya*, June 16, 1964; and interview with Genrikh Dobrovol'sky, "Kolkhoz podal isk . . ." [A collective farm has gone to court . . .], *Sovetskaya Rossiya*, August 13, 1964.

15. L. Kialeikis, "Zapretnyi plod" [Forbidden fruit], *Pravda*, August 8, 1961.

16. Ye. Volkov, "Opustit' shlagbaum!" [Lower the boom!], *Komsomol'skaya pravda*, August 26, 1961.

17. I. Korshunov, "Pravdu—v glaza" [Tell them the truth outright], *Izvestiya*, September 8, 1959.

18. *Ibid.*

19. Galina Kornilova, "Dyra v zabore" [The hole in the fence], *Literaturnaya gazeta*, September 22 and 30, 1962.

20. *Ibid.*

21. M. Arutyunov, I. Bekiyev, and others, "Vy nam bol'she ne tovarishch" [You are no longer a comrade to us], *Izvestiya*, September 26, 1961; and Yu. Feofanov, "U razbitogo koryta" [At the broken trough], *Izvestiya*, October 13, 1961. For a case of reverse—for an instance of chopping down an "illegal" orchard by a local governmental edict—see A. Gorbatov, "Zakon, topor i yablon'ka" [The law, the ax, and the little apple tree], *Sovetskaya Rossiya*, December 3, 1964.

22. D. Zaslavsky, "Umnyi Garrik" [Wise Garrik], *Pravda*, July 2, 1963.

23. L. Likhodeyev, "Yeshchyo o chastnoi sobstvennosti" [More on private property], *Literaturnaya gazeta*, August 8, 1959.

24. S. Bun'kov, "Skopidomy" [Misers], *Izvestiya*, May 21, 1961.

25. K. Skopina, "Ispytaniye blagom" [Testing through welfare], *Komsomol'skaya pravda*, March 27, 1962.

CHAPTER XVII

The Struggle Up the Stairs

1. Mariya Rozhneva, "Mera schastiya" [Measure of happiness], *Literaturnaya gazeta*, March 19, 1963.

2. Lyubov' Kabo, "Lakmusovaya bumazhka" [Litmus paper], *Literaturnaya gazeta*, October 10, 1963.

3. *Ibid.*

4. B. Pankin, "Vsyo yeshchyo mashinist . . ." [Still an engine driver . . .], *Komsomol'skaya pravda*, February 15, 1961.

5. V. Vernikov, "Spiashchaya sovest' " [Sleeping conscience], *Trud*, June 6, 1963.

6. Mikh. Koriakov, "Listki iz bloknota—Tri pokoleniya" [Leaves from a notebook—Three generations], *Novoye russkoye slovo*, November 8, 1964.

7. Vitaly Kornilov, "Mezhdu len'yu i nuzhdoi" [Between laziness and need], *Komsomol'skaya pravda*, July 2, 1964.

8. Leonid Likhodeyev, "Sem' par nechistykh" [Seven pairs of the unclean], *Literaturnaya gazeta*, June 1, 1963.

9. *Ibid.* Compare the puzzled exclamation in B. Pankin and V. Chikin, "I lozung, i obyazannost'!" [Both the slogan and the duty!], *Komsomol'skaya pravda*, January 26, 1965: "It turns out that in our country, the country of toilers and not of medieval Spanish grandees, some professions are considered practically shameful!" Among these, the two authors list laundresses, barbers, and saleswomen.

10. Aleksandr Shpeyer, "Ne mozhet byt'?" [Cannot be?] *Literaturnaya gazeta*, January 4, 1964.

11. S. Ivanova, "Shkola, roditeli i professiya" [School, parents, and profession], *Izvestiya*, November 24, 1961.

12. L. Zakharova, "O chyom mechtayet 'koroleva' " [What the "queen" is dreaming about], *Komsomol'skaya pravda*, May 15, 1963.

13. Pankin, "Vsyo yeshchyo mashinist . . . ," February 15, 1961.

14. E. Korsunskaya, "Vagon 22–71" [Car 22–71], *Izvestiya*, January 13, 1963.

15. An unsigned report of four regional conferences of Party propagandists and secretaries, "K razumu i serdtsu cheloveka" [We must appeal to man's mind and heart], *Sovetskaya Rossiya*, April 20, 1963.

16. A. Petrakova, "O geroyakh tusklo, o tuneyadtsakh yarko" [Dully about heroes, colorfully about parasites], *Sovetskaya Rossiya*, May 27, 1964.

17. G. Lalayants, "Pochemu ne uchitsia Gena?" [Why doesn't Gena study?], *Trud*, January 19, 1963.

18. *Ibid.*

19. N. Dolinina, "Semnadtsatiletniye" [The seventeen-year-old ones], *Pravda*, January 10, 1962.

20. V. Lipatov, "Chyornyi yar" [Black crag], *Novy mir*, March 1963, p. 74. For a bitter attack on this "pessimistic" novella, see Yu. Topalova, "A gde zhe nastoyashchiye lyudi?" [But where are the real people?], *Trud*, June 30, 1963.

21. V. Grebtsov, "Appetit demagoga" [A demagogue's appetite], *Sovetskaya Rossiya*, October 31, 1963.

22. M. Mikhaiylov and G. Yegiazarian, "Lichnyi interes i obshchestvennyi dolg" [Personal interest and social duty], *Sovetskaya Rossiya*, August 29, 1962.

23. O. Bitov, "Griadushcheye vstalo riadom" [The future is right next to us], *Komsomol'skaya pravda*, August 24, 1960.

24. I. Changli, "Trud, ozaryonnyi mysl'yu" [Toil, lit up by thought], *Pravda*, April 29, 1960.

25. P. Baliasov, "Razdum'ya posle ekzamenov" [Thoughts after examinations], *Izvestiya*, March 5, 1963.

26. N. Uralov, "Gordost' " [Pride], *Izvestiya*, May 10, 1963.

27. Nikolai Anikin, "Khorosheye lekarstvo" [Good medicine], *Trud*, May 11, 1963.

28. A. Rodionov, "A chto pod spetsovkoi?" [And what is under his overalls?], *Sovetskaya Rossiya*, May 30, 1963.

29. Ye. Pavlov, "Musor" [Trash], *Trud*, October 8, 1960; and V. Zasukhin, "Sovest' za tselkovyi" [Conscience sold for a ruble], *Komsomol'skaya pravda*, August 14, 1963.

30. Vadim Beliayev, "Vremia zhivoye i myortvoye" [Time living and dead], *Literaturnaya gazeta*, February 2, 1963.

31. R. Zaitsev, "Gor'koye utro yeyo zhizni" [The bitter morning of her life], *Komsomol'skaya pravda*, October 11, 1962.

32. N. Gorsheneva, "Avtor—narod" [The people is the author], *Sovetskaya Rossiya*, March 3, 1963.

33. Ilya Zverev, "Chto cheloveku nado" [What a man needs], *Literaturnaya gazeta*, August 3, 1961.

34. G. Ablezin, "Vsiakiy li trud vospityvayet?" [Is any kind of labor truly elevating?], *Sovetskaya Rossiya*, June 16, 1963.

35. Alla Trubnikova, " 'Koroli' snimayut tabel' " ["Kings" take off the timetable], *Literaturnaya gazeta*, November 2, 1963.

36. Vasily Ardamatsky, "Poriadok i my s vami" [Order and you and I], *Izvestiya*, June 21, 1962.

37. Argus, "Slukhi i fakty—O sovetskoi molodezhi" [Rumors and facts—About Soviet youth], *Novoye russkoye slovo*, July 11, 1964.

38. L. Arkhipova, "Passivnyie . . . otkuda oni?" [The passive ones . . . where are they from?], *Komsomol'skaya pravda*, April 28, 1960; and A. Cherkasov, "Predal za chetyre tselkovykh" [Betrayed for four rubles], *Komsomol'skaya pravda*, February 1, 1962.

39. Nikolai Pertsev, "Skripuny" [Squeakers], *Komsomol'skaya pravda*, June 4, 1961.

40. F. Petere, "Ot truda vse blaga" [All good things come from toil], *Izvestiya*, December 4, 1962.

41. Nikolai Sviridov, "Vozvrashchayus' k zemle" [I return to soil], *Komsomol'skaya pravda*, April 3, 1964; and Svetlana Serdyuk, "Daryu lyudiam sad" [I give people a garden as my gift], *Komsomol'skaya pravda*, June 30, 1963.

42. I. Zyuzyukin, "Binom Nyutona i . . . kartoshka" [Newton's binomial and . . . potatoes], *Komsomol'skaya pravda*, May 6, 1961.

43. N. Kalugin, "Rodnoye moye selo" [My native village], *Pravda*, December 26, 1963.

44. Vera Tkachenko, "Vishnevyie gody" [Cherry years], *Pravda*, March 22, 1964.

45. V. Ustinov, "Propisany na zemle" [Tied to the ground], *Sovetskaya Rossiya*, January 7, 1964.

46. O. Minenko-Orlovskaya, "U nas i segodnia boi" [We have a fight on our hands even today], *Komsomol'skaya pravda*, March 29, 1964.

47. V. Kokashinsky, "V pole zreniya—'tikhiye' " [The "quiet ones" are in the field of our vision], *Komsomol'skaya pravda*, December 25, 1963.

48. Galia Kovalyova and T. Gromova, " 'Serdtse ne na meste' " ["The heart is not in its place"], *Komsomol'skaya pravda*, December 27, 1962.

49. F. Pershukov, " 'Udral i ne zhaleyu' " ["I ran away and I am not sorry"], *Komsomol'skaya pravda*, January 7, 1961.

50. Unsigned, "Farmers' Training in Soviet Belittled," *The New York Times*, November 14, 1963, dispatch from Chicago reporting Professor Sudia's report at the annual convention of the Association of State Universities and Land Grant Colleges.

51. Yekaterina Lopatina, "Diplom, dolg, sud'ba" [Diploma, duty, destiny], *Literaturnaya gazeta*, June 11, 1964.

52. P. Semyonov, "Letuny s diplomami" [Deserters with diplomas], *Trud*, March 18, 1964.

53. Chingiz Aitmatov, "Sozdadim yarkiy obraz kommunista" [Let's create a bright image of the Communist], *Pravda*, March 20, 1963.

54. Unsigned, "Mera otvetstvennosti" [A measure of responsibility], *Komsomol'skaya pravda*, July 24, 1962.

CHAPTER XVIII

And the Caste Came Back

1. Alexandra Orme, *Comes the Comrade!* (New York: William Morrow and Company, 1950), pp. 60–61.

2. *Ibid.*, p. 368.

3. Oriana Atkinson, *Over at Uncle Joe's; Moscow and Me* (Indianapolis and New York: The Bobbs-Merrill Company, 1947), pp. 246–247.

4. T. Gerasimova, "I pridyot k tebe krasota" [And beauty will come to you], *Izvestiya*, February 24, 1960.

5. V. Pivovarov, "Diplom i karyera" [Diploma and career], *Komsomol'skaya pravda*, June 4, 1964.

6. V. Poliakov, "Za chto vy nenavidite Lidu?" [Why do you hate Lida?], *Izvestiya*, March 18, 1960.

7. S. Garbuzov, "Chelovek—cheloveku" [Man to man], *Izvestiya*, March 6, 1960.

8. T. Gvozdova, "Nerovnia" [Unequal], *Sovetskaya Rossiya*, January 23,

1962. *Cf.* V. Mikhailova, " 'Nerovnia' " ["Unequal"], *Trud*, January 25, 1965.

9. Mariya Loboda, "Ne k rukam delo" [Not fit for the job], *Izvestiya*, October 25, 1963.

10. G. Konyushkova, "Schastlivykh dorog!" [Here's to happy journeys!], *Krasnaya zvezda*, October 14, 1962. For an earlier summary of the problem of "unequal" marriages, see Albert Parry, "Marriage and Class in the Land of Marx," *The Georgia Review*, University of Georgia, Fall 1955.

11. E. Bokmel'der, "Konstruktor—tvorets ili remeslennik?" [Designer—creator or craftsman?], *Komsomol'skaya pravda*, November 10, 1962.

12. N. Ter-Minasova, "K rodnym penatam" [To their own household gods], *Izvestiya*, January 13, 1963.

13. Unsigned, "Uniat' inzheneromaniyu" [To stem the engineer mania], *Sovetskaya Rossiya*, October 6, 1962.

14. Anatoly Agranovsky, "Rastrata obrazovaniya" [Squandering of education], *Izvestiya*, January 20, 1963.

15. Anatoly Agranovsky, "Serzhanty industrii" [Sergeants of industry], *Izvestiya*, January 6, 1963.

16. Valery Agranovsky, "Shchepetinshchikov v opale" [Shchepetinshchikov in disgrace], *Literaturnaya gazeta*, April 2, 1963.

17. Anatoly Agranovsky, "Rastrata obrazovaniya."

18. N. Pavlov, "Pust' ne budet razocharovannykh; dumy o molodykh spetsialistakh" [Let there be no disappointed ones; thoughts about young specialists], *Sovetskaya Rossiya*, June 6, 1963.

19. P. Sablev, "Nachalo biografii inzhenera" [The beginning of an engineer's biography], *Izvestiya*, January 15, 1963.

20. Ye. Zotov, "Vo vsyom nuzhna delovitost' " [Efficiency is needed in everything], *Izvestiya*, July 17, 1963.

21. S. Vlasov, "Zakhrebetnik" [Parasite], *Komsomol'skaya pravda*, August 29, 1963.

22. D. Ogloblin, "Kandidatskaya zashchishchena, a dal'she?" [The candidate's degree has been won, but what now?], *Izvestiya*, February 28, 1960.

23. P. Chernyshev, "Tvorets ili remeslennik?" [Creator or artisan?], *Sovetskaya Rossiya*, October 26, 1962.

24. A. Torgashev, "Inzhener pokidayet tsekh" [The engineer quits the shop], *Sovetskaya Rossiya*, January 31, 1963.

25. Vladimir Kantorovich, "Inzhener ukhodit v 'bil'ding' " [The engineer leaves for the "building"], *Literaturnaya gazeta*, September 19, 1961. *Cf.* A. M. Solomatin, "Mladshiy komandir proizvodstva" [Junior commander of production], and N. N. Rodionov, "Masteru—vysokuyu kvalifikatsiyu" [Let's give a higher grade to the foreman], both articles in *Trud*, June 30, 1965.

26. T. Yakovleva, "Vopl' meshchanina" [A petty man's outcry], *Komsomol'skaya pravda*, October 26, 1962.

27. P. Filinovich, "Pravo lezheboki" [The right of the idler], *Komsomol'skaya pravda*, April 10, 1963.

28. V. V. Yermilov, "Chuvstvo obshchestvennosti" [The sense of belonging to society], *Komsomol'skaya pravda*, January 23, 1963.

29. Leonid Likhodeyev, "Sem' par nechistykh" [Seven pairs of the unclean], *Literaturnaya gazeta*, June 1, 1963.

30. *Ibid.*

31. V. Rostovshchikov, "Im, vidite li, malo" [It's too little for them, don't you see], *Izvestiya*, January 11, 1963.

32. S. Nikishov, "Vuzy—gornilo ideinoi zakalki" [Higher schools—the forge that steels ideas], *Sovetskaya Rossiya*, September 8, 1963.

33. Vl. Lidin, "Chas polivki tsvetov" [The flower-watering hour], a short story, *Komsomol'skaya pravda*, September 4, 1960.

34. Ella Cherepakhova, "Svideteli" [Witnesses], *Literaturnaya gazeta*, September 14, 1963.
35. M. Gukailo, "Zub so svistom" [The tooth with a whistle], *Izvestiya*, June 22, 1961.
36. A. Pal'm, " 'Proshu ustroit' " ["I beg to enroll"], *Komsomol'skaya pravda*, August 27, 1961.
37. V. Ponizovsky, "Dima, yego roditeli i uchitelia" [Dima, his parents and teachers], *Komsomol'skaya pravda*, March 13. 1964.
38. Yu. Sharapov, "Den' nachinayetsia s utra" [A day begins with a morning], *Izvestiya*, May 30, 1964.
39. Yermilov, "Chuvstvo obshchestvennosti."
40. Z. Markelova and Yu. Kostan'yants, "Dorogiye fontany" [Expensive fountains], *Trud*, January 26, 1962.
41. P. Bondarenko, "Professor rasshiriayet shtaty" [The professor expands his staff], *Sovetskaya Rossiya*, January 29, 1963.
42. L. Shinkaryov, "Zheton i sovest' " [A badge and conscience], *Izvestiya*, September 2, 1961.
43. E. Parkhomovsky, "Zagar is-pod poly" [Black-market tan], *Izvestiya*, June 9, 1964.
44. M. Fomenko, "S tvortsami—po puti" [Taking the same route with creators], *Sovetskaya Rossiya*, May 27, 1964.
45. V. Semyonov, "Durnyie obychai iz zhizni von!" [Let's eliminate bad customs from life!], *Trud*, March 17, 1963.
46. I. Vasil'yev and L. Kornyushin, "Svoi pirogi" [One's own pies], *Sovetskaya Rossiya*, March 21, 1963.
47. Natal'ya Davydova, *Lyubov' inzhenera Izotova* [Engineer Izotov's love], a novel (Moscow: *Sovetsky pisatel'* publishing house, 1962), pp. 118–119.
48. Alla Vinichenko, "Gore-'aristokraty' " [Would-be "aristocrats"], *Komsomol'skaya pravda*, March 1, 1961.
49. B. Bryukhanov and A. Solov'yov, "Zhak s beregov Amura" [Jacques from the Amur shores], *Krasnaya zvezda*, August 11, 1962; and D. Os'kin, "Yesli v zhilakh krov' a ne voditsa . . ." [If there is blood in the veins, and not weak water . . .], *Komsomol'skaya pravda*, May 5, 1964—to cite but two of the numerous examples available.
50. N., "Imeyu li ya pravo?" [Do I have the right?], *Komsomol'skaya pravda*, April 3, 1964.
51. I. Dement'yeva, "Schastlivyi bilet" [The lucky ticket], *Sovetskaya Rossiya*, November 13, 1963.
52. Ilya Omelichkin, "Skazaniye o levoi noge" [The tale of the left leg], *Trud*, January 23, 1963.
53. Yuly Krelin, "Smotriu s vysoty zemli" [I look from the earth's height], *Komsomol'skaya pravda*, December 30, 1964. See also Edmund K. Faltemayer, "Red Educators—A Major Problem: Producing Unsnobbish Scientists," *The Wall Street Journal*, June 25, 1963 (correspondence from Tbilisi, Soviet Georgia).

CHAPTER XIX

The Technocrats and the Arts

1. For an interesting view of experimentation in Soviet art see Richard B. K. McLanathan, "Art in the Soviet Union," *The Atlantic*, June 1960, pp. 74–84.

2. John Canaday, "Art in the Soviet: A Cold Wind Delays the Thaw," *The New York Times*, October 3, 1963.

3. "The View from Lenin Hills," *Time*, January 18, 1963, p. 26. *Cf.* Walter Z. Laqueur and others, *Khrushchev on Culture*, (London: *Encounter* pamphlet No. 9, 1963); also Priscilla Johnson, *Khrushchev and the Arts* (Cambridge, Mass.: M.I.T. Press, 1965), p. 11.

4. Priscilla Johnson, p. 9.

5. John Canaday, "A Critic Surveys the Party Line in Art," *The New York Times Magazine*, January 5, 1964, p. 64.

6. Unsigned dispatch from Moscow dated November 29, 1963, "Skul'ptor Neizvestny" [Sculptor Neizvestny], *Novoye russkoye slovo*, November 30, 1963, quoting TASS. *Cf.* Vyacheslav Zavalishin, "Skul'ptor Ernest Neizvestny" [Sculptor Ernest Neizvestny], *Novoye russkoye slovo*, April 21, 1963.

7. Editorial, "A Soviet Sculptor's Comeback," *The New York Times*, November 30, 1963.

8. Olga Andreyev Carlisle, "Poems of Anna Akhmatova," *The Atlantic*, October 1964, p. 61.

9. "Une heure avec André Voznessensky," *France Observateur* (Paris), December 13, 1962, p. 28. A slightly different version of apparently the same statement is to be found in Patricia Blake's introduction to the anthology *New Voices in Russian Writing* as part of the April 1963 issue of the London *Encounter*. She writes (p. 28): "Voznesensky recently told a *Times* correspondent that his readers are mainly members of the 'technological intelligentsia': There are millions of them in Russia now. Many of them work on sputniks and other enormously complicated machines and they want poetry to be complicated too. They have no use for rhymed editorials. . . .' "

10. Olga Andreyev Carlisle, "Literary Life in Moscow," *The New York Times Book Review*, March 14, 1965, pp. 52–53.

11. See the English translation of "Oza" by George L. Kline in *Tri-Quarterly*, (Northwestern University, Evanston, Ill.), Spring 1965, issue devoted to "Creativity in the Soviet Union," pp. 97–117.

12. Gennady Gor, "Algebra i garmoniya" [Algebra and harmony], *Literaturnaya gazeta*, February 26, 1963. Dr. Kapitsa praised Dr. Kolmogorov's work on mathematical implications of poetry in the interview, "Chelovek v mire informatsii" [Man in the world of data], *Komsomol'skaya pravda*, September 2, 1965.

13. Viktor Pekelis, " 'Algebra' uproshchayet" ["Algebra" simplifies], *Literaturnaya gazeta*, May 27, 1965, commenting on I. Gutchin, "Nesushchestvuyushchaya dilemma" [A nonexistent dilemma], *Literaturnaya gazeta*, February 26, 1965.

14. Editorial, "Spor prodolzhayetsia—slovo beryot redaktsiya" [The argument continues—the floor belongs to the editors], *Literaturnaya gazeta*, March 2, 1963.

15. I could not obtain a copy of Vladimir Turbin's book, and I quote this on the basis of Mark Frankland, "Khrushchev Faces a Khrushchevian Dilemma," *The New York Times Magazine*, May 12, 1963, p. 76. Turbin is also discussed by Mihajlo Mihajlov (*Moscow Summer*, pp. 30, 114–116, 204), who reports that Turbin's book "was printed in an edition of 22,000, an absurdly small number for the U.S.S.R., and it is impossible to find a copy today." See briefer mention of Turbin by Priscilla Johnson, *Khrushchev and the Arts*, pp. 3, 83.

16. Ilya Ehrenburg, "Lyudi, gody, zhizn' " [People, years, life], *Novy mir*, March 1965, p. 87.

17. Aleksei Surkov, "Traditsiya otkrytiy" [Tradition of discoveries], *Komsomol'skaya pravda*, May 9, 1963.

18. A. Lebedev, "Abstraktsionizm—iskusstvo obrechyonnykh" [Abstraction-

ism is the art of the doomed], *Krasnaya zvezda,* December 31, 1962. A note on the author's rank: as in the Soviet Academy of Sciences, so in the Soviet Academy of Arts, corresponding members are one rung below full members.

19. Yuri Surovtsev, " 'Pustoye oko' i blagodushnyi Ivan Ivanovich" ["Empty eye" and Ivan Ivanovich of the good soul], *Literaturnaya gazeta,* January 1, 1963.

20. M. Manizer, "Talant—dostoyaniye naroda" [Talent is the people's property], *Literaturnaya gazeta,* April 9, 1963.

21. I. Pitliar, "Poshchechina meshchaninu" [A slap in the petty man's face], *Literaturnaya gazeta,* March 18, 1961, reviewing Valeria Gerasimova's story, "Znakomoye litso" [A familiar face].

22. N. Shamota, "Svoboda sluzhit' millionam" [Freedom to serve millions of people], *Izvestiya,* March 17, 1963.

23. Granin, *Idu na grozu,* p. 152.

24. *Ibid.,* pp. 232–233. On the general subject of the literary image of the Soviet savant see Alexander Steininger, "Scientists in Soviet Literature," *Survey,* July 1964, pp. 157–165.

25. Peter Grose, "Moscow Detains Poet in Protest," dispatch from Moscow, *The New York Times,* December 18, 1965.

CHAPTER XX

How Marxist the Mood?

1. N. Bukharin, "O mirovoi revolyutsii, nashei strane, kul'ture i prochem—Otvet professoru I. Pavlovu" [On world revolution, our country, culture and other things—Reply to Professor I. Pavlov], *Krasnaya nov',* January-February 1924, pp. 171–172, 180.

2. From this paragraph on, material of this chapter was in part used by me in my article "Marx and the Doubting Comrades," *Think,* May-June, 1965, pp. 2–5.

3. Miron Petrovsky, "Khochu smotret' i videt' " [I want to look and see], *Literaturnaya gazeta,* June 12, 1962.

4. P. Yudin and others, "Nado ob'yasnit' " [It is necessary to explain], *Izvestiya,* March 8, 1964.

5. A. Bocharov, "Umnyi tovarishch chitatelia" [The reader's wise comrade], *Izvestiya,* December 13, 1964.

6. Ilya Agranovsky, "Ves' 'Kapital' " [All of "Capital"], *Izvestiya,* December 27, 1964.

7. A. Boikova, "Vnimaniye, doveriye, trebovatel'nost' " [Attention, trust, strictness of demand], *Pravda,* May 13, 1963.

8. A. Frolov, "Chtoby rodit' istinu" [In order to give birth to truth], *Komsomol'skaya pravda,* June 12, 1963.

9. A. I. Kachanov, "Serdtsa, kotoryie otdat' nel'zia . . ." [Hearts which cannot be given up . . .], *Komsomol'skaya pravda,* April 5, 1963.

10. Speech at the plenary session of the Komsomol's Central Committee in Moscow, December 14, 1962, reported in *Komsomol'skaya pravda,* December 15, 1962.

11. Speech at the plenary session of the Komsomol's Central Committee in Moscow, March 17, 1964, reported in *Komsomol'skaya pravda,* March 18, 1964. Two more years passed, and this particular situation was not any better

for Komsomol. See Theodore Shabad, "Soviet Criticizes Youth Organizers; Finds They Are Ill-Equipped to Train the Well Informed," dispatch from Moscow, *The New York Times*, January 16, 1966, quoting *Moskovsky komsomolets*.

12. An unsigned report of four regional conferences of Party propagandists and secretaries, "K razumu i serdtsu cheloveka" [We must appeal to man's mind and heart], *Sovetskaya Rossiya*, April 20, 1963.

13. *Ibid*.

14. Z. N. Nemtsova, "Revolyutsiyei prizvannyi" [Summoned by the revolution], *Komsomol'skaya pravda*, August 26, 1962.

15. Unsigned, *Moscow University in 1960—A Campus Report; Recollections of a Western Exchange Student*. Compiled by the Audience Research and Evaluation Department of Radio Liberty, Munich and New York (mimeographed, limited circulation, no date), pp. 3–5.

16. V. Ganyushkin, "Arsenal serdtsa" [The arsenal of the heart], *Komsomol'skaya pravda*, April 14, 1963.

17. S. Rozhdestvensky, " 'Kupi mne inostrannuyu rubashku' " ["Buy me a foreign shirt"], *Novoye russkoye slovo*, March 28, 1965, quoting the Komsomol newspaper *Znamia yunosti* [Banner of youth] for February 26.

18. Yu. Novikov, "Ivan Vasil'yevich beryot 'na karandash' " [Ivan Vasil'-yevich makes "a pencil note"], *Sovetskaya Rossiya*, July 9, 1963.

19. Boris Izyumsky, "Tol'ko professor?" [No more than a professor?], *Literaturnaya gazeta*, August 21, 1962.

20. A. Rudzinkas, "Riadom—starshiy tovarishch" [The elder comrade by your side], *Pravda*, January 6, 1965.

21. Z. Dubrovina, "Formirovat' nauchnoye mirovozzreniye, vospityvat' aktivnykh bortsov za kommunism" [We must form a scientific world outlook, educate active fighters for Communism], *Pravda*, May 20, 1963.

22. K. Kozhevnikova, "Otvetstvennyie za vzlyot" [Those responsible for a soaring flight], *Komsomol'skaya pravda*, March 31, 1964.

23. I. Tamm, "Poisk talantov" [Talent search], *Izvestiya*, January 3, 1962.

24. S. Khromov, "Golosuyu za talant" [I vote for talent], *Sovetskaya Rossiya*, December 23, 1964.

25. F. Burlatsky, "Politika i nauka" [Politics and science], *Pravda*, January 10, 1965; and unsigned, "O razrabotke problem politicheskikh nauk" [On working through the problems of political sciences], *Pravda*, June 13, 1965.

26. E. Sokolov, "O vremeni i primerakh s 'borodoi' " [About time and outdated examples], *Komsomol'skaya pravda*, July 11, 1961.

27. M. A. Suslov, "XXII s'yezd KPSS i zadachi kafedr obshchestvennykh nauk" [The 22nd Congress of the C.P.S.U. and the tasks of the chairs of social sciences], *Kommunist*, Number 3, February 1962, p. 27.

28. A. Chernichenko, M. Odinets, and Ya. Denisyuk, "Leninskim kursom k novym pobedam kommunizma!" [Take the Lenin direction to new victories of Communism!], *Pravda*, July 4, 1963.

29. L. Gladkaya, "Nauka ubezhdat' protiv yadovitykh primanok" [The science to argue against poisonous lures], *Komsomol'skaya pravda*, September 3, 1964.

30. Aleksandr Mikhalevich, "Spor'te, devushki!" [Argue, girls!], *Komsomol'skaya pravda*, September 4, 1964.

31. Arkady Sakhnin, "Raskayaniye opozdalo" [Repentance came late], *Komsomol'skaya pravda*, October 27, 1962.

32. Suslov, article on the 22nd Congress of the C.P.S.U., *Kommunist*, Number 3, February 1962, p. 27.

33. N. Yermolovich, "Polnoi meroi" [With a full measure], *Izvestiya*, June 14, 1963.

34. P. Neverov, "Ravnodushnomu serdtsa ne otkroyesh' " [If he is indif-

ferent, you won't open your heart to him], *Komsomol'skaya pravda*, May 24, 1961.

35. G. Zbandut, "Muskuly ubezhdeniy" [Muscles of conviction], *Komsomol'skaya pravda*, July 28, 1964.

CHAPTER XXI

But What Do They Believe In?

1. Lewis S. Feuer, "Meeting the Soviet Philosophers," *Survey* (London), April 1964, reprinted in *Dissent* (New York), Winter 1965. *Cf.* Maxim W. Mikulak, "Philosophy and Science," *Survey*, July 1964.

2. Max Frankel, "After Khrushchev—Who? What? How?" *The New York Times Magazine*, March 4, 1962, p. 66.

3. Vladimir Amlinsky, "Razgovor s 'nigilistom' " [Conversation with a "nihilist"], *Literaturnaya gazeta*, July 1, 1961.

4. V. Yemel'yanov, "Otvet pered sovest'yu" [Answer to one's conscience], *Komsomol'skaya pravda*, March 3, 1964.

5. Zinaida Schakovskoy, *The Privilege Was Mine* (New York: G. P. Putnam's Sons, 1959), pp. 299–300. On the most recent literary interest in Kafka among Soviet writers, see Mihajlov, *Moscow Summer*, pp. 19–22, 203.

6. Schakovskoy, pp. 236–239.

7. For a somewhat lengthier treatment of this subject see Albert Parry, "Soviet Technicians in Foreign Lands," *The Chicago Purchasor*, July 1964, pp. 22–25.

8. Mihajlov, pp. 33, 76, 104–114, 195–96.

9. D. Yemlyutin, N. Dolgova, and others, "Lovtsy deshyovoi slavy" [Hunters of cheap glory], *Sovetskaya Rossiya*, February 21, 1965.

10. Speech by A. A. Yepishev, *Krasnaya zvezda*, June 20, 1963.

11. Speech by Marshal R. Ya. Malinovsky, "Vospevat' geroicheskoye" [Let us sing things heroic], *Krasnaya zvezda*, February 9, 1964; and Theodore Shabad, "Soviet Defense Chief Criticizes Pacifist Trend in Artists' Work," dispatch from Moscow *The New York Times*, February 10, 1964.

12. Speech by L. S. Sobolev, "Sovetskaya literatura i vospitaniye novogo cheloveka" [Soviet literature and the fostering of the new man], *Literaturnaya gazeta*, March 4, 1965. See the same complaint, "Not too often do our writers turn to the affairs and days of our peacetime army," in Vl. Pimenov, "Gordo shagayet voyennyi chelovek" [Proudly strides the military man], *Krasnaya zvezda*, December 11, 1965.

13. P. Krivonogov, "Nash metod—sotsialistichesky realizm" [Socialist realism is our method], *Krasnaya zvezda*, January 9, 1963.

14. V. Volodin, "Igrushka—delo ser'yoznoye" [Toy is a serious business], *Komsomol'skaya pravda*, December 27, 1964.

15. See the Reverend Georges Bissonnette, *Moscow Was My Parish* (New York: McGraw-Hill Company, 1956).

16. Il. Okunev, " 'Vo istseleniye dushi i tela' " ["To heal soul and body"], *Trud*, June 13, 1965.

17. K. Pomerantsev, "Vo chto verit sovetskaya molodezh'?" [What does the Soviet youth believe in?], *Novy zhurnal*, March 1965, pp. 154–158. See also Harrison E. Salisbury, "Spiritual Key Is Hunted By Some in Soviet Science," *The New York Times*, February 7, 1962.

18. "Too Much to Ask? An Exile Writes to Khrushchev," *The Observer* (London), July 15, 1962. See also Robert C. Doty, "Defector Appeals to Khrushchev To Let His Family Leave Russia," dispatch from Paris, *The New York Times*, January 30, 1962; and "Regards from an Outcast," *Time* (New York), May 22, 1964, p. 40.

CHAPTER XXII

The Good Erosion

1. For a remarkably persuasive argument on this miscarriage of history see Leonard Schapiro, "Was Lenin Necessary?" *Commentary* (New York), December 1964, pp. 57–60.

2. J. R. Azrael, "Politics and Management," *Survey*, October 1963, p. 100, quoting Leonid Ilyichev.

3. Cf. David W. Ewing, "The Russians Yearn for the Managerial Mind," *Harper's Magazine*, January 1965, pp. 67–72. Mr. Ewing concludes by arguing that the Party means to run things just the same, no matter what privileges are being given or are yet to be given to the managers. "So far," he writes, "we have no evidence that his successors are any less devoted to the supremacy of the Party" than Khrushchev was. But it is not really any longer the question of what the Party wants or does not want. Facts are a stubborn thing, as Lenin used to say, and the facts of today and tomorrow spell out the rise of the manager at the inevitable expense of the Party.

4. Daniel Lang, "A Reporter at Large—The Peaceable Gypsies," *The New Yorker*, December 21, 1963, pp. 34–61, particularly pp. 48–54. Included in Daniel Lang, *An Inquiry into Enoughness* (New York: McGraw-Hill Book Company, 1965), in a slightly different form, pp. 153 ff.

5. Granin, *Idu na grozu*, p. 64.

6. Ye. Onufriyev and A. Kuftyrev, "Otvet 'delovym' lyudiam" [Reply to "practical" people], *Komsomol'skaya pravda*, December 13, 1959.

7. Granin, *Idu na grozu*, p. 172.

8. A. Kudriavtsev, "Byli druziyami" [Used to be friends], *Komsomol'skaya pravda*, March 22, 1964.

9. Lyubov' Kabo, " 'Kul'turny chelovek' . . . chto eto znachit?" ["Cultured person" . . . what does this mean?], *Literaturnaya gazeta*, November 30, 1963.

10. Aleksandr Solzhenitsyn, "Dlia pol'zy dela" [For the good of the cause], *Novy mir*, July 1963, p. 79.

11. K. Pomerantsev, "Chem interesuyetsia sovetskaya molodezh' " [What interests the Soviet youth], *Novoye russkoye slovo*, June 22, 1964.

12. Viktor Nekrasov, "Po obe storony okeana" [On both sides of the ocean], *Novy mir*, December 1962, p. 118. This is now available in English as *Both Sides of the Ocean: A Russian Writer's Travels in Italy and the United States*, translated by Elias Kulukundis (New York: Holt, Rinehart and Winston, 1964).

13. K. Solntsev, "Russky vklad v amerikanskuyu nauku i kul'turu" [The Russian contribution to American science and culture], *Novoye russkoye slovo*, May 1, 1960.

14. Deming Brown, *Soviet Attitudes Toward American Writing* (Princeton, N. J.: Princeton University Press, 1962), p. 187.

15. Yu. Kovalev, "Zhizn' vo mgle" [Life in the fog], *Zvezda*, August 1952, p. 185, quoted by Brown, *op. cit.*, p. 187.

16. Brown, p. 189.

17. Quoted in R. V. Burks, "The Thaw and the Future of Eastern Europe," *Encounter*, August 1964, p. 27, footnote 3.

18. Max Frankel, "Hungarians Seek 'the Good Life' " dispatch from Budapest, *The New York Times*, November 29, 1964, and "In East Germany: Economic Reform," dispatch from Berlin, *The New York Times*, December 13, 1964.

19. S. Kuzmenko, "Ispytaniye na stoikost' " [The stamina test], *Pravda*, August 10, 1962.

20. "Official Soviet Transcript of the Interview with Premier Kosygin in the Kremlin," *The New York Times*, December 8, 1965, Russian text in *Izvestiya*, December 11, 1965.

INDEX

INDEX